Botanical Illustration

THE COMPLETE GUIDE

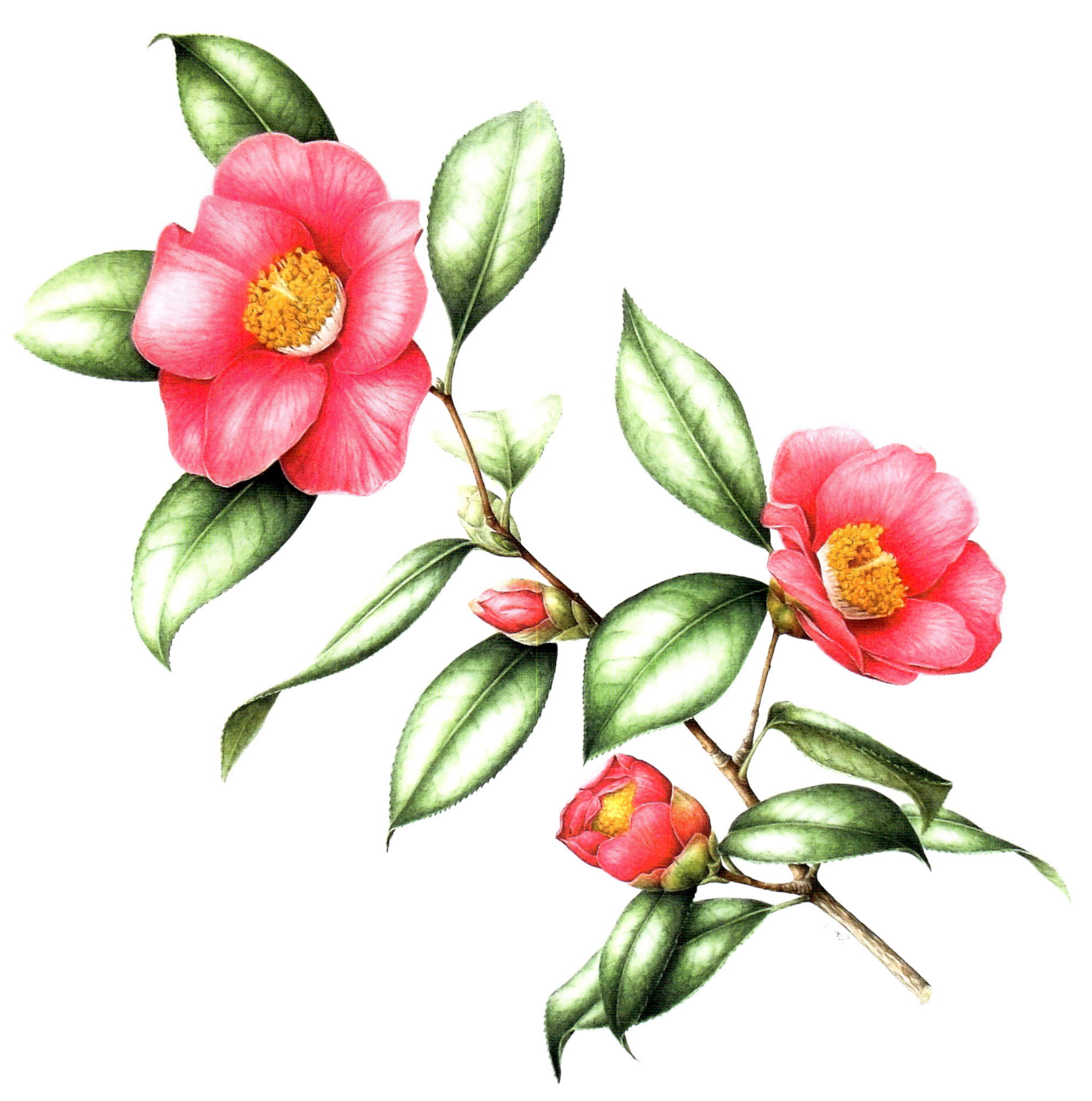

Botanical Illustration

THE COMPLETE GUIDE

Leigh Ann Gale

THE CROWOOD PRESS

First published in 2018 by
The Crowood Press Ltd
Ramsbury, Marlborough
Wiltshire SN8 2HR

www.crowood.com

Paperback edition 2023

This impression 2026

British Library Cataloguing-in-Publication Data
A catalogue record for this book is available from the British Library.

For product safety-related questions contact productsafety@crowood.com

ISBN 978 0 7198 4336 5

Frontispiece: *Camellia x williamsii* 'Bow Bells' (Leigh Ann Gale)

DEDICATION

This book is dedicated to my mother Janet Hewitt-Winch for launching my botanical illustration career after giving me a newspaper article featuring the English Gardening School's Botanical Painting Diploma course. I also dedicate this book to my grandfather Walter Winch, an exquisite draughtsman, whose precise and detailed drawing skills I was so fortunate to inherit.

Graphic design and typesetting by Peggy & Co. Design
Printed and bound in India by Thomson Press India Private Limited

Contents

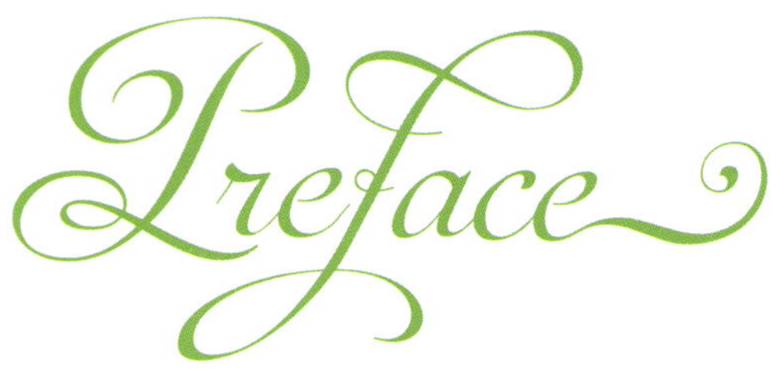

When I am teaching, a common question I am asked is how did I start in botanical illustration? I begin answering by giving my students a brief explanation of my inherent obsession and desire to see detail in art, which is something I have always strived to achieve in my own artwork. As a child, I remember feeling mesmerized as I watched my grandfather meticulously render technical drawings of complex water supply components, with exceptional skill and absolute precision, and I was never satisfied until any drawing I made contained as much detail as I could practically manage, whether I was aged six or sixteen. I studied art at school, completed a diploma in technical illustration and studied graphic design at art college, before pursuing a career as a graphic designer. Throughout each stage of my artistic career, my focus has always been about achieving a high level of detail in everything I have created. Even when I attempted my hand at a 'looser' approach to art at an evening course in flower painting, I found I still had an irresistible urge to add detail to my paintings. I eventually found the perfect opp[illegible]nity to combine this obsession with my love of pl[illegible]and flowers, and embarked upon the diploma in [illegible]ical painting at The English Gardening Schoo[illegible] at the Chelsea Physic Garden.

It is the exacting requir[illegible] precision and attention to detail which are [illegible] true, scientific botanical illustration, wher[illegible] the emphasis is on the accurate depicti[illegible] through the observed study and accura[illegible]tructures and components – often wit[illegible]agnifications and dissections to help [illegible]formation in greater detail. Because [illegible] are intended to educate and convey [illegible] to be clearly and logically devise[illegible] to be trans- ported around the [illegible]trators may

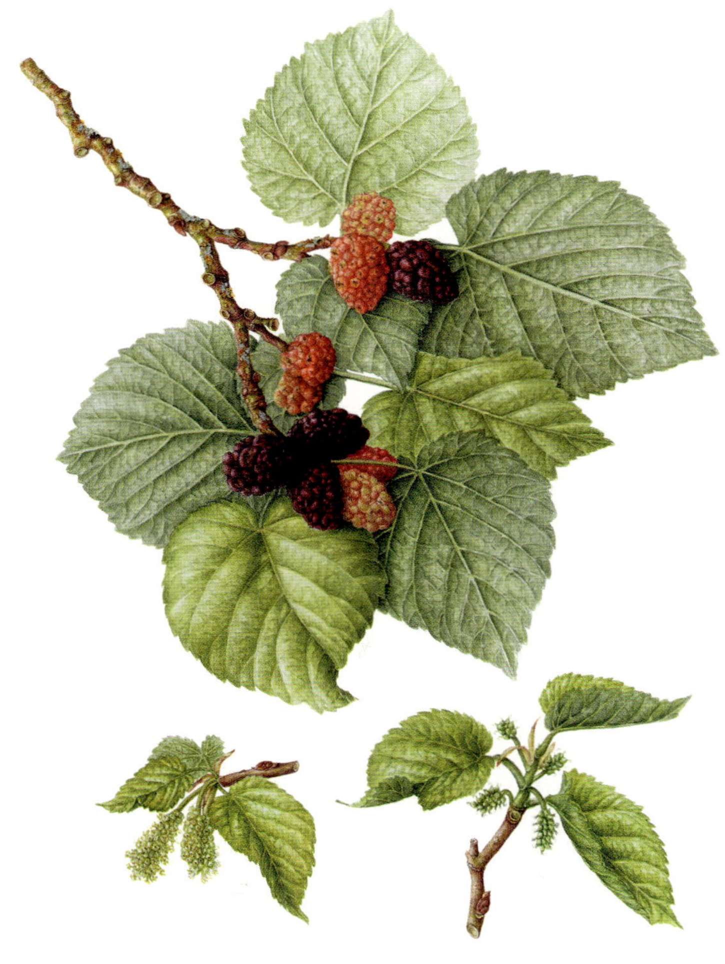

Morus nigra, Mulberries. LEIGH ANN GALE

also produce such works which are aesthetically beautiful as well. Sometimes, botanical illustration and botanical art are considered the same thing; however, in botanical art, the artist may demonstrate a more levelled persuasion to both art and science or, in some cases, predominantly art; the work is still scientifically accurate but may have emphasized artistic attributes to it at the same time.

The purpose of this book is to provide a means by which botanical illustration can be approached methodically by students, to accomplish a good, competent standard. However, it is hoped that it may also serve as a useful reference to those artists who have already gained some experience in the subject as well. It highlights the importance of the requisite skills of close observation, accurate drawing, and attention to detail, and at the same time explains and demonstrates my own personal approach to the subject which I have developed over the years. I hope this book provides you with inspiration, and proves to be a valuable resource alongside your quest to draw and paint your own botanical illustrations.

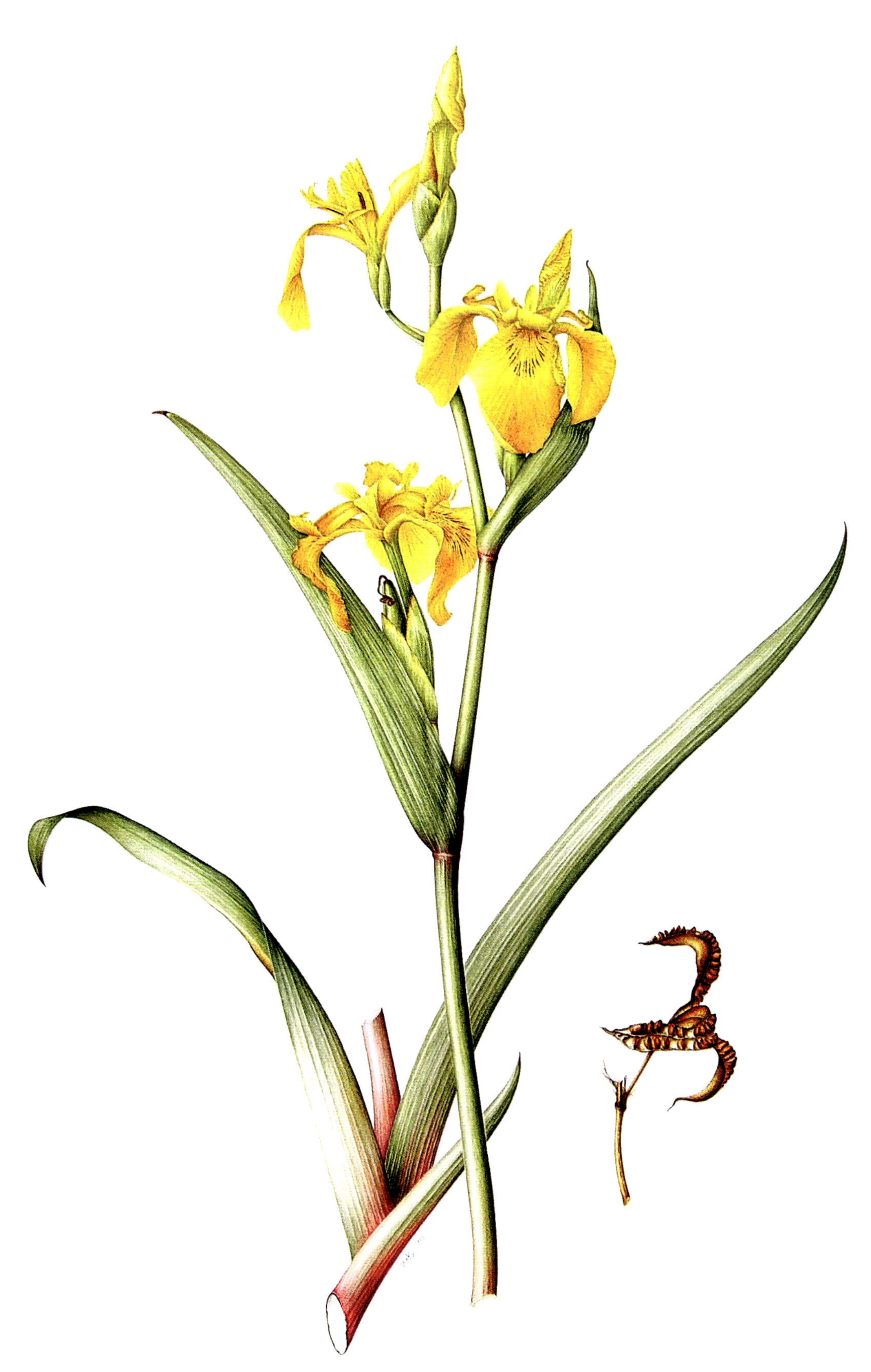

Introduction

After many years of teaching botanical illustration, it has become apparent to me that students learn significantly better through demonstration. I often sit down with a student or group of students to show them my approach, which they may in turn try for themselves or adapt to suit their own hand. In my experience, it seems that most visually aware students prefer this method of teaching, rather than any verbal descriptions of how techniques are perfected, and processes are followed. It is this realization of students' needs that this book has evolved. During discussions with many students, the overarching request for inclusion in an instruction book is that of demonstration. Therefore, I have endeavoured to include a case study; a real, worked example of a painting which demonstrates and puts into practice each of the varied stages of botanical illustration, including selection and preparation of a subject; observational drawing, composition skills, and painting processes. Using a visual step-by-step format, I have also included a chapter that deals with specific painting techniques of some of the most popular topics on which students often ponder. These are techniques that I personally have adopted over the years, which may differ from those of other artist tutors, but nevertheless offer solutions for effectively solving specific painting challenges.

To achieve competency in botanical art and illustration it is without question that a good level of understanding of botany is required. It is not necessary

Yellow Flag Iris and seeds. LEIGH ANN GALE

to obtain an abounding knowledge of the subject as a botanical artist, but you should be familiar with the basic components and features of plants and flowers, to enable you to observe and draw them accurately. Certainly, a higher level of knowledge is invaluable to produce pure scientific botanical illustrations, that may for example include finely detailed drawings of the internal workings of a species, but for this, separate texts and publications about botany are available. For the purposes of this book, it is not practical to include such in-depth information, so I have provided a section on basic botany in Chapter 3 that should be sufficient to aid most students. A botanical glossary is also included to support this, and appears at the end of the book.

In addition to the fundamental skills-based processes, I have included a comprehensive materials and equipment list for drawing and painting, and recommendations for equipment of other media such as coloured pencils and ink. Information about mounting and framing botanical paintings is given in Chapter 11. I have devoted a chapter to colour which for many, presents notable challenges, and can often prove to be a stumbling block at the painting stage. Basic colour theory is addressed, as well as guidance given on mixing colours accurately to match specimens, and how to build up and make the most of your own palette of watercolours.

Chapter 12 provides information about continuing the art of botanical illustration, including suggestions and recommendations for further learning and continued practice; exhibiting and marketing your work, and how one's own style can evolve and develop. I have included examples of my own students' work, which it is hoped will give insight into what can be achieved through committed learning and regular practice. Some of the examples represent the achievements of students who set out as complete beginners and are now establishing themselves as accomplished artists and illustrators. A list of their contributions is included at the end of the book.

The book is set out in a progressive stage-by-stage format, which for most readers will be the logical way to access the information to achieve a completed painting. However, it is also intended that the book can be dipped into; chapters can be read in isolation of others which may be of benefit to those who already have some experience of botanical illustration, and who wish to hone their skills in specific areas of the subject.

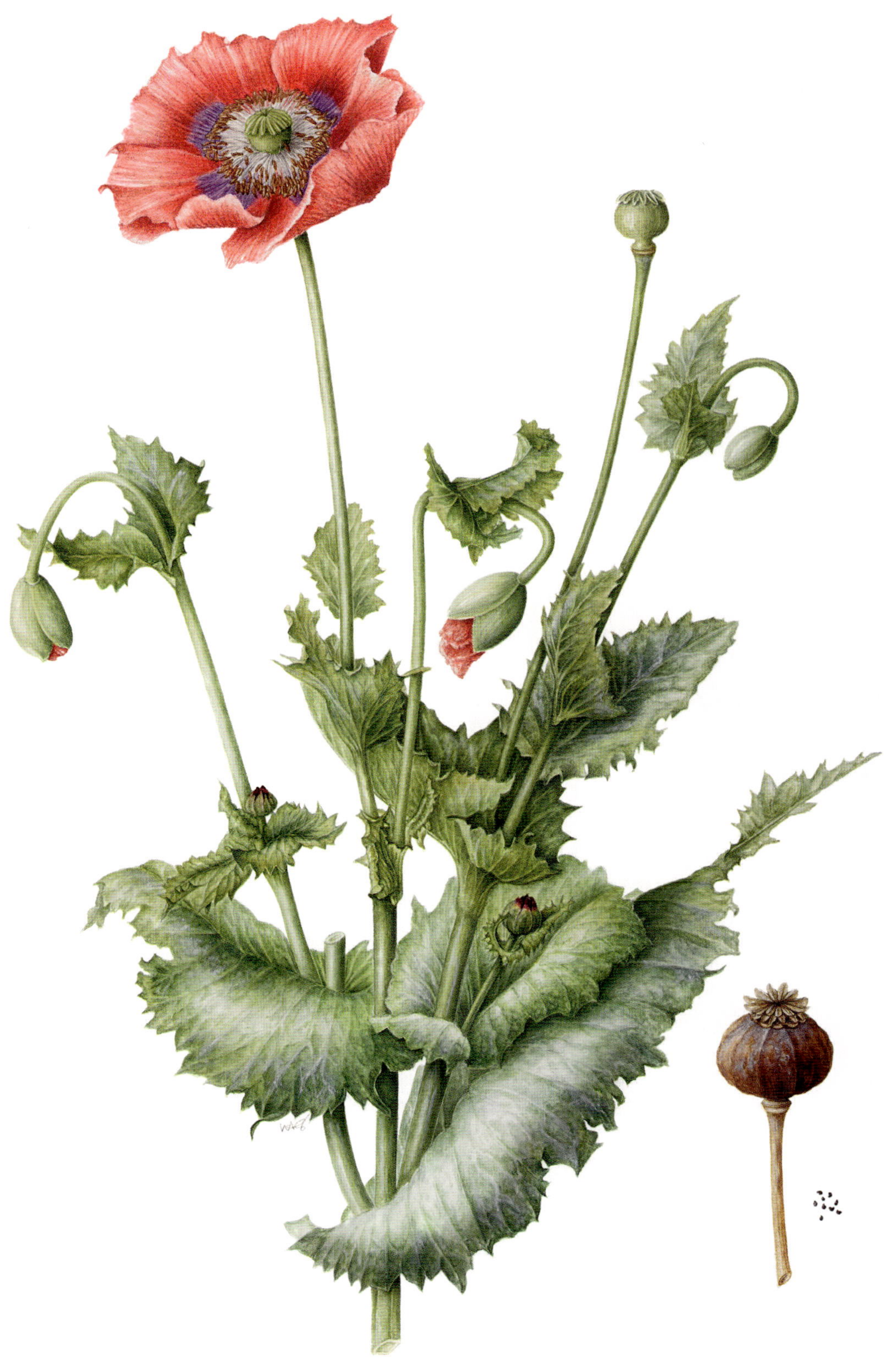

Papaver somniferum, Opium Poppy. LEIGH ANN GALE

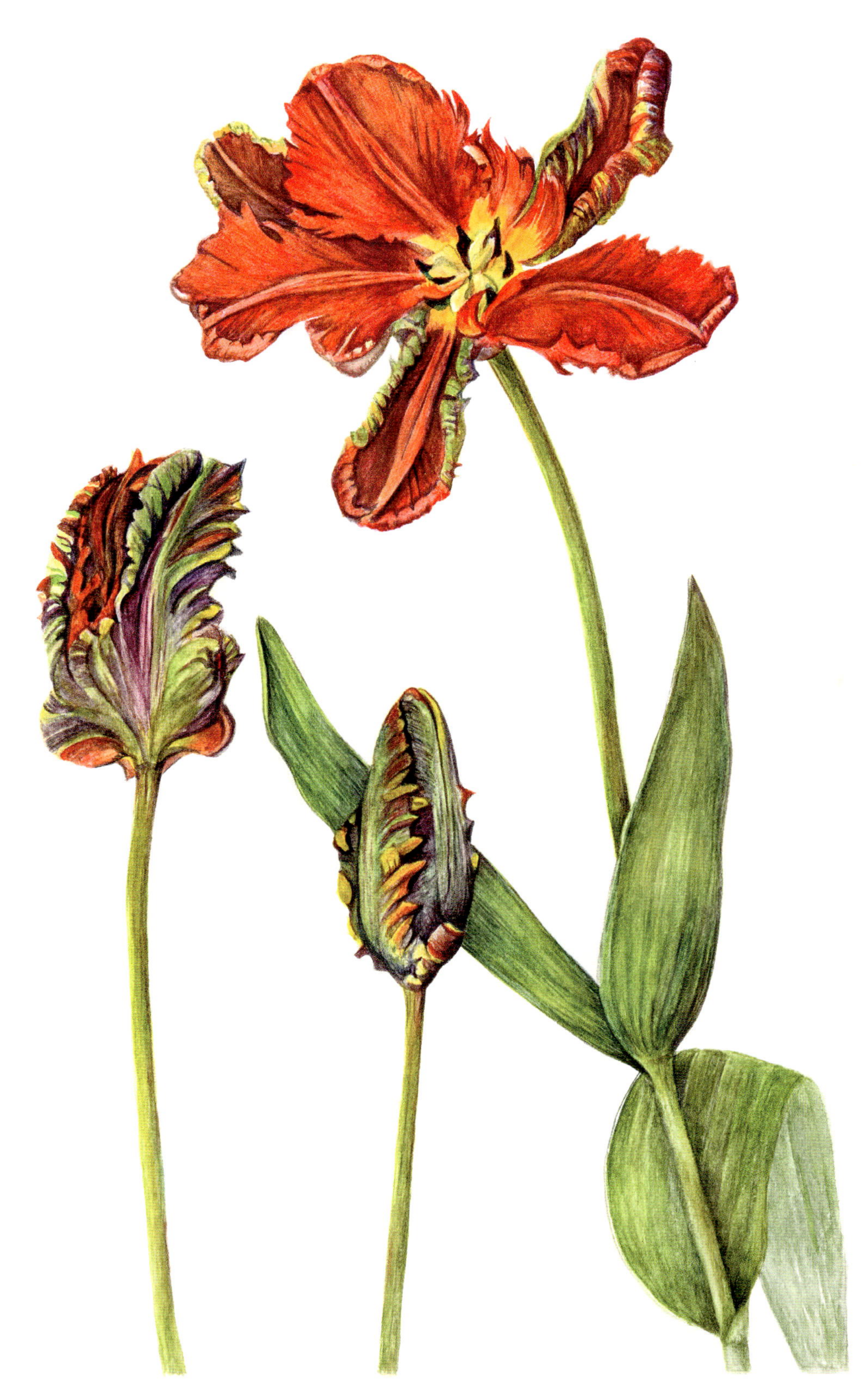

CHAPTER 1

Materials and Equipment

The hand is the tool of tools.

– Aristotle

The materials and equipment you invest in at the outset will without doubt become your trusted tools for successful botanical illustration. If you are equipping yourself for the first time then buying and building up a good selection of quality materials is by far the best option, as you will certainly achieve better results in your work right from the start. For example, selecting quality sable brushes instead of synthetic alternatives, and artist's quality watercolours instead of student colours – whilst a little more expensive – will prove their worth time and time again.

Besides pencils, brushes and paints, there are a number of other useful pieces of equipment you will find helpful. Some of these can be purchased, but cheaper, homemade alternatives can work just as well.

You will also need to consider whereabouts you will be setting up your studio or allocated workspace and how you will store your work. If you are likely to be travelling, you will need to find effective ways of carrying and storing your work to prevent it from becoming damaged.

This chapter explores a range of materials and equipment suitable for botanical illustration, and of course, you will probably come across some of your own to add as you go along.

It is important to remember that botanical illustration is not only about the practicalities of drawing and painting but how best to support your endeavours by selecting appropriate materials and equipment conducive to the task in hand.

Tulip 'Rococo'. KATE TILBURY

DRAWING MATERIALS AND EQUIPMENT

During the initial stage of the botanical illustration process, it will be necessary to make observational drawings of your subject matter. The conventional way to do this is by means of graphite pencil onto good quality cartridge paper.

PENCILS

Drawing pencils are available in varying degrees of hardness. The hardness of a pencil is determined by the ratio of graphite to clay powder content resulting in a range of soft (B) grade and hard (H) grade pencils. A pencil which is considered medium grade is known as an HB pencil, and this is the standard for most drawing activities. For botanical illustration purposes it is advisable to use a pencil from the 'H' range, since a finer and lighter line can be accomplished which will give greater accuracy and precision in your drawing. 'H' range pencils start at H and go up to 9H. It is not necessary to use the hardest '9H' option, which could potentially damage your paper. Instead, a pointed H, 2H or 3H will suffice and will produce quite a satisfactory result. It is important that during the drawing process you keep the point of your pencil sharp, by regularly using a pencil sharpener or craft knife.

You may want to consider using a 'mechanical' pencil (sometimes referred to as a 'propelling' pencil), especially if you intend doing a large amount of drawing. The advantage of this type of pencil is that the point remains permanently sharp, therefore doing away with the interruptions of sharpening all the time. The lead itself is simply propelled by an internal mechanism, which is activated by the user depressing a button on the end of the pencil. These pencils are readily available, and the different grades of lead in different widths are bought separately. As with a standard drawing pencil, choosing an H, 2H or 3H grade in a 0.3mm or 0.5mm width will be adequate for your purposes.

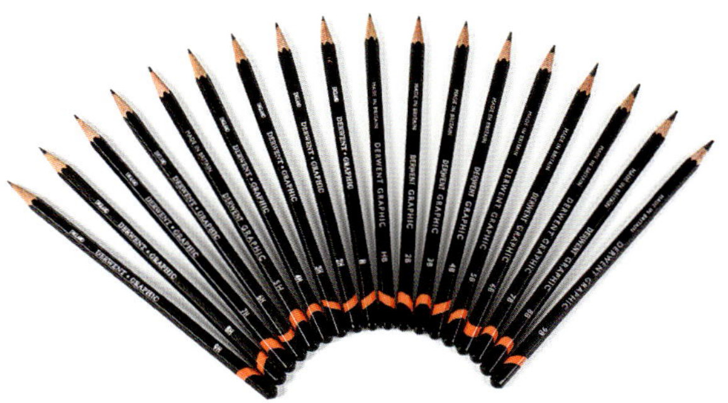

Pencils range from 9B soft to 9H hard.

Drawn lines show the difference in hardness of lead: H, 2H and 3H.

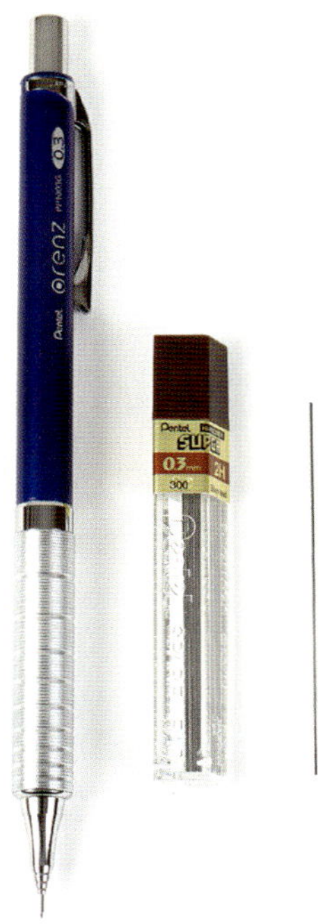

A 'mechanical' or 'propelling' pencil with individual leads.

DRAWING PAPER

The use of good quality cartridge paper is recommended for botanical drawing, but it is up to you whether you choose to use loose sheets or work in a sketchbook. Cartridge paper should be smooth textured and around 70lbs/150gsm in weight. Cheaper, thinner cartridge papers are available; however, they tend to be slightly rougher in texture and prone to scuffing when rubbing out and pencil indentation when using the necessary H grade pencil.

It is worth investing in both A3 and A4 sizes so that you can select the size suitable for the drawings you are making. Pads or books of cartridge paper are available in either case-bound or spiral-bound formats. It is fine to use either format for drawing; spiral-bound pads have the advantage of being able to turn the pages completely back on themselves.

Keeping a botanical sketchbook for all of your drawings, research, and colour notes is a very useful exercise and even the sketchbook itself can become a charming work of art in its own right. Choosing a good quality sketchbook will allow you to draw, paint, and use ink and coloured pencils, and if the paper is defined as acid free, then the longevity of your work will also be preserved. You could also use a sketchbook rather like a scrapbook, a place to keep all related findings such as pressed and dried specimens, photographs and other useful information, to help you in your quest to learn about the species you are illustrating.

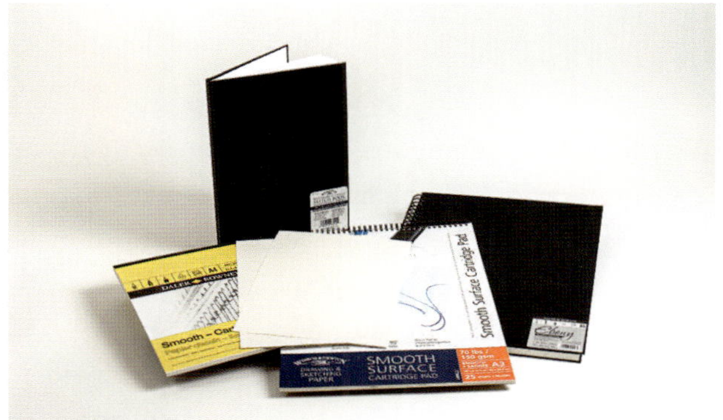

A3 and A4 cartridge paper in loose sheets and spiral- and case-bound sketchbooks.

ERASERS

Whilst you are drawing it is probable that from time to time you will need to correct any mistakes you make. It is arguable that any errors should be corrected at all, since leaving them in place is a good way of learning from your mistakes and will actually remind you of the mistake you made, thus avoiding the same error again. Although leaving errors *in situ* does have its merits, continual re-drawing can become confusing, especially when drawing fairly complex structures. If you need to erase mistakes, the best option is to do so by using a putty rubber. This is a pliable material resembling normal window putty, designed to absorb particles of graphite from the paper surface. Additionally, unlike some standard erasers, a putty rubber does not leave behind any evidence of rubbing out, which makes it ideal for keeping your drawings clean. Putty rubbers can be kneaded into any shape, for example a fine point or chisel to eradicate unwanted lines in a small space. Putty rubbers over time can become prone to hardening, or becoming soft and oily to the touch. Such rubbers can no longer be used effectively and you may find it necessary to replace them fairly regularly, however they are relatively inexpensive to buy.

Whilst a putty rubber makes the ideal eraser, a standard plastic eraser is also a good alternative. Plastic erasers are excellent for rubbing out larger areas and also have the advantage of completely eradicating pencil work. They are also neat and clean to use. Another useful type of eraser is a propelling one, rather like a propelling pencil. These are very handy for rubbing out single lines and areas of graphite from a confined space; are easy to hold and refills are readily available and inexpensive to purchase.

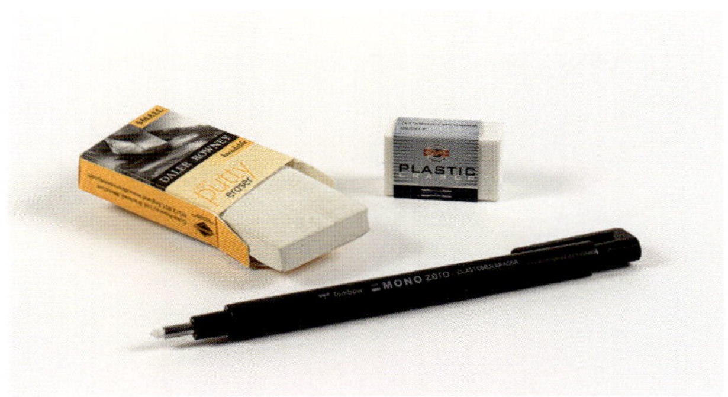

A selection of erasers: putty, good quality plastic and propelling varieties.

DIVIDERS AND PROPORTIONAL DIVIDERS

A useful aid for helping you draw accurately and to size is a pair of dividers. Looking similar to a mathematical compass, but with points on each side, you can make precise measurements of your subject matter, transfer, and mark distances onto your drawing paper.

Equally useful are a pair of proportional dividers designed especially for the purposes of enlarging or reducing drawings. By simply adjusting the central pivot to the required graduation hole, scaled drawings can quickly be made.

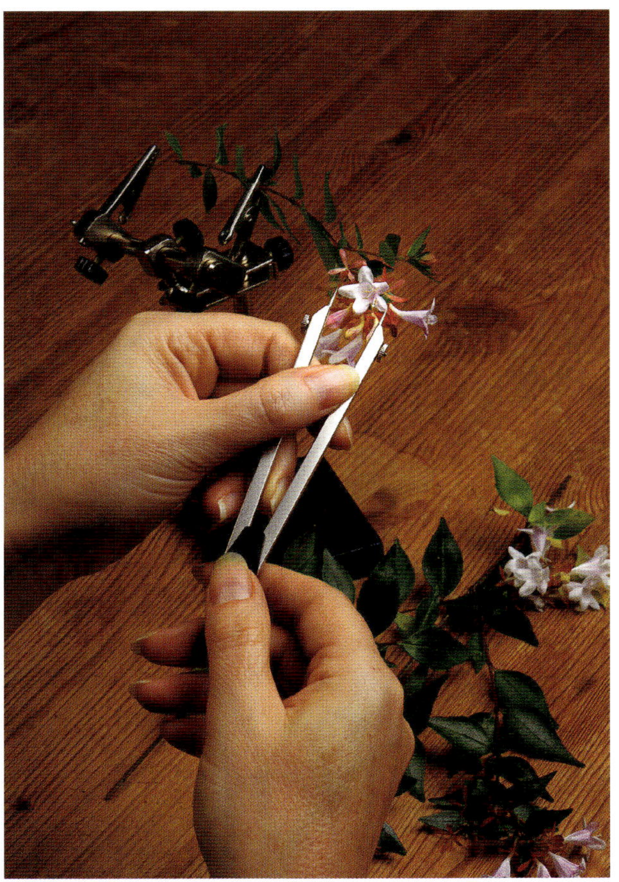

Dividers are used to take accurate measurements of a specimen when drawing at life size.

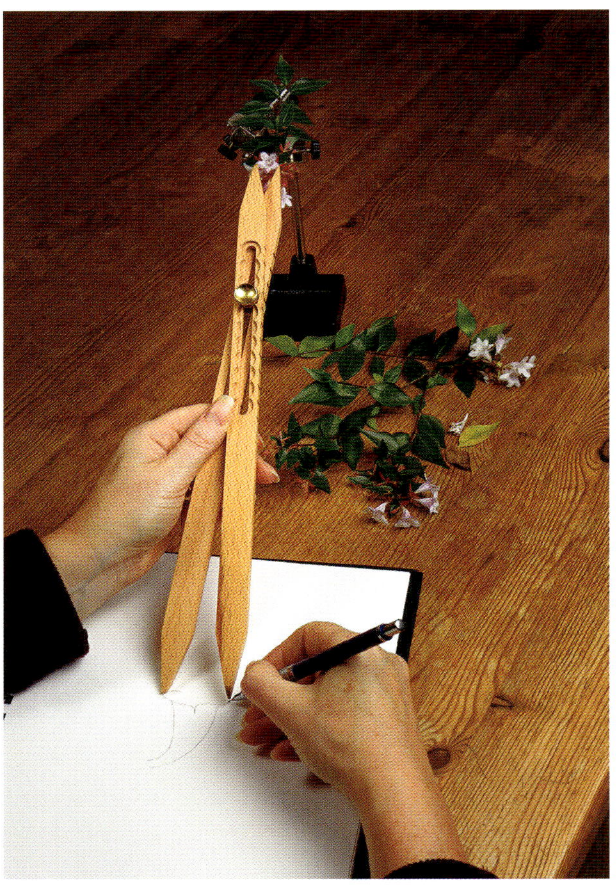

Use proportional dividers to make scaled measurements of your specimen.

PAINTING MATERIALS AND EQUIPMENT

As you progress from drawing to the painting stage you will need a variety of equipment to help you get underway. The essential materials will consist of brushes, watercolour paper and watercolour paints and you should endeavour to use the best quality you can afford. However, other items of equipment will be helpful which you can either purchase or source suitable alternatives from home to keep costs down.

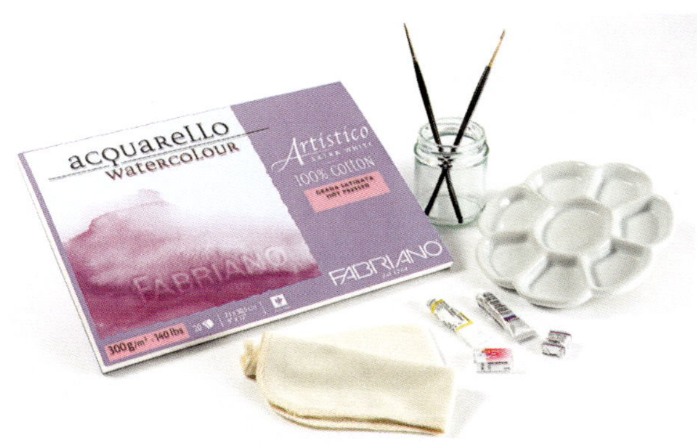

Painting materials: brushes, hot-pressed watercolour paper, watercolours, rag, palette, and water container.

BRUSHES

The finest quality kolinsky sable brushes are recommended for botanical illustration. The bristles are a natural product of the *kolinsky*, the Siberian weasel native to northern Asia. The tail hair is naturally collected, but as the animal is rare, kolinsky brushes tend to be expensive to buy. Their suitability for this type of painting, however, is evident in that they have the ability to naturally 'snap' back into position after repeated use. They also maintain a sharp point and hold paint well.

The range of brushes you will need does not need to be extensive. If you are purchasing brushes for the first time [illegible] or 3 and 1 will suffice. You can then add a size 2 and 0, more to your collection over time if you need them. There is a myth that in order to paint very finely, an extremely small brush such as 000 should be used. However, you will be able to paint [illegible]h details so long as the point of your brush forms and [ma]intains a sharp point.

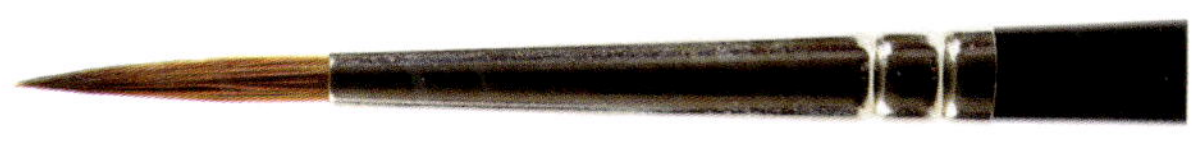

The bristles of a good quality sable brush should form a point.

The make and size of a brush is indicated on the handle.

Tips for buying [illegible]ky brushes

When you are buying b[illegible]'sider getting them from an art shop rather [illegible] Although art shops are something of a rarity [illegible]nding a good one where you can check the [ko]linsky brush before you buy it is highly recom[mended illegible] should never buy a brush with 'splayed' bris[tles illegible] bristles are a sign that the brush has been d[illegible] will not be able to paint well with it. A[illegible] will be happy to help you with purchases, so it is always worth asking for a small pot of water to check how well the brush comes to a point. Carefully remove the brush from the protective straw, dip it into some water and then rotate the bristles on the back of your hand. The point should be pin-sharp. If it is blunt or if any bristles are stray, you should not buy the brush. Look for a good alternative instead and repeat the process until you find a suitable one.

WATERCOLOUR PAPER

Selecting the correct type of watercolour paper for botanical illustration can at first appear to be quite a confusing process. There are many textures, weights and sizes to choose from so an understanding of the differences will make your job easier.

There are three categories of paper texture: hot-pressed (often referred to as 'smooth'), cold-pressed, and rough. Both cold-pressed and rough papers have a noticeable texture (known as a 'tooth') and whilst these papers are generally cheaper to purchase and good for complete beginners, their texture renders them inappropriate for achieving very fine and detailed botanical work. You will therefore need to familiarize yourself with the hot-pressed texture, which is extremely smooth by contrast, and is therefore the most suitable surface for obtaining fine painted details.

Next you will need to consider the weight of paper you need. The most common weight is 140lb/300gsm which is perfectly adequate for most botanical work. Lighter weight paper (90lb/200gsm) has a tendency to be too light and may cause problems such as buckling. Heavier weight paper (300lb/620gsm) will only be necessary if you intend applying lots of washes in your illustration. It can occasionally be necessary to stretch paper beforehand, but this would only need to be done if you are using loose sheet mid-weight paper.

Hot-pressed watercolour paper left is smoother than cold-pressed watercolour paper.

Hot-pressed watercolour paper is available in spiral pads and loose sheets.

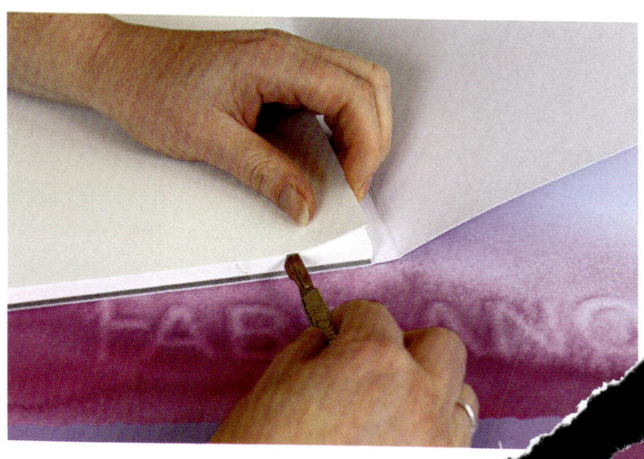

Sheets of gummed hot-pressed watercolour paper should be lifted carefully with a knife from the corner of the pad.

Acid-free, hot-pressed paper ca be bought in pads, blocks or loose sheets. If you are ly to be working at larger than 18in × 24in then yo ill have to purchase paper as loose sheets anyway, o ise blocks and pads are available in sizes upwards A5 (210 × 148mm). It is entirely up to you in whi at you buy paper. If you are new to using hot-pr per, then it may be advantageous to buy loose begin with allowing yourself the chance t apers produced by different manufacturers. tice a slight, quite subtle, colour variation pers, from bright white, off-white/ivor pale yellow. For example, Arches is m han Fabriano, but Fabriano is offered a tistico' which also vary slightly in colo down to personal choice which one y sorbency of paper

How to stretch watercolour paper

It is generally recommended that you use hot-pressed paper of at least 140lb (300gsm) weight for botanical illustration, which is regarded as the standard by most botanical painters. You will therefore not need to stretch watercolour paper all that often unless you regularly use a lot of washes or need to paint large, flat areas in your illustration.

Stretching paper is a straightforward process, but you must take care to ensure each stage of the process is followed, and it may take two or three attempts to achieve a perfect result.

You will need:

- A clean bath filled with 6in lukewarm water;
- Your watercolour paper;
- Sealed ply board (or similar);
- Lengths of brown gummed tape;
- Sponge.

Process:

1. Fill a clean bathtub with about 6in lukewarm water.
2. Gently submerge your paper, following the contours of the bath, and leave to soak for five to ten minutes.
3. Carefully lift the paper out of the water by one corner, supporting it as you go, and allowing the excess water to drip off.
4. Gently lay the paper onto a clean board (sealed ply or similar) and remove excess water with a clean sponge. Do this from the centre outwards to the edges, ensuring no air bubbles remain.

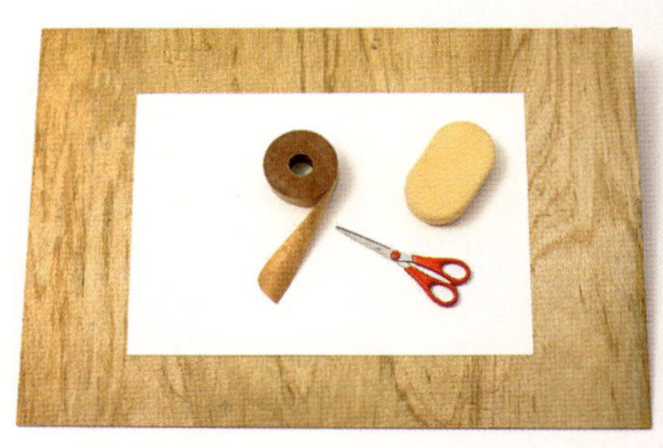

Use hot-pressed watercolour paper, sealed ply, gummed tape, scissors, and a sponge to stretch your own paper.

5. When the paper is completely flat, and all the air bubbles are dispersed, apply lengths of 2in water-soluble brown adhesive tape along the edges. You will need to wet the tape as well, so run it through the water in the bath and then hold upright so that the surplus water can drain off. (Ensure you don't hold the tape in the water for too long otherwise the gum will soak off.)
6. Carefully stick a length of tape over each edge of the paper. Make sure that the tape adheres entirely to the paper, so check for any air pockets or wrinkles.
7. Lightly use a sponge to remove excess water from the edges, taking care not to disturb the gummed tape.
8. Lay the board flat allowing the paper and tape to dry.
9. As the board dries, check for air pockets, wrinkles and lifting tape. If tape is lifting you can fix by laying an additional length of tape over the top.

also varies between manufacturers, which depends on the size that has been applied to the surface. Arches is known for its very absorbent surface, making it an ideal paper to use for building up several layers of wash. It can be quite difficult to move the paint around of this type of surface. By contrast, the fairly new Zeta paper by Stillman & Birn is much less absorbent, allowing the artist to easily move paint around the surface and to lift paint with relative ease.

Some manufacturers offer their hot-pressed paper in block form as well as sheets and pads. Buying a block of paper is a cost-effective way to buy en masse and because the paper is glued on all four sides, makes it ideal for applying numerous washes without the need to be stretched. However, it is worth bearing in mind that transferring your drawing from your sketchbook to block paper will only be possible by using the tracing method (*see* Chapter 4), so you will need to take this into account before committing to buying twenty to twenty-five in a block. Once you have completed a painting using block paper you will then have to separate the sheet from the rest of the block. This is easily done by locating the corner which is unglued, and then carefully sliding a craft knife along the edges.

WATERCOLOURS

Watercolour by definition is a pure pigment held in a water-based suspension, and is the traditional medium used by botanical artists and illustrators. The renowned German Renaissance artist Albrecht Dürer (1471–1528) painted many botanical works of art and is generally considered among the first advocates of watercolour. It has the ability to define the clarity and precision of scientific specimens in full colour making it the favoured medium even today.

Nowadays, watercolours are available in two formats; pans and tubes. The fundamental difference between them is that tubes are malleable whilst pans are dry. Whichever you choose is entirely down to your own preference; there are certain advantages and disadvantages to both.

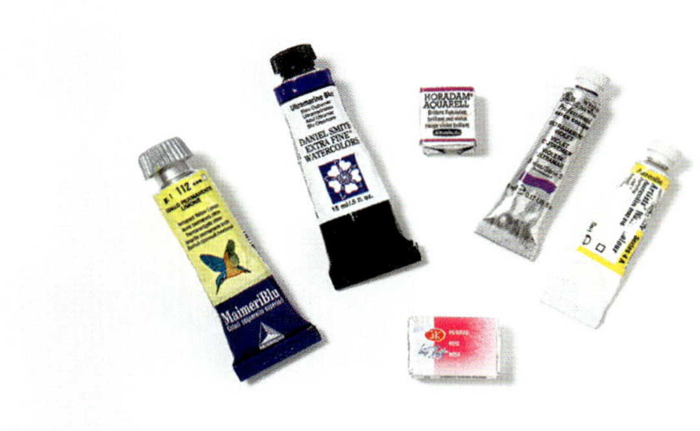

Different brands of watercolours are available in tubes and pans.

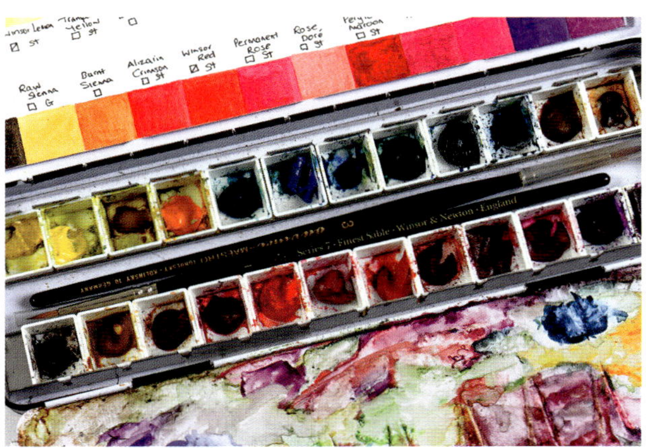

Use tube paints squeezed into empty pans to make your own palette.

TUBES

Tubes of watercolour are available in 5ml and 14ml weights, although for botanical illustration it is seldom necessary to buy the larger size. You will generally be using very small quantities of paint at any one time, so you will find that a 5ml tube will last a good while.

Tube paints contain more binder (gum Arabic) in them than pans, making them easy to squeeze onto your palette and are useful if you have large areas to cover. You will also notice that by picking up even the smallest amount of paint on your brush, the colour is immediately vibrant and intense. This is especially helpful when mixing colours together as it enables you to achieve the richness or intensity of colour quite rapidly without necessarily having to build up layer upon layer of wash.

It is quite common practice to squeeze tube paints into empty pans to make up a palette of colours. If you do this you will be able to repeatedly re-wet the colours quite easily once they have dried, although you may notice that some paints used in this way remain soft or sticky because the binder does not fully dry out. This is not a problem, and is not to the detriment of the effectiveness of the paint.

Over time, some tubes of paint can deteriorate by becoming solid. This occurs if air has been allowed to creep inside, either because there is a small puncture in the tube casing, or if the lid has not been sufficiently tightened. If this happens, it is still possible to use the paint inside like a pan, but if the paint does not adhere well to the paper, it may have dried out too much, in which case it is best to discard the tube and buy a fresh one.

PANS

The advantage of pans is that you can purchase them in a set or individually to add to your own palette. Available in both half pans and full pans, you really only need to consider buying half pans. Rather like purchasing the smallest size tube, half pans are usually more than sufficient for the needs of any botanical painter. As you unwrap each pan you will have immediate access to the colour, as there is no need to squeeze paint onto a palette.

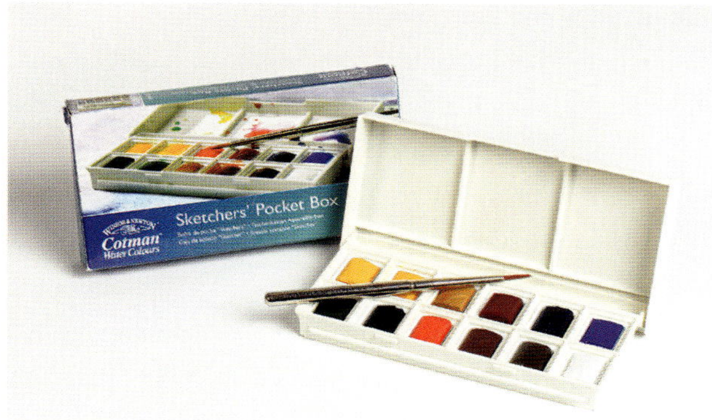

Travel sets of watercolour pans are ideal for travelling with.

Using pans can require some extra effort when mixing colours to the required consistency or quantity of colour. It is sensible to consider using an old brush to do this, as persistent use/scrubbing with a good quality brush will ruin it and its perfect point over time.

Pans are ideal for those who enjoy applying washes and are nice and portable, ideal for use when travelling or painting in a non-studio environment.

WATERCOLOUR BRANDS

There are numerous brands of watercolours on the market, but it is the artist or professional quality ranges that will offer the best results for botanical painting. Of the most popular, Winsor & Newton, Schminke, Sennelier, Daniel Smith, White Nights and Rembrandt all use the purest of pigments to ensure maximum colour intensity, brilliance and transparency. If you are new to botanical painting, it is worth experimenting with the different brands until you find one that suits you.

CHOOSING A PALETTE

If you opt for using tubes of watercolour, choosing a good palette for mixing should be a relatively straightforward process, but if you are using pans in a set then you will most likely be provided with an attached palette. Plastic and ceramic palettes are readily available to purchase in a multitude of shapes and sizes from art shops or online, but it will be a ceramic palette that will give you more success when mixing watercolours.

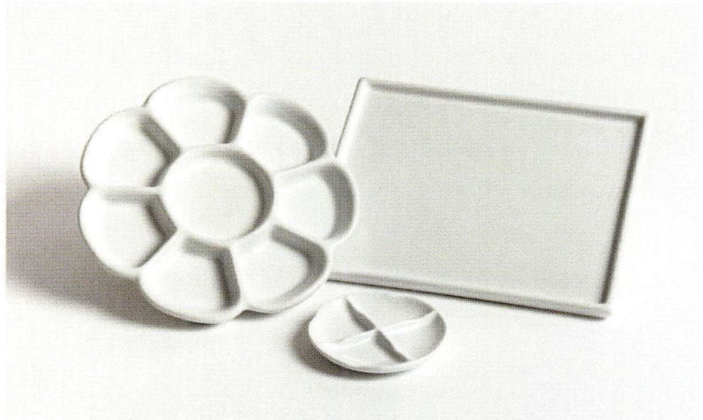

Ceramic palettes are available in different sizes and styles.

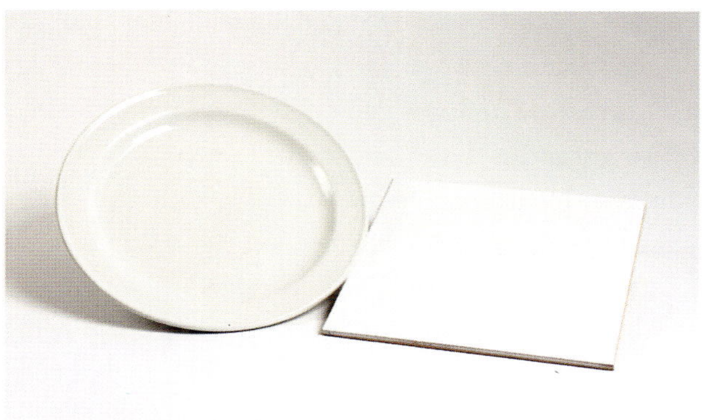

A ceramic white plate or white bathroom tile makes a cheaper alternative to commercially available palettes.

Plastic palettes, whilst relatively inexpensive, tend to stain and repel paint from the surface, rendering them hard or virtually impossible to use. It is possible that with perseverance, the plastic surface may become more accepting of paint over time. Plastic palettes are however light and durable, often making them popular choices for travelling artists.

Ceramic palettes, although heavier and more expensive to handle and carry around, provide a much better surface for colour mixing. It is possible to use a white plate or ceramic tile instead as a good alternative to a commercially available palette.

Whatever your choice of palette, ensure it provides sufficient space for holding and mixing your colours.

Whilst using your palette, it is not always necessary to clean it out after each use. Any colour remaining after you have finished painting can simply be re-wetted and used again. In fact, some artists prefer to work this way and deliberately keep their palette 'dirty', as invariably the mixes of colour left behind are so variable that they can often be used in a painting as shadow colours. However, every now and then it is a good idea to clean out your palette completely, so that you don't run out of mixing space, or contaminate and dull down individual colours.

WATER CONTAINER

The simple solution for equipping yourself with a water container is to use any clean, clear or white plastic or glass pot you have at home. Some artists prefer to buy containers which are commercially available, such as a plastic collapsible design, ideal for ease of storage or if you are travelling; a non-spill paint pot complete with a useful brush rest across the lid, and divided water pits, enabling you to permanently keep one half filled with clean water, ideal if you are using the wet-into-wet painting technique.

During painting, you should replenish your water supply regularly to avoid microorganisms from growing in it. Keeping the water clean also helps ensure your painting remains clean too. It is fine to use normal tap water. However, some artists prefer to use filtered or distilled water. This is because in some hard water areas there are significant mineral deposits or additives in the water supply such as calcium or chlorine, which can react with your paints.

When you have finished painting never leave your brush in the water. This is a bad habit that will cause the bristles of a perfectly good quality brush to become bent in a very short space of time. If you accidentally do this however, it is sometimes possible to restore the brush by suspending the bristles momentarily in boiling water.

RAGS

As you paint you will need to take excess water and paint off your brush frequently. To do this a rag is an essential piece of equipment. It doesn't have to be anything elaborate as long as it is lint free so that you avoid transferring fibres to and from your painting. You should avoid using paper kitchen towel or tissues, as these start to disintegrate once they become wet and again, fibres can easily be transferred to your painting or picked up on your brush during rinsing.

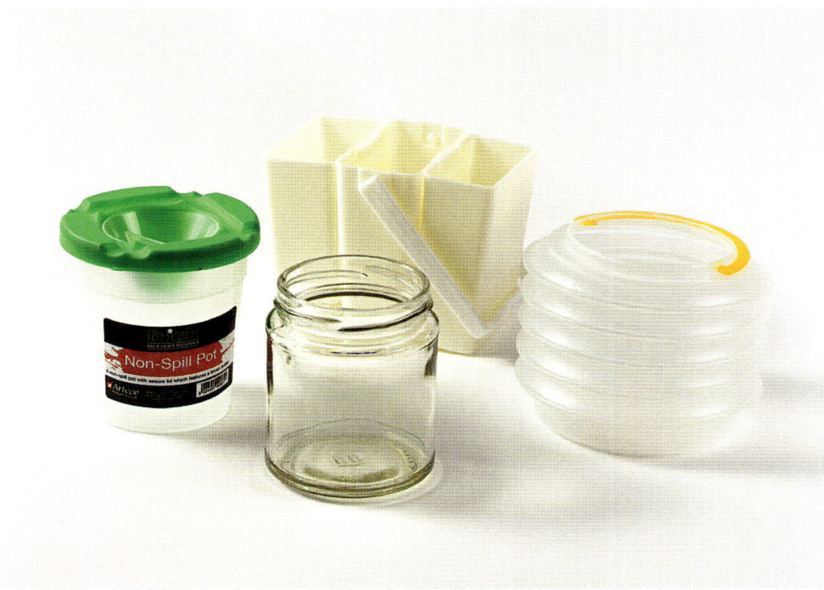

Water pots are available in different materials, or a clean, clear glass jar works equally as well.

OTHER USEFUL EQUIPMENT

Besides the obvious drawing and painting materials, there are several other items of equipment you will find useful for botanical illustration. You may even discover some items along the way that are not included in the following list. It is not uncommon for artists to be inventive and use even the most mundane of household objects to help them with their work. Items such as an upturned saucepan to stand a vase on, or a peg to clamp a specimen in place are not unheard of.

The following list of useful equipment is not conclusive, but will give you a clear indication of other items that might be useful.

ANGLEPOISE LAMP

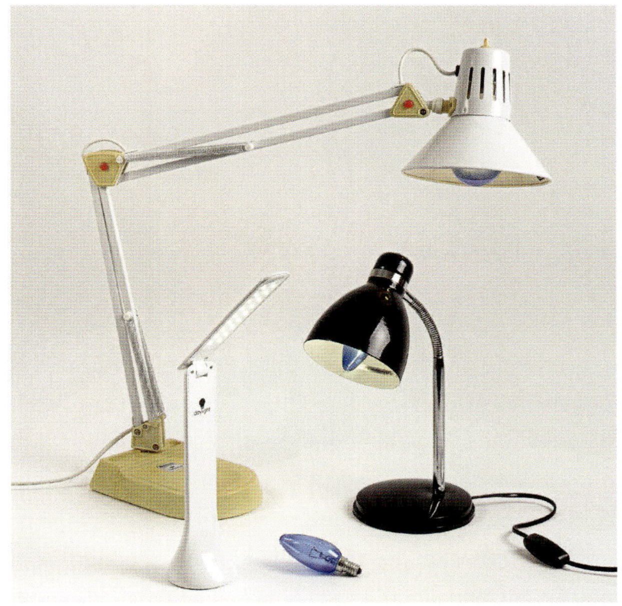

Anglepoise lamps are available in different designs, but always use a daylight simulation bulb for botanical illustration.

An Anglepoise lamp is probably the most useful additional piece of equipment to invest in. It will not only help you to see your subject matter more clearly but will also provide a directional light source onto it. During the painting process on overcast or gloomy winter days, an Anglepoise lamp will be a godsend, allowing much-needed light onto your work.

As with much equipment, there is a good selection of Anglepoise lamps available to choose from. A standard Anglepoise lamp provides quite simply light from either a screw or bayonet light bulb fitment, but more extravagant versions may incorporate a magnifying lens. Most lamps are designed to sit on your desk, but floor-standing lamps are also available.

It is vital that with any lamp, you choose a daylight bulb fitting. This will simulate daylight and therefore enable you to see the true colours of your specimen when painting.

TRACING PAPER

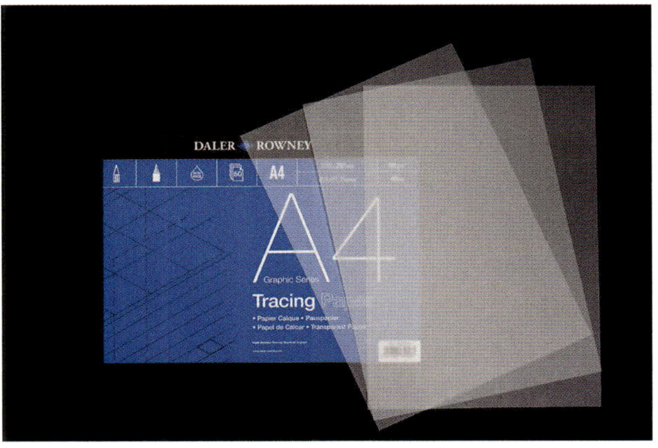

Useful tracing paper is available as loose sheets or pads.

Good quality semi-transparent tracing paper can be used during several stages of the botanical illustration process. As part of the drawing stage, a sheet of tracing paper is useful to check the accuracy of your drawing. If you can't quite see why part of your drawing looks ambiguous, re-draw the problem area directly over the top on tracing paper rather than continually rubbing out your line work. Not until you have corrected the mistake on tracing paper will you need to correct your drawing, therefore allowing you as many attempts as necessary to get it right. Remember that neatness and cleanliness are all part of creating an accurate drawing. You will only create a mess by continuing to rub out in the same area repeatedly and you also run the risk of damaging your paper.

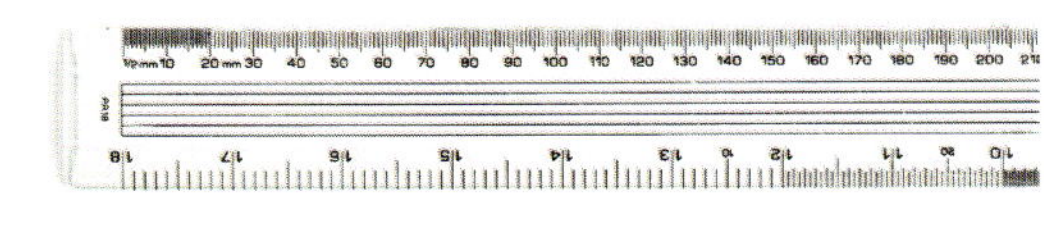

Use a plastic or metal ruler to make precise measurements.

Tracing paper can also play an important role at the composition stage (*see* Chapter 4). You can use it to assemble a master template of your drawings into a final composition, and then use either a lightbox to transfer the drawing to painting paper, or apply graphite on the reverse before tracing the image through onto painting paper.

RULER

You can use a ruler purely for making measurements at the drawing stage. Use either centimetres or inches of a plastic or metal ruler to do so. A ruler can be a useful alternative to dividers, and will give you a precise measurement to help you make accurate drawings.

You may be tempted to use the ruler for drawing the seemingly straight sides of flower stems – especially if they are long – however, this is discouraged for various reasons. Surprisingly, lines drawn with a ruler can sometimes look unnatural, or the artist may inadvertently draw a completely parallel pair of lines of a flower stem with a ruler, without observing the subtle tapering and flaring which could occur in such an example. It is good practice for botanical artists and illustrators to perfect the art of drawing straight lines, and is a very useful skill to have.

DRAWING BOARD/SLOPE

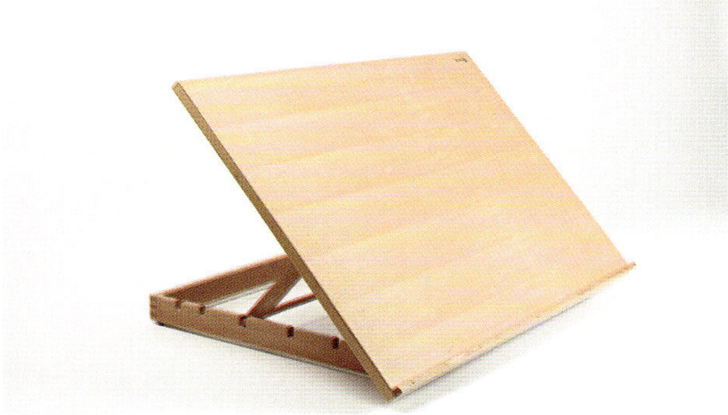

Using a drawing board can help reduce distortion when drawing your subjects and will support your paper whilst painting.

Make your own drawing slope with a length of 2in × 2in wood and a sheet of ½in thick plywood.

Many artists prefer to work at a drawing board or slope for both drawing and painting. When drawing your specimen, the drawing on the paper in front of you will appear less distorted than if you work on a flat surface. In other words, the view of your drawing is much more correct, therefore maximizing the accuracy of your drawing.

Due to the lengthy process of drawing and painting you will also find it more comfortable to use a drawing board as you will not need to bend your neck right over your work, but instead maintain a much more upright posture reducing stress and tiredness in your muscles.

If you choose to invest in a drawing board, a table-top variety should suffice. There are many types available, from fairly inexpensive options through to professional alternatives. You could also improvise and make your own drawing board or slope to work on. A piece of half-inch thick ply resting on a length of 2in × 2in wood is equally efficient as its shop-bought counterpart.

If you are travelling with your work there are now some very useful portable, lightweight drawing boards available, some featuring easy-carry handles.

LOW ADHESIVE TAPE/MASKING TAPE

Whilst you are drawing and painting it is a good idea to secure your paper to your drawing surface. You can easily do this by using low adhesive or masking tape. Masking tape that is pH neutral is easily removed from your paper without damaging it or leaving a residue. Similarly, clear, low adhesive tape allows you to easily peel it away after use, and can also be used to stick together drawings you have transferred onto tracing paper when compiling a composition master template (*see* Chapter 4). Being clear, it does not detract from the composition elements, can easily be lifted and repositioned, and can even be drawn on with a pencil.

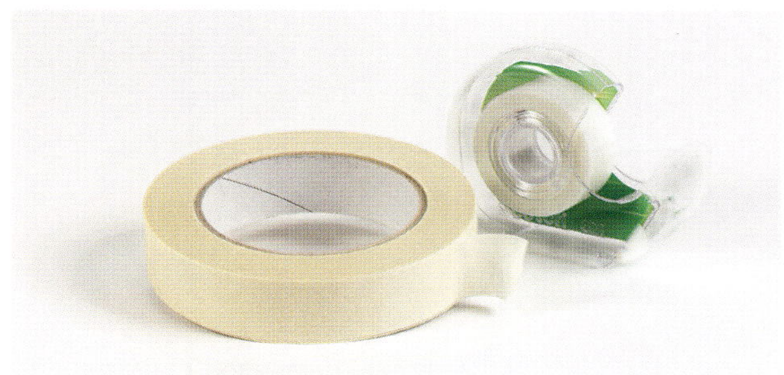

Use low-adhesive tape or masking tape to secure paper to your drawing surface.

MICROSCOPE

As a botanical illustrator it is essential to observe and draw your subject matter accurately. In the case of very small features, using a microscope or hand lens will help you see and understand some structures much more clearly. You will not need to magnify anything to the extent of being able to observe the minutiae of detail such as cell structures, but you may for example need to describe and explain specifically the structure of an anther on a stamen or perhaps the small seeds contained in a seed capsule. A microscope providing a minimum magnification of around ×20 should be sufficient for the needs of most botanical illustrators.

Basic models of microscope are reasonably priced, however if you require greater magnification models up to ×120 power are also available. Some basic models come with additional eyepieces that can be easily attached, and some, a little more expensive, have the added benefit of inbuilt illumination systems, which can be useful.

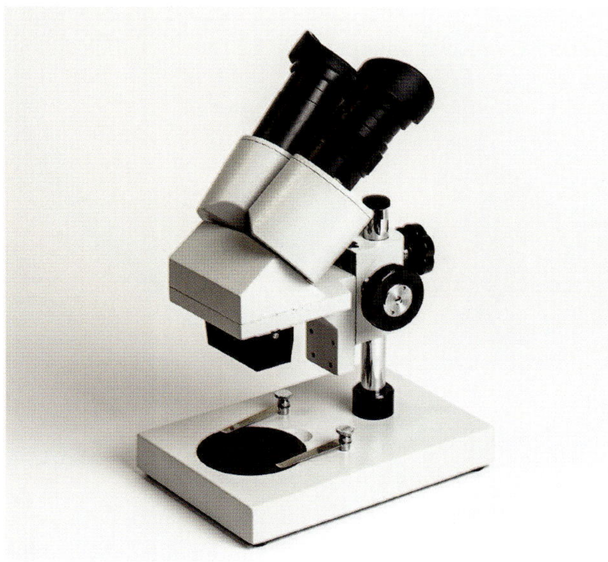

Use a microscope to make close, accurate observations of your specimens.

HAND LENS

A hand lens (such as those used by jewellers) is very helpful due to their portability, especially when observing specimens out 'in the field'. Hand lenses are available in ×8, ×10, ×15 and ×20 magnifications.

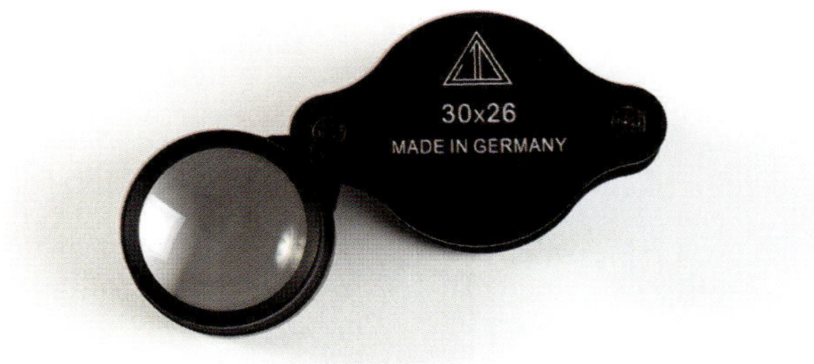

A hand lens is a convenient way to observe specimens closely, especially 'in the field'.

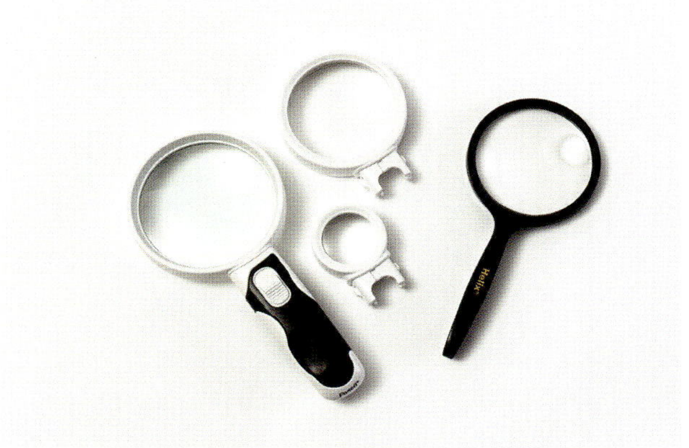

Magnifying lenses are useful for observing specimens, and are available as traditional and LED illumination options.

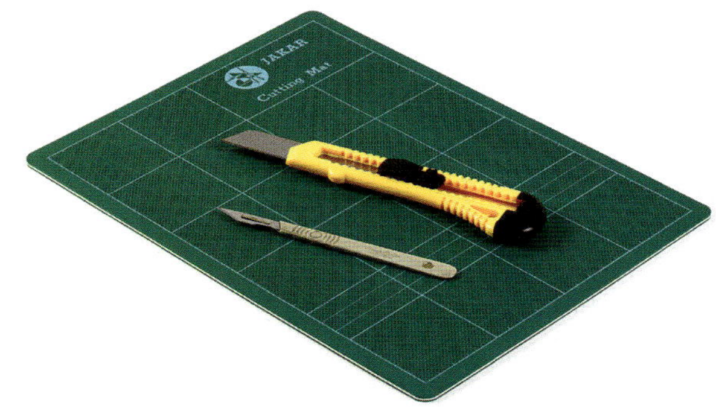

A craft knife or scalpel used on a cutting mat is a good alternative to a botanist's razor blade for cutting small specimens.

MAGNIFYING GLASS

Conventional hand-held magnifying lenses are considered as essential kit for the majority of botanical artists and illustrators. A typical magnifying glass will provide a very handy magnification of ×2 with an inbuilt additional magnification lens of ×4. Greater magnifications can also be sought, typically up to ×10 power. Available in different formats such as traditional hand-held pocket size, chest and stand (hands free), and even spectacle format, there is plenty of choice. Nowadays, many magnifying glasses also have inbuilt LED illumination.

CRAFT KNIFE AND CUTTING MAT

If you are likely to be dissecting components of your specimens, it will be necessary to use some form of blade to cut with on a cutting mat. Botanists usually use a 'double-edged razor blade' which gives a wonderfully clean, sharp cut, or you could use a craft knife or scalpel (with a size 10A blade) which both have a handle making them easier to hold. Whichever you choose, you should make sure that the blade is sharp so that you make clean cuts through your specimen. Try to avoid using blunt blades as these will cause snagging and tearing and always replace a blunt blade as soon as possible. Always take care when using any form of knife or blade and put them away safely when not in use. An effective way of storing a scalpel is to embed the blade in a cork. Artist's craft knives contain retractable blades, and razor blades can be stored safely in a sealable box.

To prevent your work surface from becoming cut, it is advisable to use a cutting mat or perhaps a piece of wood or thick cardboard. Artists' rubber cutting mats are particularly good as they are non-slip and reusable.

OFFCUTS OF WATERCOLOUR PAPER

It is well worth saving lots of offcuts of watercolour paper. These can be used to practise painting techniques and experiment with colour mixes. Painting a small swatch of your mixed colour off the edge of a scrap of paper, or around a punched hole, can when dry be held directly onto the specimen to check for likeness. If the colours of both the specimen and paint swatch merge together, you have achieved a good match.

SETTING UP A STUDIO OR WORKSPACE

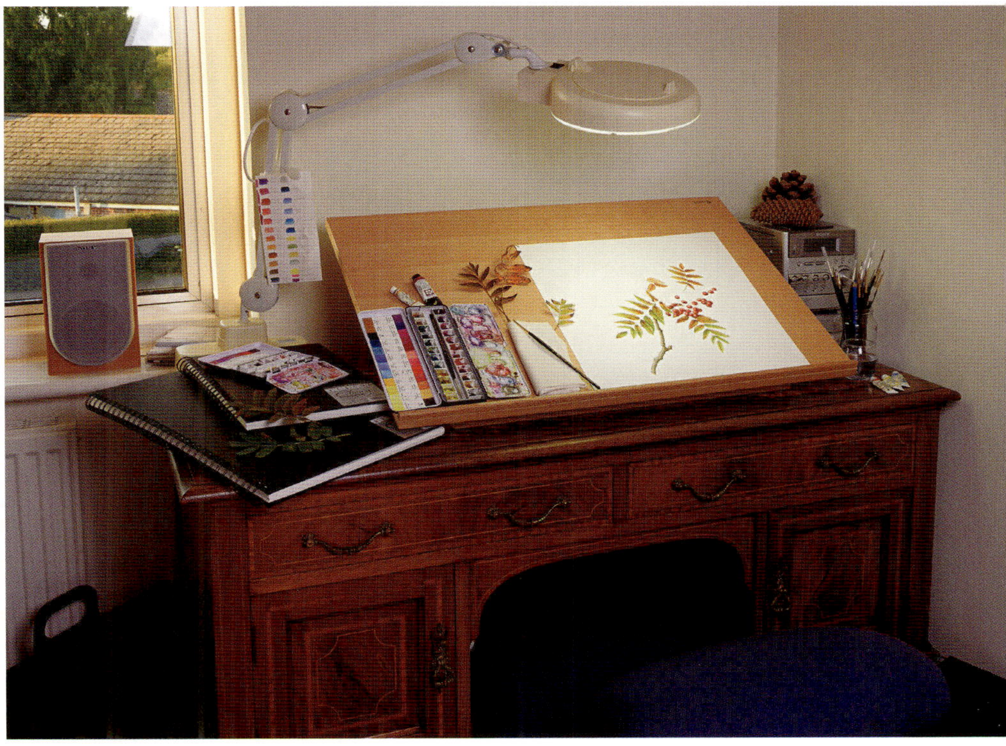

Set up your workspace so that it is conducive to botanical painting.

Choosing a good location for drawing and painting is very important. Few artists are fortunate enough to exercise the luxury of using a dedicated, fully equipped studio; some are able to utilize a spare room, but the majority are often to be found using a desk in the corner of a room, a kitchen table or one end of a dining table. Whichever is available to you, making the most of your workspace is extremely important. You will be spending many hours in the space, so it should be conducive to botanical illustration and comfortable to work in.

The convention for lighting botanical subject matter states that the light should come from the top left if you are right-handed, and top right if you are left-handed. The origins of this convention date back to when artists worked by candlelight, and needed to avoid painting in the shadow of their own hand. The convention is carried through to the present day, but is by no means a rule set in stone. Some left-handed artists happily adopt the convention for light on the top left, because that is what is generally taught (historically the ratio of right-/left-handed population in a classroom setting is 90/10).

The perfect position for your desk or work table (if you are right-handed) is in front of and to the right of a north-facing window or in front of and slightly to the left of the window if you are left-handed. Northern light in the northern hemisphere (southern light in the southern hemisphere) is the most even and constant light throughout the day; the light is softer and more diffused because the sun is less direct, which generally gives greater subtlety of modelling of the subject matter.

In addition to your desk you will need to set up your drawing board or slope with space around it for your palette, water pot and other associated equipment such

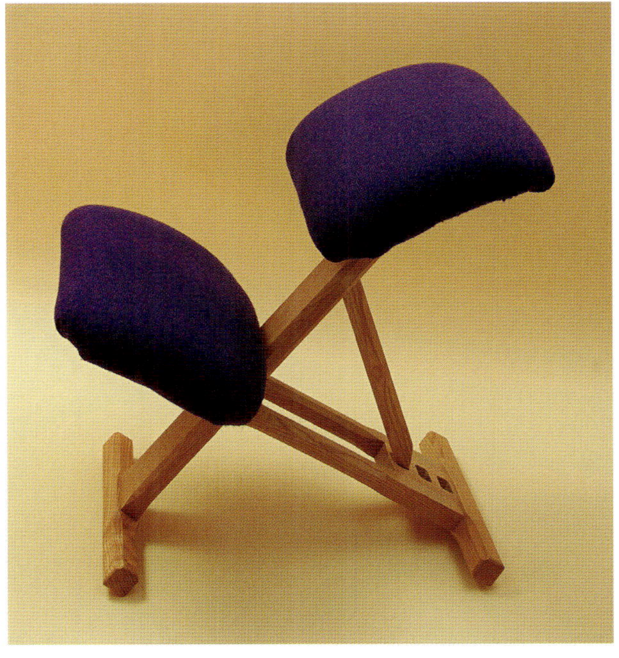

A sit/kneel stool will help you maintain a good posture whilst working at your desk.

as sketchbooks and paintbrushes. It is also a good idea to equip yourself with an Anglepoise lamp, which will be positioned slightly to the left and towards the back of your board (right side if you are left-handed).

Sitting comfortably whilst you are working is necessary to produce good work, therefore you will need something comfortable to sit on. Unless you have a suitable back-supporting chair of the right height, you may wish to consider using a sit/kneel stool. These are ideal for maintaining a good posture, and are also height adjustable.

If you have space in your studio/work room, it is a good idea to consider a second desk or table which you could use specifically for observational drawing – or, if this is not possible, using another table away from your workspace. This works well as it minimizes disruption to your painting desk, which you will be able to leave *in situ* once you are happy with the set-up. Most of your observational drawing will be done in outline, so at this preliminary stage you won't need to worry too much about the conventional way of lighting your subject. You should however ensure that there is sufficient light on this second table for you to see clearly what you are drawing, in which case another window or another lamp may be required.

Working in a clean environment is essential. You should therefore get into the habit of keeping your desk clear of clutter, dust, and other pollutants to avoid particles getting into watercolours, water and onto your work. It is a good idea to put your work away at the end of the day and to cover any unprotected paint in your palette. Pet hair can also become a problem, so keeping floor coverings and surrounding surfaces as clean as possible is advisable.

Checklist for Materials and Equipment

- Invest in good quality materials at the outset. Choose artist's quality watercolours to achieve strong, vibrant, and realistic colour matches.
- Use H grade pencils for accurate observational drawing.
- When buying paintbrushes, opt for Kolinsky sable and ensure the bristles maintain a fine point when wet. Do not buy brushes with damaged or 'splayed' bristles, and use a plastic straw to protect when not in use.
- If you live in a hard-water area, consider using filtered or distilled water for painting.
- Invest in a magnifying glass, hand lens and/or microscope to help you accurately observe and draw small details.
- Choose a north-facing window to site your desk when setting up your studio or workspace.
- When pencil shading, light your subject with a directional light source from the top left to help you identify the highlights and shadows.
- Store your work flat, either in a plan chest or sturdy portfolio.

STORAGE SOLUTIONS

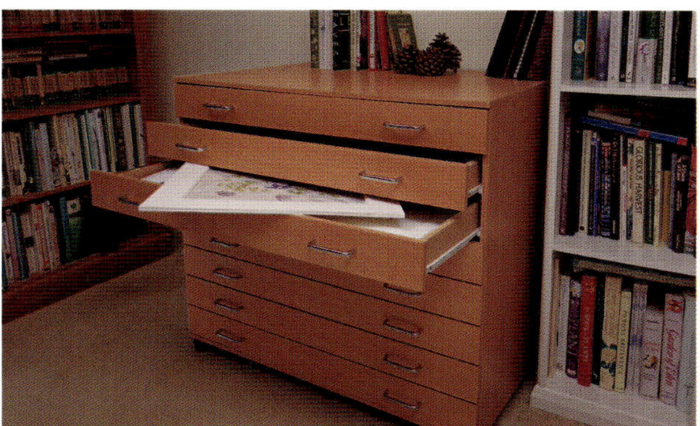

A plan chest is ideal to store your work in.

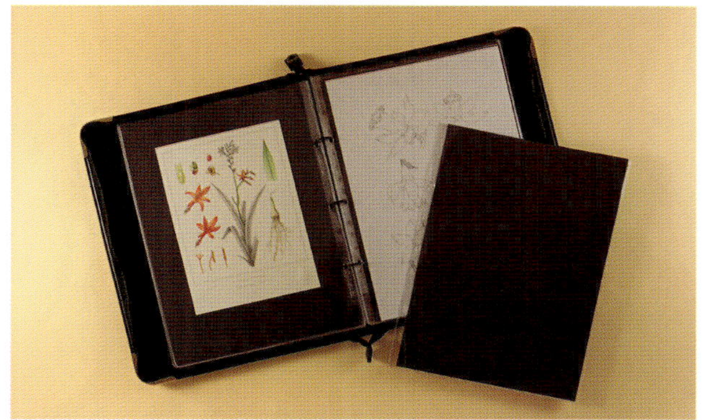

A sturdy portfolio with display sleeves is an ideal solution for storing and protecting your work.

All the time you have work in progress or have completed paintings, equipping yourself with some good storage is vital to keep your work clean, flat and out of direct sunlight. There are several options for storing work as well if you are likely to be travelling with your work.

STORAGE AT HOME

You will need to consider storage options in your workspace. If space permits, a plan chest is the obvious choice and is ideal as a long-term storage solution. You could also consider a strong, durable portfolio for storing work. There is a plethora of commercially available options but the most popular are the zipped variety, some of which can be used with display sleeves inserted.

ON THE MOVE

Portfolios are ideal for storing work if you are likely to be travelling. Heavy-duty portfolios are ideal for carrying several pieces of work include a handy shoulder strap, whilst more lightweight, thinner varieties are suitable for transporting single pieces of work. Cheaper options may need to be replaced regularly if they are used frequently.

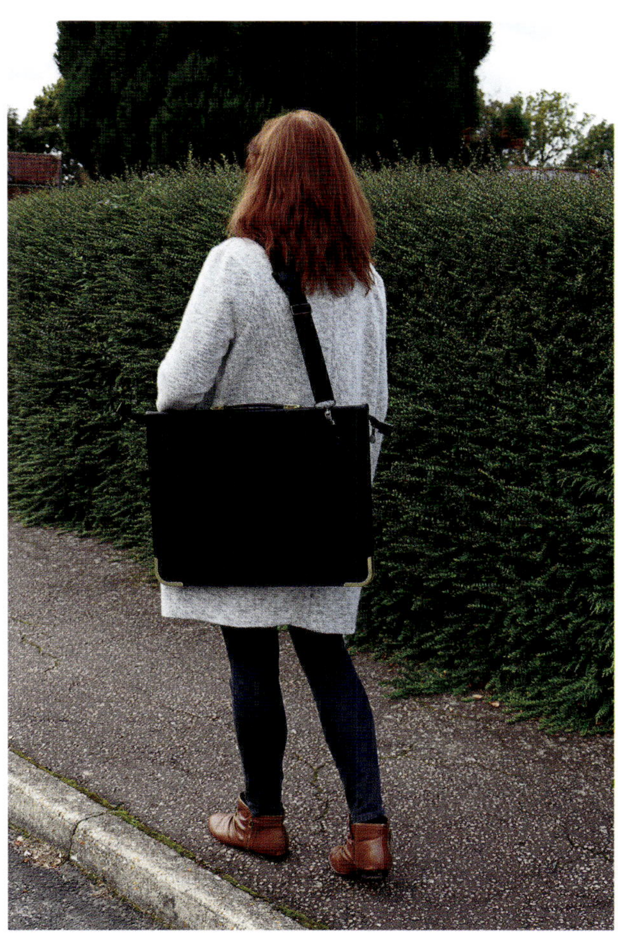

The attachment of a strap to your portfolio makes travelling with your work much easier.

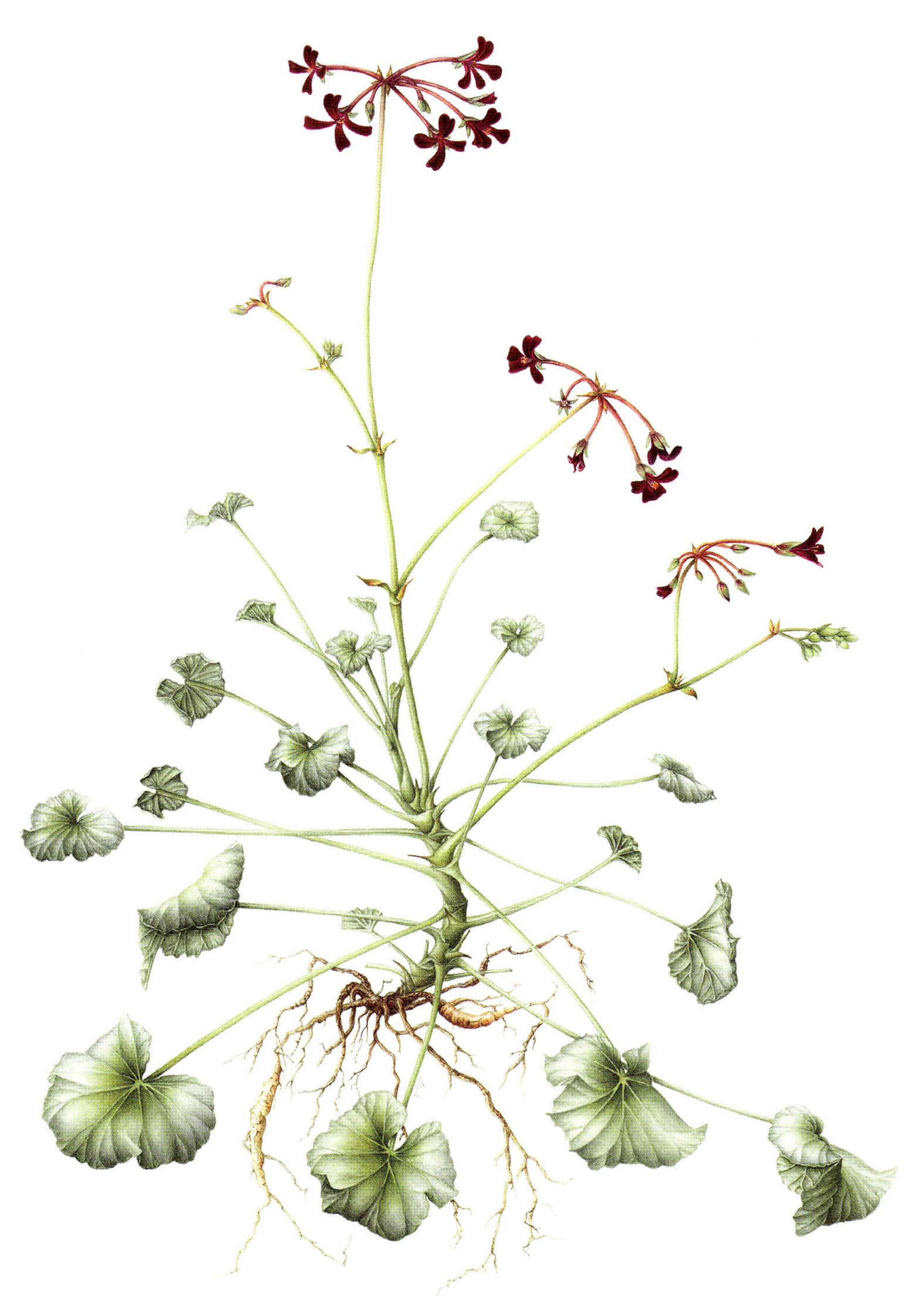

CHAPTER 2

Choosing and Preparing a Subject

Selection is the basis of all art. Nothing comes of nothing.

– James Johnson Sweeney (American curator and writer about modern art)

Choosing a subject can be a straightforward process or a more challenging prospect, depending on what the intended purpose of your illustration might be. It may be that you simply like a plant and you would like to try drawing and painting it or perhaps someone has commissioned you. If you are painting for yourself, then your subject choice may be significant in some way or you might have childhood memories of it; perhaps you grow it well in your garden or are fascinated by its colour, texture, or structure. If you intend choosing something from your garden, then hopefully it will be a fairly straightforward process to gather your plant material and prepare to draw. However, if you are illustrating a specific subject for someone else then you will need to consider how, where and when you will collect your specimens.

Remember that botanical illustration is all about being able to identify a species clearly, therefore you should carefully consider the process of choosing and preparing your subject in advance, regardless of whether you are illustrating for yourself or someone else.

In this chapter we will address not only how to go about choosing a subject but also consider the preparation process for drawing it, including research methods, collecting specimens and what to do if for example your subject is a protected or endangered species. We will also think about how to look after specimens once you have collected them, how best to take care of them when not in use, and longer-term preservation methods.

Pelargonium sidoides. LEIGH ANN GALE

WHAT SHOULD I CHOOSE TO ILLUSTRATE?

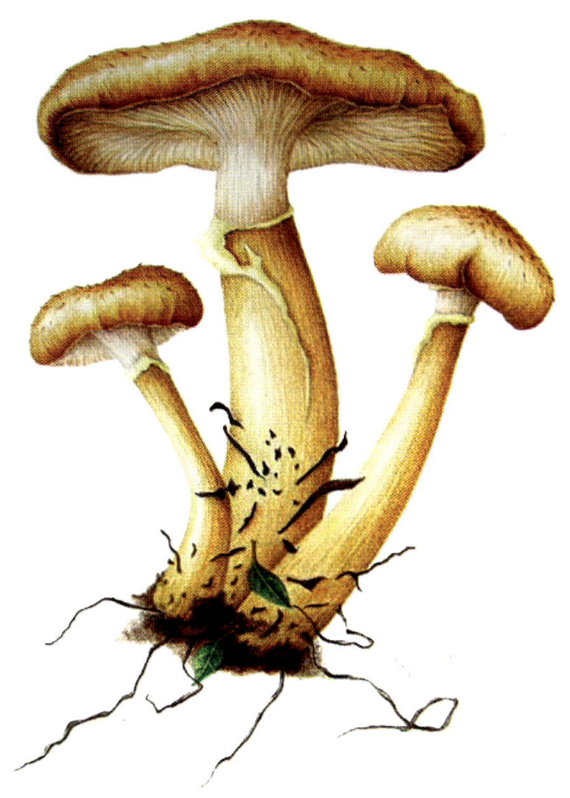

Armillaria mellea. LEIGH ANN GALE

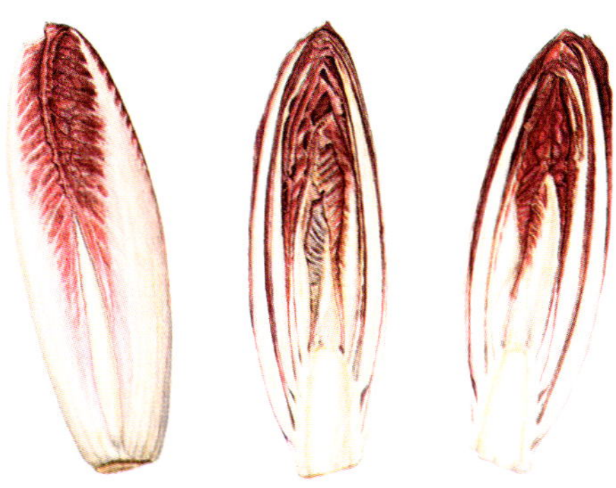

Red Chicory, *Cichorium intybus* 'Rossa di Treviso'. LINDA PITKIN

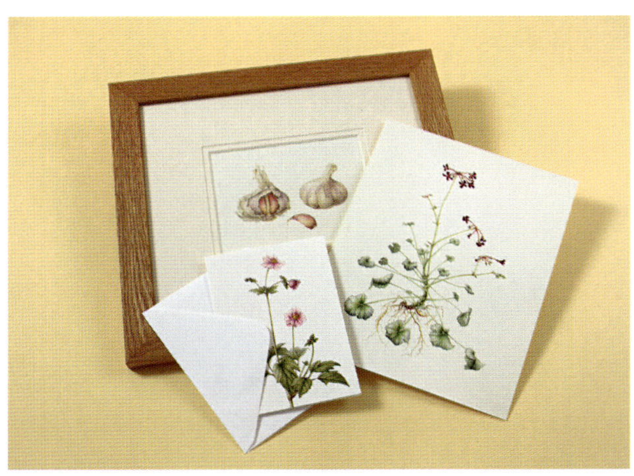

Decide on the purpose of your illustration, for example framed paintings, prints or greeting cards.

With so much choice of subject matter, you may find it hard to choose something to draw. On the other hand, if you are illustrating as a commission, then the decision may already have been made for you.

When choosing subject matter for yourself, try to choose something that really appeals to you. It may be the strong colour, texture, or growth habit that you find interesting, or you may feel inspired to draw something from your garden for example. However, if you are new to botanical illustration, then it is advisable to choose something with a relatively simplistic structure to begin with, before tackling more complex forms.

THE PURPOSE OF YOUR ILLUSTRATION

From the beginning of any project it is necessary to think about the overall purpose of your illustration. This is especially important if for example you have been asked to create an illustration to be published, exhibited, or added to a collection where the choice of subject has already been decided in advance. On the other hand, your subject choice and reason for producing your illustration may purely be a personal one. If this is the case, you will still need to consider whether you will want to mount and frame your work and if so where it might be seen, and if you intend to have it reproduced in any way, such as prints or greeting cards.

Deciding on a subject can also be dictated by how large or small it is. If it is a very small plant it may be necessary to consider painting parts of it larger than life, adding extra detail drawings and making enlargements of some of its features. You many decide you don't want to take on the extra work, so choosing a larger subject may be an option instead. In this case, considerations such as the amount of time you can devote to painting may be important, and you might have to rationalize your decisions about how much of it you do actually need to paint. This can be quite difficult when you reach the composition stage, as you will need to take care that the elements you choose to study and draw are still fully representative of the species.

Some other key considerations when choosing your subject may include whether you want to illustrate something during a specific season, the whole lifecycle of the plant or perhaps whether aspects such as the roots might need to be shown. For example, if you choose to paint ginger, then the edible root (rhizome) obviously needs to be illustrated.

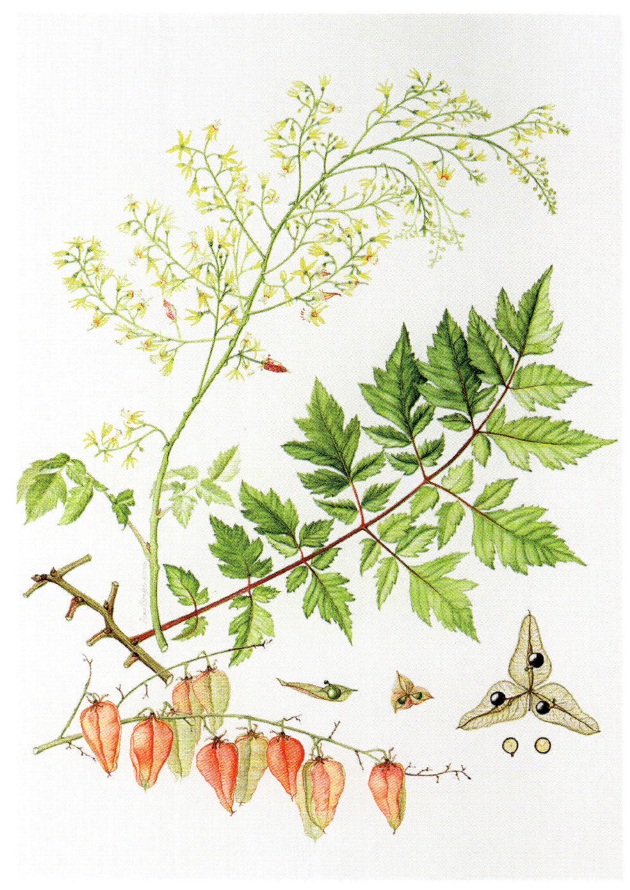

Koelreuteria paniculata. GAY BOYLE

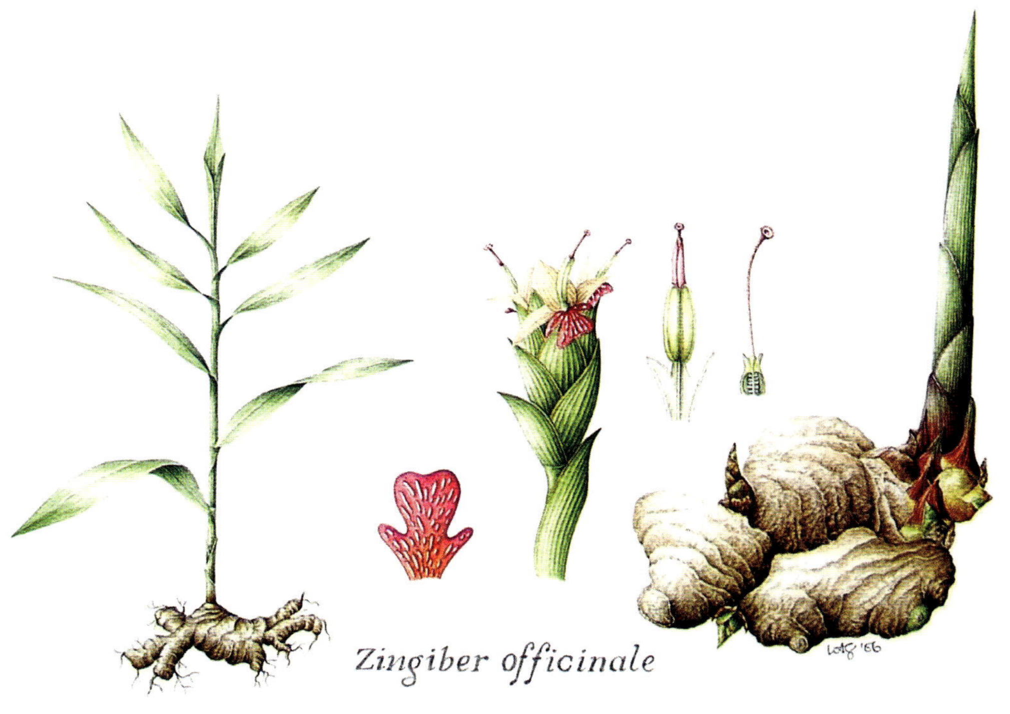

Ginger. LEIGH ANN GALE

PREPARATION FOR DRAWING

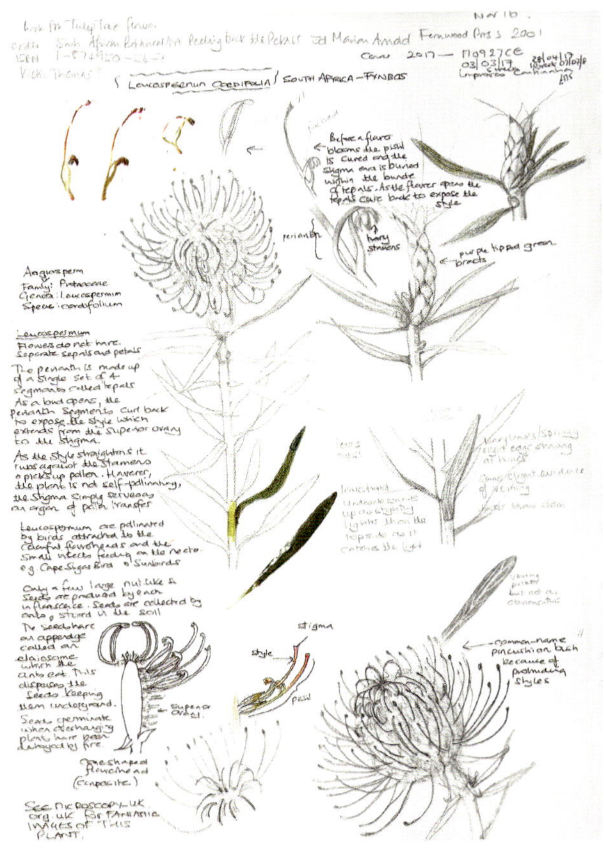

Record information about your subject in a sketchbook. Sketchbook work: *Leucospermum cordifolia*, Protea.
KATE TILBURY

Besides the drawings you make, it is useful to record supporting information about your subject matter to help you learn about it and understand it. There are several ways you can do this, such as reading and researching, recording written information, making colour reference notes in watercolour, taking photographs and so on. Any additional information you record in your sketchbook will help you ensure that your illustration will convey accurately enough information to enable your viewer to clearly identify the species.

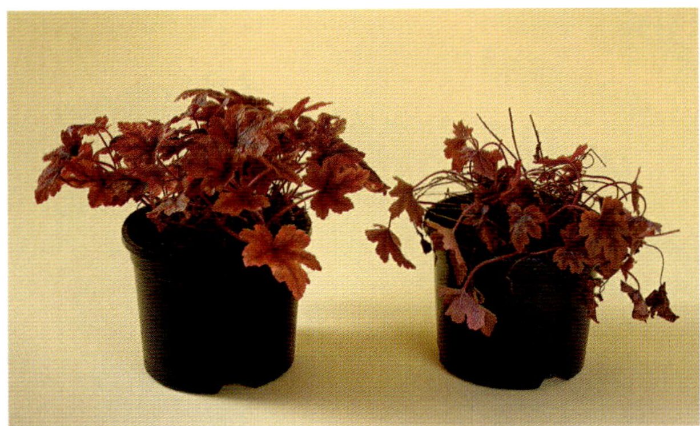

Two specimens of *Heucherella* 'Brass Lantern'; the one on the left is clearly a healthier specimen. Ensure you only select healthy specimens for drawing when purchasing plants at a garden nursery.

RESEARCHING YOUR SUBJECT

When you have decided on your subject you will need to access and select some good specimens to draw from. Carrying out some research in advance will help you make a good selection. You will need to know as much as possible about the plant, its main characteristics and growth habit; and for example, how many petals it should have and what the correct colour of the flowers should be. There are many ways to check botanical information: researching in good botany books, using reliable websites, and talking to specialist breeders are just a few ways. You should aim to record information about your subject in a botanical sketchbook.

Ensuring that the specimens you use are of good enough quality is essential. It may be necessary to find a reputable breeder, a reliable nursery, garden centre or other specialist grower who can help provide you with what you need.

Researching your subject can also lead to the discovery that your plant is a protected or endangered species such as English bluebells, slipper orchids or early gentians. If this is the case, then you will not be allowed to cut or collect any specimens by law and therefore it will

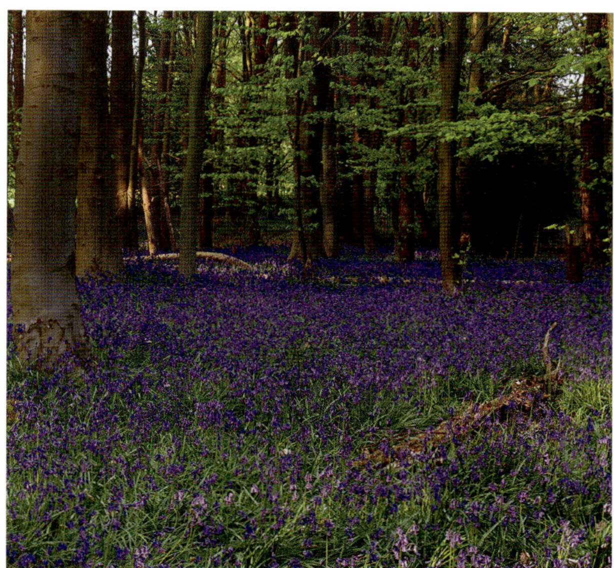

Woodland flowers such as English bluebells are a protected species.

be necessary to work 'in the field' instead. This means that you will have to draw your subject *in situ*. Making clear, accurate drawings, written notes, and colour notes will be helpful when it comes to the composition and painting processes, and it is also worthwhile taking some photographs to remind you of the plant's natural growth habit and its environment.

You will need to consider and research how you are going to access your subject. If your plant is scabious for example which grows in chalky soils, or a sedge which prefers a peat bog, then access to it could be limited. Of course, good examples of such plants may be more readily accessible at botanical gardens such as Kew or available in a national collection, but this will need to be considered during your research, and time set aside to visit, seek permission to access, and possibly take cuttings of suitable specimens. It is unwise to be tempted to 'make do' with photographs or use pictures in books to make drawings and paintings from, as you will be unable to observe, handle and investigate the species fully to understand its structures, textures and growth habit.

MAKING WRITTEN NOTES

Often, written notes about aspects of your subject matter are equally important to the drawings themselves. You can write your notes however you wish, as long as they are easy for you to understand and refer to at a later stage. You should include any measurements, descriptions about textures or smoothness of surfaces, venation of leaves, numbers of stamens and petals and so on. It is also a good idea to add in some botanical terms by referring to a good glossary, for example accurately describing the toothed margin of a leaf as 'serrated' or 'serrulated', or that the calyx of a flower consists of free or united sepals.

MAKING COLOUR REFERENCE NOTES

It is always a good idea to record the colours you can see in your specimen using your watercolours, whilst the specimens are fresh. Harvested specimens will eventually die off, no matter how hard you have tried to preserve them. Part of the decaying process includes colour fading, especially of blooms, so adding swatches in your sketch-book at an early stage will harness their true colours so that you can refer to them later during the painting process (*see* Chapter 5).

PHOTOGRAPHS

If you have a camera, it is worth taking a few 'snaps' of your subject. However, photographs should not be considered a substitute for drawing your specimen from life but rather they should serve as a reminder about it. Additionally, you should not rely on any printed photographic material for colour referencing, due to the colour calibration of any printer, which will never exactly represent the colours of your specimen.

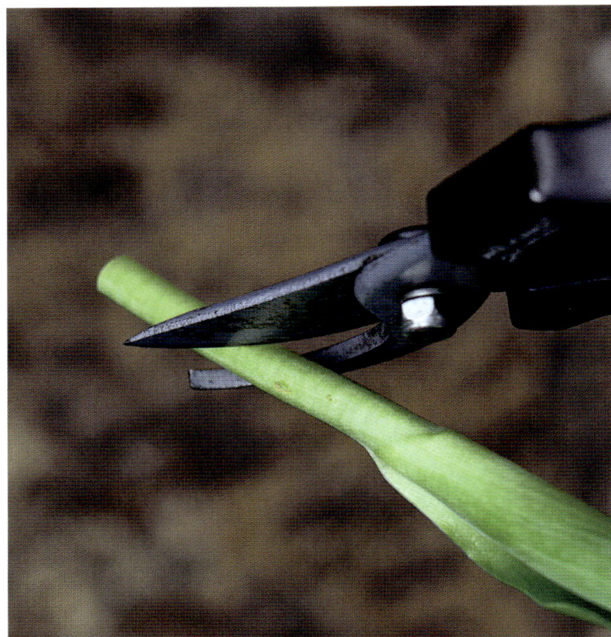

Cut stems at an angle using a clean, sharp pair of secateurs.

COLLECTING AND STORING SPECIMENS

The collection of specimens is necessary so that you can draw from life. Therefore, you should aim to collect them when they are likely to be at their best, when the weather is fine, and you are at the stage of being ready to draw them. Taking cuttings should be carried out with a good, sharp, clean pair of secateurs and you should collect all the parts of the plant you will need, for example flowers, leaves, buds, seeds, fruit and so on. The specimens you choose should be healthy, undamaged and show no signs of disease or pest infestation, as such specimens will be unsuitable for drawing. When collecting stems, always cut them at an angle. This helps to expose a larger surface area of the stem to absorb water, then be ready to immerse them into a bucket or other suitable container of fresh water. Alternatively, putting them inside a clean plastic bag, inflating it, and tying the top is another good way of preserving until you get home.

Once back in the studio you may be set up and ready to begin drawing straight away, but if not, you will need to store your specimens until you are ready. The best way of doing this is to place them into a large enough sealable

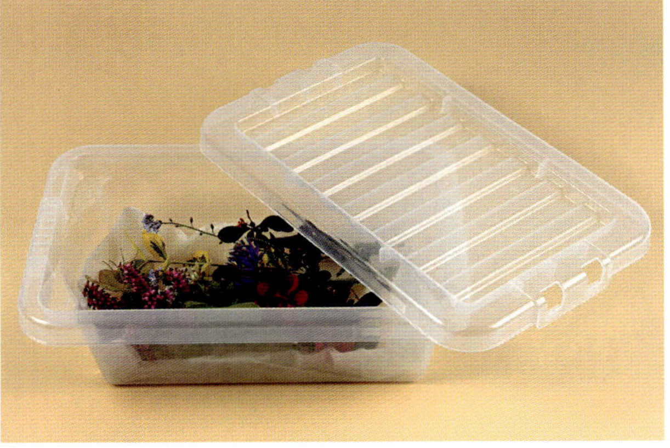

Place specimens on damp kitchen paper inside a sealable, airtight box in the fridge to keep them fresh.

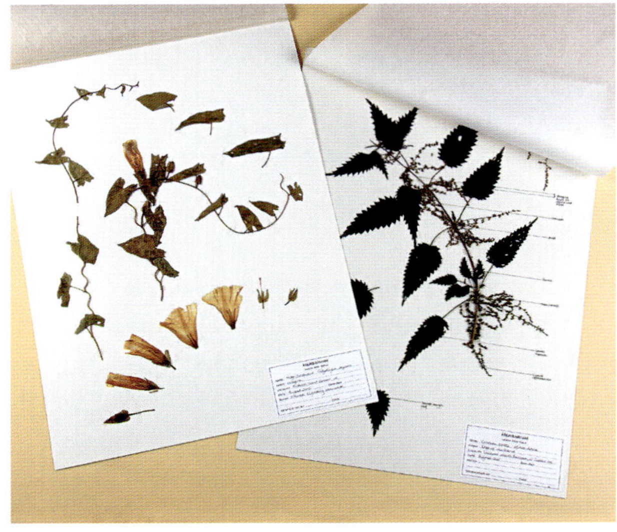

Create herbarium sheets to preserve specimens.

Toxicity in plants and avoiding injury

Many plants contain toxins, whether in the leaves, flowers, roots or indeed the whole plant. It is common for the sap in stems to be toxic which may cause rashes and other allergic reactions. Some plants have thorns and prickles on stems and heavily serrated leaves. Wearing strong gardening gloves will prevent scratches and injury. You should always take care when handling any plants or fungi and ensure you wash your hands afterwards.

container, lined with damp kitchen towel. Replace the lid carefully ensuring it is fully airtight and that no parts of your plant are trapped in the lid. It is then possible to store your specimens in the fridge for several days until you are ready to use them. From time to time, check the container to make sure the specimens are still fresh. Any signs of mould or decay should be dealt with immediately by discarding the affected parts and replacing the damp kitchen towel with a fresh piece.

PRESERVING SPECIMENS FOR LONG-TERM USE

Throughout the drawing process it will be necessary to prolong the life of your collected specimens for as long as possible. This can be achieved simply by keeping them chilled in an airtight box in the fridge (*see* Chapter 2), but you may also wish to preserve specimens for longer periods, in which case alternative methods can be used.

Herbarium sheets have long been used as a means of collecting and preserving specimens for scientific purposes. Their use to aid plant taxonomy, identify flora in geographical areas and to record historical information is widely known and in some cases, collections of herbaria are now used to record the only specimens of now extinct species.

The use of pressed specimens is a very helpful way of preserving plants for study, and can be used to help with your drawings. Pressing specimens is a straightforward process of carefully arranging the components between sheets of newspaper, placed in a flower press, or weighted with a stack of heavy books for a good length of time. This ensures that the specimens are dried and flattened undamaged. Once pressed, your specimens can be mounted onto sheets of thin card or thick paper, and labelled with information about them, such as the species name, location of find and habitat conditions, along with the date of collection.

Checklist for Choosing and Preparing a Subject

- Think about the overall intended purpose of your illustration before you start.
- Research thoroughly so that you know as much as possible about your subject.
- Be aware that some species may be protected or endangered and if so, do not pick.
- Check the labelling is correct on any shop-bought plant. If you think it may be incorrect, make enquiries.
- Only collect healthy, undamaged and pest-free specimens.
- Cut stems at an angle.
- Preserve specimens for longer by refrigerating them in an airtight container.

Once your specimen is mounted, you can use it as reference material to aid your drawings, particularly the botanical features which are often easier to identify once dried. You should take care of your pressed specimens; placing a hinged sheet of tracing paper or tissue paper over the top and keeping them flat will ensure they remain preserved for as long as possible.

Some specimens, such as seed heads, cones, or hydrangea flower heads, can simply be collected, air dried, and stored in airtight boxes to preserve them. However, fleshier specimens that are too bulky to press should be preserved in clear alcohol with added glycerine to help preserve their colour.

Case study

The decision to include a case study in the book came about after completing research with a number of botanical illustration students, who commented that it would be beneficial to see and understand the process of a 'real job' in progress. This seemed especially important for those who were new to botanical illustration or had a little experience. Therefore, throughout the book, a section at the end of each relevant chapter explains the process of creating a 'real' painting for the Nymans Florilegium archive, which aims to put the content of the chapter into context.

Nymans Gardens and the Florilegium Society

Nymans Gardens is an historic property and gardens located in West Sussex, England (it is now owned by the National Trust). In the late nineteenth century, owner and plantsman Ludwig Messel had a vision to create a vast, international collection of plants within the 600-acre estate. Messel worked in collaboration with his head gardener James Comber and together, they built the collection that today hosts many significant species from all around the world, most notably the Americas, Australasia and South Africa. This important collection is lovingly cared for by a dedicated team of gardeners and volunteers, and attracts visitors all year round.

The Nymans Florilegium was founded in 2006 by a group of botanical artists whose purpose is to record the established collection of plants growing at Nymans in botanical drawings and paintings. The recording of the notable Chilean collection in particular is a significant undertaking of the Florilegium's work.

Which plant has been chosen for the case study?

The subject for the case study is *Fuchsia magellanica*, a hardy species of Fuchsia native to Chile, in the southern cone region of South America.

There are several reasons why this species was chosen: the plant appears on the Florilegium's list of Chilean plants to be painted; the Chilean collection forms a significant part of the Nymans international collection. The flowers of *Fuchsia magellanica* are interesting enough to depict good examples of the basic shapes (cylinders, and cones especially); the botanical features including sepals, petals, stamens, style and stigma are all large enough to be recognized and drawn, and are easily distinguishable from each other; the main flower colour being pink, it takes careful thought and consideration to match accurately, and may likely require purposely bought hues to achieve a correct colour match; the leaves are typically representative of the leaves of dicotyledons, with added interest of serrated leaf margins, and red/pink petioles and midrib. The fruits are relatively uncomplicated botanically, making them easy to decipher when dissected.

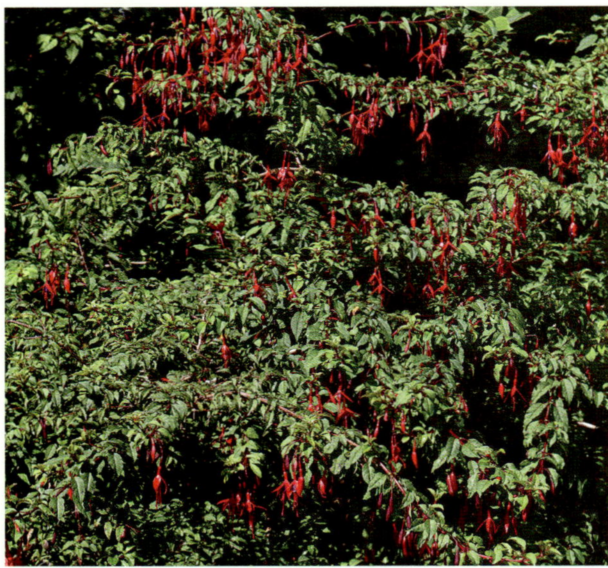

Fuchsia magellanica growing at Nymans Gardens.

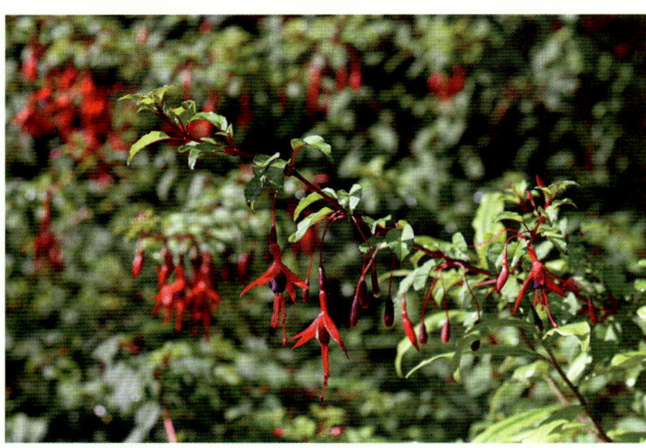

Close-up detail of a sprig of *Fuchsia magellanica*.

Research, photography, and collecting specimens

As with any subject you are considering for a botanical illustration, it is always worth carrying out a little research about the species before beginning to draw, so that you learn something about it. Having some knowledge about your plant will help align your desire and curiosity to paint it, and will ultimately mean that you understand it a little better; for example, why its growth habit is such that it is, or perhaps why the flowers are fragrant after sundown if you have discovered that moths pollinate it.

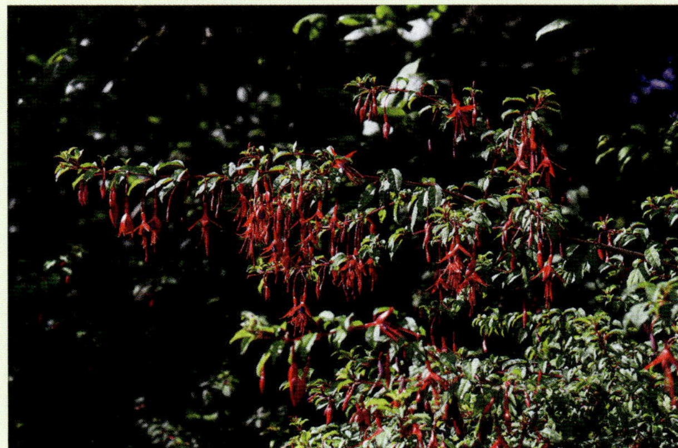

A typical branch of *Fuchsia magellanica* showing its natural growth habit.

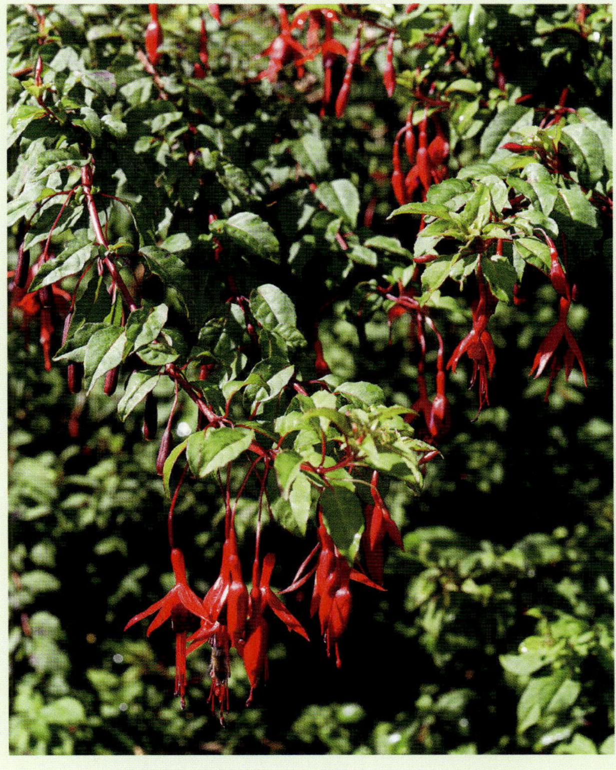

The flowers of *Fuchsia magellanica* in more detail.

We have already identified that *Fuchsia magellanica* is native to Chile, that it is hardy, and therefore makes an ideal choice for growing in the herbaceous borders of English temperate gardens; the climate is not dissimilar in Chile. There are several specimens of this plant growing at Nymans, and so the best plant was chosen to take photographs and cuttings from. Several photographs were taken, including the whole plant to show the natural growth habit, and close-ups to show more detail.

Permission was sought to take cuttings, so they could be brought back to the studio and prepared for drawing. As with many cut specimens, time is often of the essence to preserve their life for as long as possible. Other than the very woody stems of *Fuchsia magellanica*, the vegetative parts of this plant were extremely tender, particularly the flowers, which over a short period of time began to close. This made the urgency to draw them a priority and so the specimens were set up immediately in a hobby hand clamp to make habit sketches and detailed drawings of the botanical components.

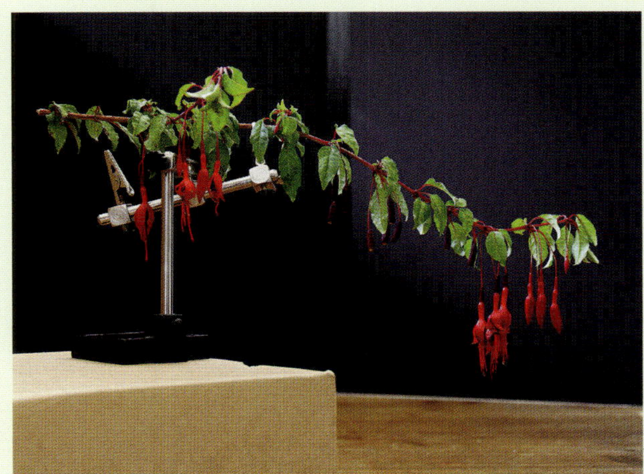

Fuchsia magellanica positioned in a hobby hand clamp ready to draw.

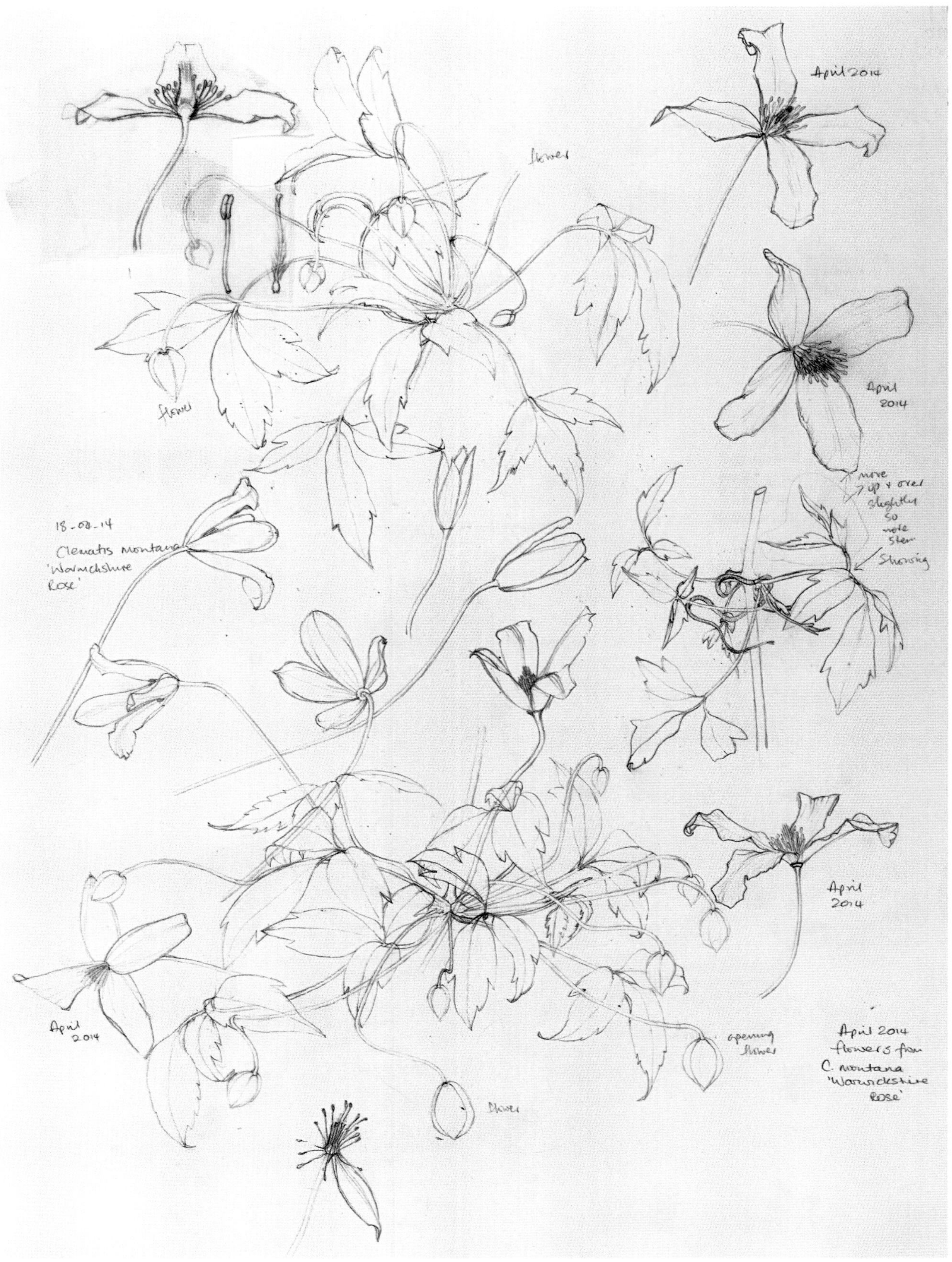
April 2014
flower
flower
18-04-14
Clematis montana 'Warwickshire Rose'
April 2014
move up + over slightly so more stem showing
April 2014
April 2014
opening flower
flower
April 2014 flowers from C. montana 'Warwickshire Rose'

CHAPTER 3

The Drawing Process

Drawing is the backbone. It is no good having a lovely sense of light and colour if there isn't the firm foundation underneath.

– Alexander Cresswell (British watercolour artist)

Reaching the drawing stage is the point at which you will need to focus and concentrate on your task ahead. It is now that you must carefully observe and record the information that your specimen presents to you in the most accurate and precise way possible, because the essence of a good competent botanical illustration lies fundamentally in the drawing. You must ensure that your drawing is correct before any painting can take place; about 75% of your illustration should be focussed on the drawing stage. If you get the drawing wrong, there will be little point progressing to the painting stage.

Now that you have chosen your subject matter, you are ready to start drawing it. It is a good idea to gather all your drawings into one place, so it is worth investing in a good quality sketchbook or cartridge pad to do so.

The process of drawing plants and flowers for botanical illustration requires a scientific and reasonably technical approach. Drawings need to be clean, crisp, and detailed, and most importantly, accurate so that they can be considered 'botanical'. It is therefore essential that you are prepared to invest time and patience into your drawing, ensuring as you go that accuracy is your key focus, and above all that you understand what you are drawing.

So that your drawings are scientifically accurate it is useful to have some knowledge of botany. Without this, you will be unable to clearly identify the botanical features you are trying to illustrate and which, quite crucially, will help others identify your illustration as the species you have studied.

Sketchbook page for *Clematis montana* 'Warwickshire Rose'. LEIGH ANN GALE

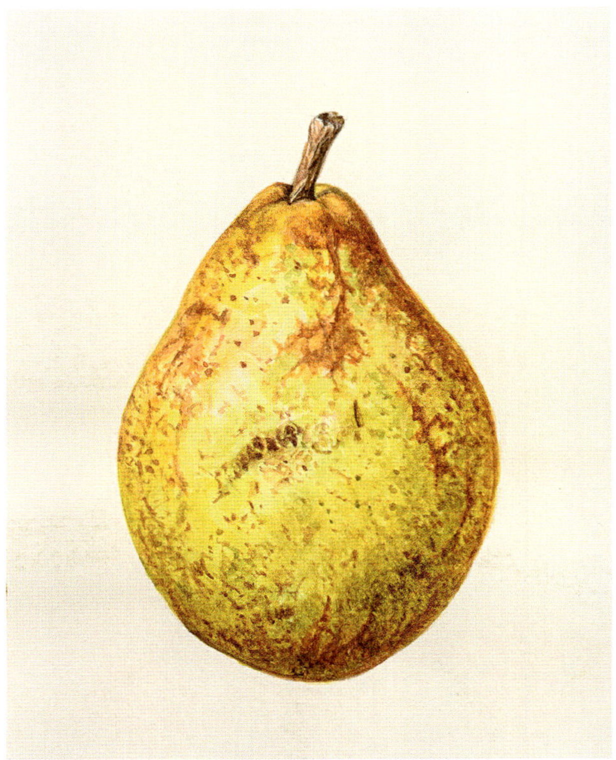

Pear 'Invincible'. VICKY SHARMAN

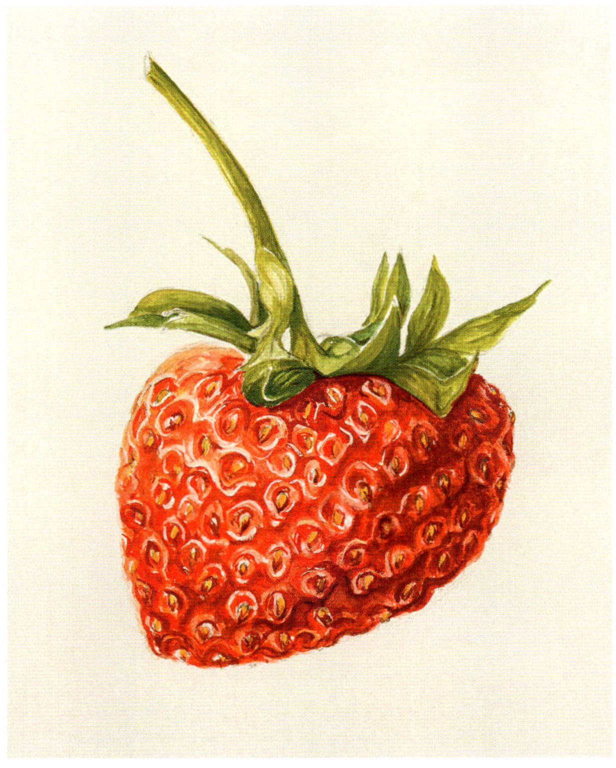

Strawberry Study. VICKY SHARMAN

In this chapter, we will break down the drawing process into several stages, and consider technical drawing aspects such as 3D shape, perspective, and foreshortening. In addition, we will think about the necessary botanical terms you should be aware of, and to help with the drawing process, consider observation and drawing techniques of botanical structures, magnifications, and dissections.

HOW MUCH DRAWING WILL I NEED TO DO?

The amount of drawing you do in preparation for composing and painting your illustration will largely be dictated by the subject matter you have chosen. Obviously, drawing a row of three cherries will demand less work than if you were to draw a sunflower for example, because the structures of cherries are quite simplistic in their shape, and less detailed in their botanical composition. However, even if your subject matter is less demanding, you should not be tempted to cut corners in the hope that just a little will do. Fundamentally, if you are completely sure you have drawn and recorded all the information that is necessary to depict the species so that it is recognizable, accurate, and drawn to scale, this will be reflected in your painting.

WHAT INFORMATION NEEDS TO BE INCLUDED?

It is good practice to observe and draw as much information about your subject as possible. This includes drawings of various components made from different angles; straight on, three-quarter views, views looking up and looking down and so on. Remember to include tonal drawings as well, to remind you of how the light falls on your subject matter. In addition to drawing, you should also take accurate measurements of botanical structures, make written notes, and add colour swatches alongside your drawings (*see* Chapter 2).

It is wise to make several drawings of the same structures but from different angles. For example, by the time you have drawn a flower from three different angles,

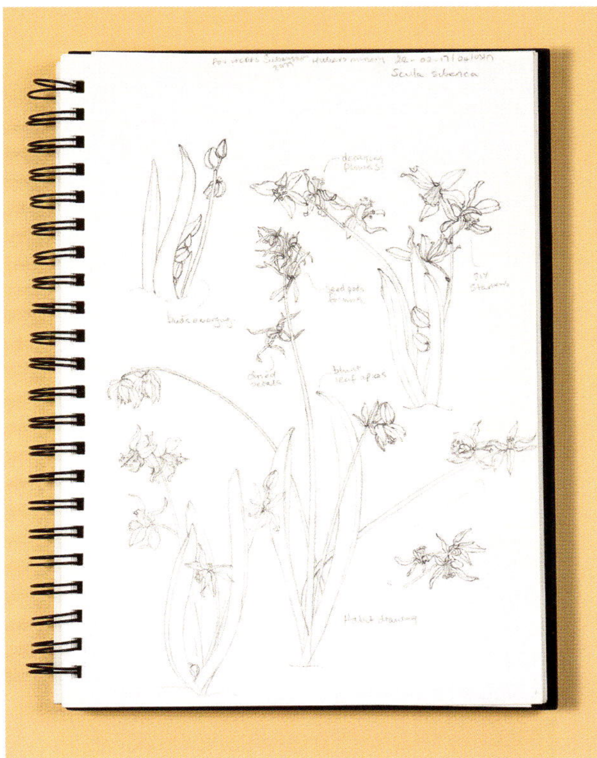

Include drawings observed from different angles in order to record as much information about your specimen as possible.

you will be very familiar with its form and structure, as well as its characteristics and unique features. The same can be said for practising your life-size drawing skills. If you find this difficult – perhaps you naturally draw slightly larger or smaller – you can help yourself by taking measurements of the width and height of the area you are drawing, and draw a box to this size on your paper. You will then only be able to draw within the specified area, thus alleviating the worry of either drawing beyond the boundaries, or drawing too small within the space.

Sometimes, components of plant structures can be quite small, so you should make use of your magnifying glass, hand lens or microscope to help you with observational drawings of those parts. You will also undoubtedly – and certainly in the case of drawing flowers – need to explore the internal workings of parts of your plant. This should be carried out with care, ensuring that any dissections you make are clean and precise, and that you use the correct equipment. Dissections, as well as magnified and reduced-sized drawings should also be

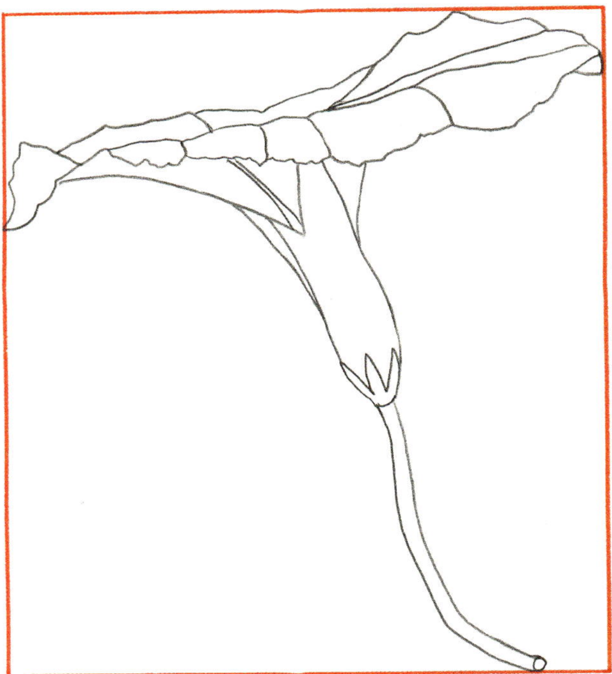

Draw a box to the width and height of your specimen to help you draw at life size.

included in your final illustration if necessary but must be drawn accurately and to scale (*see* the 'Botany' section in this chapter).

It is a good idea to imagine that the subject matter in front of you is only available to observe and record for a short period of time, then it will disappear forever. It is now down to you to record as much information about it as possible; flowers, buds, leaves, fruits, seeds, pods and so on. In theory, you should be able to paint the species relying only on all your recorded information, so it is vital that you capture every nuance of detail along the way.

KEEPING A BOTANICAL SKETCHBOOK

A botanical sketchbook becomes an integral part of the whole botanical illustration process and should be considered as a supporting working document to help you with each subject you study. It is especially important to date your work so that you don't forget when you have drawn your subject or when it has flowered, fruited, or gone to seed. If you get into the habit of supporting your drawings with written and colour notes as well, plus recording any measurements, taking leaf rubbings, adding

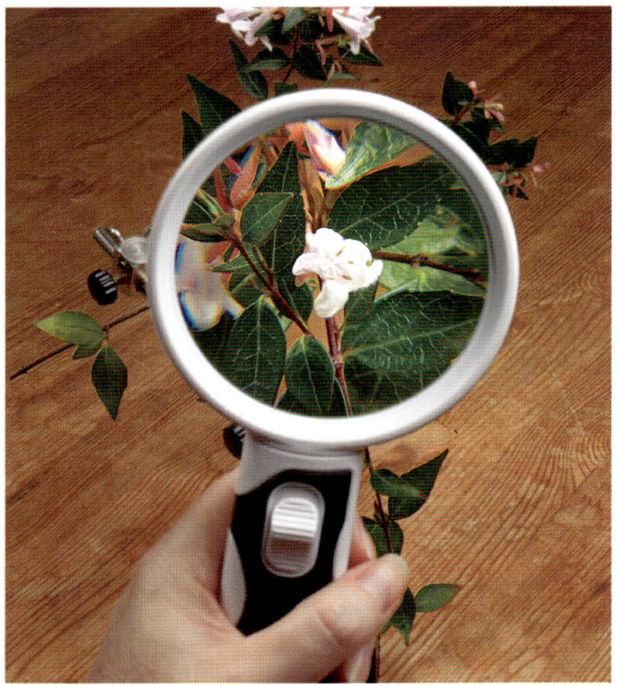

Use a magnifying glass to enlarge areas of your specimen to help you see details clearly.

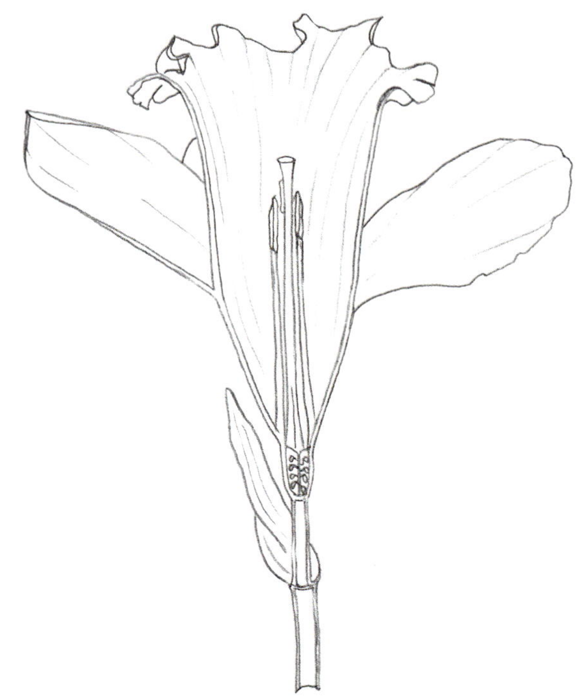

Make dissection drawings to help explain botanical information.

photographic references and so on, then your botanical sketchbook will also become a complete reference work about your chosen species.

You may not need to use the entirety of your studies for your final illustration, but you should always refer to what you have produced, in conjunction with the final painting stage of your project. Use your sketchbook liberally; it is the place to learn about and record information about your subject, practise your drawing skills, and prepare for the next stages of your illustration. Above all, it should be considered an enjoyable, fun, and rewarding part of the process of botanical illustration.

GETTING READY TO DRAW

Before you settle down to start drawing, it is worth checking that you have all your equipment to hand.

Firstly, ensure you are going to be drawing whilst seated at a large enough table. You will need space to position your specimen (either in a vase, florist's Oasis, or pin holder, or clamped in a table clamp, and if necessary either elevated or suspended by some means), and you

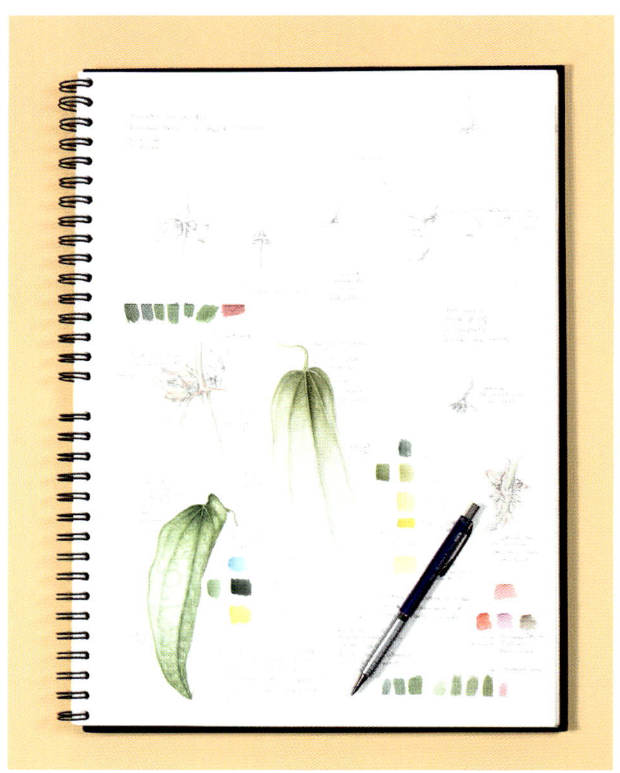

Include drawings, colour swatches, written notes, and painted samples in a botanical sketchbook.

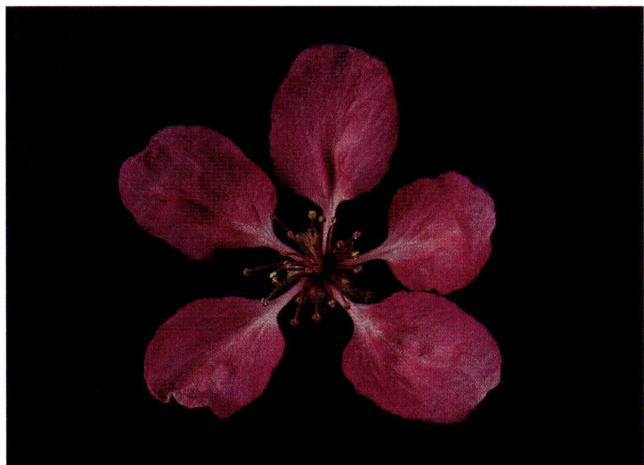

A foreshortened view of the stamens within the flower is unsuitable to identify their length, form and structure clearly.

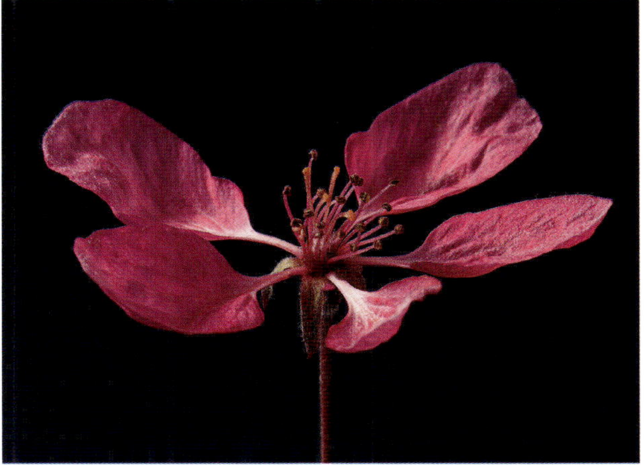

View the flower from the side to gain a clearer view of the structure of the stamens, and to identify their correct length.

should also have a comfortable seat to sit on or use a sit/kneel stool. Your lighting should be correctly positioned and if you are using an Anglepoise lamp, check that it is fitted with a daylight simulation bulb. Ensure your specimen is fresh and hasn't wilted or withered at all. You will need your sketchbook, H or 2H pencil, eraser (preferably putty), magnifying glass or hand lens, and dividers and/or proportional dividers. It is also helpful to set up a black or white hinged folding board behind your subject matter which will help ease the distraction of any background items which may interfere with your view whilst you are drawing. This can be made by using two pieces of artist's mount board (A3 or A2 size), and sealed with tape along the butted-up edges. It should be loose enough for the two boards to be folded together.

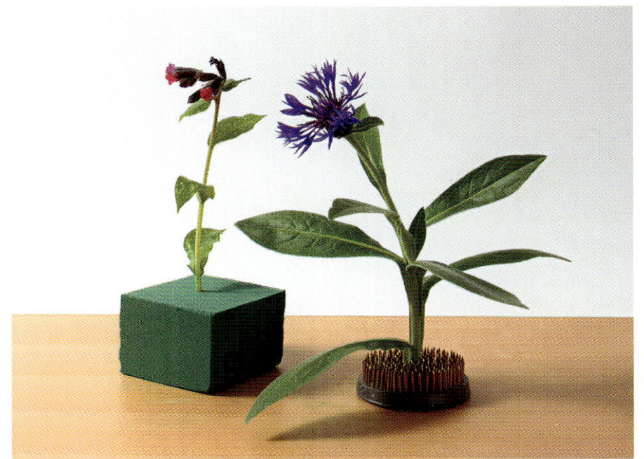

A pin holder or Oasis is ideal for holding upright growing specimens in place.

Positioning your subject matter for drawing

You will need to illustrate your subject matter in such a way that you can show all the botanical parts, including buds, flowers, leaves and so on to their full potential. This means the viewpoint from which you draw is very important, and you should take plenty of time to consider this and position the subject matter carefully. Remember that your specimen is three-dimensional. If you position it such that you are looking directly into a flower for example, you will be unable to identify the stamens clearly and draw them to show their correct length. They will not appear three-dimensional. Instead, change the angle

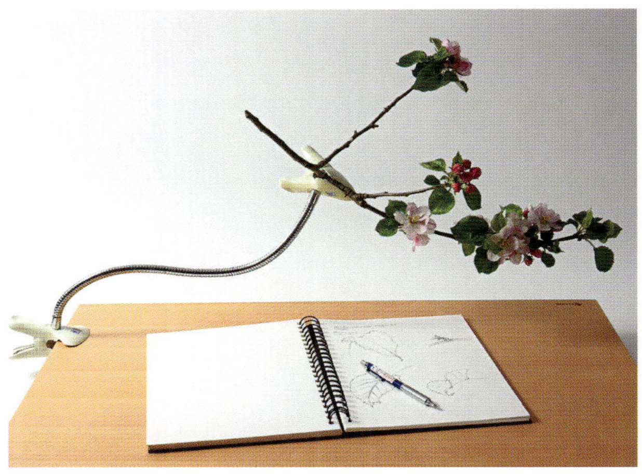

Use a table clamp to suspend a flowering twig.

of the flower so that you can view the stamens properly, perhaps by elevating the subject matter or turning or twisting it a few degrees to the left or right.

It will also be necessary to hold the subject matter in place as you draw (it is not advisable to lay it down flat on a table to one side and draw a top view of it). Think about how it grows. Do you have a whole plant that naturally grows upwards out of the ground, or do you have a flowering twig from a tree that naturally radiates outwards from one side? In the case of the latter example, you would need to suspend the flowering twig at eye level to portray it growing naturally. A table clamp is ideal for this if the stem is tough and hard wood. For most specimens of an upright growing nature, using a florist's pin holder or Oasis will be sufficient to support your specimen. If you have soft wood or succulent stems to suspend then a 'Helping Hands' hobby tool with clips may be suitable.

Warming up

Sometimes, artists like to 'warm up' before starting their drawings. A style of drawing which consists of large, loose, and freestyle movements involving the use of the whole arm (hand, wrist, elbow, and shoulder) helps to free up and flex the muscles before drawing. This is often a good idea as the type of drawing necessary for botanical work can cause the arm, shoulder, neck, and back muscles to tense up and become uncomfortable if care is not taken. Botanical drawing consists of tight, relatively small, and detailed drawing which involves movements primarily from the hand and wrist, and it is easy to sit in one position for a long time without realizing your muscles are tensing.

As you undertake what can often be a lengthy drawing process, ensure you move positions regularly, take regular breaks to stretch your muscles, and remain hydrated.

MAKING OBSERVATIONAL DRAWINGS

The drawings you make are referred to as 'observational' drawings, and they will need to be exactly that. They should be the result of carefully observed information about your specimen, kept primarily as line drawings for clarity, and drawn to scale. Some parts of your drawings will include mathematical technicalities such as perspective and foreshortening, to convey the illusion of 3D in a realistic way. You may also need to include magnified or dissected drawings to explain structures in more detail, and create tonal drawings to help you identify highlights and shadows on your subject.

It will be essential to really observe your subject matter carefully, understand the functions of the structures and identify botanical features accurately.

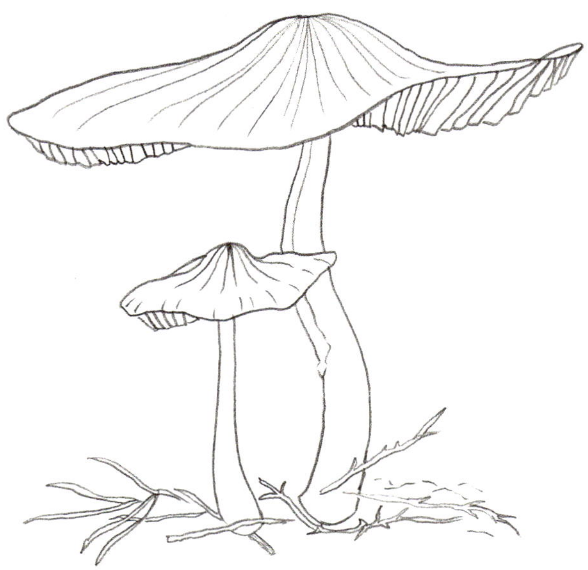

Keep observational drawings as line drawings.

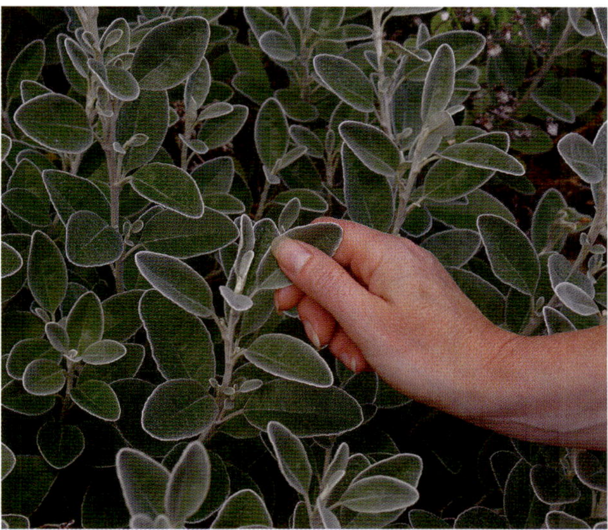

Touch the surfaces of leaves to determine their texture and to identify which side the veins are most prominent.

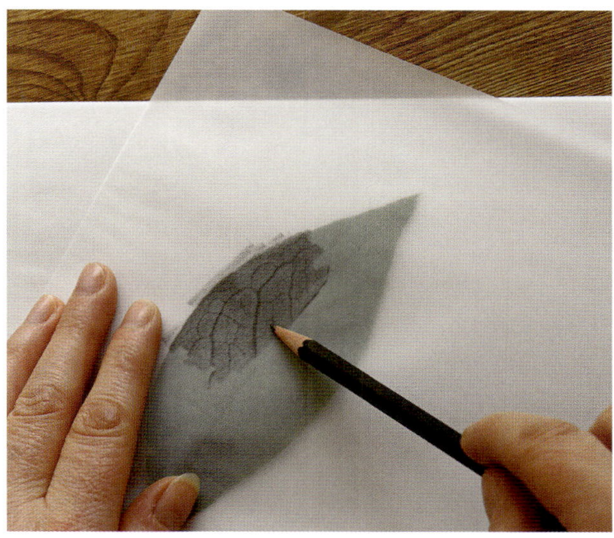

Make a leaf rubbing to help you identify leaf venation.

LOOKING AT THE STRUCTURES OF YOUR SPECIMEN

It is usually a good idea before you attempt any drawings at all to take plenty of time to study your subject matter thoroughly. This will include not only close visual observation but in most cases, physically touching it as well. A lot can be learned simply by feeling surface textures with your fingertips. For example, in the case of drawing veins on a leaf, it would be helpful to rub your fingers over the veins on the top and underside, to detect on which surface the veins feel more prominent. You will also feel the texture of the leaf blade itself, which may be smooth, hairy, waxy and so on. You could also make a leaf rubbing at the same time, which may clearly identify the venation and the structure of the veins individually; this could help further with your ability to draw them accurately.

FIRST DRAWINGS AND CORRECTING ERRORS

As you begin to draw it is likely you will feel some nervousness about doing so, especially if this is a new discipline for you. It is strongly advisable to set yourself several small drawing tasks to begin with, before tackling more challenging drawings. Simplistic structures such as apples, pears or mushrooms make good first subjects as they are representative of some of the basic 3D shapes described in this chapter, and should be relatively straightforward to draw. Remember you should aim to draw your subject at life size.

As your drawings progress, you will probably find that you will need to alter them in some way, in other words amend or correct them. It is recommended – especially at the outset – that you do not rub out too much. Instead, re-draw the subject, perhaps more than once until you are satisfied you are making more representative and accurate drawings. Resisting the urge to rub out mistakes at this stage will help you to see and remember any mistakes you made previously, which is beneficial in the learning process. Do this several times for the first few

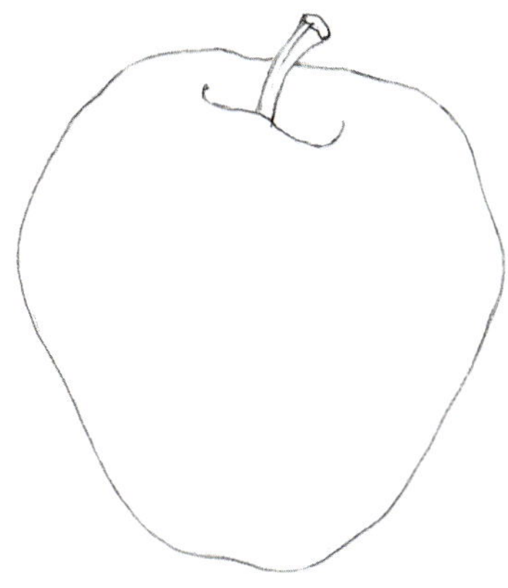

An apple depicts a spherical basic shape.

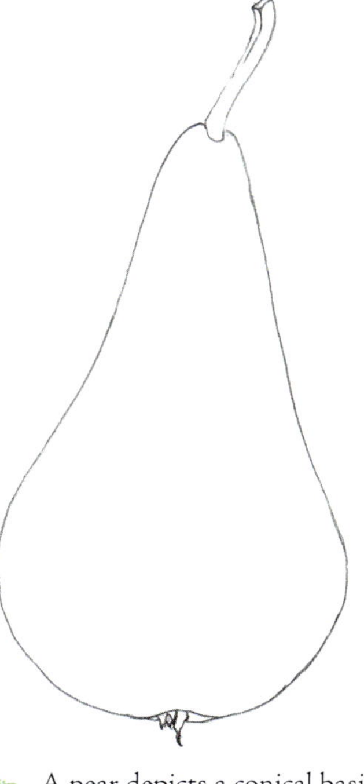

A pear depicts a conical basic shape.

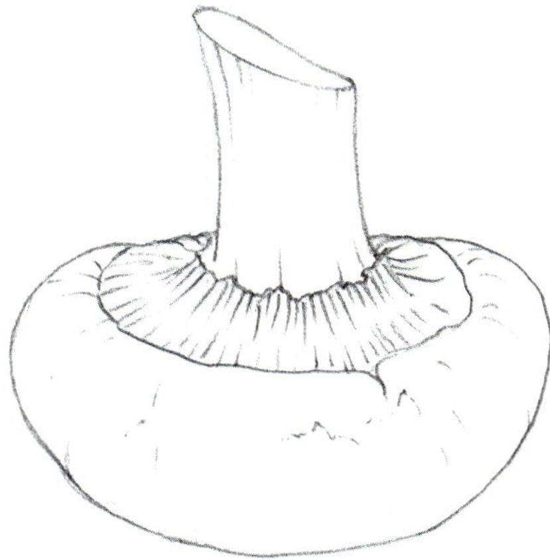

A mushroom depicts both a cup and cylindrical basic shape.

botanical drawings you create, and with practice, you should develop your proficiency and confidence in accurate observational drawing. When drawing larger, more complex structures, you will on occasion need to correct some minor mistakes. If you need to correct errors, use a putty rubber to do so, which will be kinder on the drawing paper and prevent damaging the fibres quite so much. If the error is too large, often it is easier to simply re-draw the incorrect section directly to one side, indicating with a written note or arrow that you will need to replace the incorrect part with the correct version when you create a template drawing at the composition stage.

OUTLINE DRAWINGS

The best way to make initial observational drawings is by drawing in outline. You should aim to draw your specimen at 100% – life size – unless there is a good reason not to. If the subject is naturally very small or very large, then additional magnified or reduced drawings should be considered. Use your 2H or H pencil for drawing, as they will ensure your lines remain crisp and refined. You can use either a very sharp pencil or a propelling pencil to do this. Outline drawings provide you with an opportunity to add sufficient detail, and when you specifically have a more complex structure to draw, you will also be able to illustrate the finer nuances of your subject matter with relative ease.

Your drawings should convey all the details of your specimen, for example showing the veining on a leaf such that it naturally tapers towards the margin, or showing the correct number of petals or stamens in a flower.

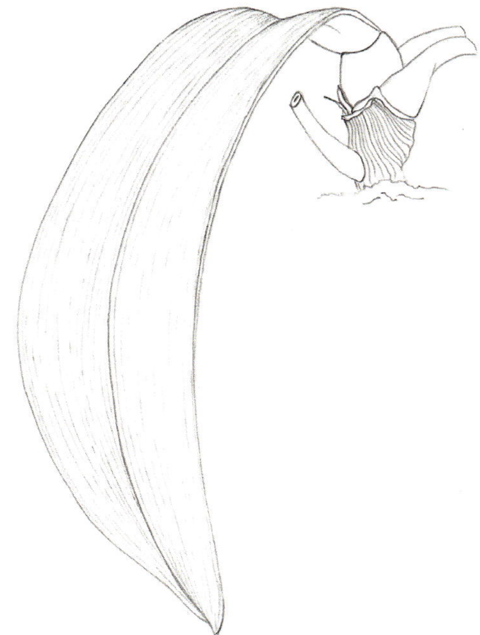

Ensure you capture information such as the tapering venation of a leaf in your drawing.

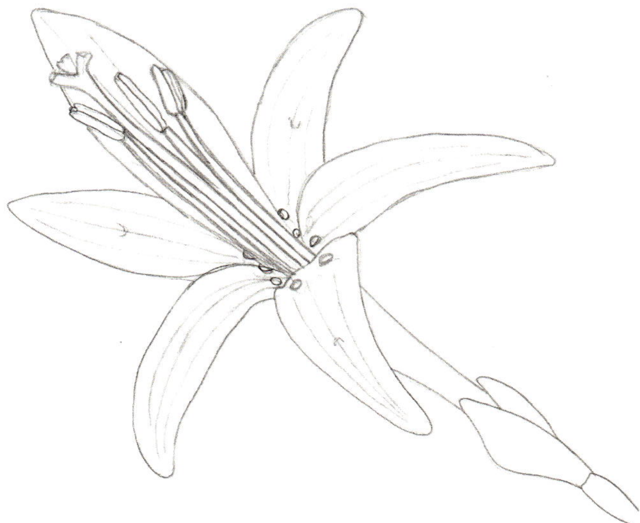

Indicating the correct number of stamens in a flower at the drawing stage is essential.

HABIT DRAWINGS

In most cases, you should aim to make a 'habit' drawing of your subject. This is a drawing of the plant, usually in its entirety, which helps to depict the species more readily and its natural growth habit. It is not always possible to include a full habit drawing, perhaps the species is very large, the structure rather complex or there are numerous flowers or leaves. If this is the case, then you should select part of it instead, and consider adding a small reduced-sized graphite drawing to the illustration.

You should ensure that the specimen you choose for your habit drawing is a good selection. It should be typical of the species, healthy, and disease free.

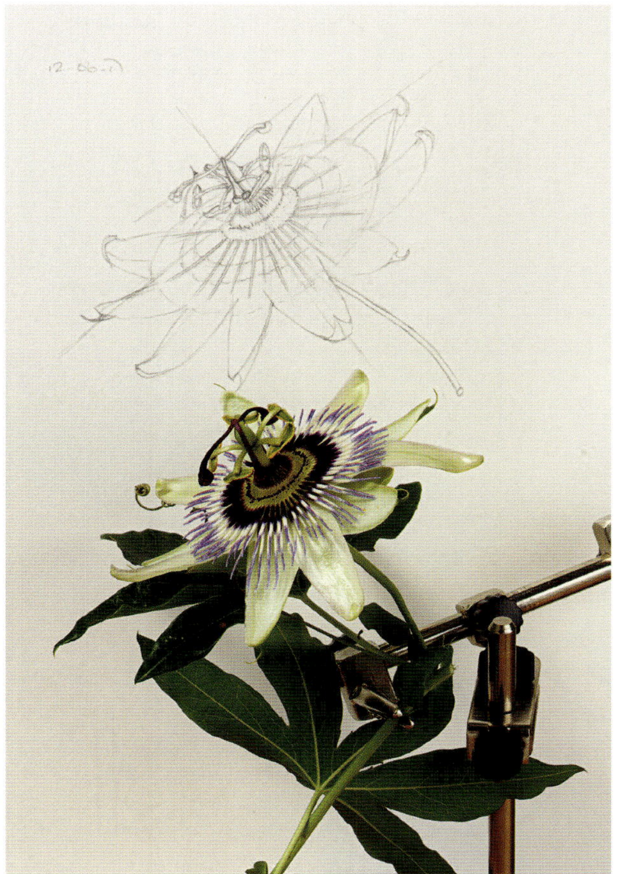

Make accurate habit drawings representative of the species to depict growth habit.

MAKING ACCURATE DRAWINGS

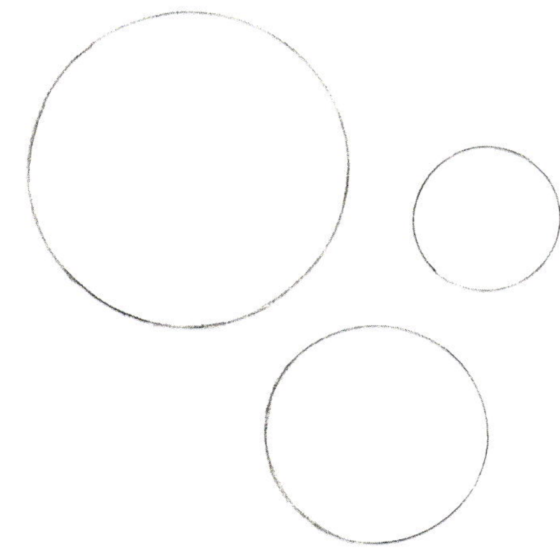

Practise drawing different sized spheres.

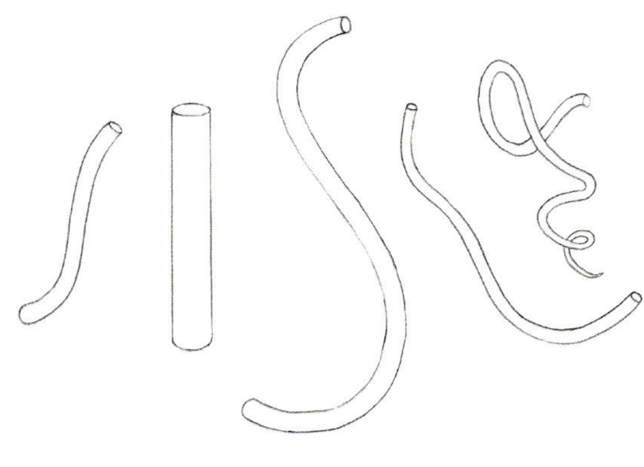

Cylinders are not only representative of straight stems; they may be curved as well, such as tendrils on a climbing plant.

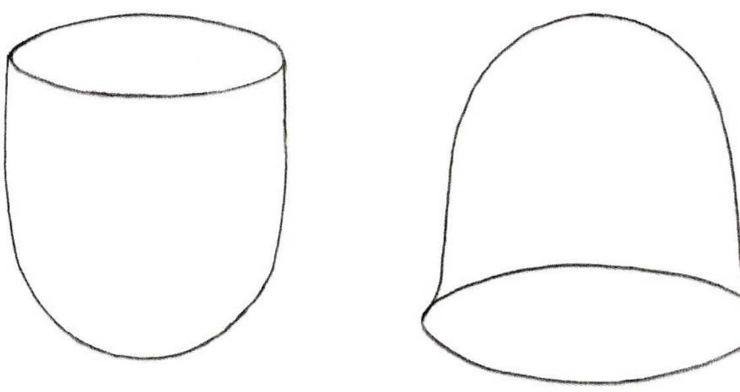

Upright cup shapes are evident in flowers like tulips and crocus, but also appear upside down in flowers such as bluebells and fritillaries.

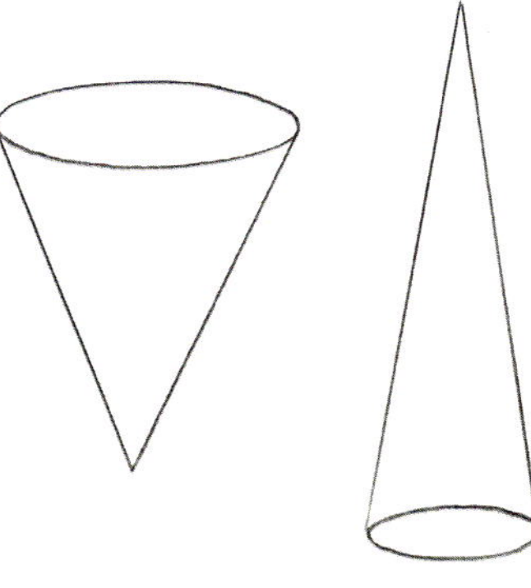

Cone and upside-down conical shapes can be identified in lilies and pears.

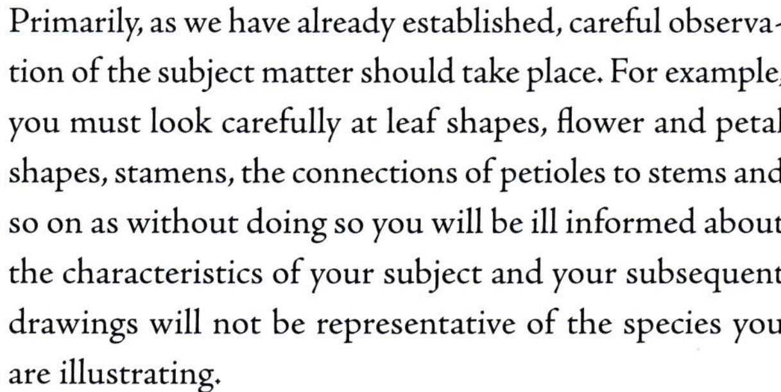

Primarily, as we have already established, careful observation of the subject matter should take place. For example, you must look carefully at leaf shapes, flower and petal shapes, stamens, the connections of petioles to stems and so on as without doing so you will be ill informed about the characteristics of your subject and your subsequent drawings will not be representative of the species you are illustrating.

One of the most difficult things to do in botanical illustration is to create accurate drawings. The process requires a methodical, informed approach, but also one of a fundamentally technical nature.

Coping with the technical aspects of botanical drawing, such as 3D structures, perspective, and foreshortening can be challenging, especially if this is a relatively new concept to you or you have previously been accustomed to looser styles of drawing. The ability to think and draw technically – and subsequently with accuracy – can be learned through practice and repetition to gain confidence and precision. Breaking the process down into small, simplified tasks is by far the easiest way to begin; you should feel at ease if you make mistakes in the process.

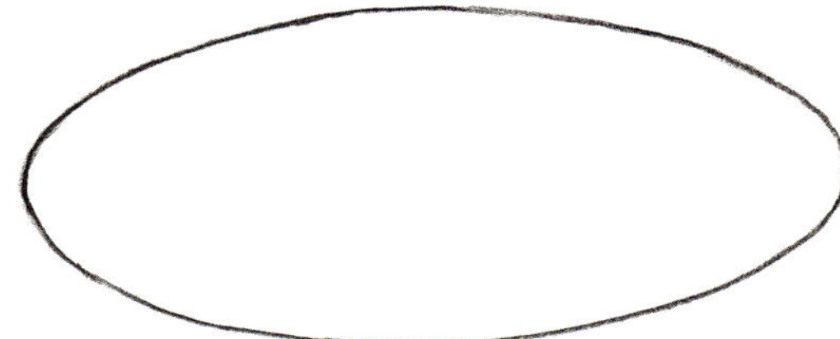

Ellipses drawn correctly should consist of no straight lines or angles.

LOOKING FOR BASIC 3D SHAPES

Part of the observation and drawing process will be your ability to identify what we refer to as 'basic 3D shapes'. This is the starting point of a botanical drawing. These shapes, which include a sphere, cylinder, cup and cone are considered to be the most common three-dimensional structures which you will come across. Being able to identify them in botanical specimens will help enormously when you begin to draw, and your initial drawings should always be based on them. For example, the shapes identifiable when drawing a Japanese anemone or a tulip would consist of a cylinder for the stem and a cup for the flower. Similarly, a weigela or lily flower would comprise a cylinder for the stem and a cone for the flower.

It is worth spending some time just drawing the 3D shapes by themselves from different viewpoints, which will maximize your investigations of parallel line, symmetry, and ellipses.

Understanding the properties of ellipses especially, with no angles or straight lines in them, should be evident in your drawings. They should be sufficiently convincing to allow your viewer to see them without any ambiguity.

Practise drawing ellipses from different angles so that they are accurate. Only once you have drawn the basic 3D shapes *in situ* should you begin to add the structural lines of your subject matter, for example adding the individual petals to the anemone or weigela flower.

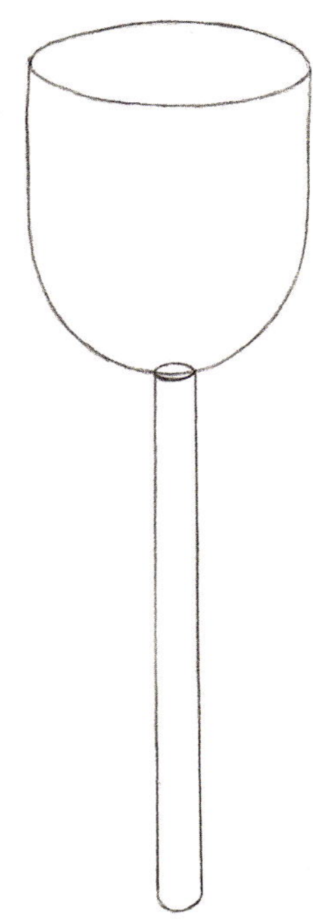

Draw the basic shapes of your subject first, as your starting point.

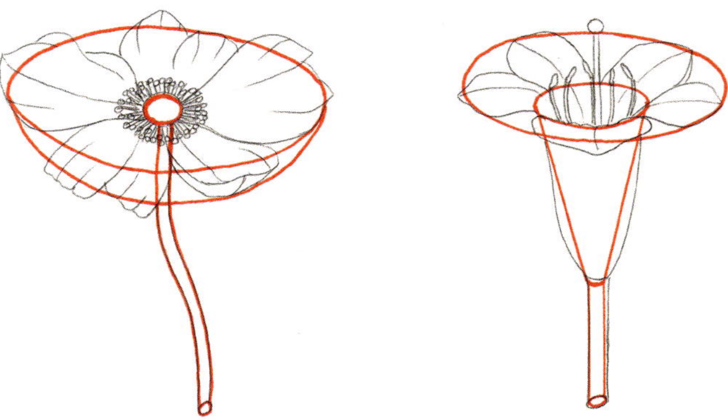

Add details such as petals over the top of the basic shapes.

SYMMETRY

Many flowers are said to be symmetrical if they can be divided in half and both halves are identical. There are two types of symmetry, known as radial (actinomorphic), when a flower can be cut in half in any direction and both halves are identical, and bilateral (zygomorphic), when a flower can only be cut in half lengthways for both halves to be identical. A few flowers and some leaves are

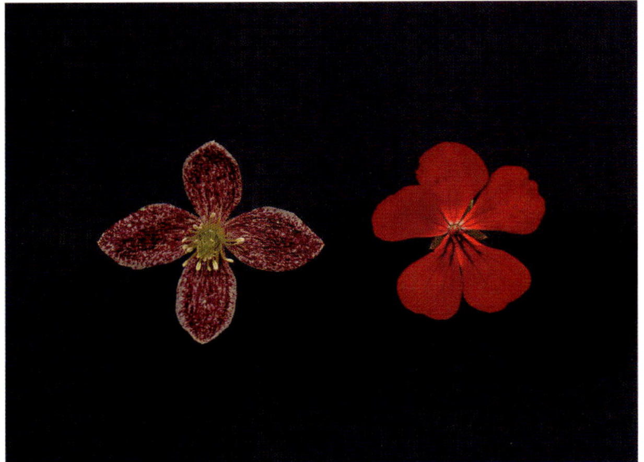

Radial actinomorphic symmetry and right: bilateral zygomorphic symmetry.

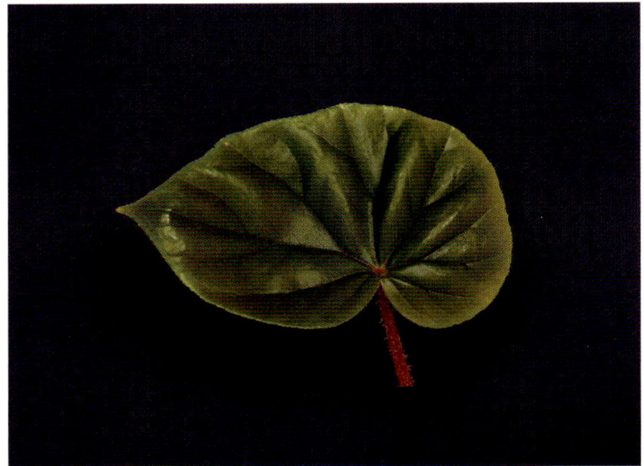

Begonia leaves are good examples of asymmetrical symmetry.

asymmetrical, meaning that no symmetry exists at all. Identifying the symmetry of your specimens therefore is fundamental. You should always check carefully against your specimen, ensuring the type of symmetry you are describing is accurate.

DRAWING LEAVES

When you draw leaves you will have to observe 3D structures that are generally much flatter than most floral structures. Although they may vary in thickness and shape, many leaf structures are also quite intricate, with serrated margins, textured surfaces, and fine networks of veins. You will also notice that some leaves are symmetrical, whilst some are asymmetrical, so this adds to the complexities of drawing them.

As many leaves contain a midrib, this often makes a good starting point. By drawing the length of the midrib accurately first, and noting whether it tapers to a point, you will be able to draw the rest of the leaf to the correct size. Once the midrib is drawn, you should then plot the positions of the lateral veins, noting whether they may be opposite or alternate, and then draw the leaf margin including any serrations. Extending the lateral veins to the correct lengths and adding the secondary veins will complete your drawing.

Whilst drawing leaves, you should also note any foreshortening that is visible, and include this in your drawing (*see* the 'Foreshortening' section in this chapter).

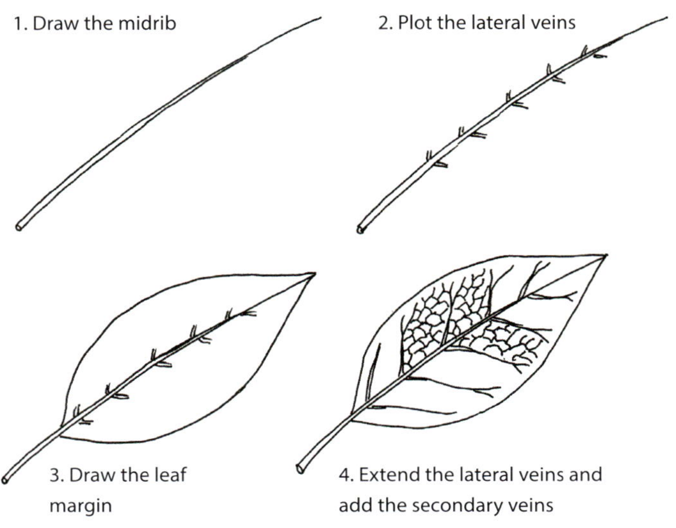

Step-by-step method to drawing leaves effectively.

PARALLEL LINES

In some cases, your drawings will warrant the skill of drawing parallel lines convincingly. For example, the parallel lines of a flower stem, although you should be mindful that not all stems are completely parallel, as some taper towards the top or may even become wider on the approach to a node junction.

An easy way to draw parallel lines is to start by drawing the full length of one of the lines. Then, slowly begin to draw the second line, but instead of watching your pencil, follow the direction of the first drawn line with your eye, approximately half an inch ahead of your pencil. You will notice how your hand naturally follows the direction of the first line, keeping an equal distance from it to the end.

PERSPECTIVE

Perspective drawing is a way of representing how 3D objects appear to get smaller as they get further away, eventually converging at what is referred to as the vanishing point on the horizon line. The illusion of perspective is such that objects appear to alter realistically in depth, width, and height over distance.

You will not encounter a great deal of perspective when viewing your subject matter, because you will only see a relatively short depth of field. However, you should be aware of perspective, understand what it is, and how to draw it as on occasion you may need to incorporate it, if for example you draw a scene of natural habitat behind a close-up drawing of your subject matter.

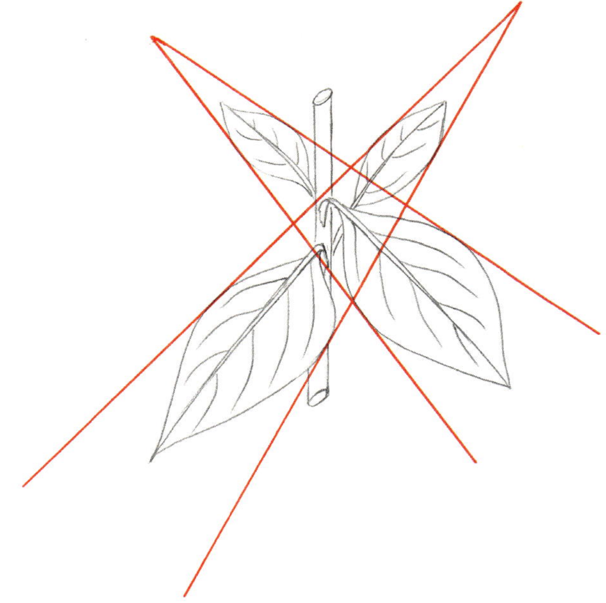

If necessary, add perspective to your drawing to increase the depth of field.

FORESHORTENING

An object is said to be 'foreshortened' when it presents a view of itself that is less than its actual length, width, or height.

The ability to draw objects when they are foreshortened relies on being able to convince your brain that is how they need to be drawn, since your brain will automatically try to tell you otherwise. This can be a challenging concept and one that requires you to literally draw what you see in front of you. Closing one eye when viewing your subject can help, as you will see the compression and distortion of the shape more clearly. However, you must ensure that you always close the same eye, otherwise the position of the subject will alter, by moving either to the left or right.

The best way to tackle foreshortened drawings for the first time is to consider drawing a single object such as a simple leaf from different viewpoints. You will see how at eye level the line drawn for the midrib is very short. It is necessary to draw the midrib as short as this so that the optical illusion is created of the leaf projecting forward. Compare these examples of foreshortened leaves, and

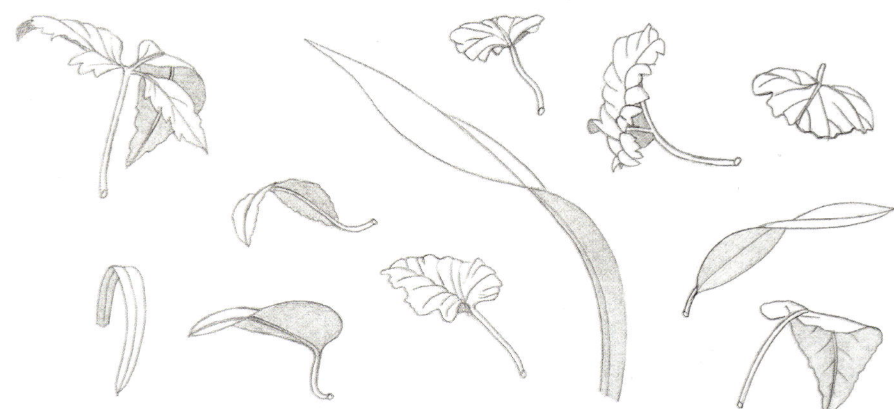

Practise drawing specimens with foreshortened views.

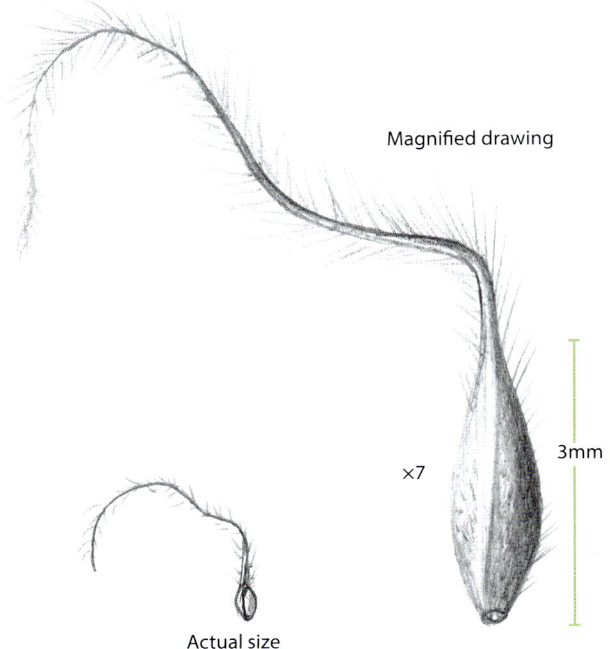

Indicate the size of an enlarged drawing using a magnification or scale bar.

note how the midrib is at its shortest when the leaf is viewed closest to eye level, and how it alters in length as you look down on it from a higher viewpoint. As you embark on drawing your subject matter, make sure that you use foreshortening techniques to make your drawings convincing and naturalistic.

DRAWING TO DIFFERENT SCALES

Many botanical textbooks contain scaled drawings that are helpful in explaining information about the size of plant components, and which otherwise may be too complex to comprehend at life size. If you need to make drawings larger or smaller, it is advisable to keep the process as simple as possible by choosing a scale that is easy to understand. For example, a magnified drawing could be drawn at ×2 or ×3, with its magnification written alongside, or indicated by using a scale bar positioned next to the drawing. A scale bar is drawn neatly next to the specific botanical component it refers to, and consists of a single straight line, with 'T' bars drawn at either end. Indicate the measurement using millimetres, ensuring it is the life-size measurement of the component.

A scaled-down drawing (typically if the specimen is too large to be drawn at life size) can be shown in a similar way, either ×0.5 or ×0.75 or indicated with a scale bar.

To help you make accurate magnified and reduced-sized drawings, use a pair of proportional dividers, setting the scale appropriately. You can also use a microscope to help you study details for drawing magnifications.

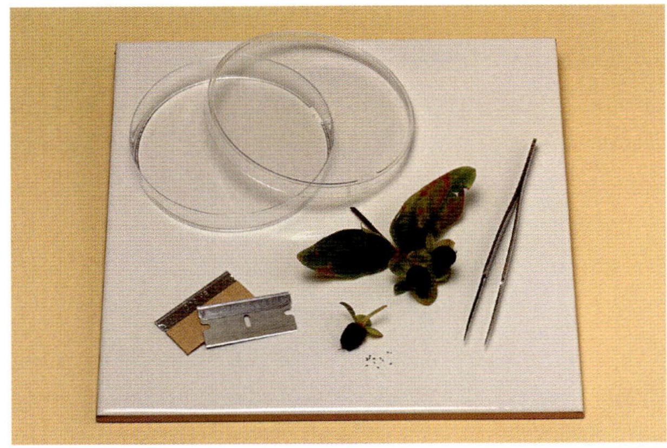

A small selection of dissecting equipment is helpful when investigating the internal components of specimens.

DISSECTIONS

Taking apart a flower, seed pod or other structural component of your subject matter to analyse, and subsequently draw, will be a necessary process from time to time. Including some dissections in your illustration also helps to explain information about your species, especially if the components are small (in which case they can be magnified as well). Use a microscope or hand lens to help you.

To make successful dissections it will be helpful to have a small selection of dissecting equipment. You will find the following tools useful:

- Scientific tweezers (forceps) for holding and removing components;
- Single blade razor blades, for dissecting specimens;
- A specimen dish;
- A white ceramic tile for cutting on.

If you have a plentiful supply of your subject matter it may take several practice attempts at dissecting before you achieve a satisfactory result. Look carefully at the dissected material before drawing it, remembering to keep all line work clean and precise. Many botanical dissection drawings are made in ink, but it is quite acceptable to use pencil or paint for the task.

Make different dissections; longitudinal (lengthways) and transverse (widthways) to obtain different views of your subject matter.

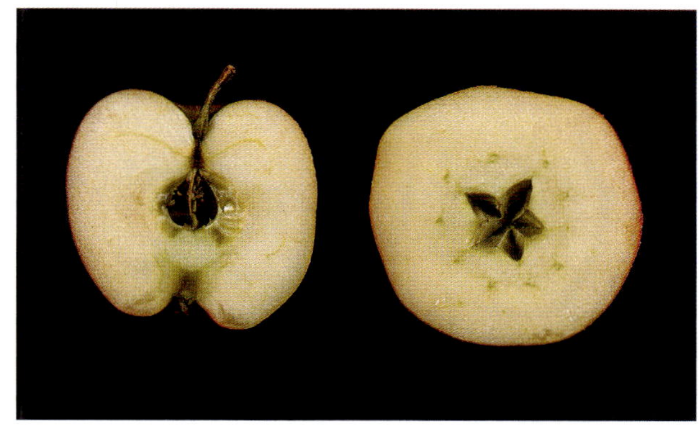

Left: a longitudinal section LS; Right: a transverse section TS.

TONAL DRAWINGS

In addition to an outline drawing, prepare a graphite tonal drawing in advance of painting, to remind yourself where highlights and shadows fall.

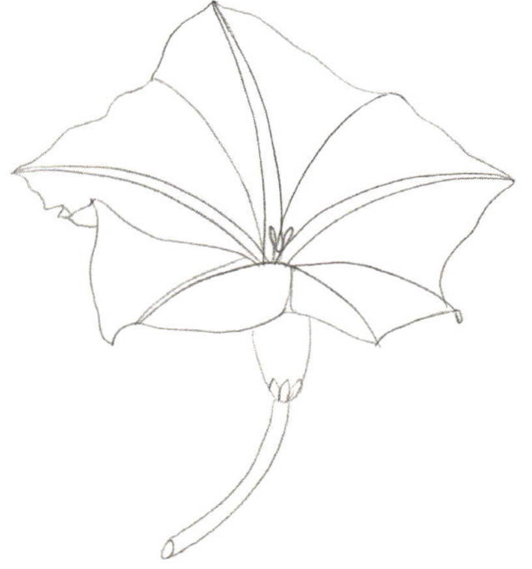

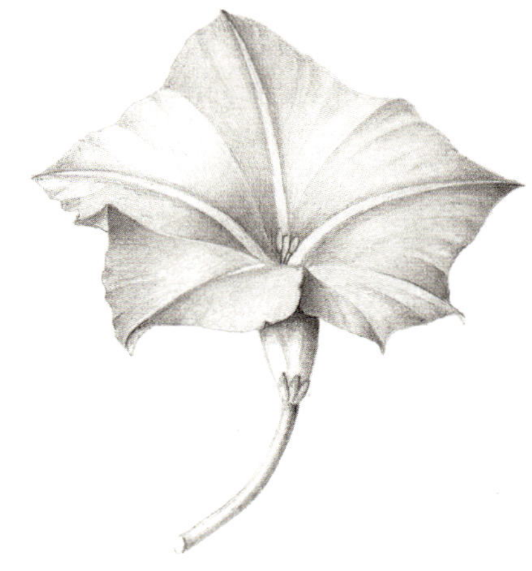

For many proficient artists, making shaded, tonal drawings in addition to outline drawings is often bypassed. This isn't an act of laziness but simply shows that the artist feels confident in progressing to the composition and painting stage without the need to make tonal drawings beforehand. However, for those who are new to botanical illustration this stage of the drawing process is necessary and advised, so that you can carefully observe how the light falls on your subject and where the highlights and shadows appear. By creating a tonal drawing in advance of painting you will essentially be doing all the hard work beforehand, as you should be able to translate the tones you have made in pencil directly into colour when painting.

LIGHTING YOUR SUBJECT FOR TONAL DRAWINGS

So that you can see the highlights and shadows on your subject clearly, you will need to set up your lighting correctly. As described in Chapter 1, your lighting should either be from the top left or top right, depending on whether you are left- or right-handed. You must ensure that you maintain the same lighting position throughout the process of making tonal drawings. It is important that you do this, otherwise the highlights and shadows will alter, causing confusion and incomprehensible lighting. If you rely on your light source from a window, remember that the contrast between highlights and shadows will remain most consistent if you use a north-facing aspect.

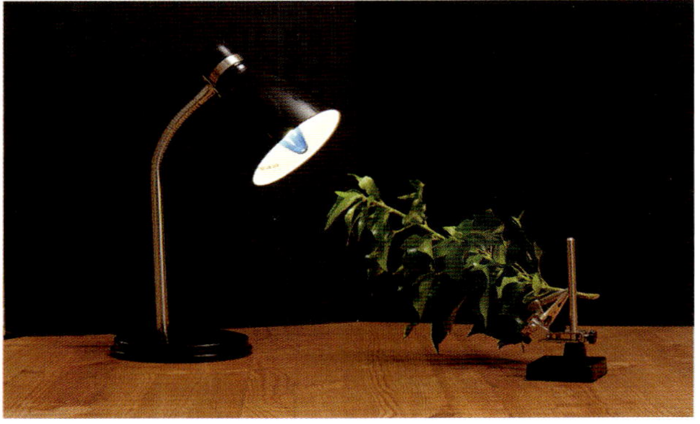

Light your subject correctly, for example from the top left, using a directional light source.

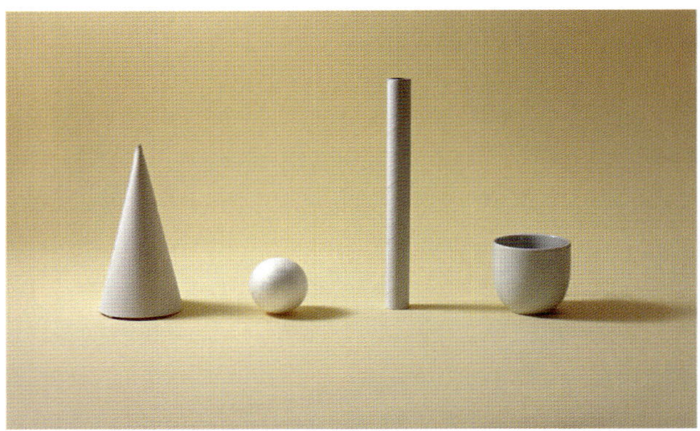

The four basic shapes: cone, sphere, cylinder and cup lit from top left.

SHADING THE BASIC 3D SHAPES

It is worth practising shading the basic 3D shapes to bring them to life. Think carefully about the lighting on them (set up some models if it helps), then set about representing the highlights and shadows by shading with your H or 2H pencil. Look at the examples here to see where the highlights and shadows appear when each shape is lit from the top left. The opposite happens when the shapes are lit from the top right.

Your goal is to create the smoothest gradated tone you possibly can. This can be achieved by drawing numerous small, elliptical marks, at the same time as carefully adjusting the pressure of your hand on and off the paper. The result should be an area of gradated tone with no 'holes' (white paper) showing through, and no hard, visible pencil lines.

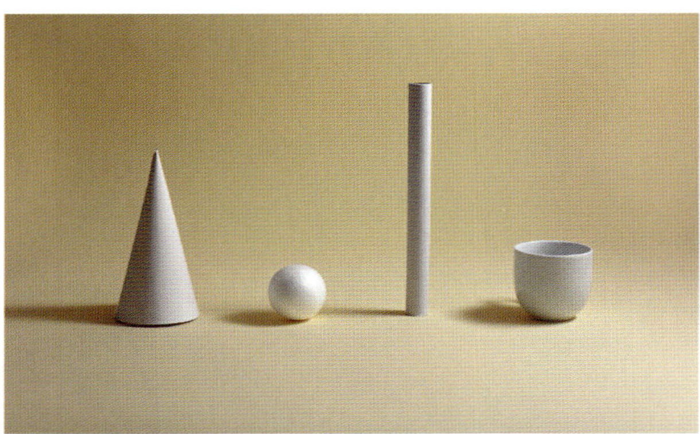

Note how the shadows and highlights switch to the opposite side when the four basic shapes are lit from the top right.

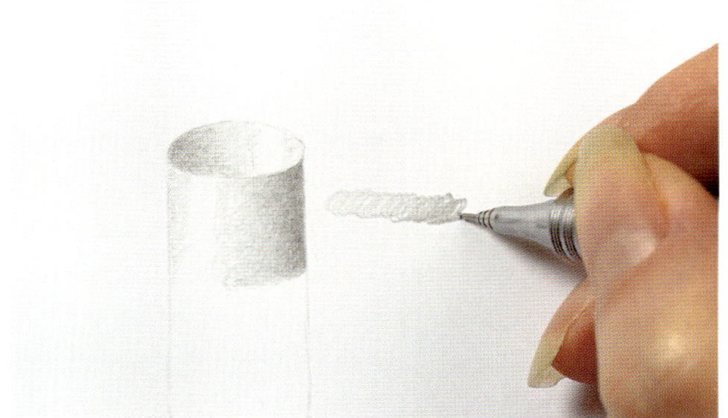

Using small, round, elliptical movements, create smooth, graduated tone using an H or 2H pencil.

The highlight appears in the top left quadrant of a shaded sphere.

Try to keep a straight, vertical shape for highlights on long, straight cylinders.

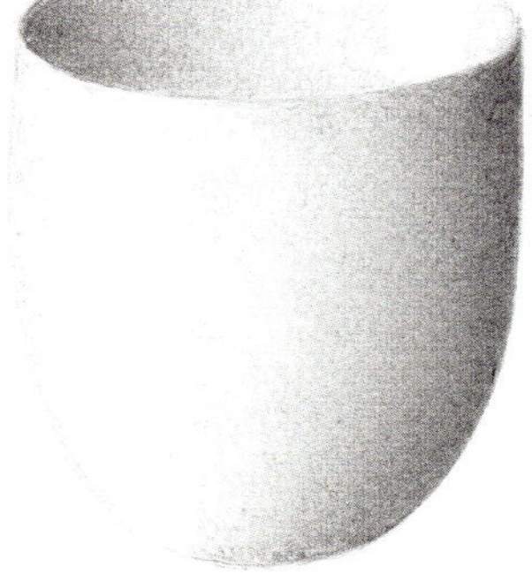

Follow the contour of the curved side to create a convincing highlight on a cup.

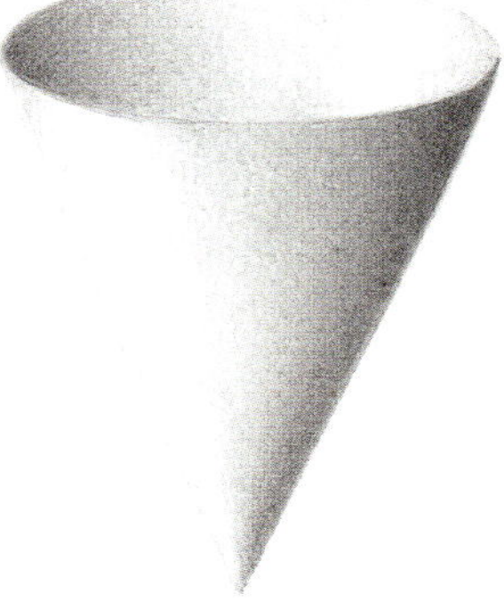

Taper the shape of the highlight towards the point of a cone.

Creating a tonal bar to help with shaded drawings

Identifying the darkest and lightest tones in your drawing and replicating them in a tonal bar will help you see out of context the range of tones you have used. If they all look similar, then you need to adjust them in your drawing to make the variation between dark and light greater. This will help you describe the 3D structures of your subject matter more clearly.

To create a tonal bar, start by looking at the range of tones you have used in your drawing. Identify the darkest and the lightest, and how many other tones lie in between.

Draw a small square for the darkest tone (1cm × 1cm) and shade the square with the darkest tone you have identified in your drawing.

Add another square of the same dimensions abutting the first square, and shade it in the next darkest tone.

Repeat the exercise until you have identified each tone. You will probably have around four to six squares.

Now look carefully at the tonal bar you have created, and consider the range of tones. Are they all similar? Is there one very dark tone and the rest are very light or vice-versa?

If necessary, alter the tones in your drawing so that there is an even gradation from dark to light/light to dark. Don't be afraid to make your darkest tone darker, and the lightest tone lighter.

A typical tonal bar should look like this:

A shaded tonal bar showing six increments.

BOTANY

Coping with the botany in botanical illustration demands a basic knowledge of this exacting science. Without a fundamental awareness of botany, it will be much harder to make accurate drawings and subsequently accurate illustrations, but how much knowledge will you really need to have?

Surprisingly, you will not need to know every single botanical term that exists, but you will need to know a reasonable amount about plant morphology and plant anatomy. An understanding of how botanical components within structures function and how they work in relation to one another, and the purposes of such components, is helpful during the drawing process.

Much botanical knowledge can be learned on a project-by-project basis by using reference material such as a good, reliable glossary, so that over time botanical terms will become more familiar and you will have a greater understanding of botany as you produce increasingly more illustrations. However, learning some basic key information – especially about flowers and leaves – is useful from the outset.

PLANT TAXONOMY

Plants are classified using a ranking system developed by Carl Linnaeus, a Swedish botanist of the eighteenth century. Linnaeus is often referred to as the 'father of taxonomy'.

The classification and naming of plants exists so that species can be distinguished from one another, according to their distinguishing features. Linnaeus achieved his system by using a method of division and subdivision, of which the principle ranks include: kingdom, division, class, order, family, genus, and species. To help you recognize whether you are referring to a family, genus, or species, it is worth becoming familiar with the word endings. For example, the family name will end in '*-aceae*'. Often, a family may be divided into subfamilies, ending in '*-oideae*', tribes, ending in '*-eae*', and subtribes, ending in '*-inae*'.

As a botanical illustrator, you will mainly be concerned with the family, genus and species ranks. Being able to identify family characteristics, as well as learning which genus your plant belongs to, and finally the species name, will be the most valuable information to know.

Unless your plant is already accurately named (this should be checked and double-checked – especially if you have purchased a plant from a garden nursery, where labelling can easily be switched through customer handling),

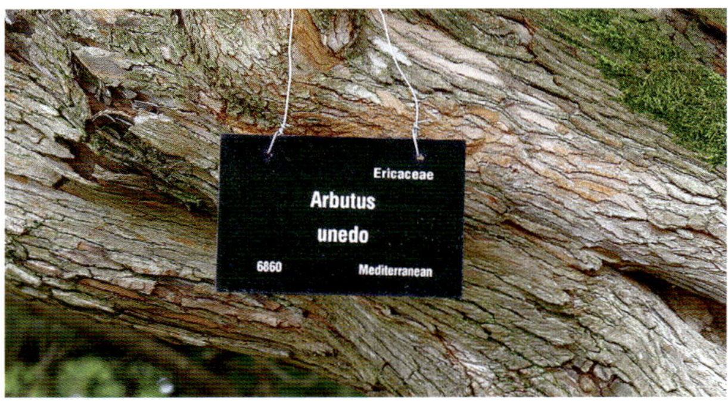

Species labelling according to the ranks of family, genus, and species. The plant's native country is also specified.

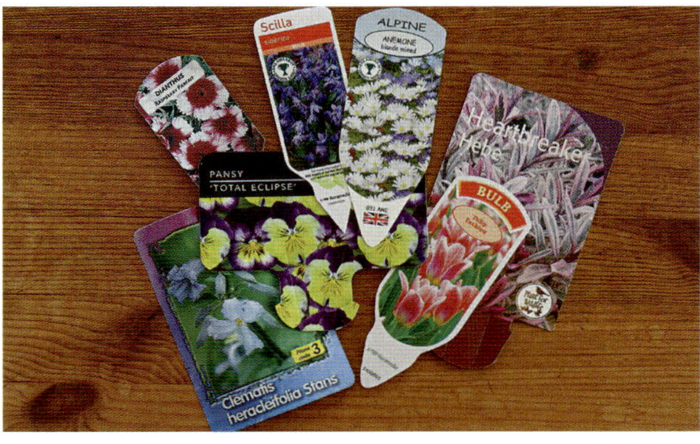

Check the labels of nursery-bought plants in case the labels have been misplaced.

you may have some investigation work to do so that you can correctly identify your plant. You may have to rely on a dependable source, such as the RHS Horticultural Database and RHS Plant Finder web pages.

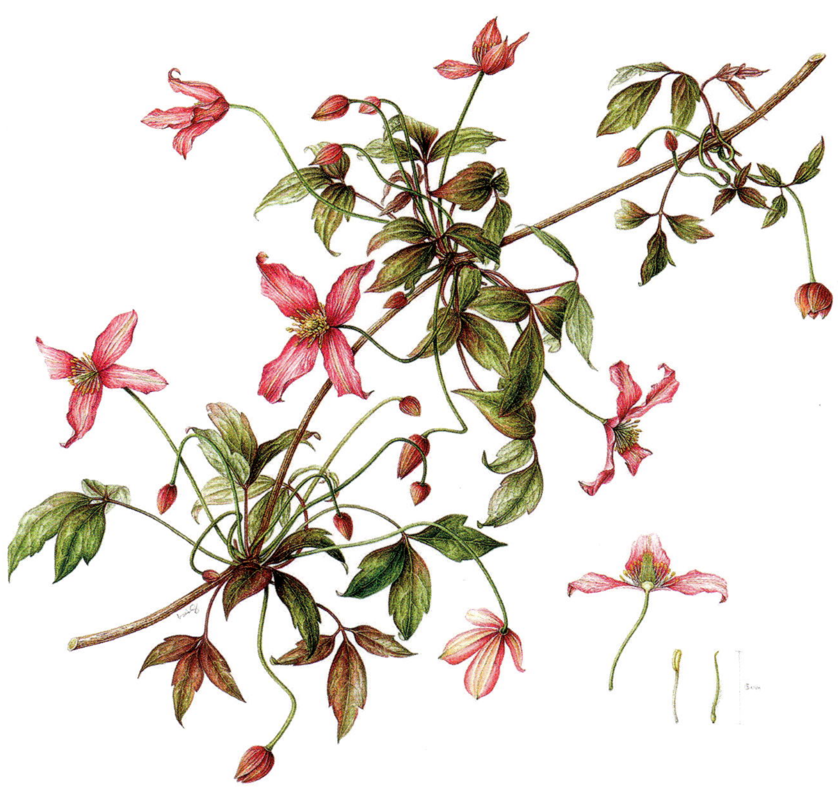

Clematis montana 'Warwickshire Rose'. LEIGH ANN GALE

WRITING BOTANICAL NAMES CORRECTLY

The botanical name of a plant should always be written following the conventional method devised by Linnaeus. A plant name will consist of the genus name, which always begins with a capital letter in italics, as in *Clematis*. This is followed by the species name written all in lower case italics, as in *Clematis montana*. If you are listing several examples of the same genus, it is acceptable to abbreviate the genus name to the initial capital letter followed by a full stop each time as in *Clematis montana, C. armandii, C. alpina*.

In some species, a cultivar name is added after the species name in roman type with initial capital letters, and inserted between single quotes, as in *Clematis montana* 'Warwickshire Rose'. A cultivar, or variety, is the term used for the selection of certain characteristics that remain consistent during the propagation process. However, not all cultivars evolve from propagated means. Some cultivars may also evolve naturally in the wild. In the example above, we know that *Clematis montana* 'Warwickshire Rose' was named by garden designer John Williams from Warwickshire, who found what was believed to be a seedling of *Clematis montana* 'Rubens' growing in his garden in the early 1990s, but it had particularly long, narrow tepals of a deep pink hue, together with flushed bronzed leaves. As well as the Warwickshire reference, he also named his new find after his mother, Rose.

In the case of hybrids (the result of two plants being cross-pollinated) the indication is such that an 'x' (in roman type) is inserted between the names of the plant parents, creating a hybrid formula. For example, for hybrids that are propagated from plants of the same genus, the formula would read: *Pelargonium lobatum* x *P. fulgidum*. Sometimes, the offspring hybrid is given a new name. In this instance, it becomes *P.* x 'ardens'.

If hybrids are created from plants in different genera, then the new hybrid is given a new genus name followed by a new species name. An upper case 'X' is put before the new genus and species names. For example, X *Amarygia parkeri*, which is a hybridization between *Amaryllis belladonna* x *Brunsvigia josephinae*.

MONOCOTYLEDONS AND DICOTYLEDONS

One of the very first things you should learn in botany relates to the categories of plants you will come across. The differences between monocotyledons and dicotyledons can be identified in the structural features of plants,

	MONOCOTYLEDON	DICOTYLEDON
Flowers (Petals)	Usually formed in threes	Usually formed in fours or fives
Leaves	Parallel veins	Branching veins
Roots	Generally fibrous roots	Tap root as well as other roots
Stems	Sporadic arrangement of vascular tissue	Organised arrangement of vascular tissue

The differences between monocotyledons and dicotyledons.

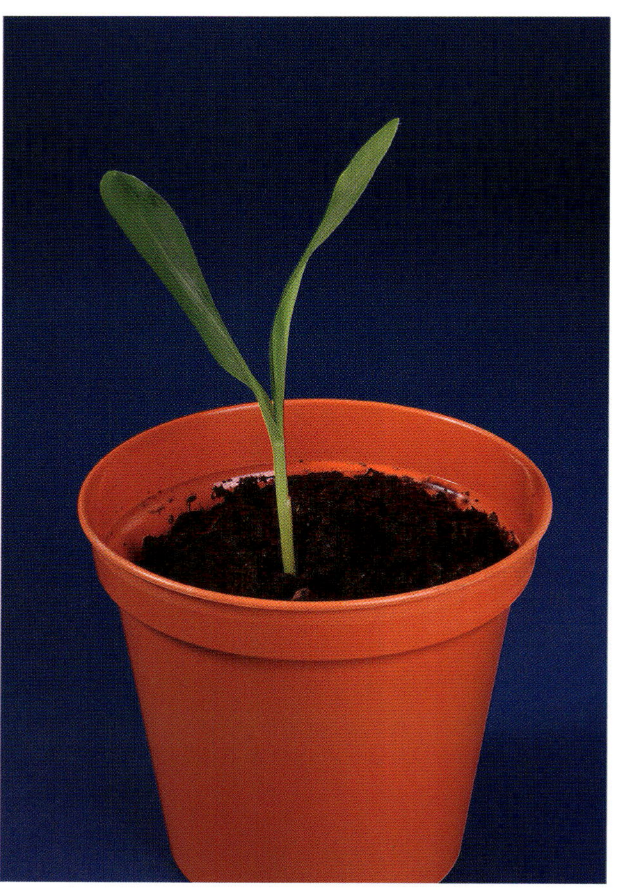

A monocotyledon plant sweetcorn showing parallel veins.

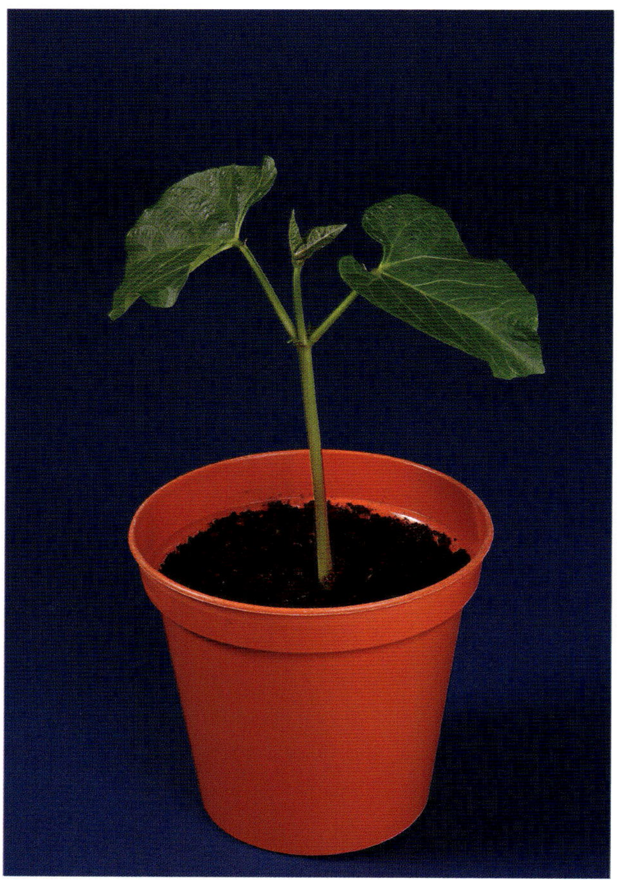

A dicotyledon plant runner bean showing branching veins.

such as the flowers, leaves, roots, and stems. Whether a plant forms as a monocot or a dicot all depends on what happens in the internal embryo of a seed. In most plants, the embryo will contain either one cotyledon or two (seed leaves). To determine whether you are studying and drawing a monocot or a dicot you will need to look at the differences carefully.

IDENTIFYING BOTANICAL STRUCTURES

There will be several botanical structures that you will be frequently drawing during your illustration projects. Flowers, leaves, and stems will repeatedly appear as common components, and from time to time you will also need to be able to recognize the features of fruits and seeds, especially if you are illustrating the lifecycle of a species.

COMMON FAMILY FEATURES

As you become more practiced, you will begin to notice similarities in the characteristics of plants occurring in specific families. For example, the ray-florets and disc-florets of the *Asteraceae* (Daisy) family – such as the dandelion, gerbera and chrysanthemum; the standard, keel, and wing petals of flowers, and dry, dehiscent legumes in members of the *Fabaceae* (Pea) family – such as the sweet pea, broad bean and Judas Tree; and the generally edible fruits of the *Rosaceae* (Rose) family, such as apples, blackcurrants and strawberries.

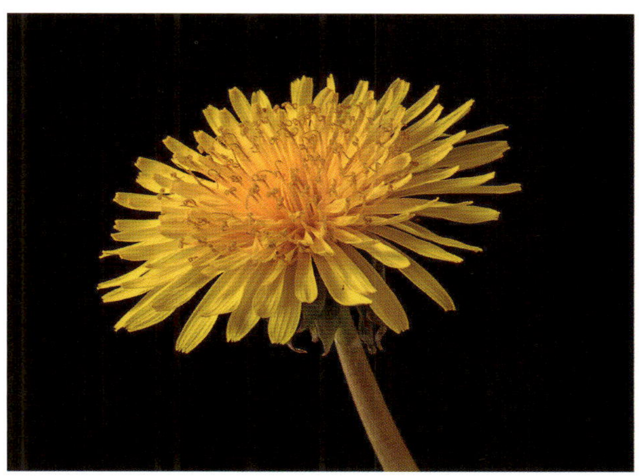

The *Asteraceae* family: features include ray and disc florets. Dandelion, *Taraxacum officinale*.

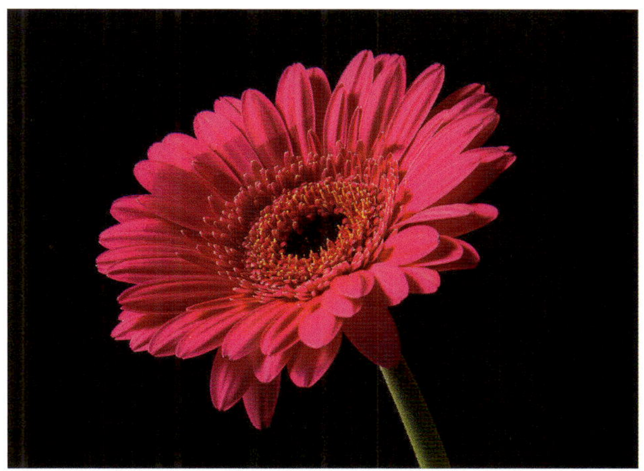

Asteraceae family: Gerbera.

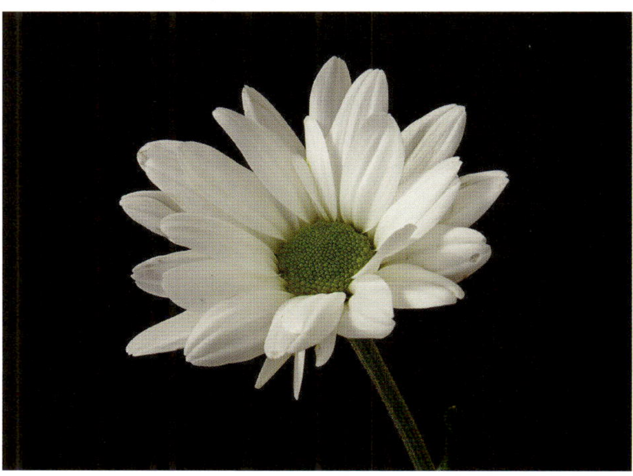

Asteraceae family: Chrysanthemum.

FLOWERS AND THEIR STRUCTURES

Probably the most common type of flower you will encounter is a complete (hermaphrodite) flower. A complete flower is one that contains both male and female reproductive organs. Species bearing complete flowers are referred to as hermaphroditic.

In some species such as *Ilex* (Holly), separate male and female flowers are borne on separate male and female plants (dioecious), and in some species, such as *Alnus* (Alder), male and female flowers are produced on the same plant (monoecious).

It is important that you can recognize these differences when you are drawing flowers, and ensure you include drawings of both individual male and female flowers if the species is dioecious or monoecious.

The botanical structures of a complete flower

In a typical complete flower, the floral anatomy can be identified in three whorls, namely, the gynoecium, the

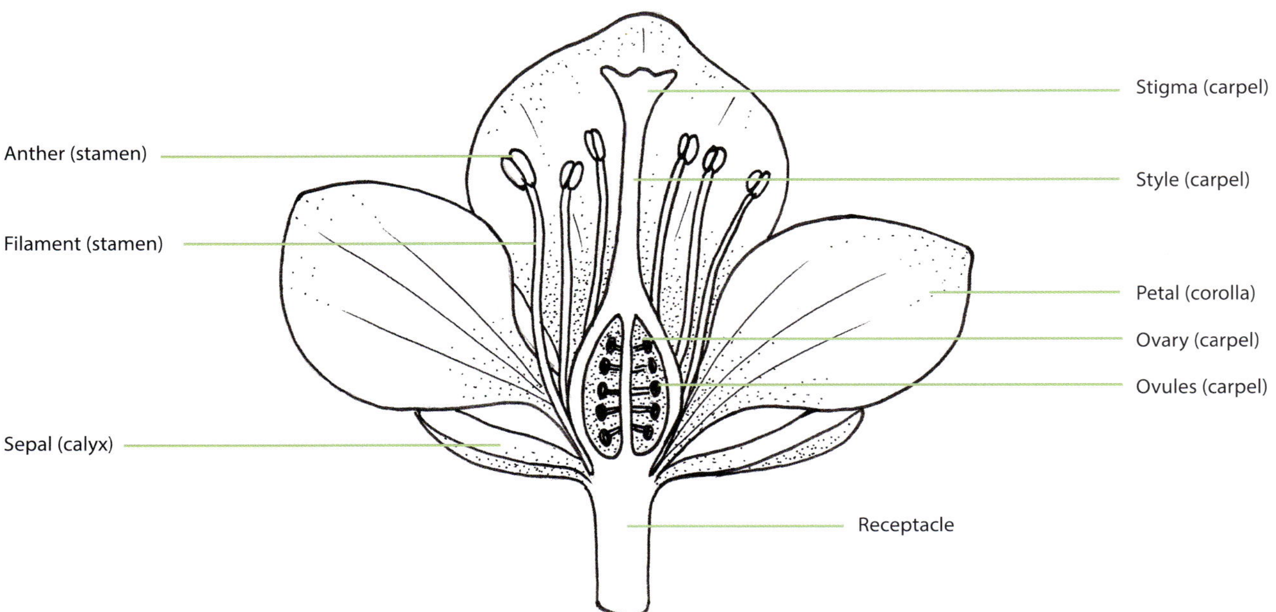

Diagram showing the botanical components dissected of a typical complete flower.

collective term for the centrally located female reproductive organs comprising of one or more carpels; the androecium, the collective term for the male reproductive organs consisting of stamens; and the perianth, the outer whorl of non-reproductive parts comprising a corolla and a calyx.

The assemblage of components in each whorl include the following:

- Gynoecium – carpel (female) – stigma, style, and ovary
- Androecium – stamen (male) – anther and filament
- Perianth – corolla (non-reproductive) – petals
- Perianth – calyx (non-reproductive) – sepals
- Receptacle – (non-reproductive) – the expanded top of a flower stem at which point the flower parts are attached.

LEAF STRUCTURES

There are numerous shaped leaves and you will no doubt discover many of them when drawing. However, shape is not the only defining feature of a leaf. Texture, thickness, and venation should also be observed and considered when drawing leaf structures. The cell structures of leaves are complex, and you will not normally need to worry about them, although it may be useful to learn a little about these internal workings so that you understand for example how photosynthesis takes place, how water loss is prevented or how water and minerals are transported around a leaf.

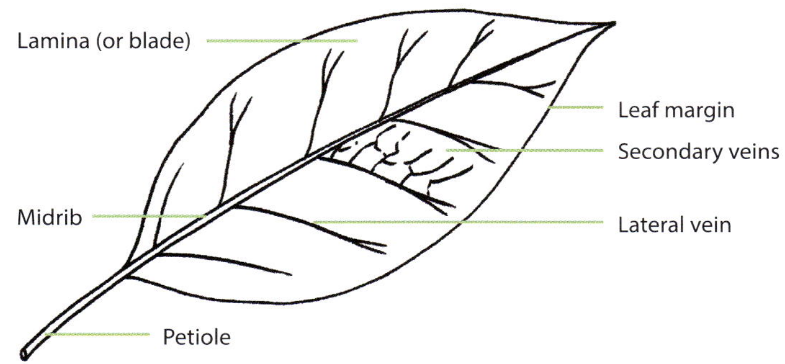

Diagram showing the botanical components of a leaf.

It is useful to be able to identify the various outer botanical components that you can see, as the presentations of these will vary considerably from leaf to leaf.

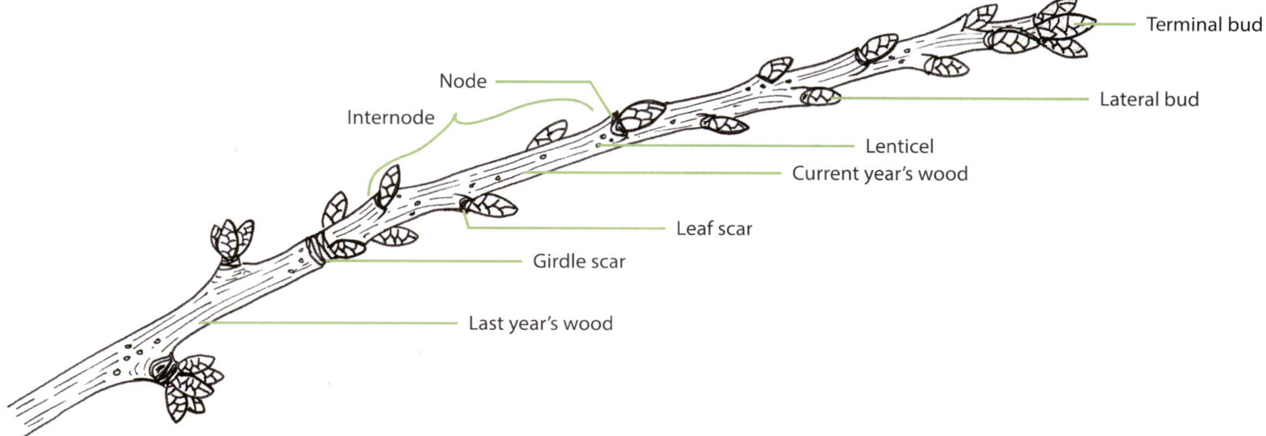

Diagram showing the botanical components of a winter twig.

STEM STRUCTURES

Stems, twigs, and branches perform a vital role in the external morphology of plants, providing a means of support and elevation to flowers, leaves, and fruits. They also act as a transportation system for water and nutrients upwards from the roots.

Stems are generally considered to be woody or soft in texture. Typically, soft wood stems are associated with younger, fleshier plant growth, whilst harder, woodier stems tend to be associated with older, sustained growth and that of larger, mature shrubs and trees.

Whether the stems you are drawing are soft or woody, there will be similarities in their structures. Stems are normally divided into nodes and internodes. The nodes are responsible for producing the leaves, buds and sometimes roots. The internodes are simply the areas between one node and the next.

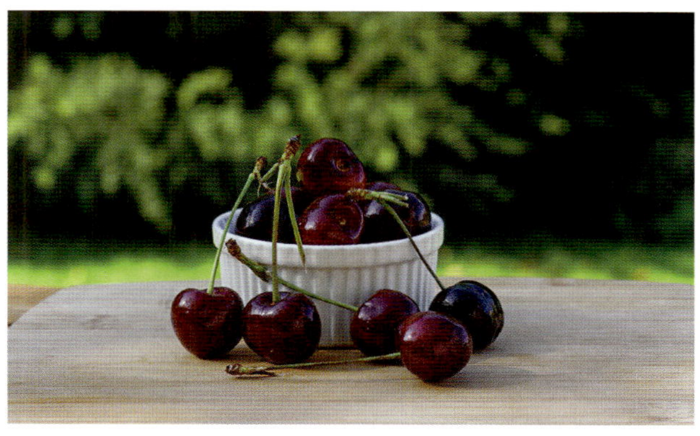

Cherries are fleshy, simple fruits.

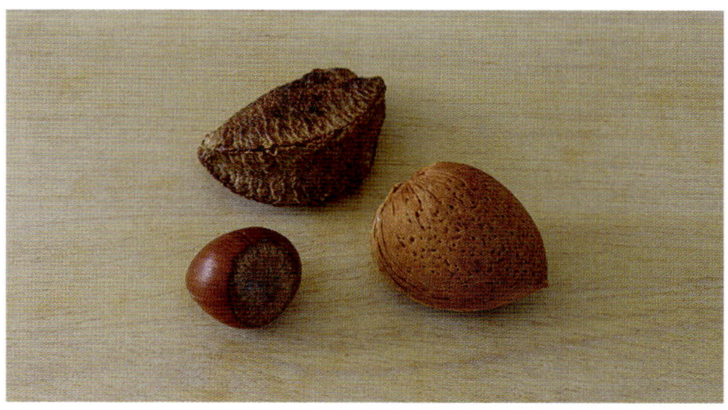

Brazil nuts, almonds and hazelnuts are examples of dry, simple fruits.

FRUITS AND SEEDS

The fruits and seeds of plants are the result of pollinated flowers. Unless a flower is pollinated it will not bare either. If your subject matter has produced fruits and seeds, it is a good idea to add them to your illustration, as you can provide yet more information about the development of the species and how lifecycles ebb and flow.

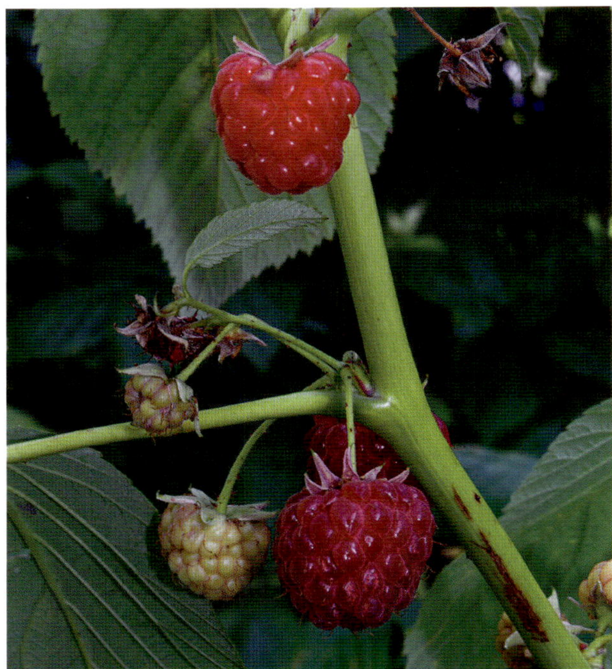

A raspberry is an example of an aggregate fruit.

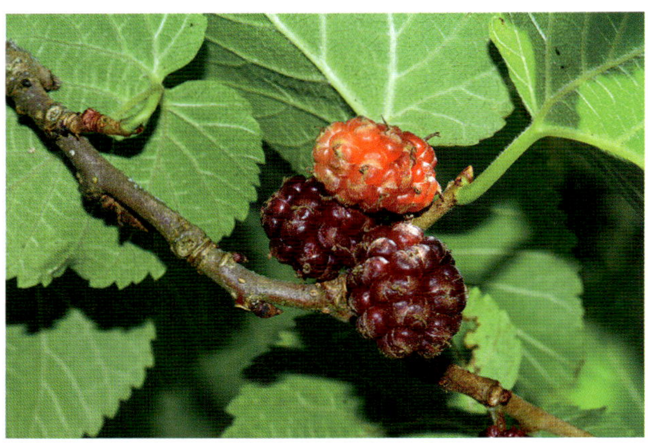

A mulberry is a multiple fruit.

It is important that you do not become confused with the difference between fruits and seeds, so it is worth spending some time checking what you have in front of you to draw. It is the formation of fruits and seeds that indicates the main difference between the two. In a flower, it is the ovule(s) that develop into the seed(s) after fertilization, whilst the ovary develops into the fruit (often the edible part). This type of fruit is known as a simple fruit because it has formed from a single flower, and may be fleshy or dry. Examples of simple fruits include cherry (fleshy) and nut (dry).

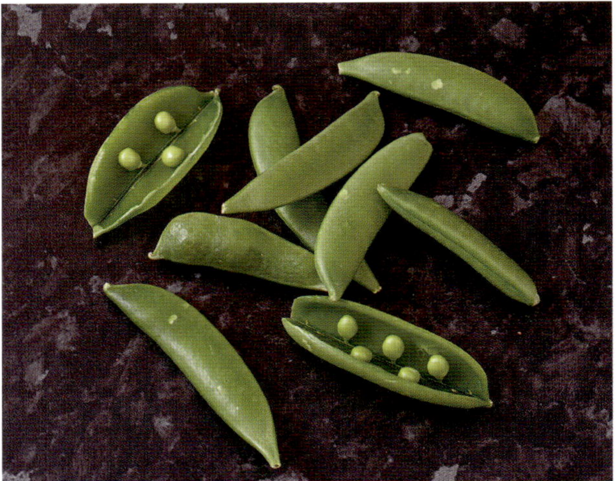

Legumes, such as peas, are dehiscent fruits.

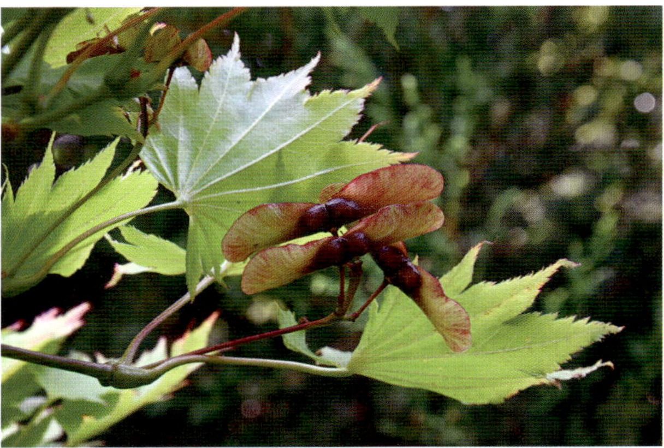

Acer samaras are indehiscent fruits.

Other types of fleshy fruits include aggregate fruit, formed from a single compound flower with several ovaries as in blackberry or raspberry, and multiple fruits, formed from an inflorescence (after flowering known as an infructescence) as in fig and mulberry.

Further examples of dry fruits can be categorized as dry dehiscent fruits or dry indehiscent fruits.

The term dehiscent means to split open naturally, and this process occurs on maturity of the fruit, for example in a legume such as a pea or runner bean, when the pod splits open to reveal the fruit inside.

Indehiscent fruits are those that do not split, such as the winged samaras of *Acer* (Maple) or *Fraxinus* (Ash), and the nutlets of salvia and other members of the *Lamiaceae* (Mint) family.

FRUIT STRUCTURE

The structure of a fruit includes the usually edible layers of the epicarp, the outermost layer (normally the skin), the mesocarp, (the central fleshy layer), and the endocarp, (the layer surrounding the seed which is often woody and inedible).

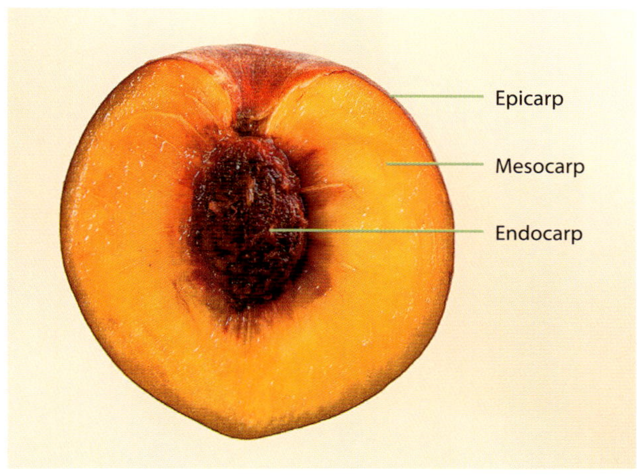

The various layers of a peach that form the pericarp.

SEED STRUCTURE

Once pollination has taken place the ovule(s) within a flower will develop into seed(s). Sometimes, two coats of a seed are formed from the ovule, one outer known as the testa, and an inner one, known as the tegmen. However, some seeds may have only one coat present.

Additional components of seeds that you may need to draw include the funicle, a stalk-like attachment which once connected an ovule to its placenta, and the hilum, the small scar left behind where the seed was once attached to the funicle.

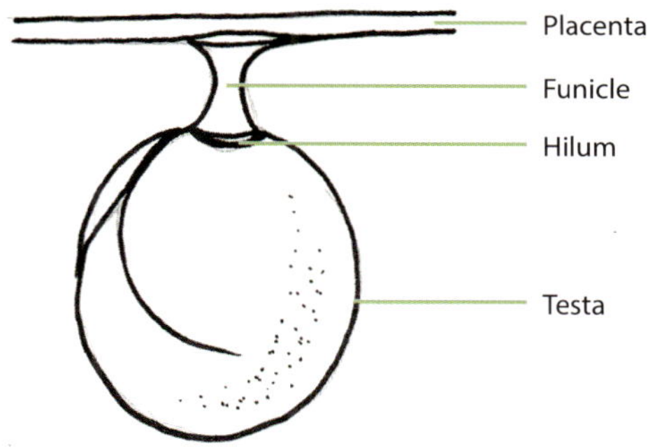

Diagram showing the botanical components of a seed.

POLLINATION

Pollination is essential for plant reproduction and survival. Without it, our plant species would die out including essential crops that we rely on for feeding the world's human population.

Pollination is a process of the transferral of pollen from the male stamens to the female stigma, and commonly carried out by insects such as bees, butterflies, and moths. However, some plants rely on other insects such as flies and wasps, and even beetles and ants. Some vertebrates too including bats and birds also pollinate other species, and mammals such as monkeys, rodents and lizards help with this vital role.

It is helpful to have some knowledge of pollinators and pollination, especially if you intend to include drawings of pollinators in your illustration. Always use a trusted source to help with your research and study of anthecology, since you should never illustrate an incorrect pollinator with your plant.

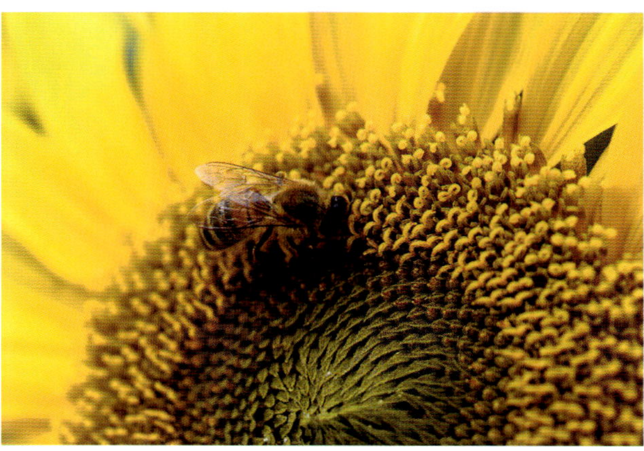

The process of pollination is essential for plant reproduction and survival.

SEED DISPERSAL

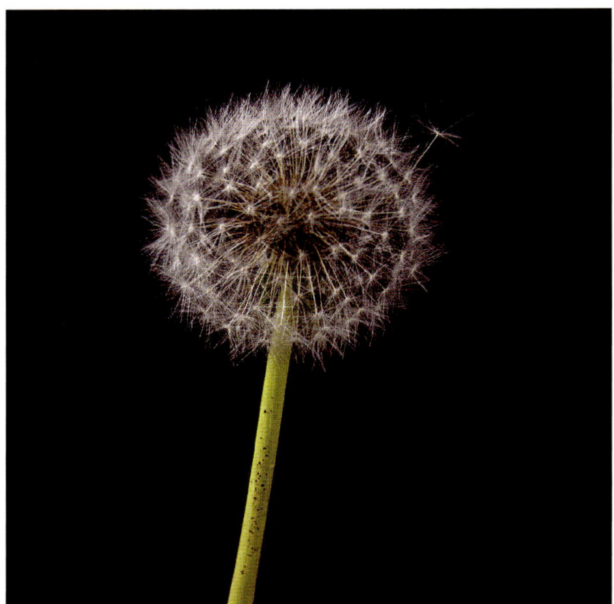

The feathery pappus of a dandelion seed uses the wind to aid its dispersal.

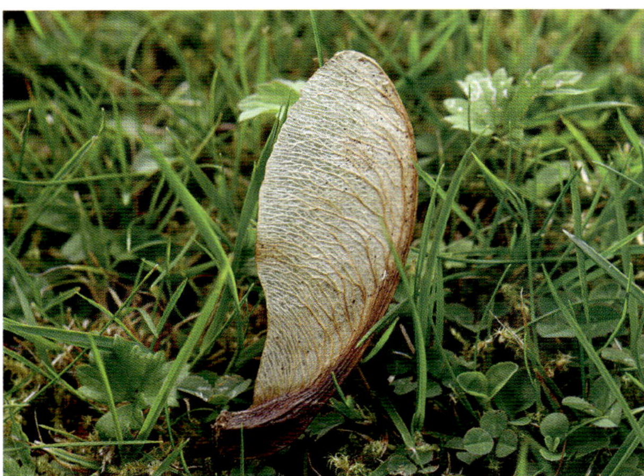

The winged seed of a single sycamore samara familiarly known as a helicopter relies on the wind for seed dispersal.

As with pollination, the future survival of plants is reliant on the process of successful seed development and dispersal. Seed dispersal only takes place once the seeds have been generated and are ripe. Effective seed dispersal is achieved when maximum transferral distances from the parent plant are possible, allowing maximum efficiency of migration distances. This allows future generations of species to spread and grow if the conditions are correct, in a variety of regions of the world.

There are several methods of seed dispersal, including wind, gravity, animals, water, and explosive means. Examples of these include:

Wind – dandelion, using a feathery pappus (a modified calyx consisting of hairs and scales) to aid dispersal over long distances; a single winged sycamore samara uses the wind to propel it along.

Gravity – apple, and other heavy-coated seeds such as coconut, which may then roll away to gain more distance from the parent plant.

Animals – buttercup, using small hooked achenes to attach to animal hair and succeed in vast, rapid seed dispersal.

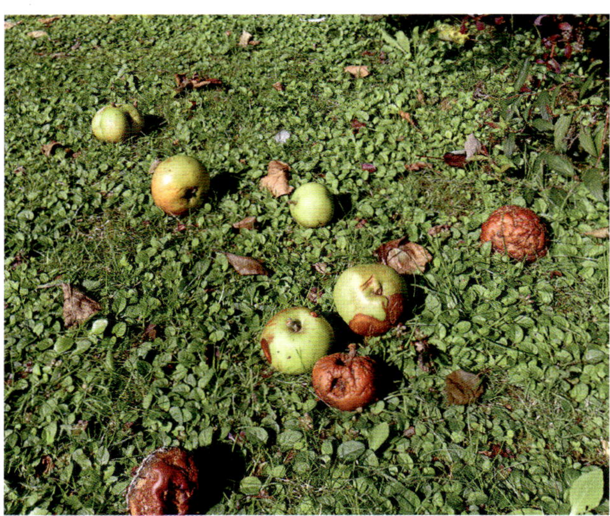

Seed dispersal by gravity: an apple will fall to the ground and roll away from the parent plant.

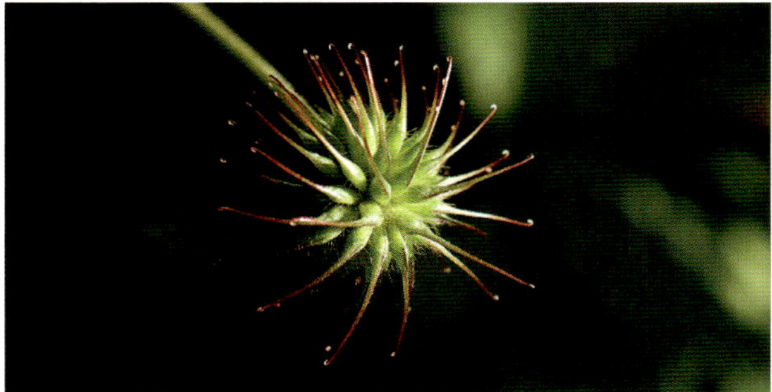

Buttercup achenes rely on their hooks to attach to animal hair to aid dispersal.

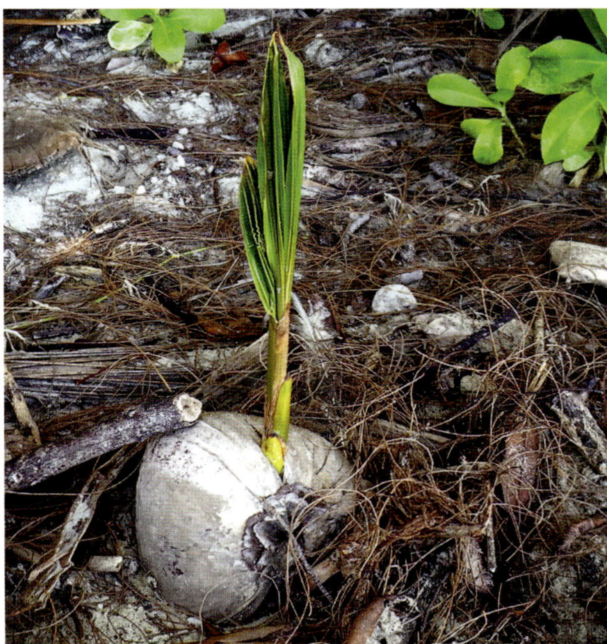

The seed of a coconut palm may have travelled many miles in water before settling on dry land to germinate.

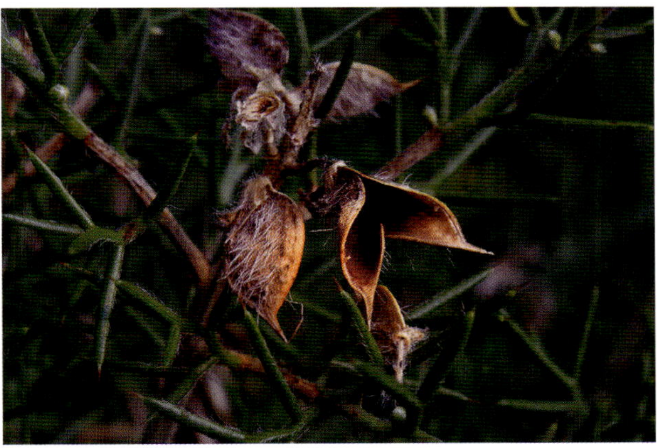

Gorse pods use ballistic methods to eject their seeds.

Water – palm trees, using the effect of oceanic currents (if they grow by water) to transfer seeds many miles, often to other continents.

Ballistic – gorse, using the internal tension within the seed pod to generate an explosive action when dry, allowing the seed to disperse over several meters.

Whilst it is not essential that you learn about seed dispersal specifically, you may find it helpful when drawing seeds, especially when drawing their structures, which are indicative of the method of seed dispersal, for example samaras (often known as 'helicopters'), with their winged appendages.

Checklist for The Drawing Process

- Check that your drawing space is set up satisfactorily, for example lighting, equipment, and specimens.
- Position your specimens suitably; suspend or elevate them if necessary.
- Consider 'warming up' before beginning botanical drawing, by making larger, looser style drawings.
- Study the structures of your subject matter before drawing (use a magnifying glass if necessary); look for the basic 3D shapes.
- Use a putty rubber to correct errors.
- Make outline and tonal drawings, as well as habit drawings of your subject matter.
- Pay attention to technical drawing aspects such as perspective and foreshortening.
- Consider including additional drawings in your final illustration, such as magnifications and dissections.
- Ensure you use the correct dissecting equipment for dissecting flowers.
- Learn some botanical terms based on a good glossary.
- Familiarize yourself with the botanical features of complete flowers and leaves.
- Look for similar features within botanical family groups.
- Name and label plants correctly, using italic and roman type.

Case Study

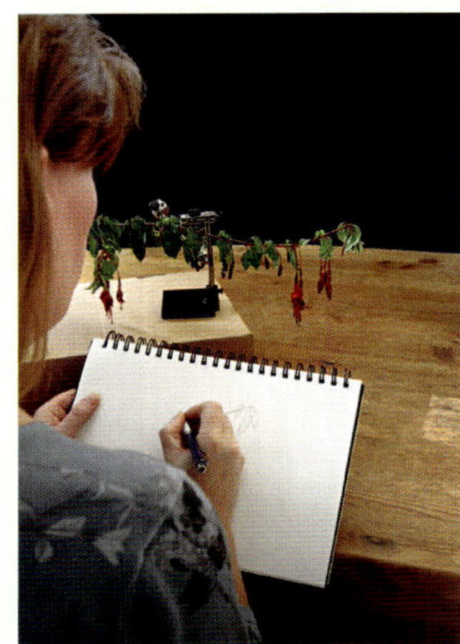

Habit drawings of *Fuchsia magellanica* were made as quickly as possible.

The next stage for the case study included the drawing of specimens collected from Nymans. Back in the studio, the specimens were set up urgently (due to wilting) on a table and held in a hobby hand clamp ready to be drawn. It was important to check that the angle of the specimen in the clamp represented the growing habit of the plant at Nymans. A black alcove was positioned behind the specimens so that interference of surrounding items in the studio did not inhibit the process of accurate drawing. The drawings were compiled in an A3 sketchbook so that they could be used as reference material during the composition and painting stages.

Observational drawings

With the specimens rapidly deteriorating, it was apparent that drawings had to be made quickly so that as much information as possible could be recorded. Reference was made to the photographs taken of the plant growing *in situ* at Nymans, so that several flowers could be drawn in an open position. Several outline habit drawings were made from the collected specimens that would provide plenty of scope to produce a good, naturalistic composition later on. Individual leaf studies were also made, so that the serrated leaf margins could be accurately recorded and drawn, and different views of the leaves could be incorporated into the composition. This was important, because many of the leaves tended to naturally curl, and so the composition would clearly have to include foreshortened views of these leaves. One or two tonal drawings were also made of the leaves and flowers, to reinforce an awareness of where the highlights and shadows occurred.

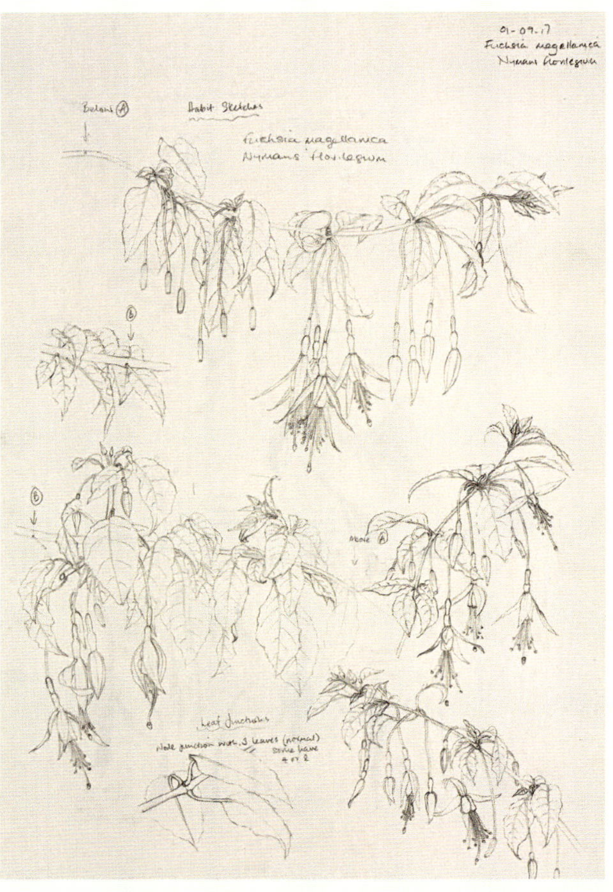

Several habit drawings were made of *Fuchsia magellanica*.

Botany

It is always important to have a good, basic understanding of the botanical features of the species being studied, so some time was spent investigating these of *Fuchsia magellanica*. The flowers and buds were drawn, dissections were made of the flowers and fruit using a botanist's blade and subsequently drawn, and enlarged drawings of the stamens, style and stigma were also made to show close-up details.

Fuchsia magellanica is classified in the family *Onagraceae*, the Evening Primrose family, which includes species such as Clarkias and Willowherbs. The diagnostic features of the family include four sepals, four petals, usually four or sometimes eight stamens and a style and stigma. The ovary when developed as a fruit (or berry in the case of our plant) consists of four carpels, which contain the ovules.

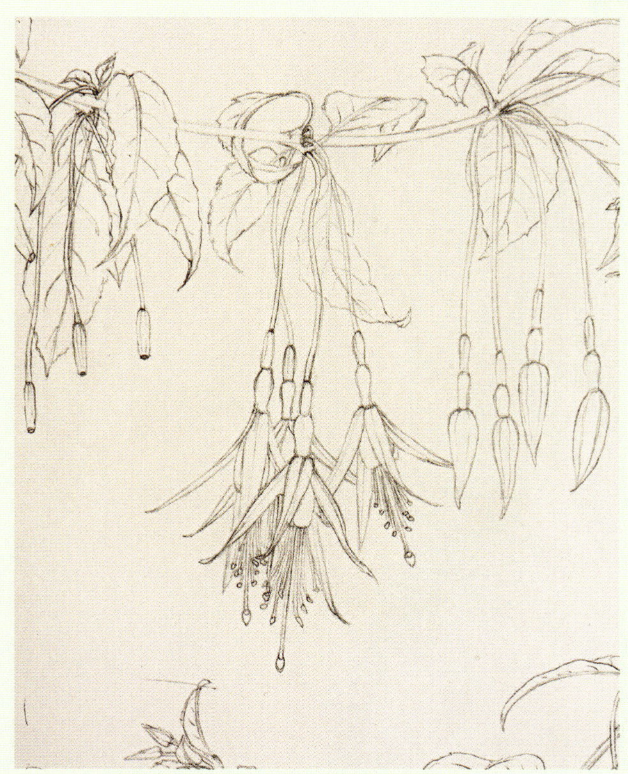

Attention was paid to the botanical accuracy of drawings, using outlines only.

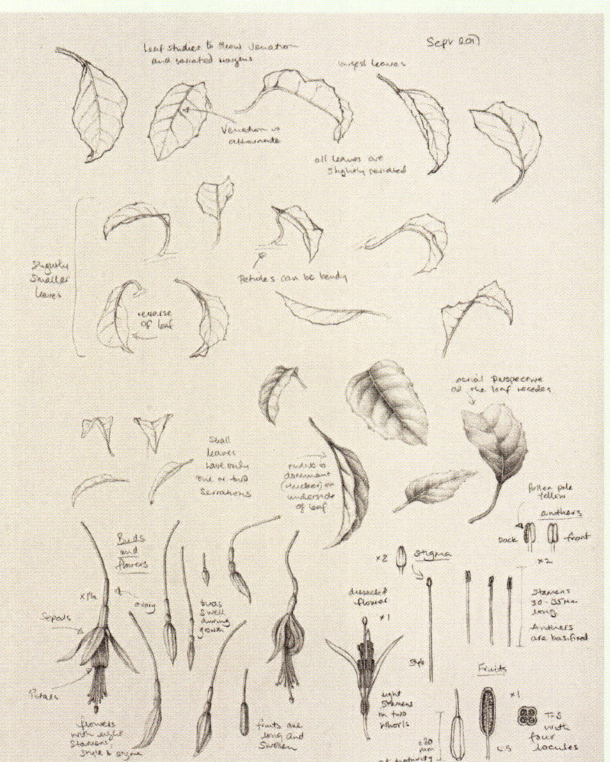

Individual studies of the leaves, flowers and other components were made.

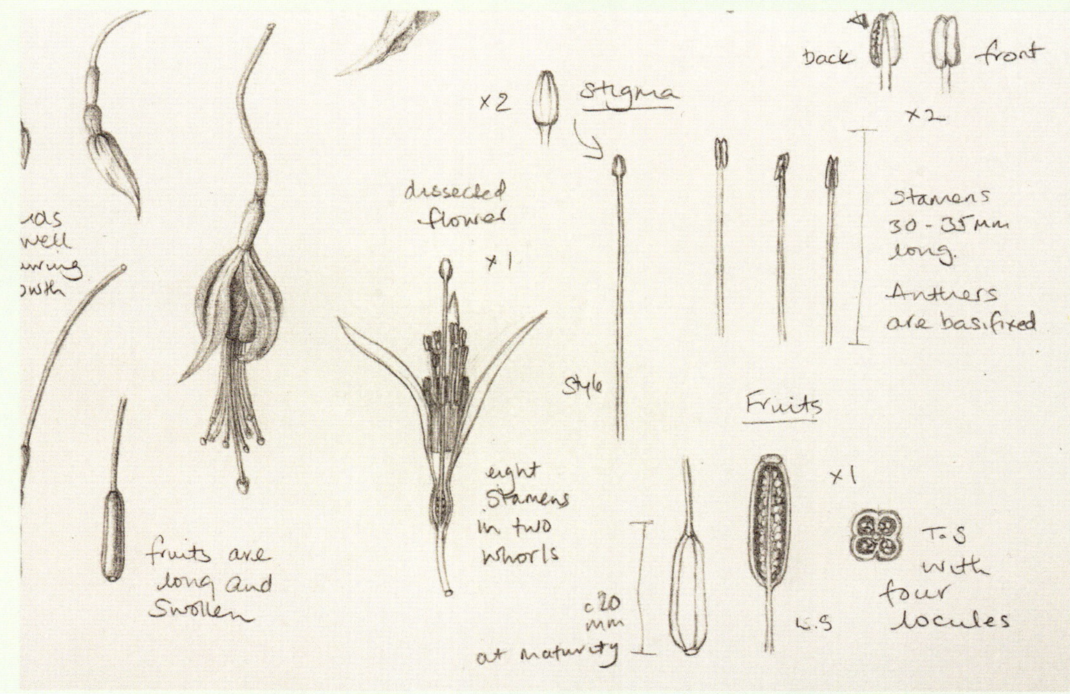

Dissections and enlargements of the botanical components were observed and drawn.

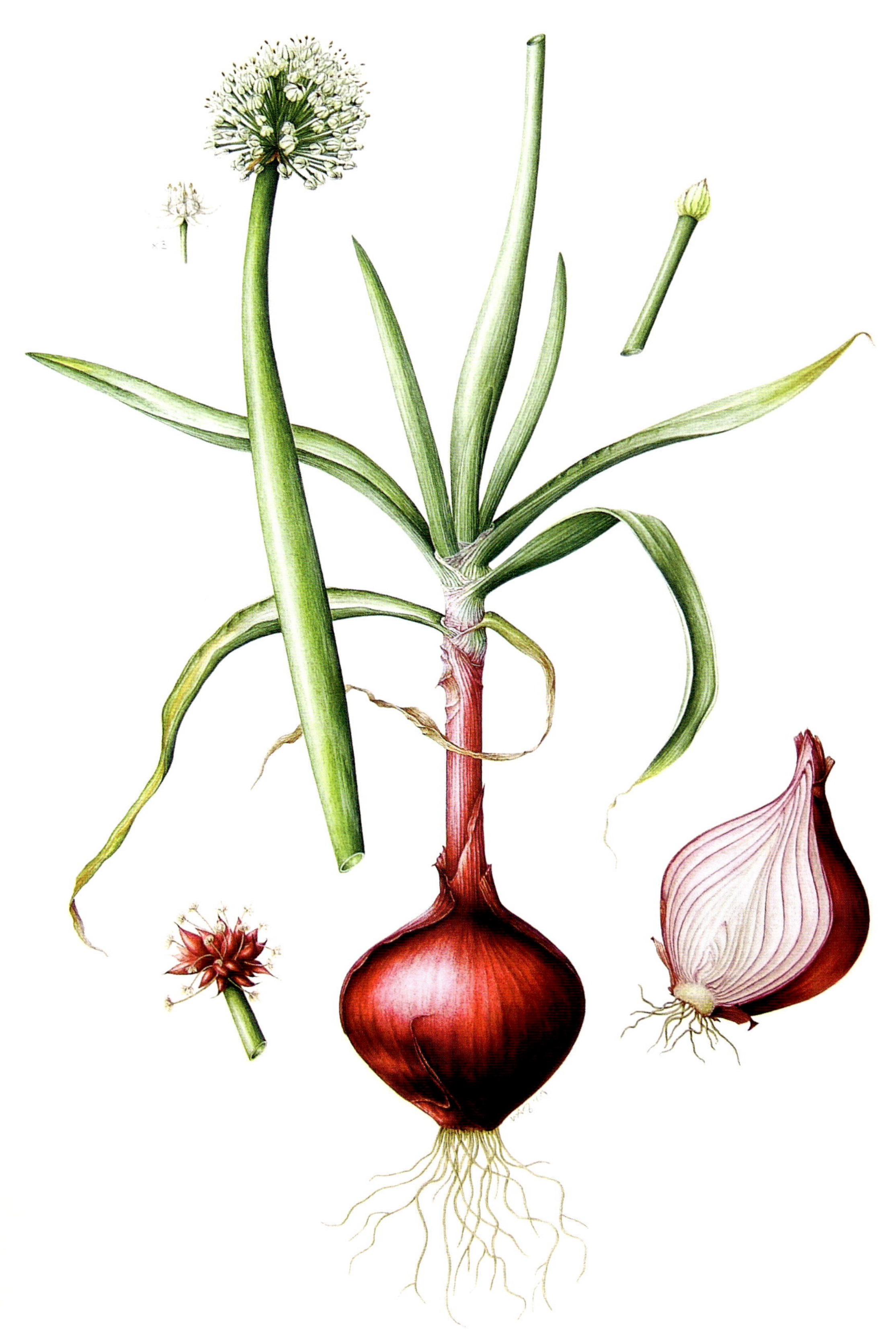

CHAPTER 4

Composition

Composition is the gravity that holds a painting together.

– Frank Webb (Artist)

Composition is rather like a link in a chain. In botanical illustration it is the stage between drawing and painting, the stage at which you will need to engineer a final layout for your illustration before you can begin the painting process.

During the composition stage there will be several processes to consider, but thinking about the content without forgetting about the overall function of your illustration will be the most important. Creating a suitable composition can be a time-consuming process, as you will need to think about many things. To begin with, you will have to choose carefully particular drawings made from your observational studies in order to depict the species accurately, followed by considerations such as creating a focal point; how the 'negative' or 'white space' will work; the distribution of colour across the entire composition and how much space to leave for your margins, for example. Finally, towards the end you will also need to think about how you will transfer your drawings onto watercolour paper ready for the painting stage.

By the end of the whole process you will have established the vital link – an aesthetic composition that clearly defines artistic quality combined with scientific accuracy.

Red Onion Study *Allium cepa*, now in the collection of the Hunt Institute for Botanical Documentation, Carnegie Mellon University, Pittsburgh, USA. LEIGH ANN GALE

WHAT IS COMPOSITION?

You may have heard people referring to 'the composition' when viewing and analysing works of art. They may say 'it's a good composition', 'the composition works well' or conversely, 'the composition doesn't work', but what are they referring to? To a degree, composition can be purely subjective, either someone likes what they see in front of them or they don't. However, as an artist creating a composition, you should be aware that there are several conventional practices that can be used to help establish an agreeable and logical solution.

Composition in the context of botanical illustration means the way in which the illustration is organized, specifically of the information necessary to inform and educate us about the species in question. We have already established that the drawing process produces well-observed and accurately drawn studies, so it is the choice of these drawings and their arrangement on the paper that will define the composition. As you practise, you will discover that creating a good composition doesn't merely involve popping a few images together and accepting the first layout that you come up with. Instead, it is about making well-informed and suitable choices to fulfil the function of botanical illustration.

As well as being the stepping-stone between drawing and painting, composition can also be thought of as the 'design' of your illustration. Design takes thought and time, planning and adjustment, and often re-design, so you should be prepared to sit down and carefully consider what will produce a good, workable design.

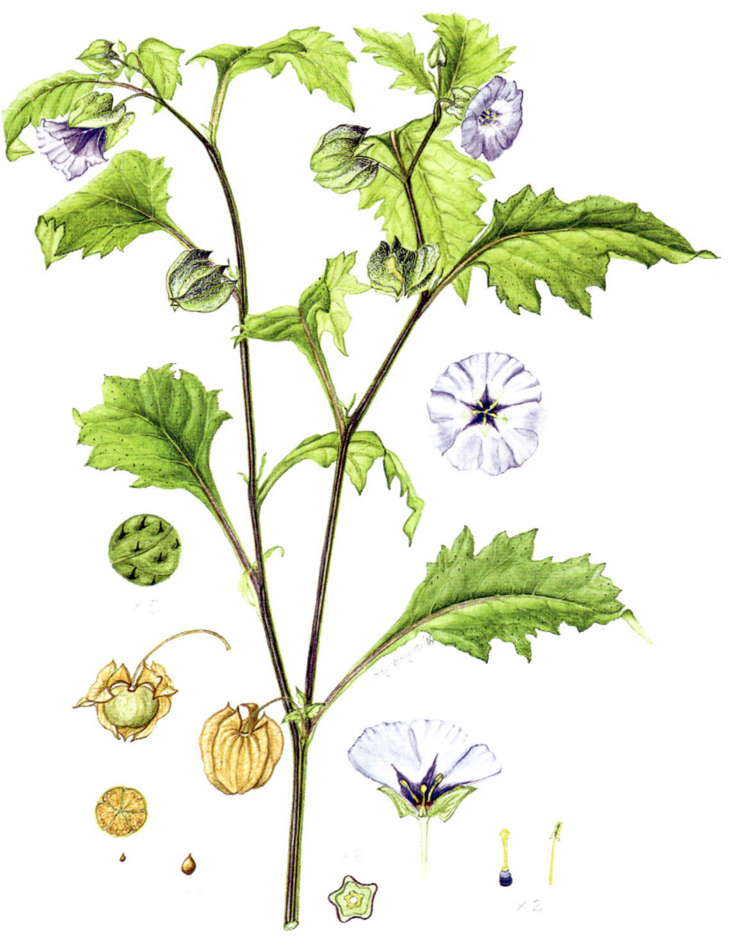

Nicandra physalodes. GAY BOYLE

THE COMPOSITION PROCESS

Throughout the drawing stage it is possible that you may have had a few ideas about how your final illustration could look when it is finished. You may have 'composed' a picture in your mind, so to speak. Perhaps you can envisage your illustration composed in a less conventional way, maybe because you have seen other botanical illustrations that have a more contemporary feel about them which appeals to you. For example, setting your illustration on a paper size that might be square or very long/tall and narrow, rather than on the more conventional landscape or portrait rectangular format. Maybe you admire the work of a particular artist and how they depict their imagery, or you like the idea of creating regimental lines from left to right or top to bottom to give a more abstract feel.

Whatever you have in mind, traditional, contemporary, or otherwise, it will be necessary to work your way through the composition process in a logical and methodical way, remembering all the time the reasons why you are creating your illustration.

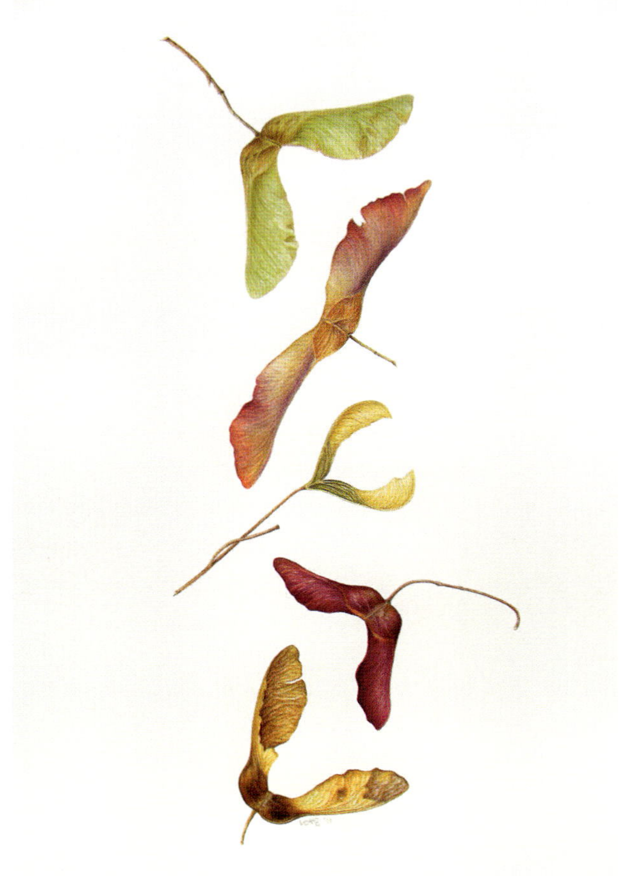

Double Samaras. LEIGH ANN GALE

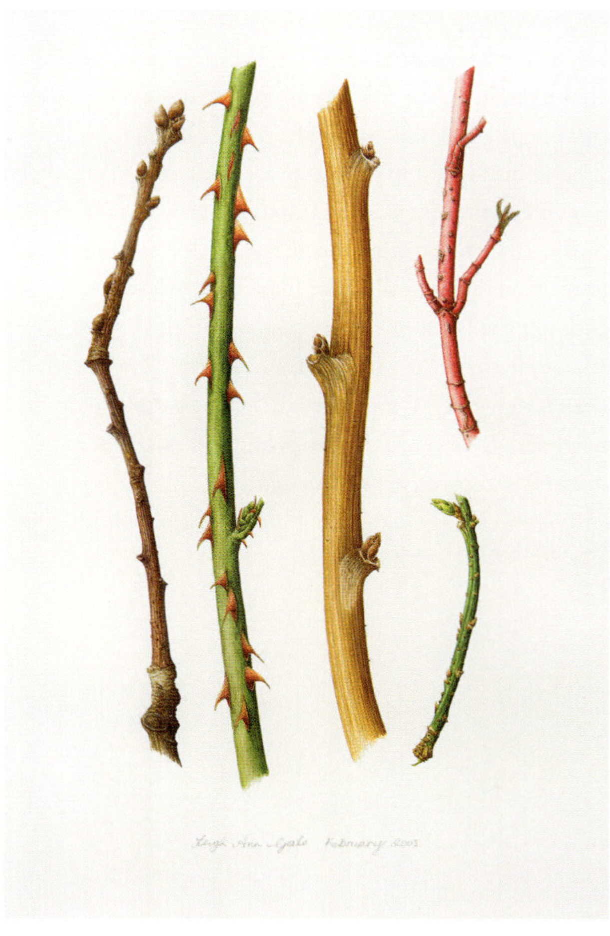

A contemporary composition depicting winter twigs. LEIGH ANN GALE

CHOOSING YOUR DRAWINGS

Hopefully, you will have produced plenty of drawings of your subject matter: habit drawings, close-up details, enlargements of specific botanical features and so on, as well as drawings from different angles. If you have kept a botanical sketchbook it is likely that you have also made some written and colour notes about aspects of your subject matter, and possibly taken some measurements or labelled botanical features from a glossary, to help you understand some of the structures and their functions. These will all be helpful when selecting your drawings and shouldn't be ignored. There was a good reason why you wrote a note, measured the width of an open flower or jotted down specific information about a growth form – to remind you about the importance of the information and to include it in your composition.

In a conventional sense, the composition primarily should include a habit drawing, which will quite possibly become the focus. Showing how the plant grows gives a precise indication of how it presents itself in its natural growing environment, what its natural growth pattern may be like, and the positions of all the botanical components in relation to each other. For most of the time you should produce the habit drawing at life size in the composition. However, if your plant is typically very small or very large then it may not be practicable or even possible to do this, in which case you will need to produce enlarged or reduced drawings to convey the information.

Other drawings to consider using will be those that describe fruits or seed pods. This is especially relevant if for example you are illustrating the life cycle of your subject, and these drawings will also create further interest by introducing more colour, shape, and texture. You may also need to describe in detail – perhaps as an enlargement – some of the finer botanical structures of your plant if they are particularly small or are of a more complex nature, such as the arrangement of stamens comprising their filaments and anthers, and styles supporting their stigmas. Additionally, you might need to include a drawing for example of a dissected flower, such as a primrose, showing whether it is pin-eyed or thrum-eyed. These are just a few examples of the drawings you should consider using in conjunction with your habit drawing, but ultimately, your choice of drawings will dictate the next steps of the composition process, and how you resolve to illustrate your subject matter effectively.

The positioning of any extra magnification and dissection drawings should be decided now, during the composition stage. You should have a clear idea how they will form part of your overall composition before you illustrate them. It is usually best to try and include them where they relate most to the content of your illustration. For example, positioning an enlarged drawing of a stamen, style, and stigma near painted flowers often works well. Alternatively, as in more traditional illustrations, you could arrange them in a more linear style, usually along the bottom of an illustration, which gives a very neat and 'arranged' feel to the work. This idea is often used in very scientific illustrations that contain many magnifications and dissections.

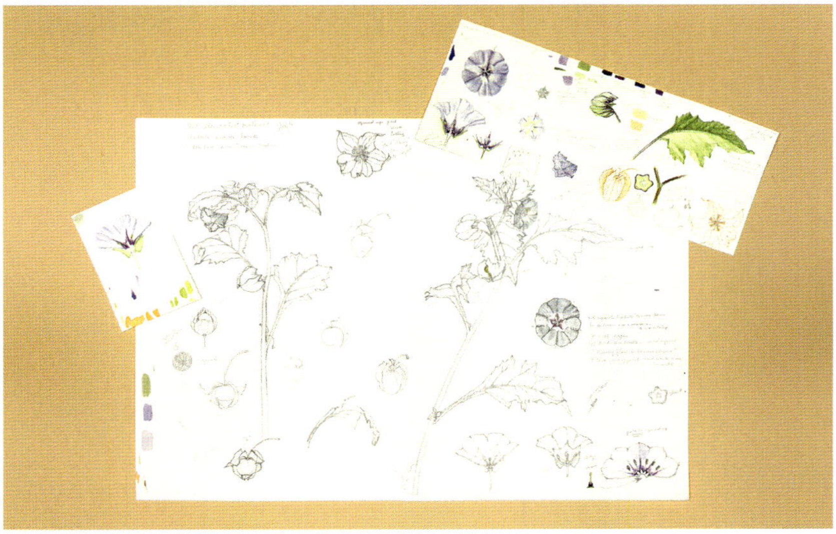

Selected drawings, including habit, dissection and enlargements for a composition. *Nicandra physalodes* sketches. GAY BOYLE

TRYING DIFFERENT IDEAS

It is a good idea to begin arranging your composition by trying out several ideas first. You could do this very quickly by making some thumbnail sketches to get an idea of how your illustration could look, or you could start by tracing off the drawings you will be including in the composition, cutting them out and trying different layouts. (It is generally not a good idea to draw an arrangement directly onto watercolour paper as invariably you will want to try some alternative layouts, and the paper fibres could potentially become spoiled by continuous rubbing out.) Using the method of tracing your drawings, ensure you capture all the lines within your drawing (a good way of checking this is to occasionally lift the tracing paper away from the drawing and you will notice any missed lines). If you are tracing a particularly complex drawing it can be helpful to tape down the tracing paper over the drawing in one or two places first, using low-grade adhesive tape. This will stop the tracing paper from slipping as you hold it in position.

When you have traced off all the drawings you need, cut them out and keep them flat. You will then be able to move the pieces around into different positions to come up with alternative layouts for a composition. If it helps, take quick photos or photocopies of each one to remind you of the possibilities. As you go, think about the overall shape that each drawing makes, the orientation of the illustration, for example landscape or portrait, and the sequencing of each drawing (in other words what goes next to the preceding drawing, especially when illustrating a lifecycle), and how the colour is likely to be distributed throughout the overall composition. You could also try turning over one or two of your traced drawings to see how the shapes fit together, but only do this if there is clearly no distinguishable back and front to your subject.

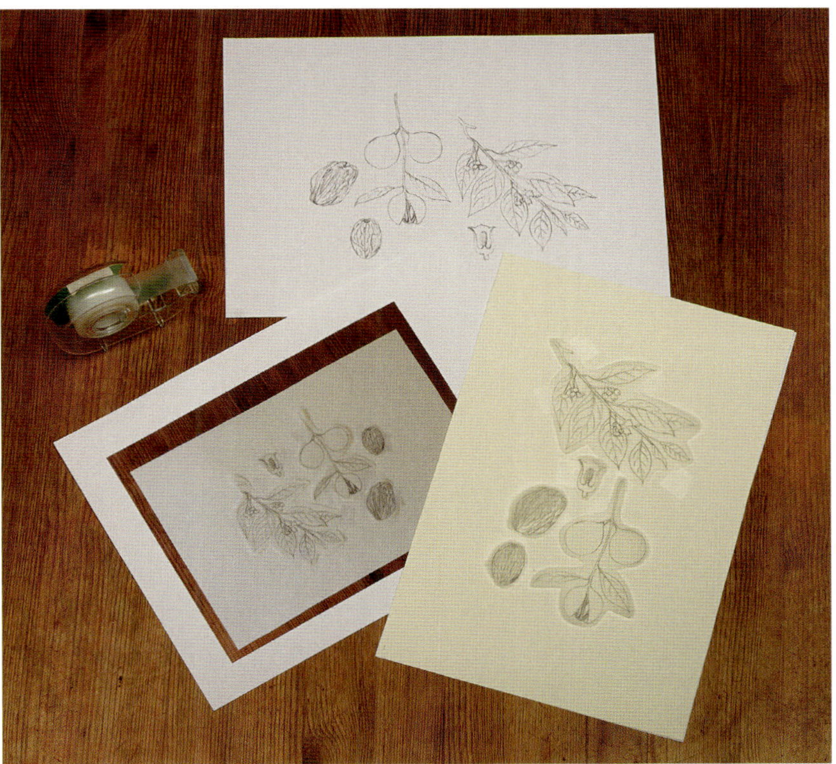

Try making different arrangements for your composition, taking photos or photocopies of them to remind you of what they were.

Creating thumbnail sketches

Creating thumbnail sketches is a very useful and quick way of working out initially whether your composition ideas may or may not work. If you have done other types of art or design, you might already be familiar with this technique, but if not, have a go at trying some before you continue with the rest of the composition process.

To create thumbnail sketches simply draw on a sheet of paper an outline to represent the edge of your watercolour paper, approximately 4in × 2in for portrait size or 2in × 4in for a landscape format, and roughly copy the drawings you are going to include into an arrangement. You can do this as many times as you like, trying the drawings in different positions each time. If it helps, add in a little tonal shading to emphasize some of the 3D shapes such as stems and buds, or to visualize the colour distribution, a little shading using coloured pencils can be used. This will help you achieve an overall 'feel' for how things will look in the composition. Once you have produced several thumbnail sketches you should have a clearer idea about what could and couldn't work in a composition, and you will be able to discard any straight away that clearly don't work. Mark each of your ideas with a cross or a tick, to remind you of those that are composition possibilities and those that you can easily discard. Producing thumbnail drawings can also help build your confidence about the whole composition process, especially if this way of working is new to you.

When you are ready, you can start to arrange your composition based on the thumbnail sketch that works best, following the process described in this chapter.

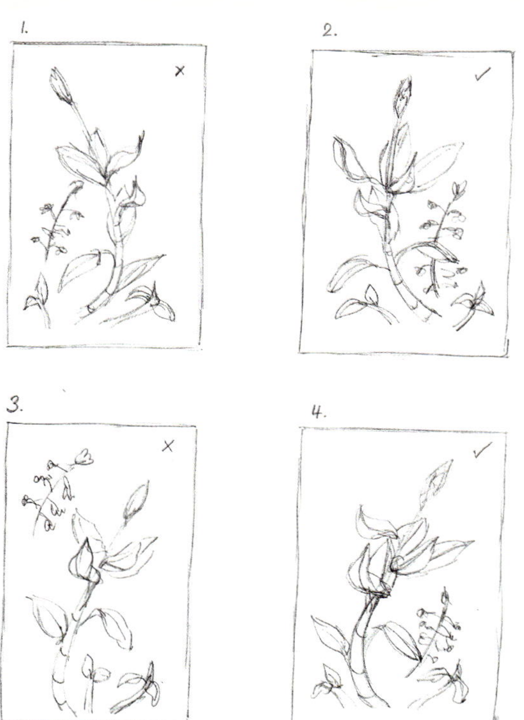

Create thumbnail sketches of your ideas for compositions.

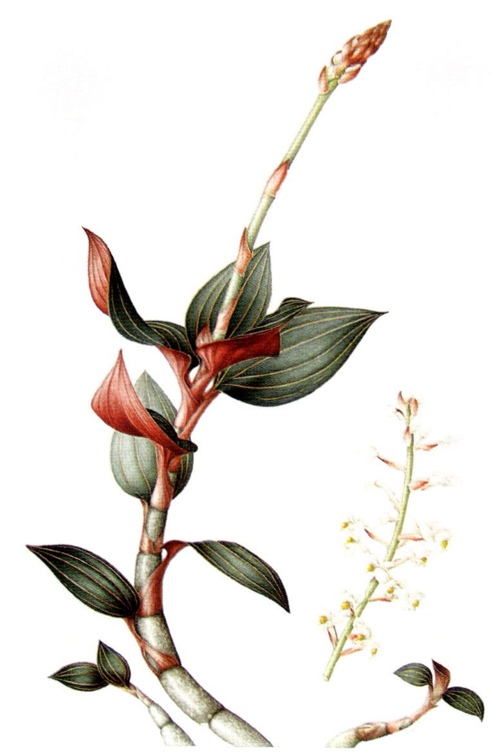

Final composition and painting. *Ludisia discolor* 'Red Velvet'. LEIGH ANN GALE

CREATING A FOCAL POINT

You will need to ensure that your composition works well in an artistic sense and creating the focal point should be your primary concern. To do this, it will be necessary to create a focal point, a point at which the eye will finally rest after it has 'read' your illustration, and which holds your viewers' attention.

If you have created some thumbnail sketches you may already have a good idea of which aspects of your subject matter will become your focal point. For example, a single open red poppy amongst surrounding buds and foliage, a white rose cleverly depicted against several leaves or a string of black bryony berries entwined amongst their foliage. In most cases the focal point of a botanical illustration that depicts flowers or fruits will be the flowers or fruits themselves – usually included within the habit illustration.

To help find the position for your focal point it is important to understand how the eye moves around when initially viewing a picture. If the eye is trained to read from left to right and write in the same way, then it will also track visual information from left to right. The converse is true; those who read from right to left will also scan an image in the same way. Most likely, you will find that your focal point will gravitate towards the centre of your composition, because that will become the area of emphasis that pulls your viewer's eye into the picture.

You can use many strategies to decide where your focal point should be. The positioning of a dominant colour, most notably red, towards the centre of the picture will make the focal point dominant, because red is a bright, warm and vibrant colour. Introducing a contrast of different shapes, tones and textures will also help draw the eye, as will contrasting the size of objects next to each other or considering the size of the gaps left between elements (known as the 'negative' or 'white' space).

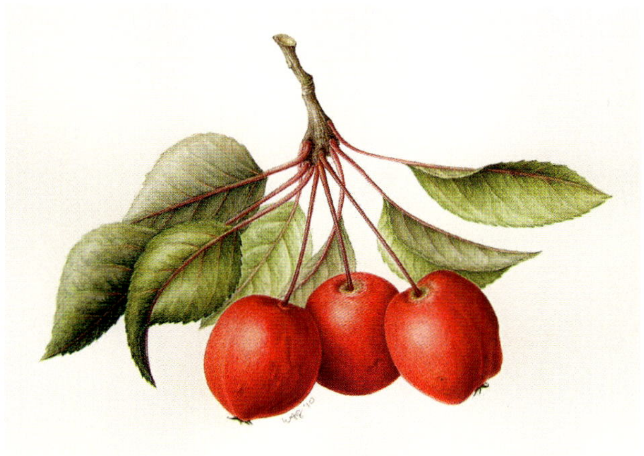

Create a clear focal point in your composition. Crab Apples. LEIGH ANN GALE

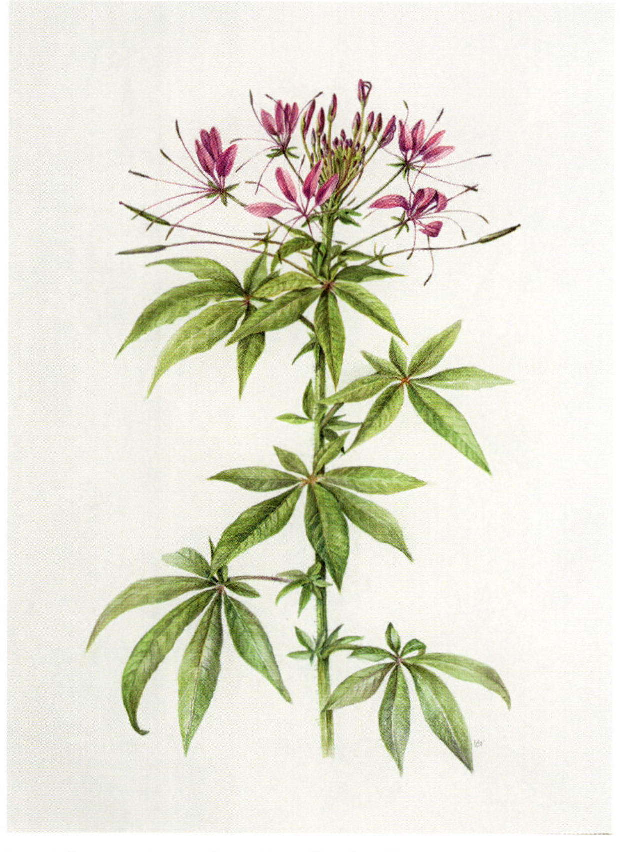

Cleome spinosa, American Spider Flower. KATE TILBURY

COLOUR DISTRIBUTION AND BALANCE

You will need to consider how the colours within your composition will harmonize. Artists generally refer to colours as either 'warm' or 'cool' depending whereabouts in the colour spectrum they fall (*see* Chapter 5). A fair balance of warm and cool colours should be introduced into your composition; some subjects such as a sprig of holly with its red berries and green leaves will produce a natural harmonization of warm and cool colours, creating a well-balanced distribution of colour, especially as the red berries themselves could also become the focal point because red is a strong, dominant colour.

Sometimes, colours are described as being weighted as 'light' or 'heavy'. For example, yellow, being a much lighter colour becomes insubstantial when compared to dark brown, which is much heavier in darkness and density.

If you have a contrast of light and heavy colours to distribute in your composition, try to keep the lighter ones towards the top and the heavier ones towards the bottom, to avoid the composition looking top heavy. You can achieve this easily if for example you are painting a single yellow tulip with its bulb, but if you are using several colourful elements, then you will need to spend more time evaluating the colours and how they will be distributed to achieve an equally balanced composition.

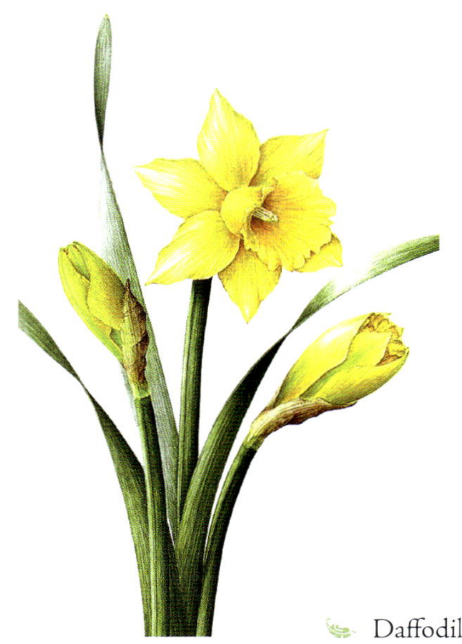

Daffodils. LEIGH ANN GALE

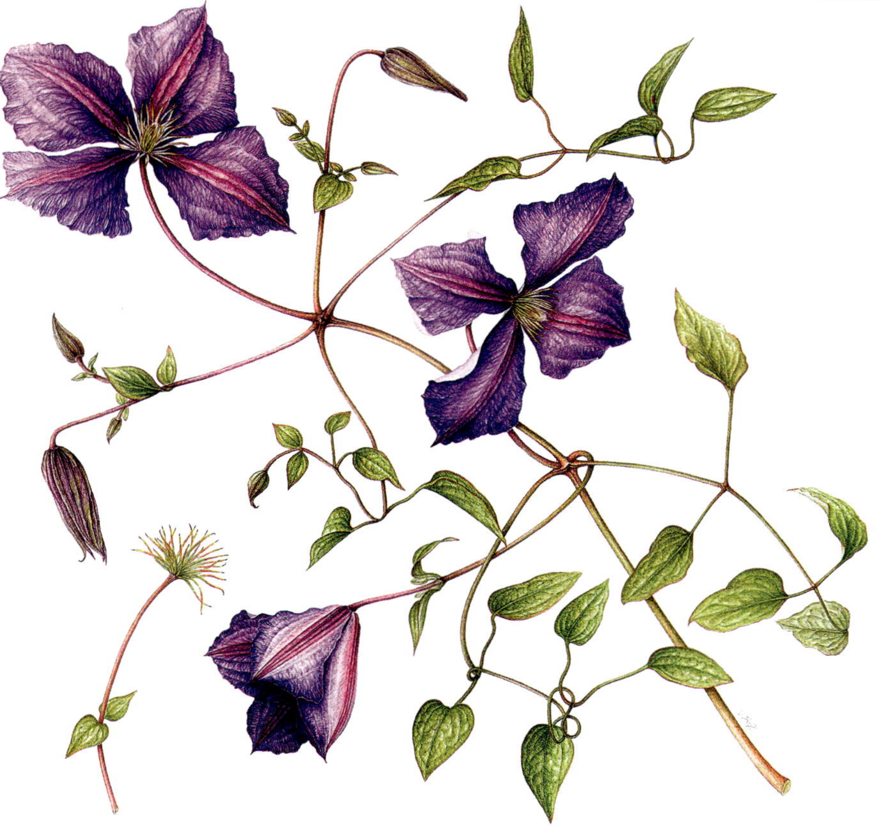

Clematis 'Jackmanii'. LEIGH ANN GALE

NEGATIVE SPACE

When composing a picture, it is often easy to just concentrate on the placement of the content without considering the space that surrounds it. This space, known as 'negative' or 'white' space, is an integral part of your composition, so as you practise laying out your ideas, you should be aware of it and how you can use it with maximum effect in your composition. Negative space is just as relevant as the subject itself.

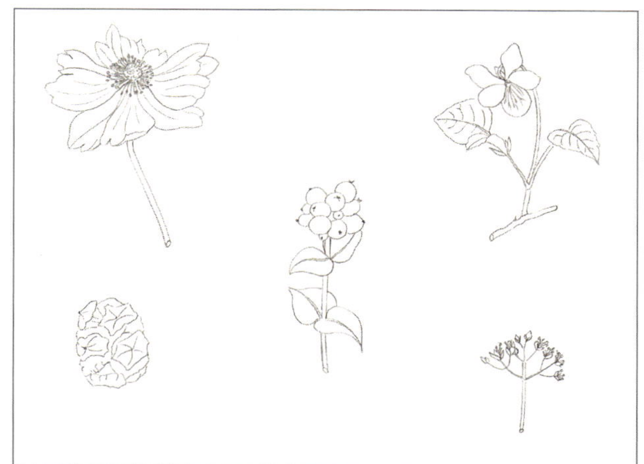

Thinking about negative space in your composition is key. Here, there is too much space between the elements in the composition, making it feel unbalanced.

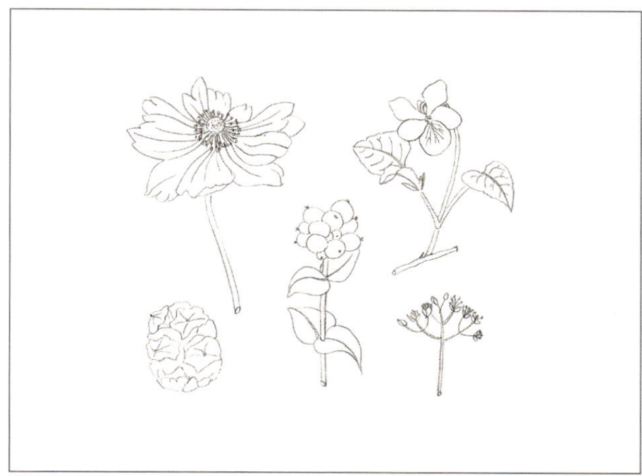

By bringing the elements closer together, the gaps are minimized, and the composition is balanced.

You will often find that the overall shape that one element makes (the outline of your drawing) may fit neatly near another, rather like fitting the pieces of a jigsaw together. This is of great value and can be used to create 'pathways' through your design which help the viewer's eye move around your picture.

Try to avoid leaving large amounts of negative space at the centre of your design. Remember, there is a strong possibility that this area will accommodate your focal point. Additionally, beware of making the negative spaces too large. There is often a tendency by less experienced artists to leave considerable amounts of negative space, believing that everything needs to be separated out, and be given room 'to breathe'. Try not to fall into this trap as you will immediately unbalance your composition – especially if you are leaving clear margins around the outside. If you find that the margins around the outside are visually considerably smaller than the visual negative space, move the elements closer together to reverse the distribution of negative space and re-establish a balanced design.

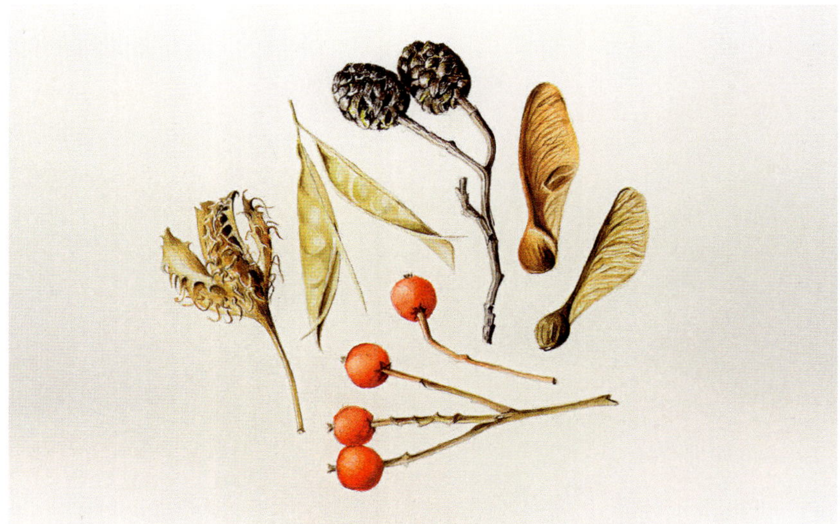

Effective use of negative space in a painting. Seeds composition.
ELANOR WEXLER

The 'Rule of Threes'

Artists often work at composition using the 'Rule of Threes'. This is when three elements (or another odd number: 5, 7, 9) are known to create more visual impact than equal numbers of elements in a picture. This is because when scanning an image with the eye, it is more difficult to segregate an odd number of elements; it takes longer for the brain to organize the content, and visually, it is generally considered more appealing. For example, three or five flowers illustrated rather than two or four will produce a greater visual impact. If an even number of elements are used, the brain can easily separate and compartmentalize the information into equal sections, meaning that the composition is less coherent. You may have noticed that other creative people use the rule, for example gardeners, designers, and florists. It is worth studying examples of botanical illustration to see how the rule works and using the Rule of Threes in your own composition.

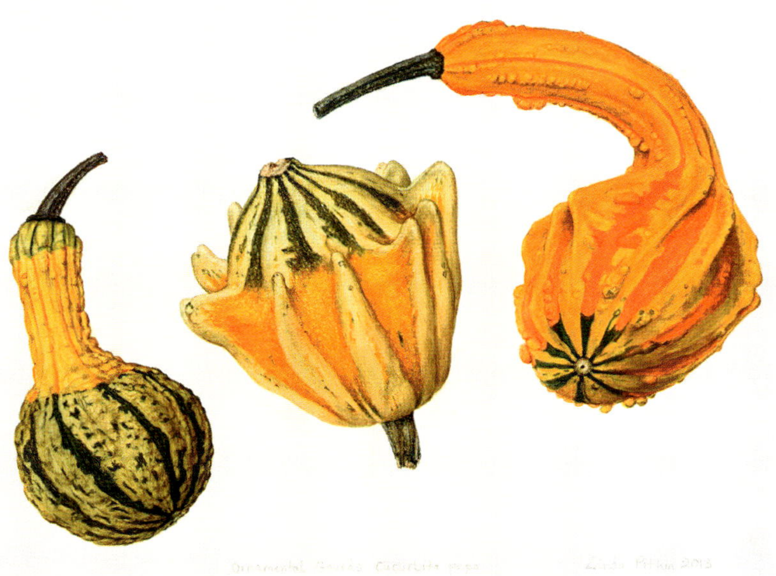

Example of using three elements in a composition. Ornamental Gourds, *Cucurbita pepo.* LINDA PITKIN

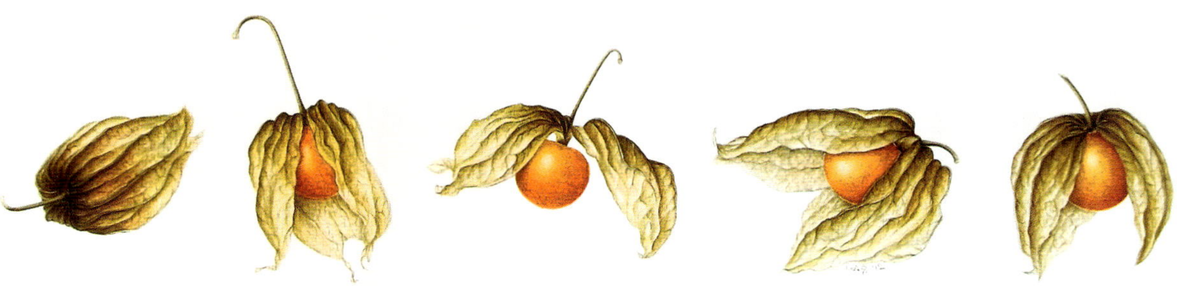

Example of using five elements in a composition. *Physalis.* LEIGH ANN GALE

MARGINS AND BLEEDING OFF

Most of the time you will not be painting up to the very edges of your watercolour paper. If you are going to mount and possibly frame your work, you will want to leave some space at the sides, across the top and along the bottom to lay the mount over the top. There are no rules about how much space you should leave but instead, visually, the margins should look comfortable on the eye and be proportionally balanced against the content of the picture. It is widely accepted that a slightly deeper margin should be left across the bottom edge, which gives an optical illusion of it being equal to that of the side margins.

In some cases, you might want to consider 'bleeding off' part of your image on one or more sides instead of leaving a clear margin. 'Bleeding off' is a term used in graphics to describe how imagery extends beyond the page, but it can also be used in botanical illustration to refer to part of the painting that touches the edge of the paper or mount. Bleeding off is useful when you need to explain that more of the plant exists beyond what you have observed.

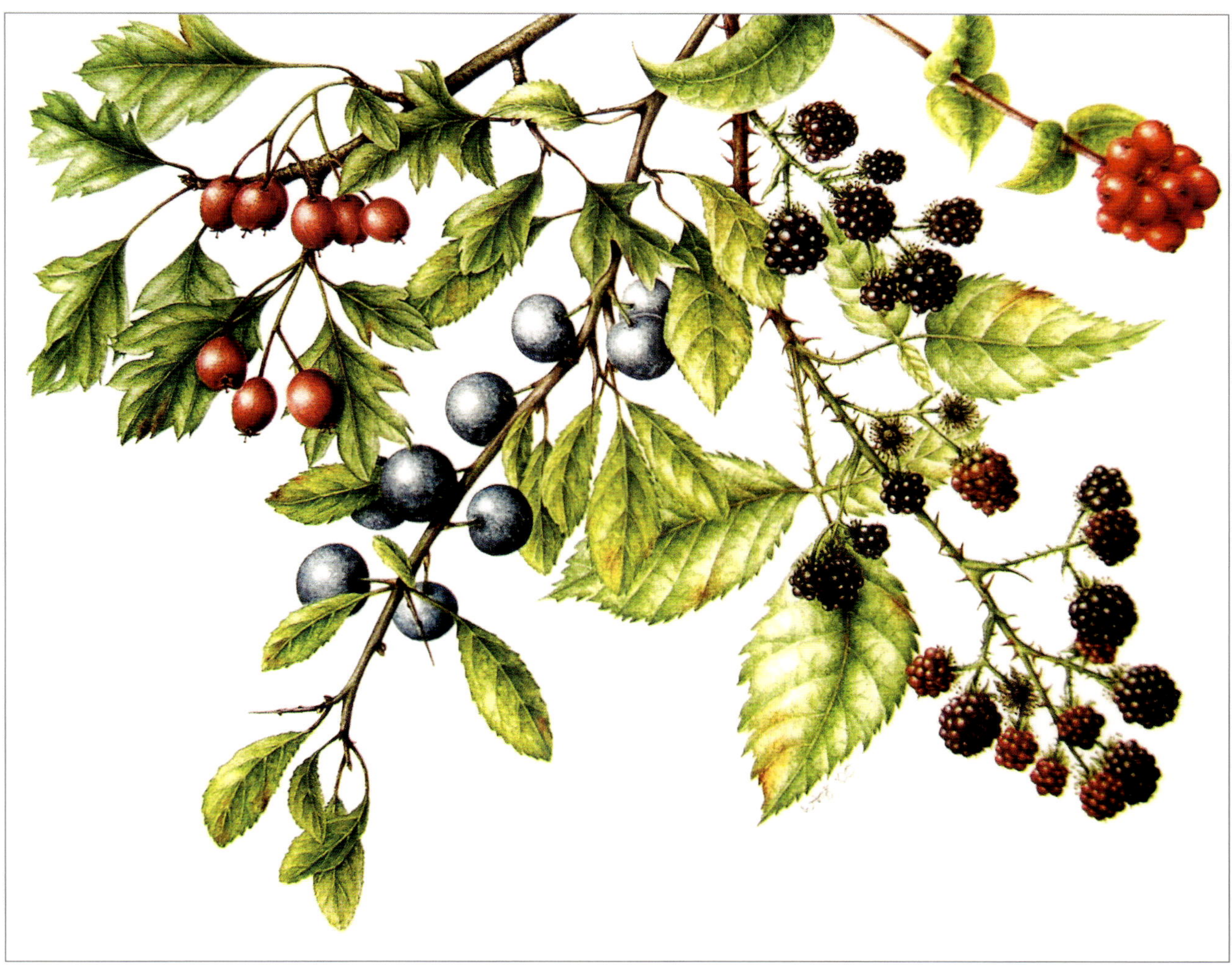

Bleeding off imagery helps to explain that more of the plant(s) exists beyond the boundary. Autumn Fruits. LEIGH ANN GALE

FINALIZING A COMPOSITION

Once you are satisfied that your composition works, and your traced drawings are all in position, you will need to join them all together. This is easily done by using pieces of low-grade adhesive tape, and ensures you don't move any of the drawings in the process. You now have a master template of your composition.

After creating your composition, it is always a good idea to check what you have done. It is worth doing this the following day or even two or three days later especially if the arrangement is quite complex. Up until now, you have had much to think about; creating a good composition can be an intense and lengthy process, so a fresh eye the following day can reveal some parts which may not be working so well and which you may simply have missed previously.

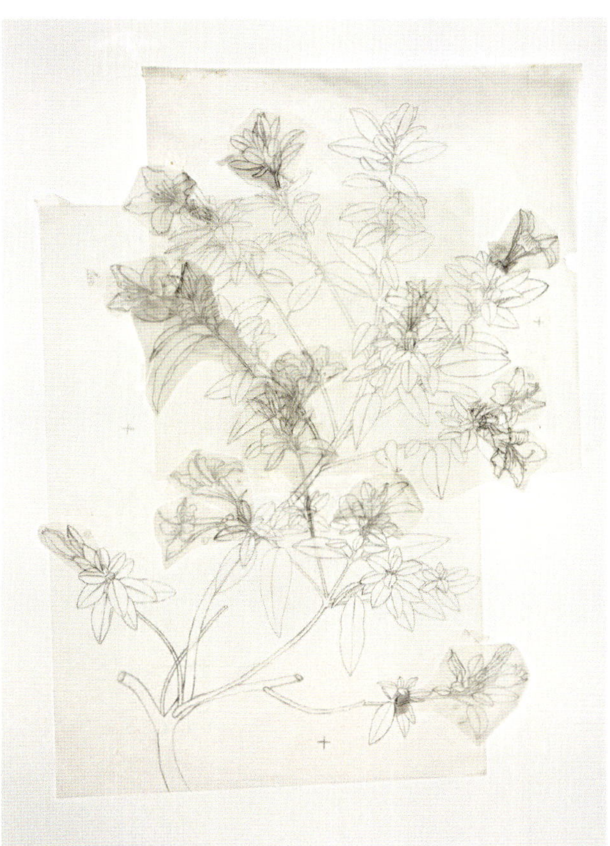

A master tracing paper template of a final composition, ready for transferring to watercolour paper.

The composition of your illustration is the final stage before beginning to paint, so it is well worth investing some extra time to make sure you have not made any obvious errors. A few common problems to look out for include:

- The edges of two leaves against each other. Either move one leaf away slightly or completely overlap it.
- Two visual parallel lines very close together. Alter the angle of one just a little to change the shape of the space between.
- Bleeding off in the wrong place. If you are bleeding off part of your illustration, avoid doing so in the very corner where your mount will be positioned.
- Repeating information. For example, you don't have to show all the flowers completely open if it is perfectly feasible that at any given time, there could additionally be buds, partially opened flowers and spent flowers on the same sprig.

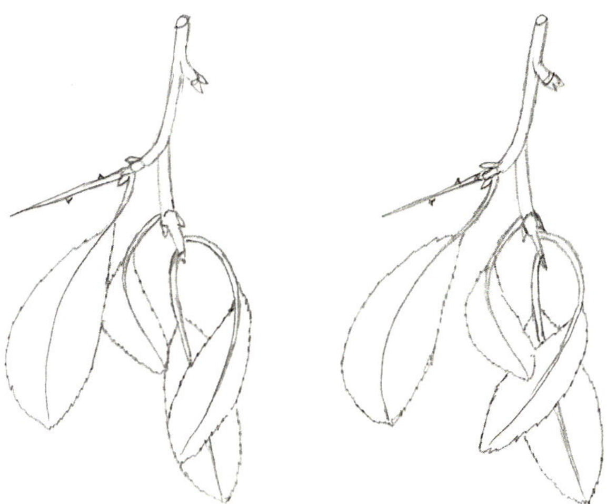

Avoid the edges of leaves touching by moving them completely away from each other or overlapping them.

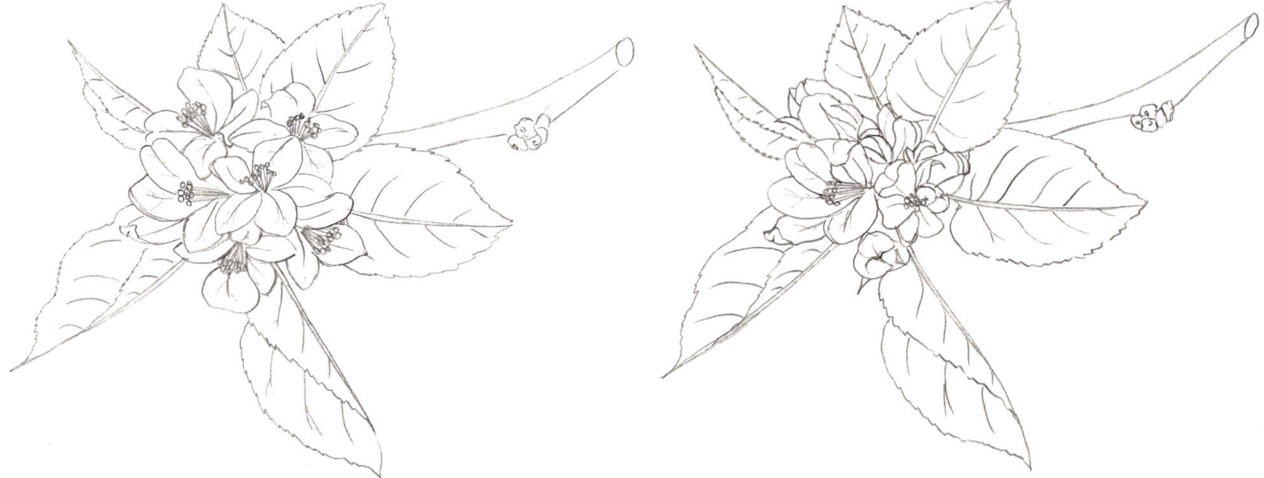

Do not repeat information unnecessarily. If it is feasible on your specimen, include several growth stages of the flowers, such as buds, open flowers, and spent flowers.

- Crossed stems, especially in the centre of the composition. It is best to avoid crossed stems if possible, as the eye becomes immediately attracted to them and they can become confusing. However, some plants (such as winter jasmine) naturally grow with crossed stems in which case, try to ensure you minimize the crossed stems and move them away from the centre of the composition.

TRANSFERRAL PROCESSES

Now that your composition is complete, and you have created a template, you will be in a position to transfer the image onto watercolour paper in order to begin painting. There are alternative ways of doing this but the most common include using a lightbox and the tracing method.

Using a lightbox

The cleanest and most effective way of transferring your image is to use a lightbox. These are available commercially and nowadays obtainable in many different sizes. You could also construct your own quite cheaply by using a wooden box, adding a fluorescent tube, and laying opaque glass or white Plexiglas over the top.

To use a lightbox, simply lay down your template onto the surface, turn the light on and position your watercolour paper over the top. When positioning the paper, make sure you leave sufficient clear space around the edges so that a mount could be added later. It is worth taping down the tracing paper template with clear tape on the surface of the lightbox, to stop it sliding around. It is also a good idea to wash and dry your hands thoroughly before tracing as this will avoid transferring any oils from your hand onto your paper, which could in turn repel paint. Check that you can see the drawn lines from your template through the paper, and strengthen any that are too light either by pressing a little harder with your pencil or using a black ink fineliner pen. Once you have positioned your template on the lightbox, add two or three registration marks (simple crosses such as +), and then trace these off lightly first, before you begin to trace your image. Registration marks can be rubbed out later, but will help you re-register your image should you knock it out of position during the transferral process.

Ensure you trace the image quite lightly. Stop occasionally to see how you are doing, as it is easy to alter the pressure of your pencil and press harder without realizing. The lines that you make should be just visible on the paper. You should also check that you transfer all the lines. Again, stop, and by carefully lifting the edge of the paper, you will notice if you have missed any lines. If you have, go back, and add them in.

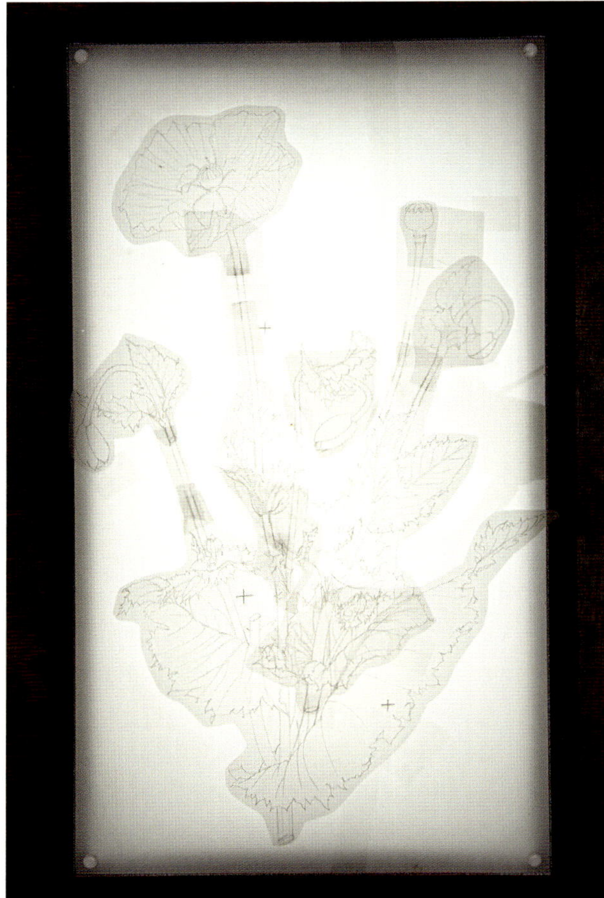

Add two or three registration marks to your traced template.

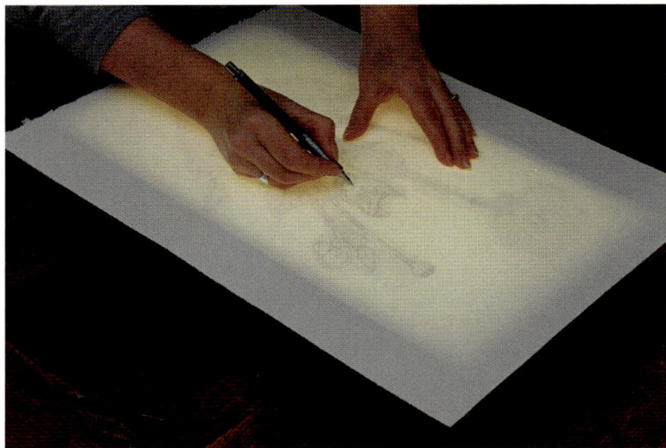

Lightly trace off the image on a lightbox.

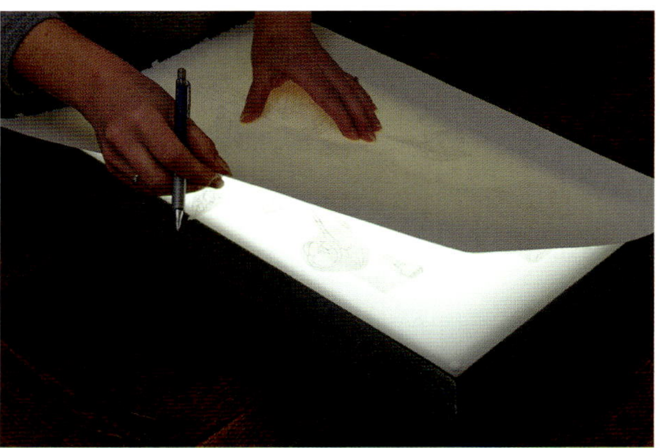

Check that you have traced off all the lines by gently lifting the paper away from the lightbox.

Once the whole image is completed, carefully remove your watercolour paper and double-check all the lines have been transferred. You are now ready to start your painting.

As an alternative, you could also try using a sunny window for transferring your image. Use the same method as for using a lightbox, starting with taping your original onto the window.

The tracing method

A popular transferral method is to using tracing paper. This is very straightforward but can be less accurate and a little messy.

You will need to ensure that your original drawing is already on tracing paper (your template). Turn over the tracing paper and begin scribbling with an HB pencil over the lines.

When they are all covered, turn the tracing paper back to the front and carefully position it onto your watercolour paper, making sure not to go too close to the edges. Re-trace over the lines carefully, gently lifting the tracing paper every now and then to check that you haven't missed any.

If you are transferring a complex image, it is advisable to lightly draw several registration marks to the tracing (*see* 'Transferral Processes: Using a lightbox' in this chapter).

When you have finished tracing, gently remove any loose particles of graphite from the watercolour paper by blotting with a putty rubber. You can now begin your painting.

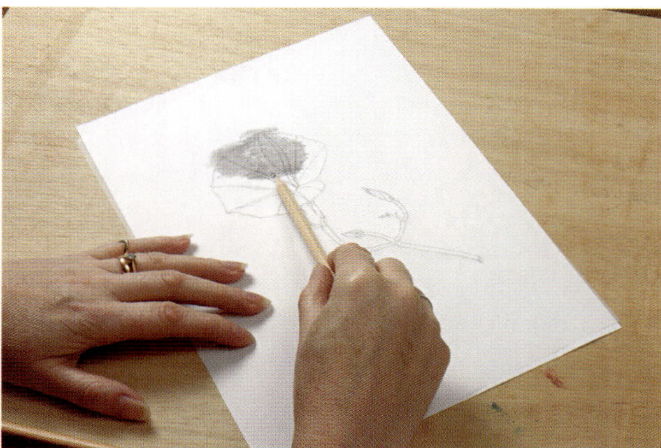

Once you have traced your image, reverse the tracing paper and 'scribble' over the lines using an HB pencil. Ensure you cover the entire image.

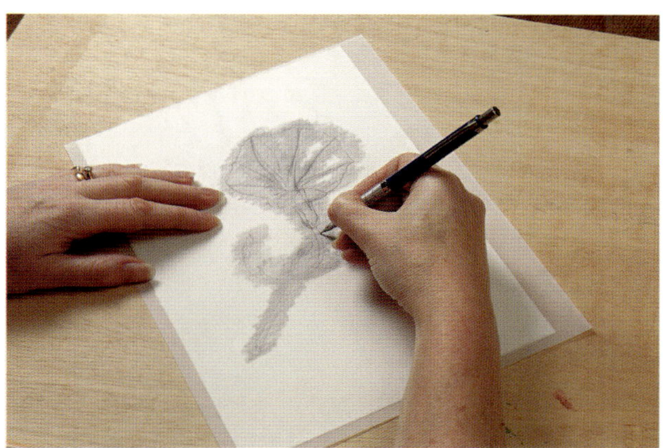

Turn the tracing paper back to the front, and carefully retrace the image onto hot-pressed watercolour paper.

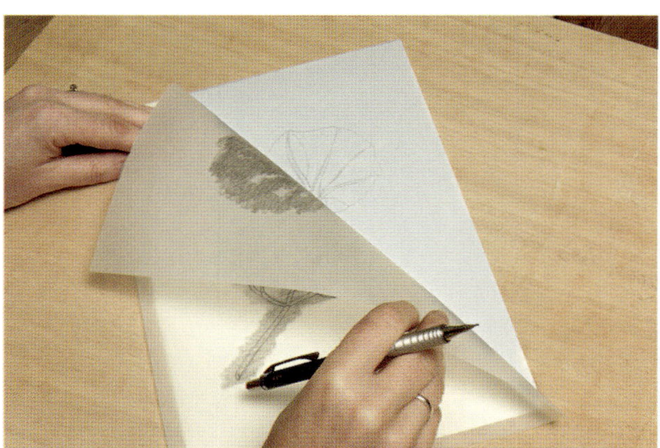

Check you have transferred all the lines of your image.

Checklist for Composition

- Allow yourself plenty of time to complete the process of composition.
- Choose relevant drawings from your observational studies, which should include a habit drawing.
- Consider making thumbnail sketches at the start, eliminating those that don't work along the way.
- Establish at the outset which features of your plant will be your focal point, remembering that the focal point doesn't always have to be completely central.
- Be conscious of the cool and warm colour distribution in your composition and try to balance it evenly. Consider the 'weight' of the colours to ensure you don't create a top-heavy feel.
- Allow the negative space to work in conjunction with the imagery itself. Create leading 'pathways' to help the eye move around the picture.
- If you intend leaving clear margins around the outside, ensure the size of them is proportional to the negative space within the composition.
- Bleed off part of the image if you want your viewer to understand that the subject extends beyond the boundary of your composition.
- Double-check your composition a day or two later, correcting any common errors you come across before transferring to watercolour paper.
- When transferring your image allow room at the sides for your margins and for a mount to be positioned over the top.

Case Study

It is often the case that an amalgamation of images will be necessary to create a good final composition. In our case study, it was necessary to do this, and so all the habit drawings that were made were traced off carefully. It became apparent that the final composition would most likely be a landscape format, due to the natural lateral growth habit of the flowering stems of *Fuchsia magellanica*. Most flowering stems consisted of leaves, berries, flowers, and buds, and so it was important that these should all be included in the final composition. The pendulous nature of the flowers, buds and berries was very attractive, but it was the open flowers in the composition that would become the main focal point.

Care was taken to ensure the tracings of all the habit drawings were made as accurately as possible, using a 2H pencil, and once completed, were neatly trimmed out. An arrangement of the tracings was then made, paying attention all the time to reflect the realism of the specimens and how they would appear on the bush in nature, and to ensure all the relevant growing parts could be seen on the flowering stem. Other important botanical features to check were the attachments of flower stems and leaf petioles to the main stem, that they were all representative of the species, and the sizes of the leaves, that they progressed from the larger, mature leaves to smaller, very tender leaves at the growing tip.

After a final arrangement of the tracings was made, a master template was created, by carefully attaching all the tracings together with clear tape. In total, this consisted of seven parts.

Once assembled, registration marks were added in one or two clear spaces, and the template was transferred to a light-box and secured, ready to be traced onto painting paper. A sheet of Arches 140lb/300gsm hot-pressed watercolour paper was cut to size and positioned over the image.

The registration marks and the image were then traced off using a 2H pencil, taking care to keep the lines as light as possible, and the registration accurate. Once the entire image had been traced, a final check was made to ensure all the lines had transferred; any missing ones were added in.

On completion of the transferral process, the image was removed from the light box and set up on the drawing board in the studio ready to begin the painting process.

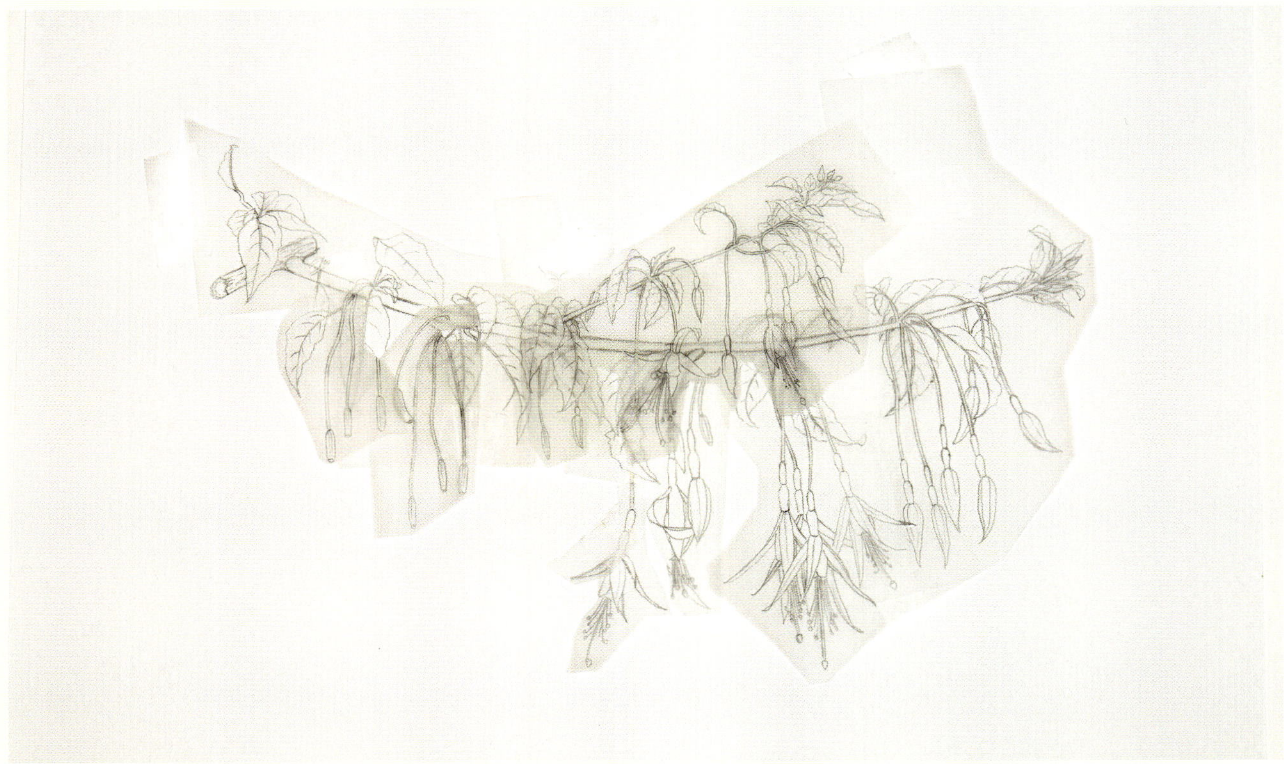

Once the composition was finalized, it was traced off in sections, stuck together and ready to be transferred onto watercolour paper.

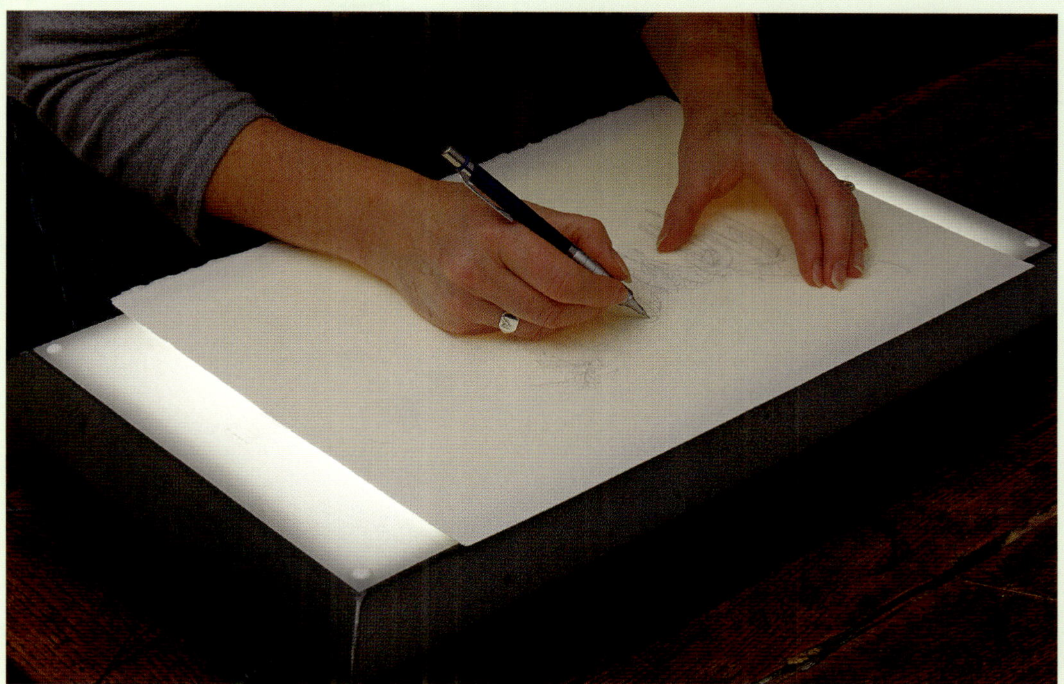

The image was carefully traced off onto hot-pressed paper using a lightbox.

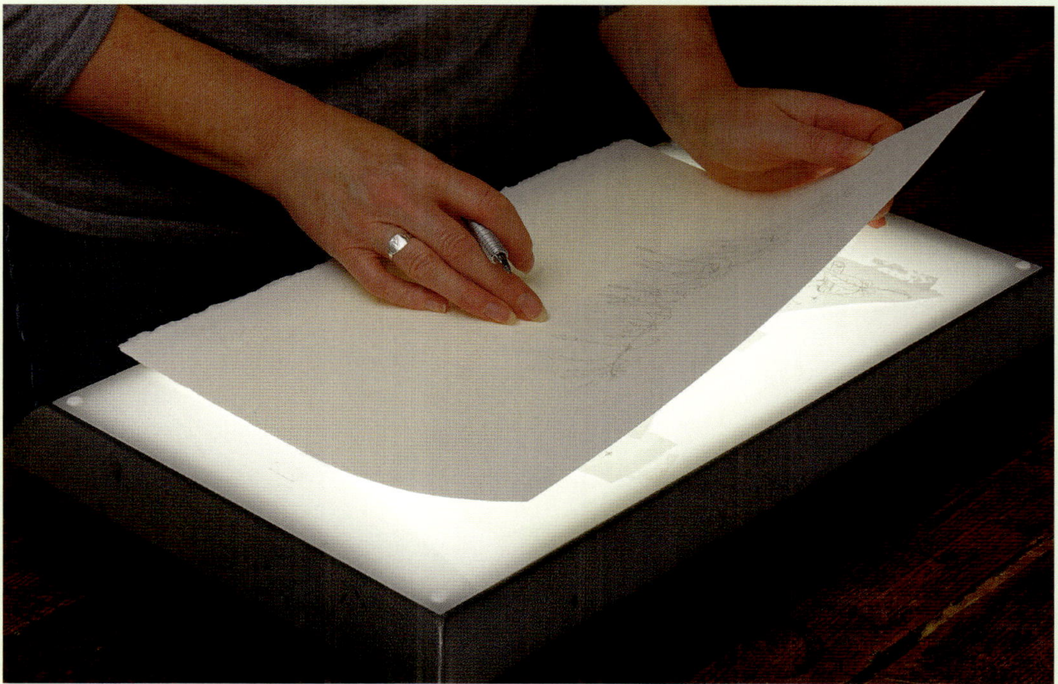

Once the image was traced off on the lightbox, a check was made to ensure no lines had been missed.

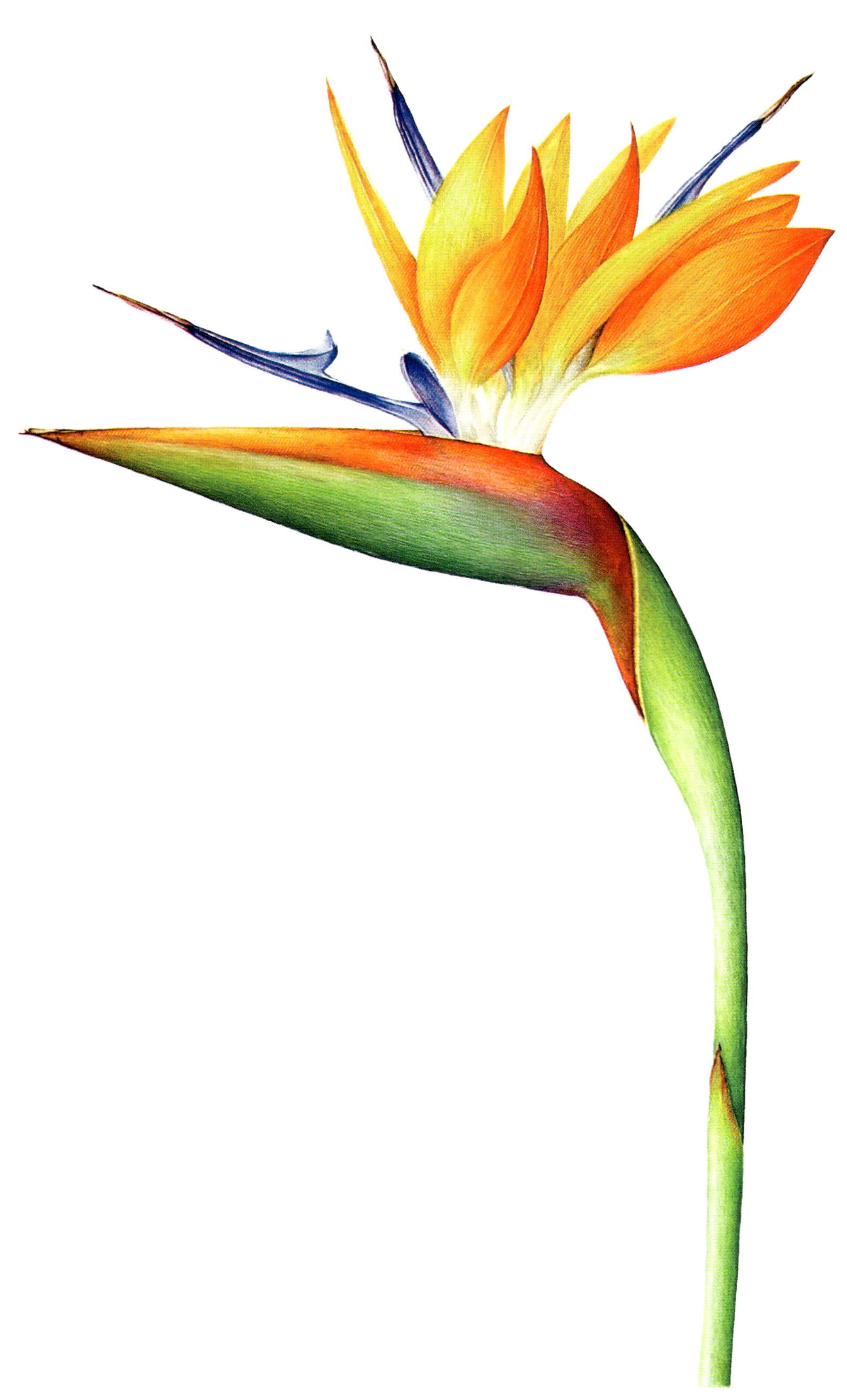

CHAPTER 5

All About Colour

When the colour achieves richness, the form attains its fullness also.

– Paul Cezanne (Post-Impressionist painter)

It is often without doubt that colour is taken for granted in our world. After all, it is something with which we become familiar from such an early age, when we learn that objects are coloured and that the world is a colourful place. We associate specific colours with certain aspects of life such as red representing heat and danger, blue representing water and the cold, and yellow representing sunlight and warmth. For botanical painters, colour is an incredibly important issue because along with form and structure, it is one of the most defining features of a species.

Evidence suggests that individuals see colours slightly differently from one another, so for example although five different artists may describe a red tulip as being 'red', they will all most likely see very slightly different hues. However,

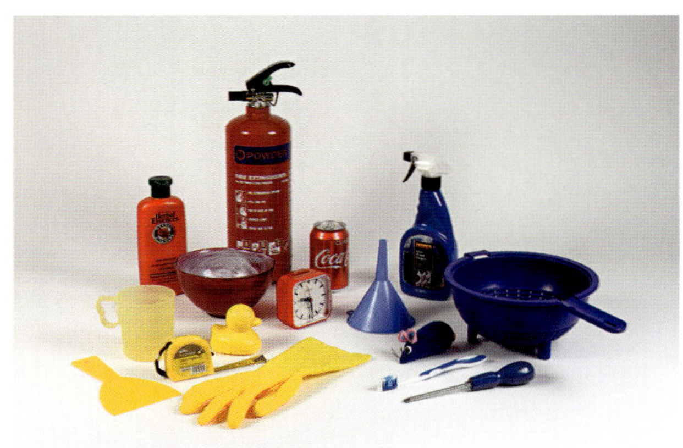

We take for granted the varying shades of colour of everyday items, and associate colours with different aspects of life, including, red – danger and heat; blue – water and cold; yellow – sunlight and warmth.

Strelitzia reginae, Bird of Paradise. LEIGH ANN GALE

The Colour Wheel

Sometimes referred to as the colour circle, the colour wheel is simply a means by which the colours of the spectrum can be illustrated, showing the relationships between the different groups of colours: primary, secondary, opposite (or complementary) and tertiary colours.

You will observe the use of yellow, red and blue as being the primary colours, arranged around the wheel at three equally spaced intervals. In between each primary colour the secondary colours appear: orange, violet and green, and between each of the primary and secondary colours lies a tertiary colour.

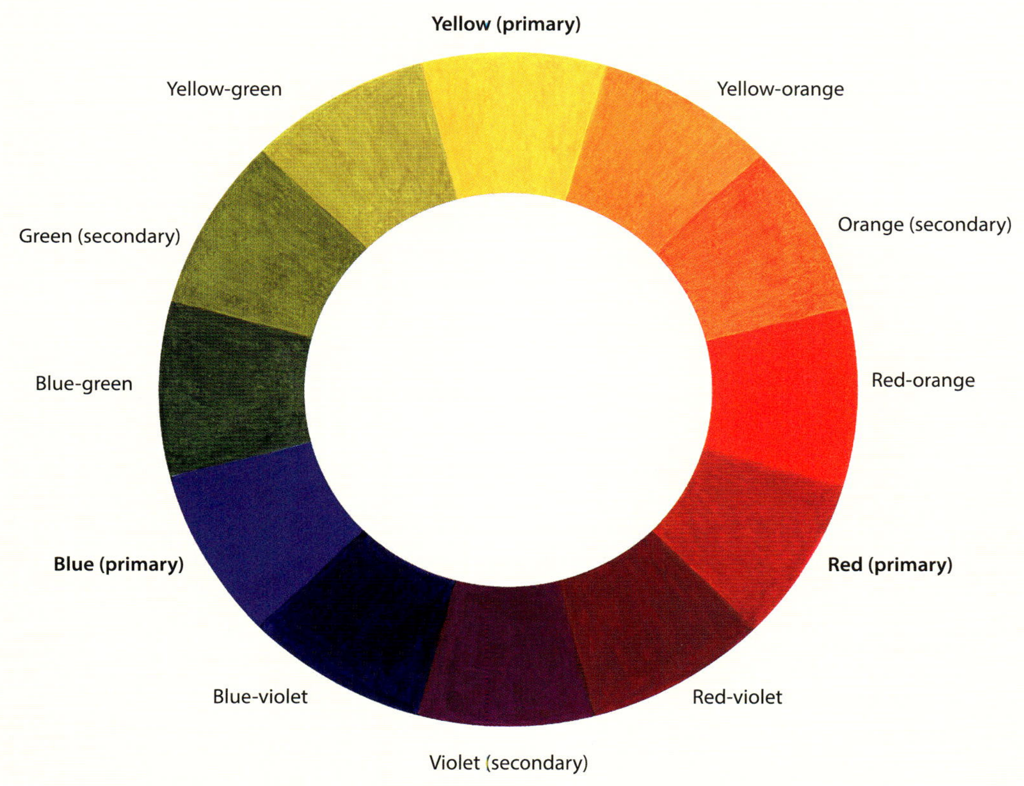

these differences are generally so subtle that they may not be consciously noticed; botanical painters should however work hard to match watercolour mixes to the colour of the specimen in front of them as closely as possible, considering all the subtle nuances of tone and shade.

A basic knowledge of the colour wheel, including primary, secondary, complementary and tertiary colours, will help you in your quest to achieve a complete likeness of colour to specimens, so it is worth taking the time to familiarize yourself with colour theory if it is new to you. Additionally, learning about the individual properties of your watercolours will help you understand what they are capable of, their limitations and how to work with them. In time, it is also a good idea to create some of your own colour charts and establish a botanical palette.

In this chapter, you will learn all about colour as well as some of the properties and features of your watercolours and colour mixing. We will also think about studying colours in botanical specimens, selecting the correct colours for colour mixing and matching, and how to set up a botanical palette. These essential skills will give you a basic, fundamental knowledge and appreciation of colour for botanical illustration, enabling you to put paint to paper with confidence.

COLOUR THEORY

Throughout history, references to 'colour theory' have been recorded, but it was Isaac Newton's principles of colour in the eighteenth century, when the visual effects of combined colours from light and prisms were scientifically explored, that our concept of the theory of colour in an artistic context exists as it does today.

THE PRIMARY COLOURS

RYB (red, yellow, blue) form the principle triad of colours on the artist's colour wheel. This group of colours are termed 'the primary colours' because it is believed they are capable of mixing all the other colours on the colour wheel. The primary colours form the basis of colour theory.

The primary colours of yellow, red and blue.

THE SECONDARY COLOURS

OVG (orange, violet, green) form the second triad on the colour wheel and are termed the secondary colours, since each is created from two primary colours:

- Yellow + red = orange
- Red + blue = violet
- Blue + yellow = green

It is worth noting that to create a good, true violet, the choice of red and blue primary colours is significant. Artists are often disappointed to discover their mixed violet turns out a turgid brown colour; it is likely the choice of primary red contains too much yellow. If you plan to make your own colour wheel, follow the indicated colours on the colour wheel here to achieve a good representation of violet.

The secondary colours of orange, violet and green.

TERTIARY COLOURS

Least known of the groups of colours are tertiary colours. This set of colours is useful since they provide an extremely wide array, including some earthy tones. The tertiary colours are achieved by mixing a primary colour with its immediate secondary colour neighbour on the colour wheel. For example:

- Yellow + orange = yellow-orange
- Blue + violet = blue-violet

When naming tertiary colours note that the primary and secondary colour names are given, joined by a dash (-), with the primary colour being named first.

COMPLEMENTARY (OPPOSITE) COLOURS

Complementary colours, otherwise known as opposite colours, are simply the pairs of colours which appear opposite each other on the colour wheel: yellow and violet, blue and orange, red and green. These are important colour combinations as they are often relied upon to produce shadow colours in botanical illustration, for example a shadow colour of violet applied delicately to the yellow of a daffodil gives a natural grey shadow without 'muddying' the vibrancy of the yellow in the daffodil.

It is worth noting that although in theory green and red are complementary colours, when it comes to creating shadow colours, this mix results in a somewhat dirty brown colour. It is recommended that adjusting the complementary colour towards violet on the wheel will achieve a more naturalistic shadow colour for botanical illustration.

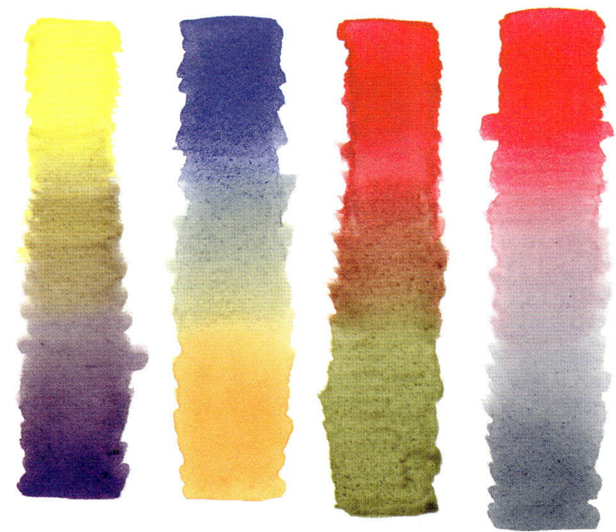

The complementary (opposite) colours of yellow/violet, blue/orange, red/green and red/green altered with blue.

HUE AND COLOUR

You will find that some colours are referred to as 'hues', which can be confusing to the novice artist. The term 'hue' relates more specifically to the pure spectrum of colours consisting of violet, indigo, blue, green, yellow, orange and red (commonly familiar as the seven colours of the rainbow). 'Colour' is a more general term used for the whole subject of colour, even black and white, and all possible combinations of these colours.

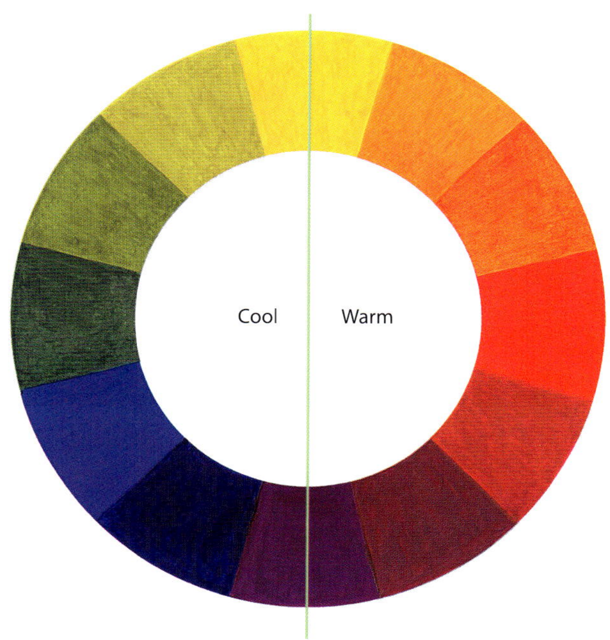

The colour wheel indicating cool and warm colours.

WARM AND COOL COLOURS

Colours are often referred to as either 'warm' or 'cool' and this distinction is clearly seen in the colours included under each heading. It is widely accepted that warm colours generally consist of yellows, oranges and reds with associations linked to the sun, heat, and fire, whilst the cool colours of greens, blues and some greys are associated with the cold, water and ice. Notice that the complementary duos of colours consist of one warm and one cool colour, for example green and red and blue and orange, and that the division of warm and cool colours splits the colour wheel in two.

Colour theory suggests that warm colours stand proud in a painting, whilst cooler colours noticeably recede.

HIGHLIGHTS AND SHADOWS

Using techniques in your painting to create highlights and shadows will bring your illustrations alive, and will greatly emphasize the 3D form of your painted subject matter. Acquiring a basic concept of highlights and shadows, and being able to identify them successfully, will give you greater confidence to apply them in your work.

We see highlights and shadows on a subject because of how the light falls upon it. As we know, a directional light source positioned from the top left-hand side (top right-hand side if you are left-handed) is how we should light our specimens for painting purposes. Observe where the highlights and shadows occur in this example.

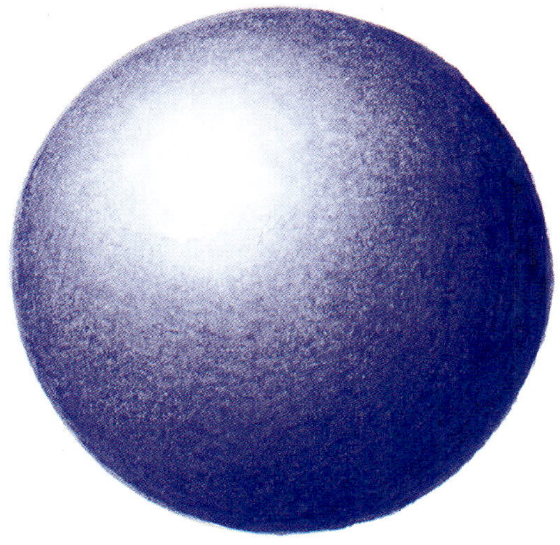

The positions of highlights and shadows on a painted sphere.

Highlights

Lit from top left, we see in the example above that a highlight occurs in the top left quadrant of the sphere. This happens because the light is reflected off the highest point on the rounded surface, therefore making the colour of the surface appear lighter. The highlight that you see on your subject matter may be sharp and bright or diffused and dull, depending on the surface texture.

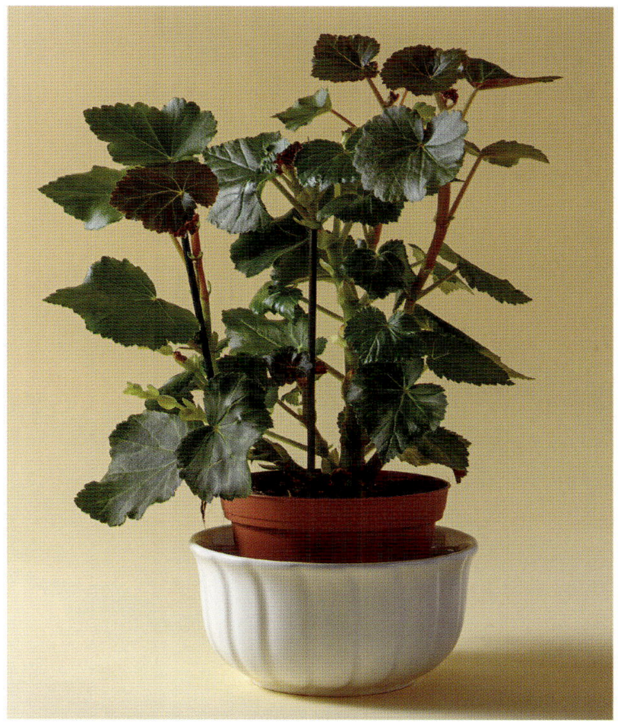

Shadows are noticeable against overlapping leaves and along veins and midrib.

Shadows

Shadows are the opposite of highlights. In other words, the surfaces of the object that are not being hit by light are in shadow, they appear darker. This usually occurs on the opposite side to a highlight on rounded surfaces, but you will also notice pockets of shadow occurring when objects or leaves overlap one another, and along one side of a leaf vein or midrib for example.

SHADES, TINTS AND TONES

Defining shades, tints and tones of colour can appear somewhat confusing but learning the differences can help you understand whether you need to use a shade, tint, or tone of colour in your work.

Shades

In colour theory, a shade is simply a colour or hue with black added to it. However, as we now understand that neutral black does not exist in nature, you will be able to make your own shades by adding your own mixes of black. As you grow more confident in the use of

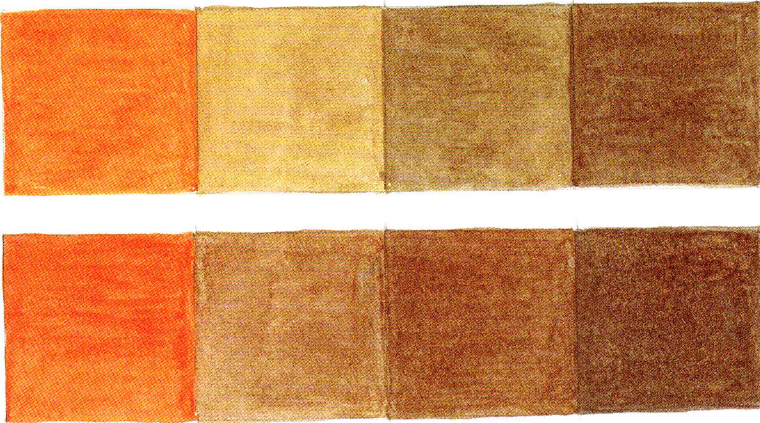

Shades are created by adding 'cool' black (top) or 'warm' black (bottom) to a colour.

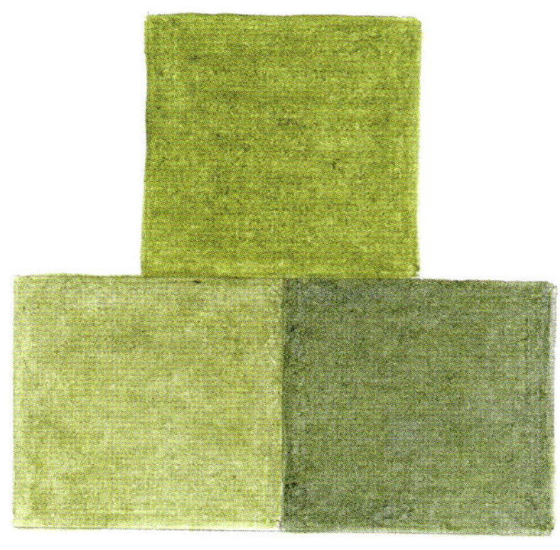

The addition of grey makes warm and cool tones.

Simply dilute the colour with water to make tints.

watercolour, you will learn to make shades reasonably quickly if you mix a combination of the three primary colours and green together, adjusting the ratios of each to give a cool or warm black. Very subtle shades may be required, and can be obtained by adding only small quantities of paints together.

You will notice when purchasing paints that some have a reference to a 'shade' in their name, for example Winsor Blue (Green Shade) and Winsor Blue (Red Shade). This reference indicates that Winsor Blue can be purchased as either a cool or warm colour, by the addition of green (cool) or red (warm) pigments to the base colour.

Tints

The addition of white to a colour or hue results in a 'tint'. However, the use of white in botanical illustration – because of its opacity – should be avoided as much as possible otherwise pastel colours are obtained. To overcome the problem and create a tint effectively, simply dilute the colour by adding more water to it. This will ensure your colours remain bright and vibrant as much as possible.

Tones

Dark and light tones are achieved when theoretically speaking, both black and white are added to a colour or hue. A greater addition of black than white will give a dark tone, whilst a greater addition of white will give a light tone. The tone then appears as a grey, as the combination of black and white make grey.

In botanical illustration, you can make your own grey – either warm (by adding more yellow to your mixed black) or cool (by adding more blue to your mixed black), but you could also use a pre-mixed grey instead. The most common of the commercial greys are Davy's Gray (warm) and Payne's Gray (cool). To avoid obscuring the transparency of your colour mix, you should only use small amounts of these greys since they are both opaque. Practise your colour mixing before applying to your illustration.

COLOUR SATURATION

The saturation of a colour is determined by how intense, bright, and vivid it is. At full saturation, the colour is at its purest, whilst with decreased saturation it appears to be washed out, taking on a grey, dull effect.

Colour saturation can be easily achieved using watercolour. Simply by adding grey to the pure colour, you will reduce the saturation.

Adding more and more grey to a colour will make it less saturated.

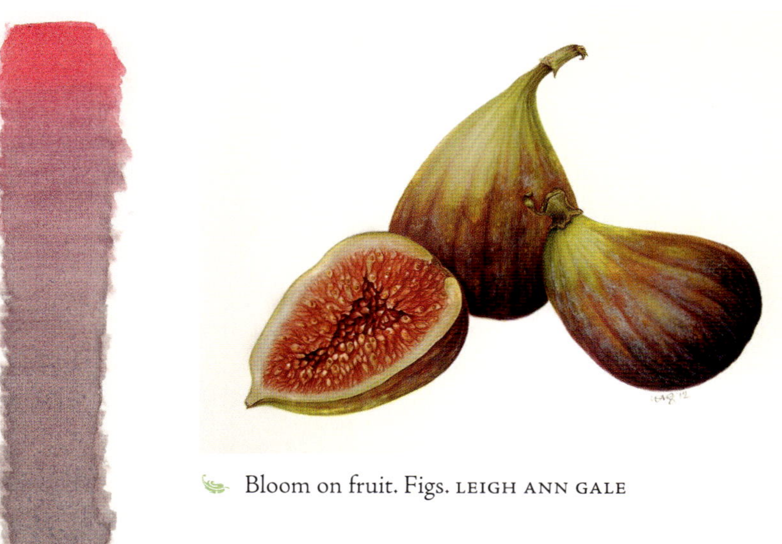

Bloom on fruit. Figs. LEIGH ANN GALE

THE USE OF BLACK AND WHITE PAINT

Black and white are not defined as true, specific colours but are usually included in most sets of watercolour paints and regarded as 'colours'. Black is the result of the absorption of all the colours of the visible spectrum but does not reflect any light back to the eye, whilst the opposite is true of white, which is the result of all the colours combined of the visible spectrum but does reflect light back to the eye.

Use a pale blue tint on the highlight areas of shiny leaves. *Camellia x williamsii* 'Bow Bells'. LEIGH ANN GALE

Black paint

The black paint contained in a shop-bought watercolour set is a neutral black (usually Lamp Black, Mars Black, or Ivory Black). It is considered 'neutral' because the ratios of colours used give it neither a warm or cool tone. Neutral black does not exist in nature, so you will therefore have little use for it in a set of watercolours. Instead, you should mix your own blacks to replicate the naturally occurring blacks that you may come across in your subject matter.

White paint

White paint is an opaque 'colour' (sometimes referred to as body colour), which if added to the purest transparent pigments will cause the colour created to become semi-opaque. A somewhat 'chalky' or 'milky' flat-looking colour is obtained, which is less desirable for botanical illustration. However, there is more leniency towards the use of white paint, which can be used for specific techniques such as bloom on fruit (*see* Chapter 9), or mixed with a small quantity of colour for painting hairs on a specimen. White paint can also be used effectively when painting subjects such as gourds, which naturally have an opaque pastel colouring. It is recommended that highlights, typically on fruits or shiny leaves, should not be made using white paint as the effect can look rather clinical and unnatural. Instead, leaving the paper white and then tinting the highlight area at the end of painting with a faint wash of colour gives a more naturalistic and real effect (*see* Chapter 9).

LEARNING ABOUT YOUR WATERCOLOURS

Whilst the differences between student's and artist's quality watercolours are discussed in Chapter 1, it is worth knowing a little about the properties of your watercolours, what they are capable of, and how to work with them. The technical specifications of each colour are usually explained in the manufacturer's guidelines, but familiarizing yourself with which of your paints are opaque, transparent, staining or granulating can help immensely when selecting colours for your palette and for your painting.

OPACITY AND LIGHTFASTNESS

Recognizing the differences between opaque and transparent watercolours and how lightfast a colour might be is very important when it comes to the process of colour selection in botanical painting. The colours in your finished painting need to be strong and vibrant and able to withstand medium exposure to daylight, so it is worth taking the time to learn a little about your paints in advance to help you make well-informed colour choices for your botanical palette.

Opacity

When purchasing your watercolours, you will notice that some are indicated as 'opaque', 'transparent' or sometimes 'semi-opaque' or 'semi-transparent'. Some manufacturers indicate the opacity of their colours using a symbol, so you should familiarize yourself with their system.

Opaque colours are normally more associated with gouache however; it is the addition of fillers such as Chinese White which are used to make some watercolours opaque. This addition is often referred to as 'body' colour. The opacity of a watercolour will depend on the amount of 'body' colour added to the pigment and they are therefore usually cheaper to buy than transparent colours. It is recommended that botanical painters use pure, transparent colours wherever possible, as they allow the light to pass through the paint to make it 'glow' on the paper. Certainly, there may be occasions when an opaque

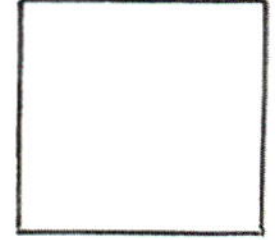 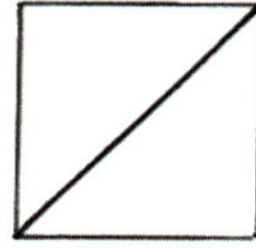 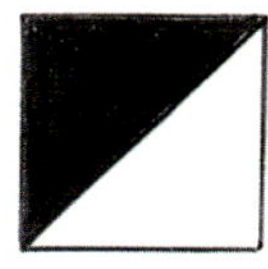 

The Winsor & Newton system of opacity: transparent, semi-transparent, semi-opaque and opaque.

Test for Opacity

If you are unsure whether your watercolour is opaque or transparent, simply paint a thick swatch of it over a line drawn with a black marker pen on white paper. If you can quite clearly see the paint sitting over the black line obliterating it, then your colour is completely opaque. Conversely, if you see little or no evidence of paint sitting on the line, then your colour is semi-transparent or completely transparent.

Indicate the opacity of your paint next to a swatch of it when labelling a colour chart of your paint box.

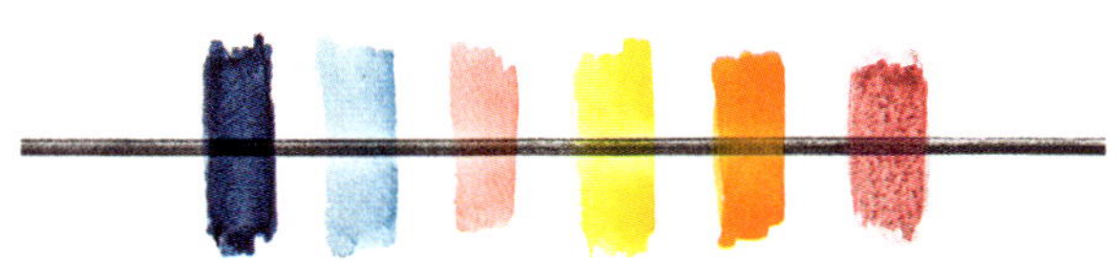

Paint watercolours over a black marker line to determine their opacity.

colour is actually required, for example when painting pumpkins and gourds, in which case opaque colours will be consciously sought. You will find that the Cadmium range of colours (C. Yellow, C. Orange, C. Red) are ideal for such purposes.

Lightfastness

The lightfastness of a watercolour relates to how well the pigment resists changes in exposure to light. This will depend on the chemical composition used to create the pigment, and its concentration.

Lightfastness is indicated by an ASTM rating (American Society for Testing and Materials). This international standard is used for all mediums including watercolour with I being the highest lightfastness available and V the least. It is accepted that ratings of I and II however are considered as permanent for artists' use.

Occasionally, you may discover that a colour has not been assigned a rating. This usually means that the colour has not yet been tested against the ASTM standard, rather than it necessarily lacking in lightfastness.

PERMANENCE

Manufacturers have their own grading systems and criteria for measuring permanence, but as a guide, pigments are usually graded between extremely permanent/very good through to fugitive. (Relatively few fugitive colours exist, but if you come across them and need to use them, use should be kept to a minimum and laid as base washes.) Permanency is generally related to how durable the pigment is when laid on paper or canvas with a brush, and how well it behaves when displayed under glass, in a dry atmosphere.

GRANULATION AND STAINING

Granulation and staining are features of some colours. It is useful to know what you are dealing with so that you are not surprised or 'caught out' during painting, when you discover small particles of paint remaining on the surface of your paper, or that you find it extremely hard to lift a colour from your paper.

Granulation

You will often come across the term 'granulation' associated with watercolours. Some artists, such as landscape artists, specifically use paints that granulate to add textured effects to their paintings, most often to skies and seas. Granulating paints are most effective used on cold-pressed paper, when the hard particles sit in the toothed surface. They are generally associated with the earth colours, such as Raw Umber and Raw Sienna, but several blues including Ultramarine, Cobalt Blue and Cerulean Blue also contain granulating properties.

Granulation effects are used less by botanical painters because usually a smooth texture of paint is required instead. However, there are occasions when granulating paints could be used effectively, such as adding tiny dark speckles to dry, autumn leaves.

Staining

'Staining' refers literally to the fact that some pigments stain very easily once applied to paper making them difficult to lift or move. This typically occurs in pinks, maroons, and reds. The staining property of a colour could be minimized with a prior application of lifting preparation before painting begins (*see* Chapter 7).

MIXING WATERCOLOURS

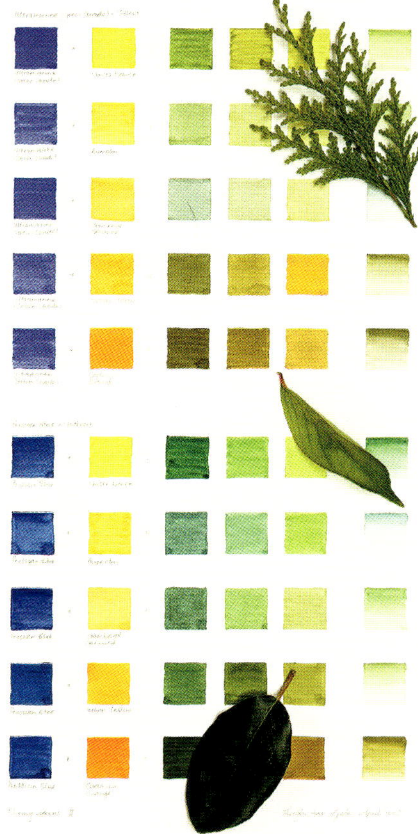

Make a greens colour chart to match the hues of your green specimens.

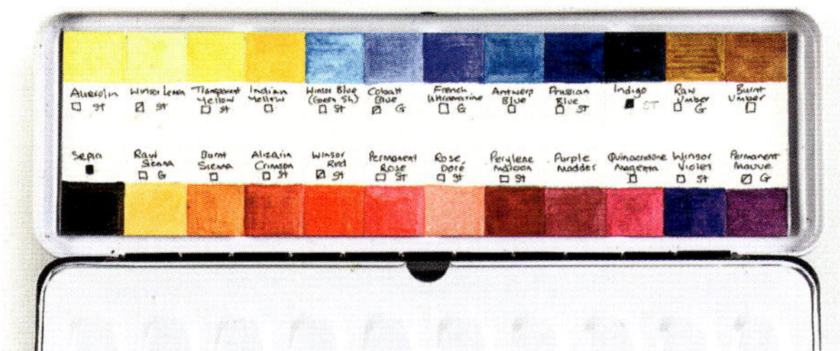

Make a colour chart of the paints in your paint box.

The most effective way to become proficient at mixing watercolours is simply to practise. It is only through the discipline of continued practice that you will become familiar with the properties of all your watercolours and build the confidence to mix them accurately. Specific techniques such as dry brush work and wet-into-wet are discussed in Chapter 7, but the basic application process of paint onto paper can be accomplished through some basic exercises before attempting a complete botanical illustration.

If you are completely new to watercolour painting, it is worthwhile in the first instance to literally play about with your paints. Try mixing them with different quantities of water so that you discover differences in colour intensity; mix colours together randomly to learn how they react with each other. Are you using a granulating paint? Can you see the effect on the paper as you use it?

You could also practise mixing watercolours by making a colour wheel like the one shown in this chapter, or try making some tertiary colours by mixing primary and secondary colours together.

CREATING COLOUR CHARTS

Once you feel confident about mixing watercolours generally, it is a good idea to equip yourself with one or two colour charts for referencing. An essential colour chart to create early on is one for different shades of green mixed from all the blues and yellows in your palette. Keeping this nearby and using it to help you mix a specific leaf colour for example will help you quickly identify the different combinations to make the various greens you can see. Other colour charts to consider creating are for the additional secondary colours of violet and orange.

As well as colour charts, it would also be useful to make a chart of the colours you have in your paint box. A simple format of named painted blocks of colour will remind you of what each colour looks like, and useful information such as the opacity, staining and granulation properties can also be included.

MIXING YOUR OWN BLACKS

We have already identified that neutral black is not defined as a true 'colour' and does not exist in nature, but you may find on occasion you will need to paint 'black' specimens, for example, blueberries and blackberries, cherry laurel berries, or maybe a more exotic looking plant such as a 'black' Aeonium. Upon close inspection you will discover that such 'black'- looking specimens are instead formed of many dark colours which give the illusion of being black. When this happens, it is best to analyse the colours in the specimen very carefully, then identify these individual colours in your palette, and set about mixing them together.

You will notice the temperature of the black, whether it is cool as in the example of sloes (blue) or warm as in the example of Hypericum berries (red). You will need to experiment with making your blacks as accurate as possible, adjusting the ratios of colours accordingly to create warm and cool tones.

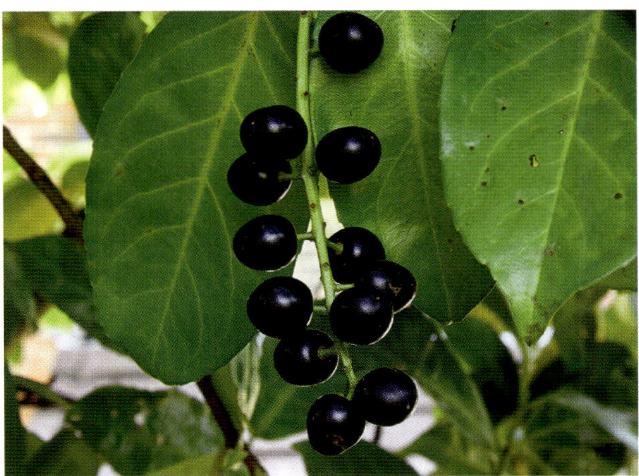

Carefully identify the colours that make the black you can see in a specimen, such as Cherry Laurel berries.

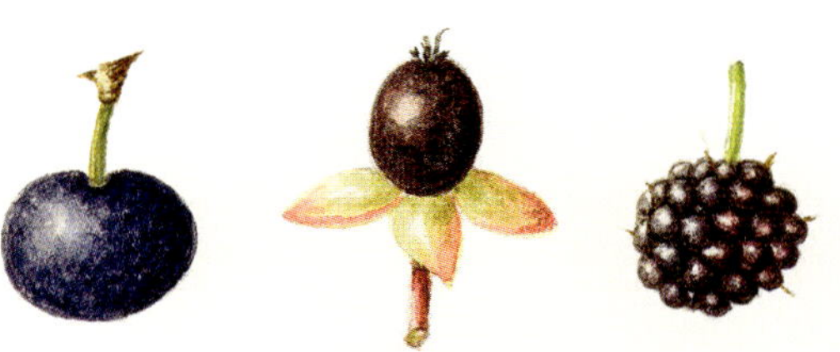

The temperature of 'black' ranges from cool to warm in sloes, Hypericum and blackberries.

Making Neutral Black

Although you will be making your own blacks in botanical illustration, it is a worthwhile exercise when learning about the accuracy of mixing ratios of paint to try making a neutral black. Neutral black is neither cool (blue) nor warm (red), so testing your ability to mix the correct ratios of colour accurately is excellent practice – and challenging. Try the following exercise:

Create an intense mix of Ultramarine, Alizarin Crimson, Burnt Umber and a pre-mixed green such as Permanent Green, Winsor Green or Viridian, using what you believe to be the correct ratios of each to make a neutral black.

Once you think you have mixed the combination accurately, test your result by creating a tonal bar ranging from 100% to 1%. Start with the solid colour (100%) and slowly dilute the mix with increasing amounts of water until you decrease the saturation to 1%.

Once the paint is dry, look carefully to see how accurate you have been. If your mix is too cool, add more Alizarin Crimson; if your mix is too warm, add more Ultramarine.

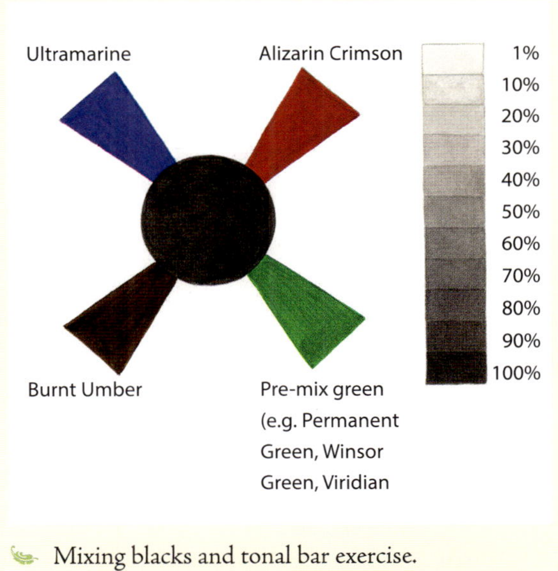

Mixing blacks and tonal bar exercise.

LOOKING AT COLOUR IN BOTANICAL SPECIMENS

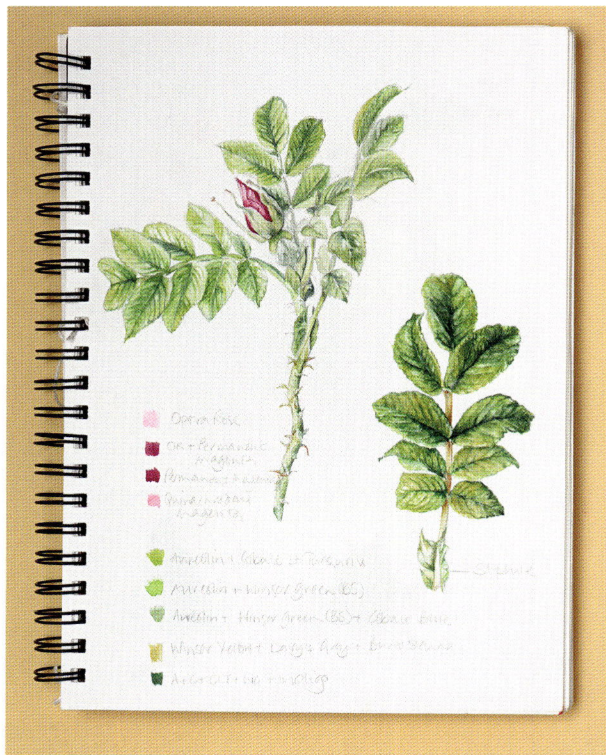

Adding colour mixes to your illustration in your sketchbook will remind you of the colours you have used. *Rosa rugosa*, sketchbook study. VICKY SHARMAN

Two examples of reds, one with more yellow and one with more blue.

An integral part of any botanical illustration is the authenticity of the colours you select and mix to make a perfect colour match to your specimen. Alongside your drawing and compositional skills, the acquired skill of colour recognition is a key process in making your illustration look true and realistic. It will take some time to become proficient in identifying the colours you need to mix, but eventually through careful observation of the specimen, practice, and perseverance, you will succeed. Being as knowledgeable as possible about colour theory also plays a large part in this process. Eventually, your careful analysis of colour in botanical specimens will become so acute that you should find it virtually second nature to identify the colours you need to use from your palette.

MAKING THE RIGHT COLOUR CHOICES

Making the correct paint colour choices will largely come from your experience of being able to recognize cool and warm colours in colour theory. Judging for example out of two reds that you may have, which contains the most yellow or blue, will help you make an informed colour choice when matching the relative warmth or coolness of red in a specimen. It is critical that you analyse the colours in your specimen carefully, and you should be prepared to experiment with different mixes until you become familiar with your paints.

DIFFICULT COLOURS

It is possible that on occasion you will find it very difficult to identify the exact colours you need to make a successful colour match. This is especially true of the colour pink. Whilst in theory you would be able to make pink, trying to obtain an accurate mix for matching to the bright, vivid pink of a Hottentot Fig flower for example could prove fruitless. In this situation, it is best to buy an additional colour to add to your palette, selecting the closest of an array of pinks available, to give yourself every opportunity of making a good colour match. You may discover that even though you have found and bought the closest premixed pink, you still have to add another colour(s) to finalize the mix to make it completely accurate.

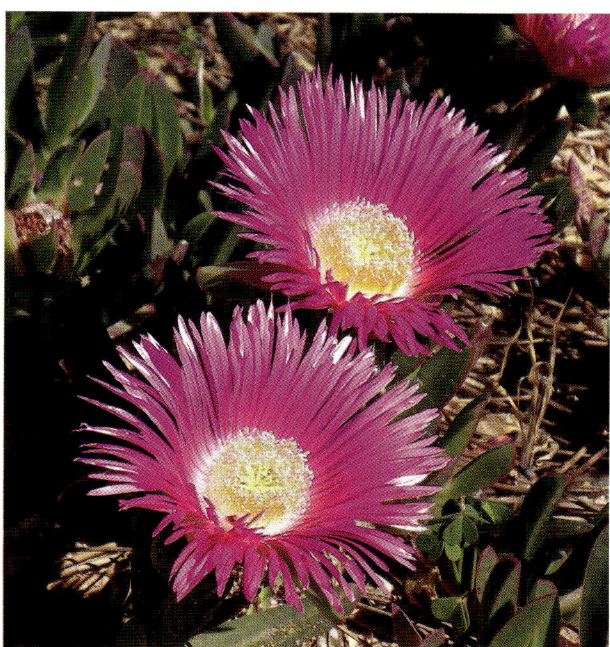

The bright pink colour of some flowers is difficult to make from the primary colours alone. Invest in a premixed pink to help with colour mixing and matching. *Carpobrotus edulis*, Hottentot Fig. MALCOLM ELLIOTT

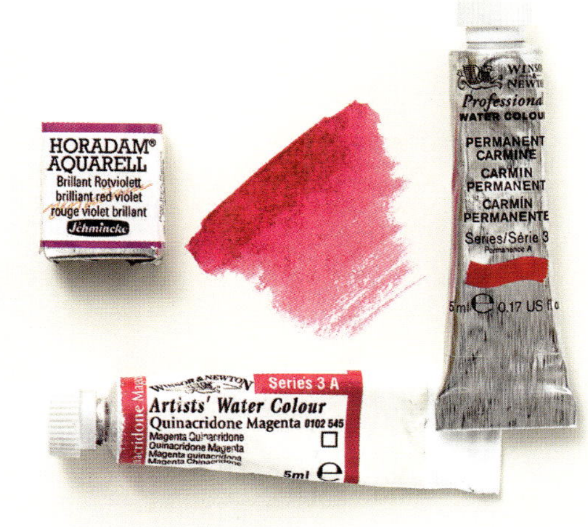

You may need to purchase a pink for accurate colour mixing when painting pink coloured subjects.

CREATING A BOTANICAL PALETTE

If you already have a few watercolours, then it is best to start with them – discarding black and white if they are included – and practise the colour mixing exercises recommended in this chapter. If the tubes are old, you may find that some have dried out and become solid. However, you will still be able to use them like this simply by cutting open the tube casing and using the paint inside, rather like a pan. Obviously if your existing paints are already in pans, you will not have this problem as they are already dry.

If you are seeking to buy watercolours for the first time it is worth establishing a set of colours specifically for botanical illustration. There is no need to buy a full set of colours in one go, but to build your palette starting with the primary colours.

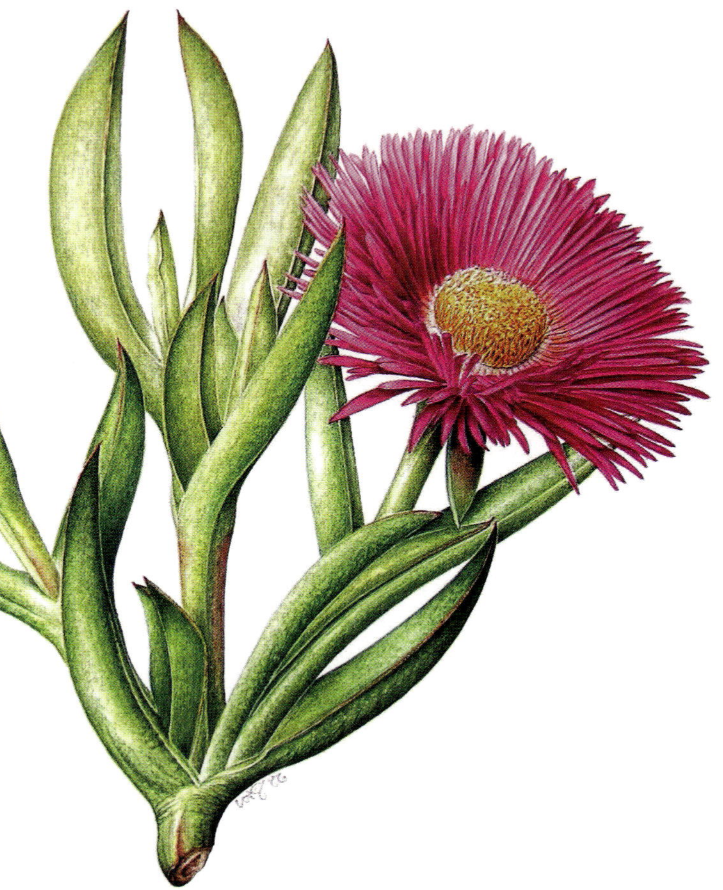

Hottentot Fig. LEIGH ANN GALE

Colour selection

With so many colours to choose from, it can be difficult to know which you need to include in your selection. A botanical palette of watercolours should primarily consist of colours that are representative of the naturalistic and earthy colours of nature and should in the mainstream be transparent. Avoid numerous colours that are opaque such as Cadmium Yellow, pre-mixed vivid greens such as Hooker's Green and Viridian, and neutral black.

To get started, surprisingly, you will need very few colours. As we have learned, the primary colours of red, blue, and yellow when mixed in various combinations will make a multitude of colours, so your palette should primarily consist of these. You could quite successfully get by and produce a vibrant botanical illustration just with primary colours. When you are ready, expand your range by adding some extra colours:

- Primary colours: Alizarin Crimson, Ultramarine or French Ultramarine, Aureolin
- Additional colours: Rose Dore, Prussian Blue, Indigo, Winsor Violet, Winsor Lemon, Burnt Umber, Raw Sienna, Sepia
- Optional colours: Payne's Gray, Davy's Gray
- Useful colour: Permanent Green (for making black).

Of course, you may wish to expand your palette even further, especially as you begin to paint more and more subjects.

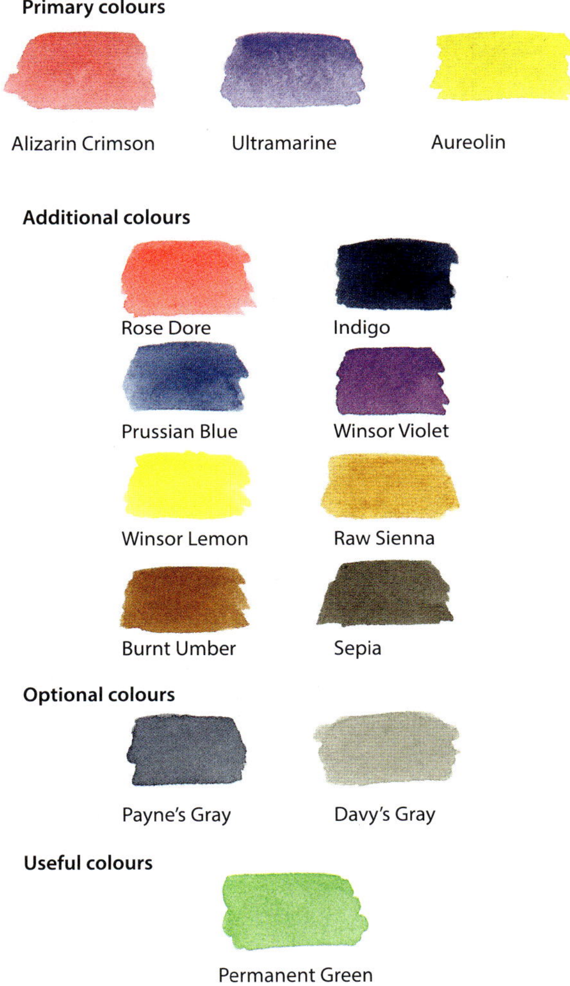

Recommended colours for creating a botanical palette.

Building your palette

It is worth considering at the outset whether you would like to use tubes or pans; there are advantages and disadvantages to each (*see* Chapter 1).

An excellent way of building a palette is to purchase an empty metal paint box capable of holding either half pans or whole pans of paint. These are available in the following configurations:

- 12HP / 6WP
- 24HP / 12WP
- 36HP / 18WP
- 48HP / 24WP

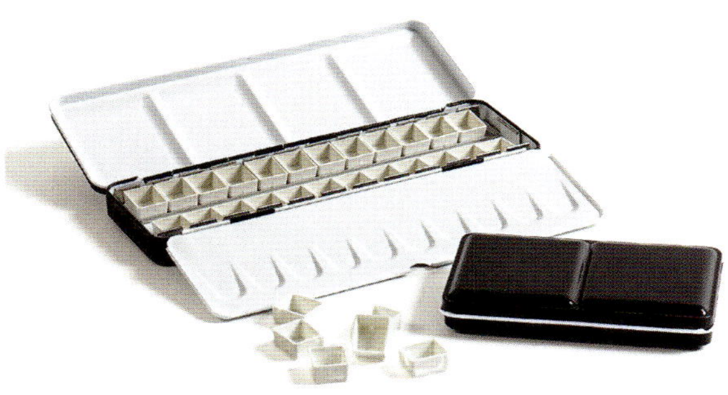

Build your own palette by purchasing an empty metal paint box which holds either half or whole pans.

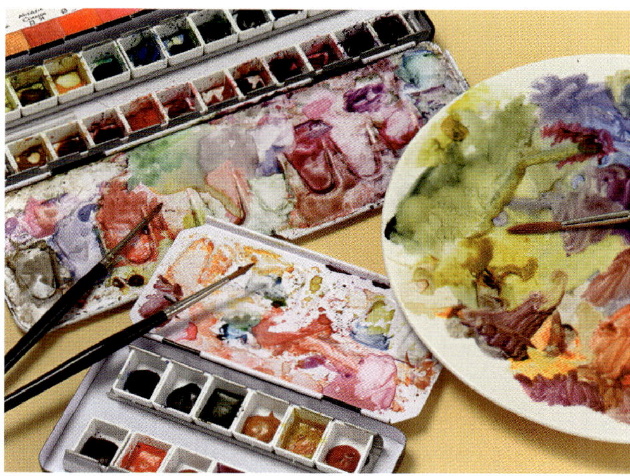

Retain unused paint in your palette for future use.

These paint boxes have the capacity to hold a brush in the centre and have two fold-out mixing palettes.

Alternatively, purchase the same metal tins together with empty half pans, then squeeze paints in each from your selected tubes.

Once you have set up your palette and have started using it, don't be tempted to clean away any unused paint after you have finished painting. Not only is this wasteful, but the mixed colours left behind will offer useful hues to add as shadow colours to your work. However, you should ensure that you keep your palette in a dust-free environment, especially during long periods of non-use, and if you need to clean an area to mix a brand new colour, then you should do so.

Checklist for All About Colour

- Learn colour theory.
- Familiarize yourself with the specific properties of watercolours and know their limitations.
- Practise the exercises for colour mixing in this chapter.
- Do not use neutral black. Instead replicate the natural warm and cool blacks in nature.
- Use white paint only for specific painting techniques (refer to Chapter 9).
- Test the opacity of your colours if there is no reference on the packaging.
- Practise mixing watercolours together before starting to paint an illustration. Check the likeness of your colour match by painting on the edge of a scrap of paper and holding it against the specimen when dry.
- Create some colour charts, particularly of your palette colours and shades of green using blues and yellows.
- Add pre-mixed pinks to your palette to ensure accuracy when colour matching to pink specimens.

Case Study

Creating a palette of colours for a painting is of great importance and should be decided upon before beginning to paint an illustration. Making studies of the individual components of the plant, and working out their colours, helps inform the entire colour palette for the whole illustration. You will usually find that a fairly limited palette is needed, as many of the colours will appear in several parts of the plant. For example, in our case study, it is clear that a purple/red colour is dominant not only in the berries, but also the tip of the flowering stem, the flower stems (pedicels) themselves, and the leaf petioles.

One of the most challenging aspects of painting *Fuchsia magellanica* was the ability to observe, mix, and match the colours of the pink flowers accurately. The sepals of the flowers are a rich, vibrant pink/red, which would be hard to mix using primary colours alone, and so a pre-mixed pink would be used instead. To achieve the colour vibrancy, Winsor and Newton's Quinacridone Magenta was selected, but by itself it is a relatively cool pink. The addition of Winsor Red was necessary to inject some warmth, and to achieve a better colour match. The colour mixed for the sepals would also be used for the stamens and the style in the flowers.

The internal petals of the pink/purple Fuchsia flowers are equally as vibrant as the sepals, so this needed to be shown in the selection of colours to paint them. Schminke's Brilliant Red/Violet was chosen as it is bright and vivid, and mixed with a little Winsor Violet.

Matching the leaf colour was also challenging. It is quite easy to simply mix up a green for the leaves you are painting without paying attention to how the colour may vary between leaves, so this was checked for the case study. It was noted that there was some variance in the green of the leaves, particularly in the younger leaves growing towards the tip of the specimen, which were a fresher, more yellow green, compared with more mature leaves growing elsewhere. A duller grey/green was observed on the underside of the leaves, so this would also need to be reflected in the painting. The final colour selection for the overall hue of the leaves consisted of Winsor and Newton's Transparent Yellow, Winsor Blue (Green Shade) and a little Cobalt Blue. The addition of extra Transparent Yellow in the mix for the younger leaves would be used, and the addition of Winsor and Newton Davy's Gray would be sufficient to dull the green on the underside of the leaves.

In addition, a little Winsor and Newton Raw Umber would be needed to tint the very tips of the Fuchsia berries, and used in addition to Winsor Red for part of the flowering stem; in addition to dulling the green for the underside of the leaves, Davy's Gray could be used to indicate the pollen on the tips of the stamens, and shadow colours such as Winsor and Newton Indigo and a little Winsor and Newton Sepia could be used on the underside of the stems to create a more rounded 3D appearance.

The final selected palette of the main colours to paint *Fuchsia magellanica* include: Winsor Violet (W&N), Perylene Violet (W&N), Quinacridone Magenta (W&N), Winsor Red (W&N), Brilliant Red/Violet (Schminke), Transparent Yellow (W&N), Winsor Blue (Green Shade) (W&N), and Cobalt Blue (W&N).

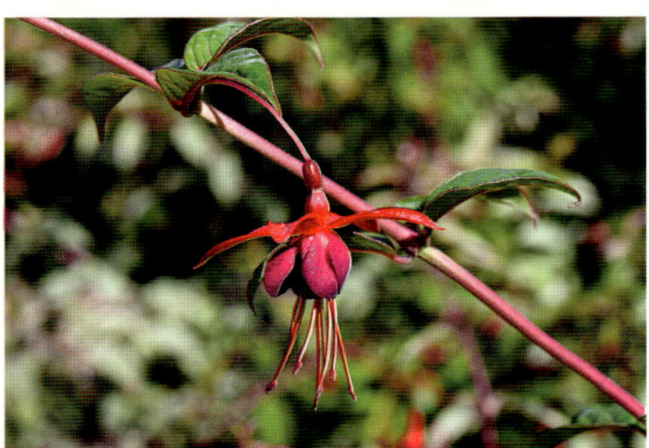

A close-up of a single flower, to help with colour matching.

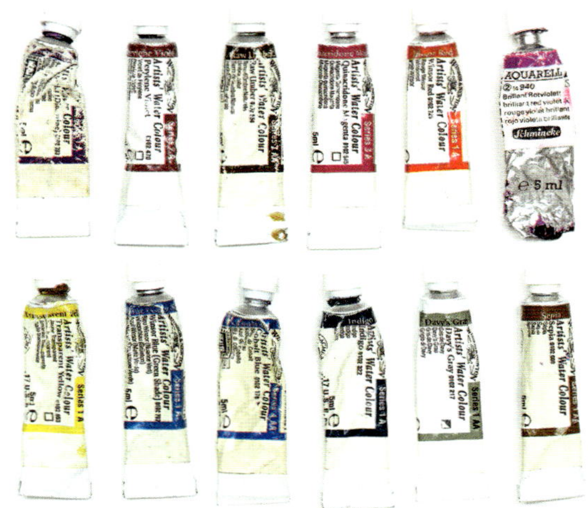

The selected palette for *Fuchsia magellanica* includes: Winsor Violet, Perylene Violet, Raw Umber, Quinacridone Magenta, Winsor Red, Brilliant Red/Violet, Transparent Yellow, Winsor Blue (Green Shade), Cobalt Blue, Indigo, Davy's Gray and Sepia.

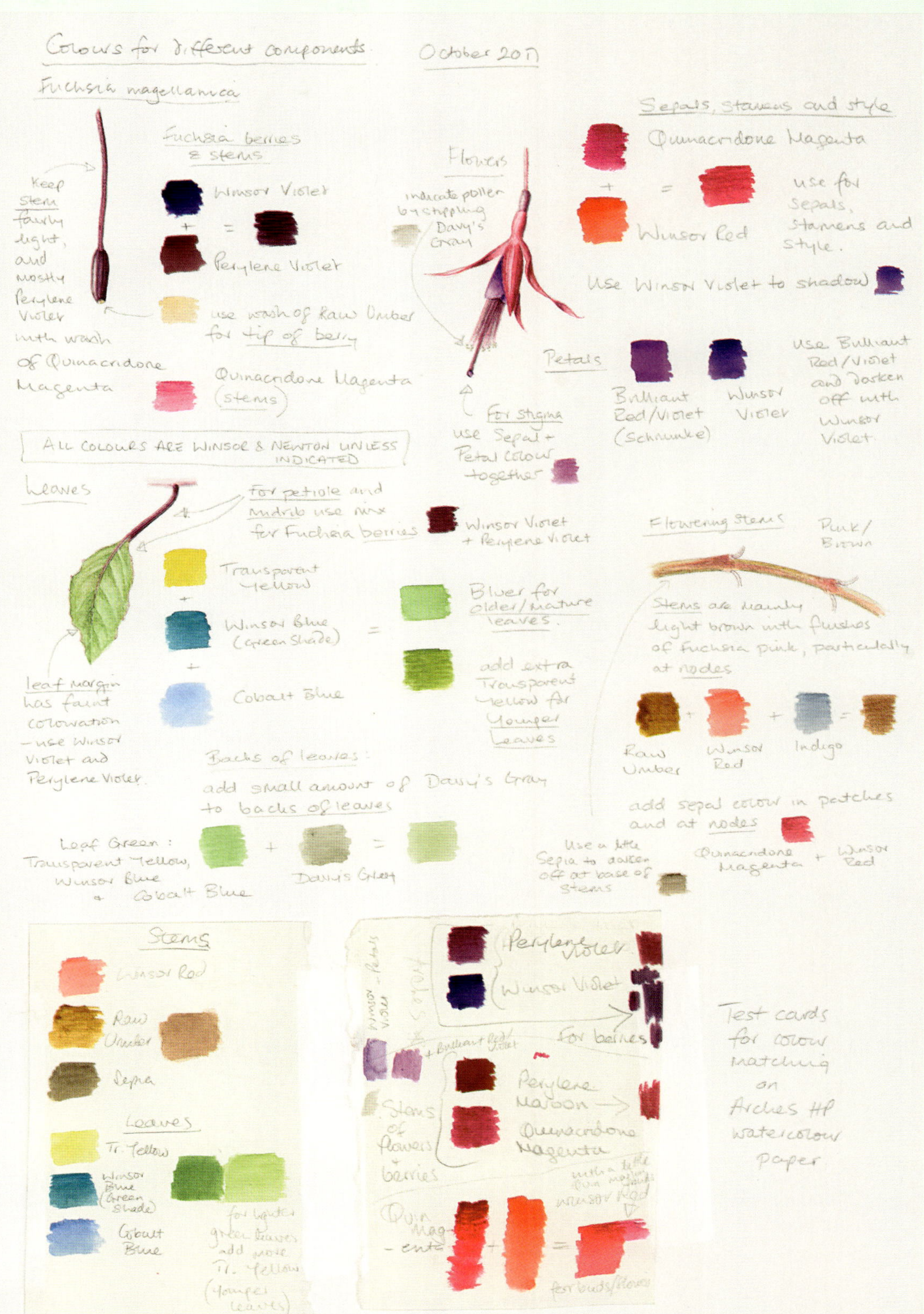

Colour mixing and references to selected colours, including written notes for *Fuchsia magellanica*.

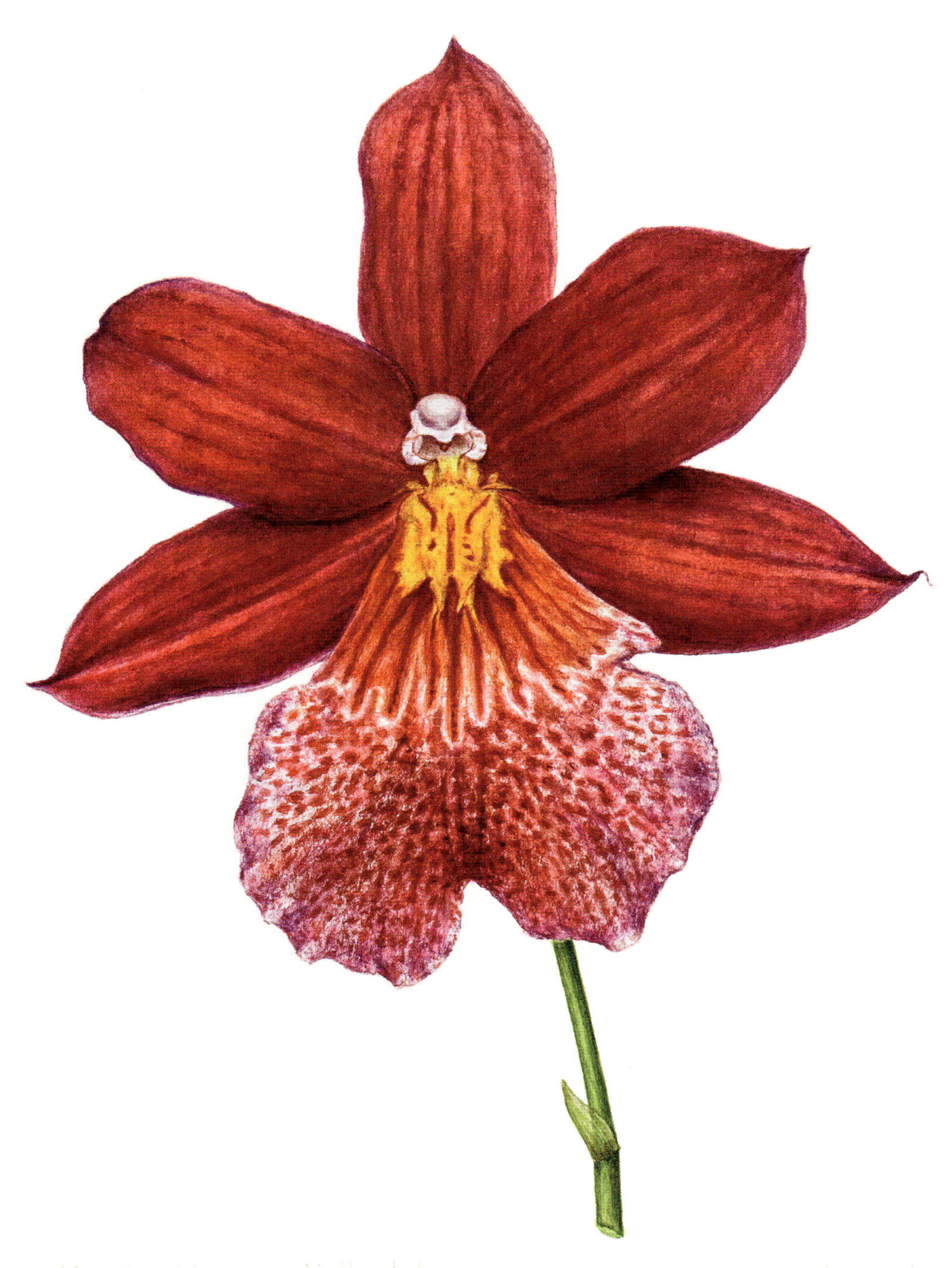
Orchid Oncidopsis Nelly Isler

CHAPTER 6

Preparing to Paint

The best preparation for good work tomorrow is to do good work today.

– Elbert Hubbard (American artist, writer, and publisher)

After finalizing your composition and transferring your drawing to painting paper, you will be ready to begin painting. You will need to check that you have everything to hand, and decide whereabouts on your paper you will actually make your first brush strokes. If you are new to botanical painting, then it is wise to do some initial practice on some spare paper first, so that you will feel confident about painting your final piece. Even seasoned artists can feel a little nervous about starting a new painting and may even feel apprehensive about their ability to do so if they haven't painted for a while.

Part of the preparation process should include organizing your workspace efficiently so that you have everything accessible: your sketchbook, specimens, and painting equipment, as well as your lighting, palette, water pot and rag (*see* Chapter 1). You will probably also want to think about some initial techniques to use to start your painting off. Will you use a wet-into-wet approach to lay down some first washes? Or will you tackle some small, fairly indiscreet areas with more detailed dry brush painting first? It is important to make these preliminary decisions so that you have a strategy in place for progressing your work. It is also important to remember that for each artist, the approach is slightly different. There is no right or wrong way to begin your painting, but above all you should feel comfortable and confident to start.

Here we will discuss aspects of the preparation for painting process, which you should aim to address and include each time you start a new painting.

Orchid x *Oncidopsis* 'Nelly Isler' (flower enlarged). LINDA PITKIN

ORGANIZING YOUR WORKSPACE

You will spend many hours at the workspace you have set aside for painting, therefore it is very important that you make it as comfortable and as conducive as possible. Your desk or work table should be well lit, either with natural light from a window or a daylight simulation lamp to the top left of your desk, or top right if you are left-handed and you should gather all your equipment together, such as brushes, palette, sketchbooks and so on. It is worth spending some time setting everything up until you are happy with the arrangement around your drawing board or slope (*see* Chapter 1).

STARTING A PAINTING

It is always wise to start your painting when you feel at your best. For some artists, this may mean getting up early because they function better in the mornings, whilst for others starting later in the day suits them better. You will want to ensure you feel relaxed and fully alert, so that you keep a clear mind to concentrate on what you are doing. It is no good feeling tired, exhausted, or stressed as your concentration levels will be affected; you may feel tense when holding your brush and you will be prone to making mistakes. Although botanical illustration usually requires you to be seated and remain virtually still, it is important that you regularly take breaks, stretch, and exercise your shoulders, arms, and hands. It can be very easy to find yourself clenching your brush or sitting awkwardly, so try to be conscious about this as you are painting.

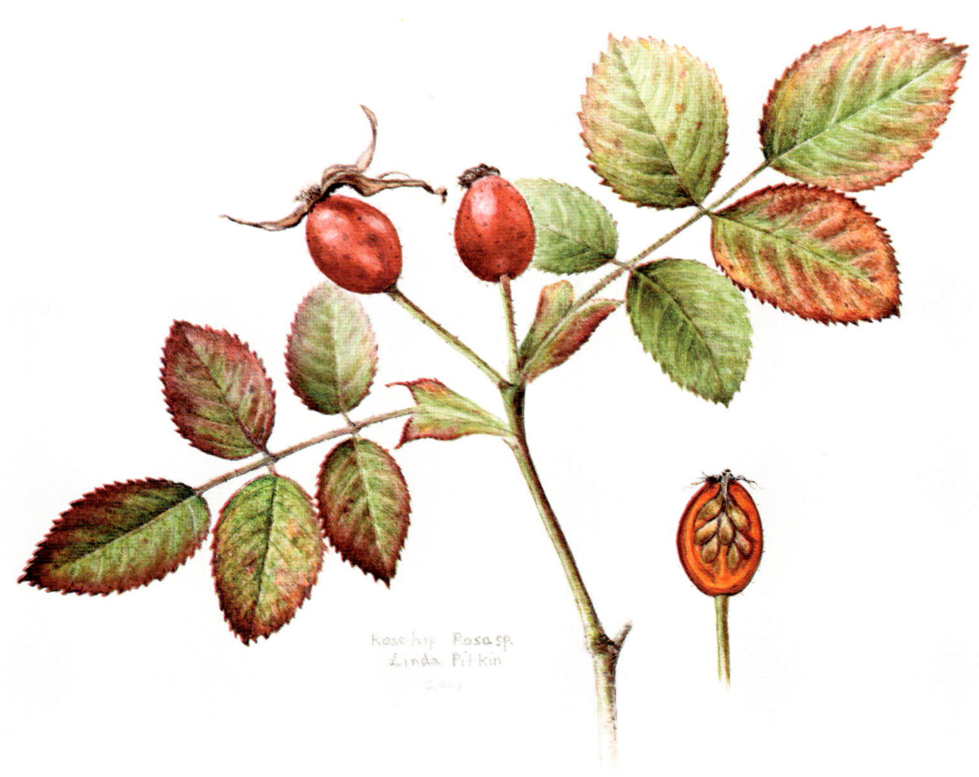

Rose Hips, *Rosa* sp. LINDA PITKIN

THE 'BLANK SHEET' SYNDROME

Whether you are just starting out in botanical illustration or you have been painting for some time, it is very common to experience 'blank sheet' syndrome. Being faced with a sheet of paper – despite your drawn image upon it – can cause a feeling of panic and anxiety, especially if you are a very visual artist and can envisage the finished painting in your mind. Trying to fathom out how you will get from A to B – from drawing to finished painting – can be quite bewildering. If you find yourself experiencing this it is best to try and work out what is causing you to fear the blank sheet in front of you. Is it a case of 'will I be able to paint well enough?', 'what happens if I make a mistake?', 'will my painting be good enough if I compare it with someone else's'? These are all common questions to ask yourself and are perfectly normal. You will naturally want to paint as well as you possibly can, which demonstrates your passion and commitment to your work.

You will discover that having some strategies in place to deal with 'blank sheet syndrome' will help you overcome your fears, and enable you to make a start on your painting. Here are a few suggestions to consider:

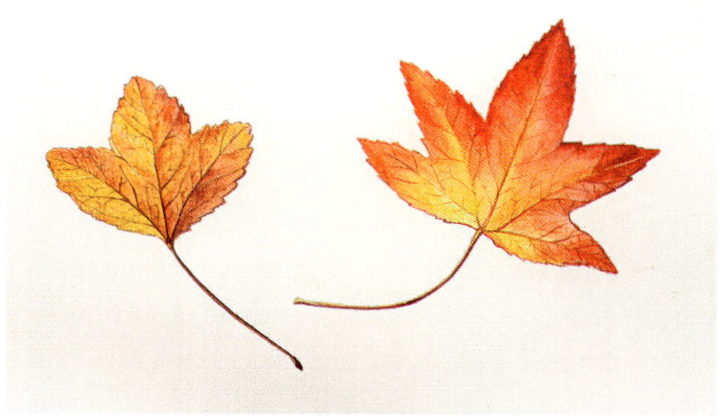

Autumn Leaves. ELANOR WEXLER

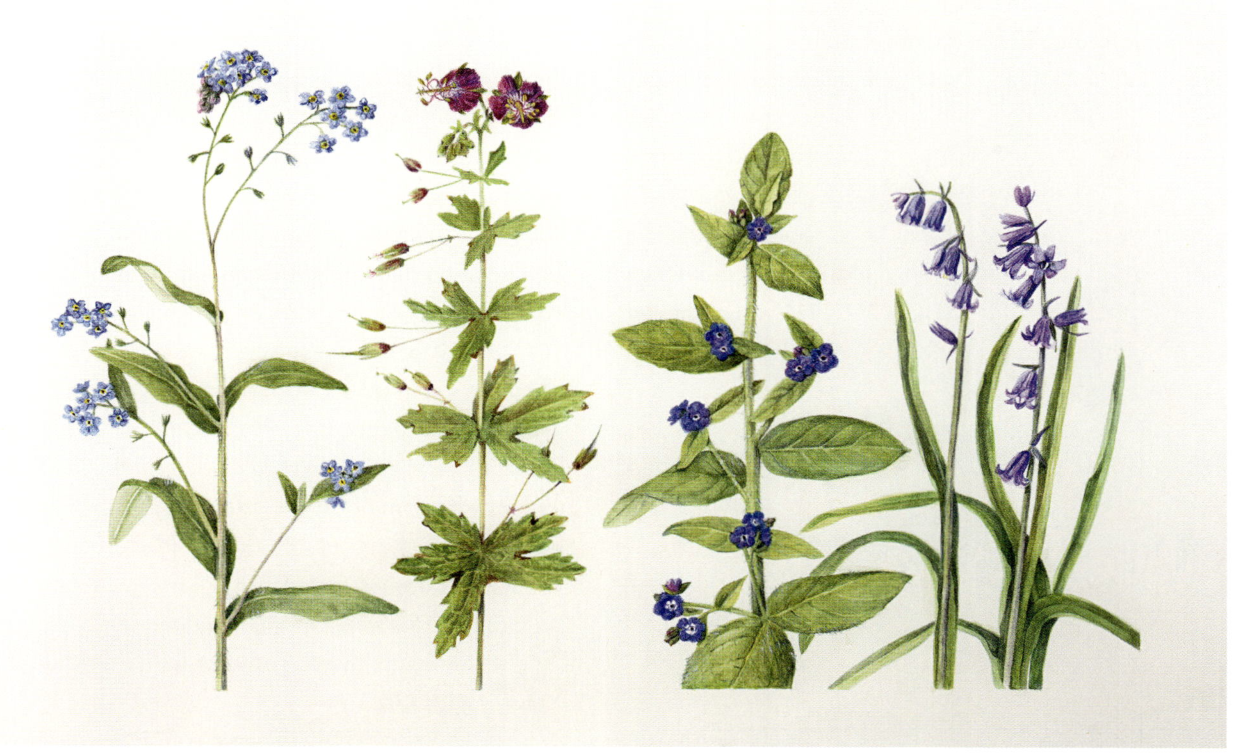

Wild Flowers in my Garden: *Mysotis sylvatica* – Forget Me Not, *Pentaglossis sempervivens* – Alkanet, *Geranium phaeum*, *Hyacinthoides non-scripta* – Bluebell. KATE TILBURY

1. If you are new to botanical painting, ask yourself what your measure is. Is this your first painting? If so, then you have nothing to measure against, or compare to. Until you try painting for the first time you won't know whether you will have a natural aptitude or will need a little extra practice; allow yourself a chance to learn 'on the job'; practise beforehand on spare pieces of paper; do not be tempted to rush, and above all, don't be afraid of making mistakes. If you are painting purely for your own pleasure, enjoy the process, and take your time (you probably won't have a deadline).

2. Botanical artists and illustrators usually set the bar quite high for themselves, which is a very natural response to the practical side of the painting process. Due to the nature of the subject, there is often a feeling of added pressure to 'get it right'; to make your painting completely accurate and exquisitely executed on your first attempt. Experiencing these feelings will naturally contribute to encountering 'blank sheet syndrome'. Remember that getting to a good, proficient standard (if this is your objective) will take time and plenty of practice, and there will be mistakes along the way.

3. For those who have painted before, but still experience these feelings before starting a painting, think of how you have faced the challenges of painting in the past. Did you have a clear idea of how you would go about starting the painting beforehand? Did your strategy work? Did you cope with it? If the answers are 'yes', then you can confidently apply the same methods this time. If, however, the answers are 'no', then you should address the issues you had problems with, and consider some different approaches. Try to think of different ways you could work this time and test them out. Perhaps you could begin your painting when you have less on your mind or are feeling more relaxed; if you have a deadline then consider setting yourself some mini targets by working through your painting in small sections; plan ahead and always allow some contingency time if you do have a deadline to meet. Maybe you could also change the starting point on your new painting. Perhaps create some extra initial washes or try not including them at all, or allow yourself plenty of extra time to practise if you are tackling an entirely new subject and are not sure if you will achieve the results you want.

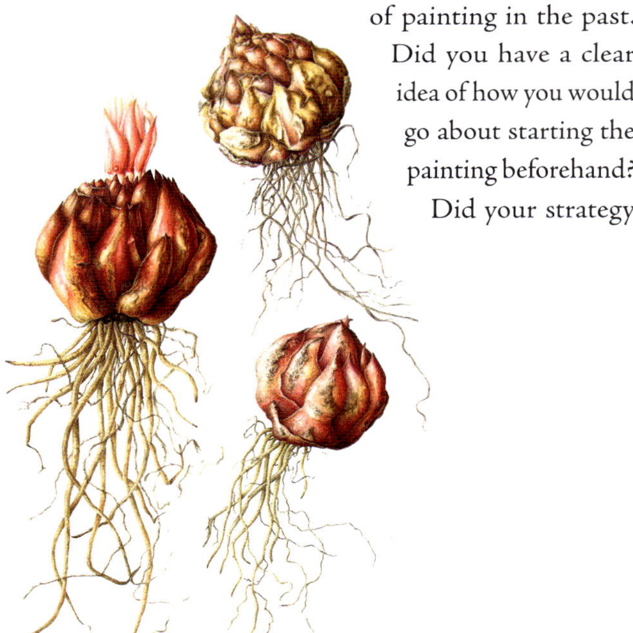

Lilium Bulbs. LEIGH ANN GALE

There are many ways to alter your working method, so experiment with new ideas to see what works well for you.

WHERE DO I BEGIN PAINTING ON THE PAPER?

It may seem obvious, but choosing the starting point to make your first brushstrokes is an important consideration. Choosing your starting point is different for every artist, but it is quite likely that whatever your starting point, it will physically be a natural comfortable position for your hand to be in. This is because your hand will rest in a position that is already familiar to you (as in writing for example), and you will feel that you have most control to operate your brush. However, this is not to say that you should without question begin painting at this particular place on your paper. It may be more appropriate for you to begin your painting at the centre, top, left, right or even the bottom of the paper depending on the content of your subject matter. For example, before painting the foliage of poppies or morning glory, it may be critical to paint the flowers first as they are very short-lived. You will want to ensure you capture them at their best before they fade.

The choice of where to begin your painting therefore is completely up to you. There are no fixed rules and you should practise what comes naturally to you personally.

Checklist for Preparing to Paint

- Organize your workspace efficiently; ensure you can sit and work comfortably.
- Ensure you have access to your sketchbook and any other materials you are using, including your specimens, close to hand.
- Be in the right frame of mind to begin your painting. Don't work if you are tired, exhausted, or stressed.
- Overcome the 'blank sheet' syndrome by strategizing a new or different approach; address previous issues.
- Make your first brush strokes in a logical place, either to suit the comfort of your hand or ascertaining from the content of your subject matter the most urgent point.

Case Study

Now that *Fuchsia magellanica* was finally ready to paint, it was necessary to prepare the workspace in the studio so that painting could begin. Checking that everything that would be needed was set up and close at hand was a priority, including the work surface and seating. Working on a drawing board positioned centrally on the desk would be the easiest and most comfortable position to work in, given that the painting process would be likely to involve many hours. A sit/kneel stool was also set up at the correct height to maintain a good posture during painting. In addition to watercolour paints, brushes, palette and a water pot, the sketchbook used to record and draw the subject would also be needed and close to hand, ready to refer to when painting.

In theory, it should always be possible to paint an illustration entirely from sketchbook drawings and notes if necessary, especially if a painting is to be completed out of season when specimens may not be available. This would be entirely possible for the case study as thorough observations, drawings and notes were made of the subject. However, as the painting was to be completed in season, it would be prudent to use the specimens as well as the sketchbook drawings and notes in this instance. Therefore, an Anglepoise lamp would also be needed to light any specimens correctly if they were brought into the studio.

It is always difficult to plan exactly where on the paper to begin painting, and this can cause some anxiety. It is often helpful if there is an obvious starting point, as in the case study, where the flowers and berries would most likely be chosen as they are the most perishable parts of the plant.

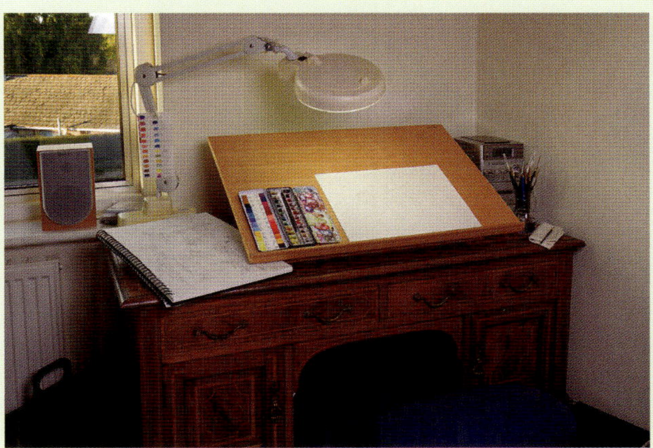

Once the image was traced onto hot-pressed watercolour paper it was ready to paint.

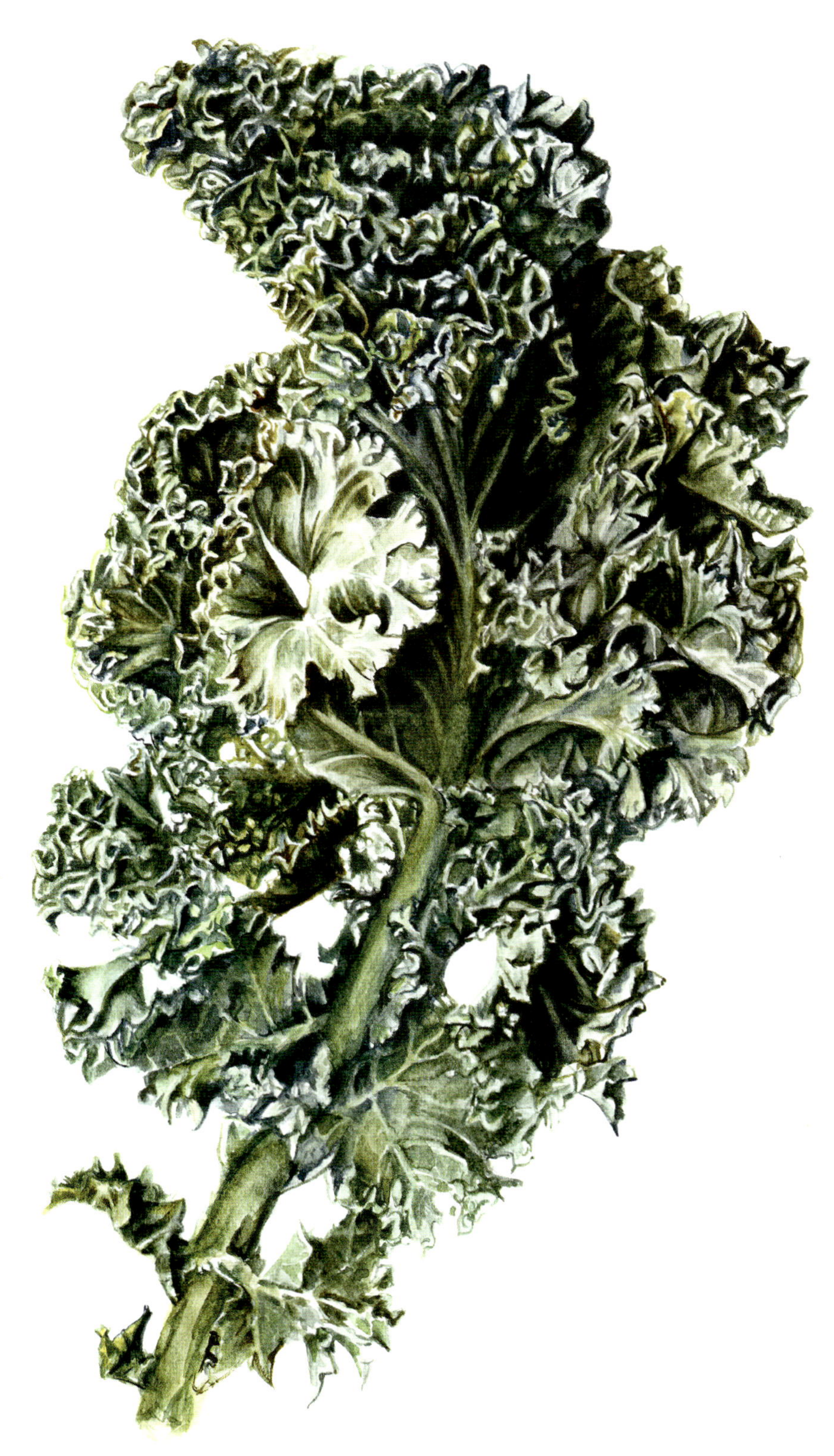

CHAPTER 7

Developing a Painting

Go on working, freely and furiously, and you will make progress.

– Paul Gauguin (French Post-Impressionist artist)

Now that you have made important key decisions about your approach to painting your illustration, it is time to put your strategies into action. You should make sure you are in the right frame of mind for developing your painting, as this will set the tone for your continuation and progression through each stage.

If this is your first botanical painting, remember to allow yourself the opportunity to make mistakes and learn from them. So often, new artists panic at the slightest hint of making a mistake, but all you need to do is to stay calm, continue, and rectify any mistakes in due course. After all, that is how we can learn so much; never look upon mistakes as failures.

Achieving a completed, finished painting in botanical illustration requires lots of patience and time, and many processes right from the outset when you choose your subject. The painting process alone will require you to work through several different stages such as modelling and adding fine details, but to achieve these you will also need to consider the techniques you will use and whether you use any preparations such as ox gall liquid or gum Arabic to help you. You should also become familiar with learning how to deal with common problems that may arise during the painting process, such as hard water lines around washes or paint lifting off unintentionally.

This chapter deals with the different stages of developing your painting including ideas for different techniques, modelling and achieving a sense of 3D, and how to deal with common problems. Through practice, you will become familiar with the process of botanical painting, and learn to develop strategies that are suitable for you as an individual.

Kale Leaf. VICKY SHARMAN

PAINTING TECHNIQUES

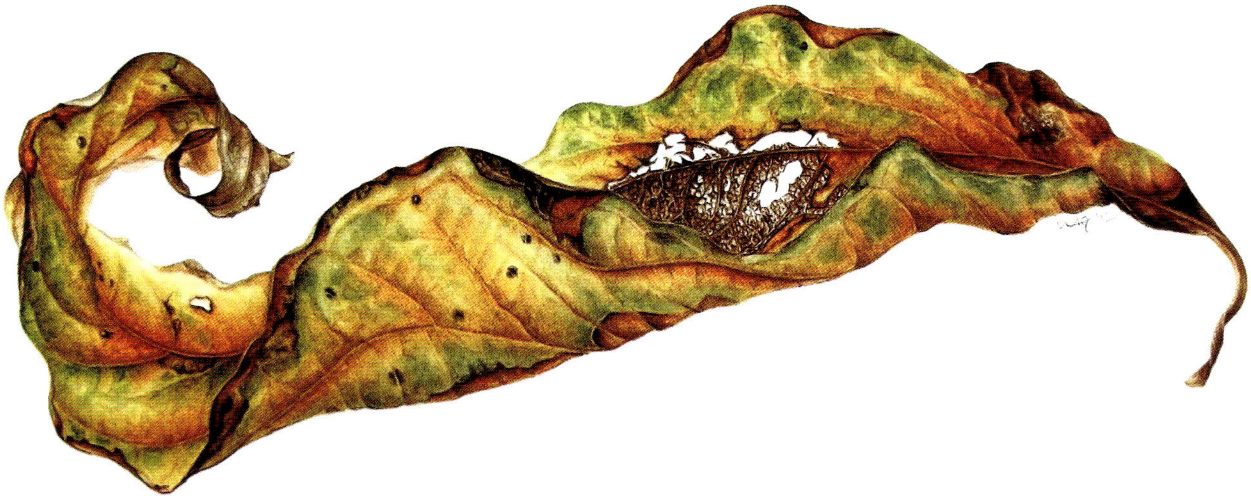

Avocado Leaf. LEIGH ANN GALE

One of the most common questions a botanical painter may hear is, 'how did you paint…?', especially if the viewer is an aspiring artist or student themselves. You have probably admired an artist's work yourself and asked the same questions if you have visited an exhibition or gallery when the artist is present, or you have read up about different methods and techniques an artist uses. It is valuable knowledge to understand how effects are achieved in botanical illustration and usually even more so if you can see them being demonstrated at close hand by an artist.

Developing technique will happen differently for each artist, and proficiency will occur at different rates. Some artists love using specific techniques whilst others loathe them, so the skills you develop will be entirely unique to you. You may even discover that you can create some of your own as you practise and become more confident with your painting.

It is important that you always use relevant techniques for illustrating your subject, so it is worth investing time and effort into familiarizing yourself with several different techniques and putting them into practice. This will also help you to develop your confidence in botanical painting.

There are two key painting techniques that you will most likely use in botanical illustration. These are the wet-into-wet and dry brush techniques.

THE WET-INTO-WET TECHNIQUE

If you have done some watercolour painting before you may have already come across the wet-into-wet technique. It is often used in looser styles of painting when a blend of colours is required. The process of applying wet paint into damp water on the paper will produce soft, diffused edges of colour, which gently merge together. However, predicting the results of the wet-into-wet application takes skill and practice to achieve the desired result.

In botanical illustration, this technique is generally used to create soft merges of background colours, typically for those of autumn leaves for example, and usually serves as a preliminary technique over which dry brush detail may be added afterwards. The effects of a successful wet-into-wet application can be beautiful, so it is well worth pursuing the technique to perfect it.

Before committing yourself to your actual illustration, practise the technique following the method described here on scraps of paper first. Here, the technique is demonstrated on an autumn leaf:

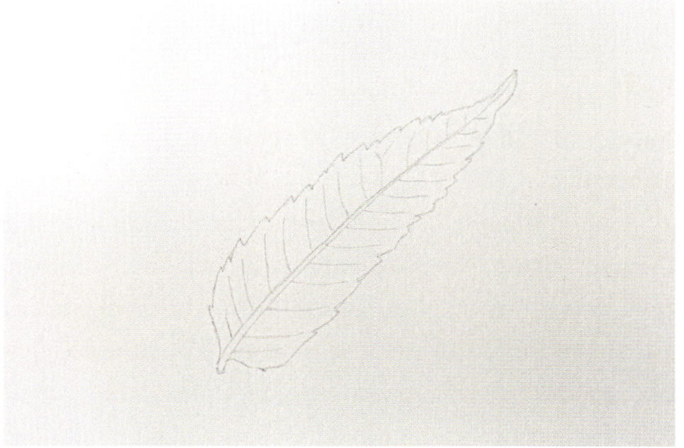

Step 1. First complete an accurate drawing, including the positions of the midrib and lateral veins. Remember to keep the graphite line light, especially if you are painting a predominantly yellow or orange leaf. Identify the main colours of your leaf, and mix quantities of them up in your palette. Make the solutions fairly dilute. You will need two pots of clean water for this technique. Paint the area to be painted with clear water and wait until it starts to soak into the paper. (Ensure your paper lies flat for this process.) Using the light to help you, note when the water has soaked the paper sufficiently so that it resembles a lustre, rather like an eggshell surface.

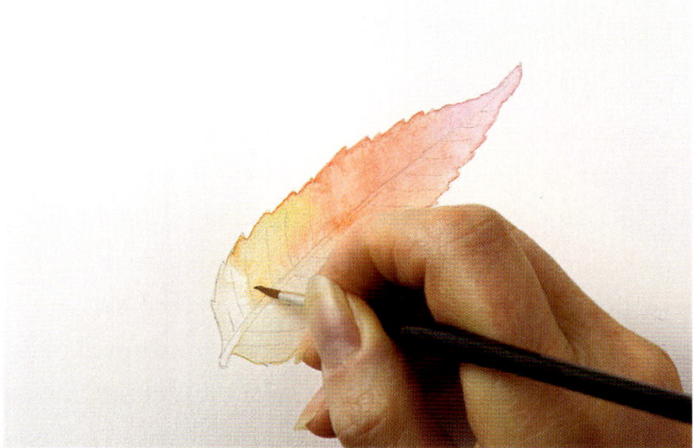

Step 2. Begin to drop in the different colours over the leaf. Use the second pot of water to rinse your brush each time you change colour. Don't worry about applying paint over the veins at this stage. Assuming you are using transparent colours, you will still see just enough pencil work underneath to guide you when painting them in more detail later on. It is important that you drop the paint into the damp surface at the correct time. If you do this too early, the water will be too wet, and the paint will quickly travel to the margins and cause a strong line when dry; if the paper has dried too much, the paint will not spread sufficiently.

You may need to practise the technique several times before perfecting it, so allow yourself plenty of time to do this. If it helps, write notes against each attempt stating what did and didn't work.

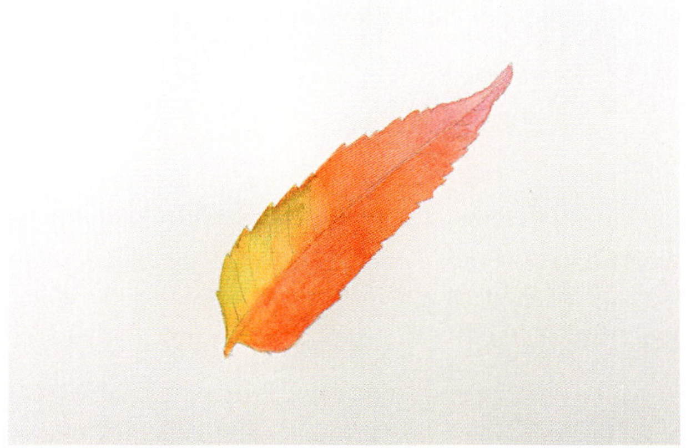

Step 3. Once the paper has totally dried, repeat the process, building up the intensity of colour as you go, and feathering the edges of colours together if necessary whilst the paint is still damp. Pay attention to any highlight and shadow areas on the leaf, adding extra shadow colours if necessary. Allow each application to dry thoroughly.

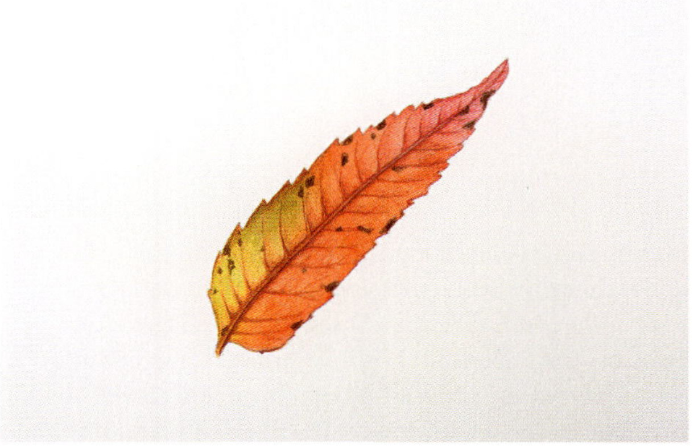

Step 4. Finally, depict with dry brush work the midrib and lateral veins by carefully using a virtually upright pointed brush, and lightly indicate only a selection of secondary veins. Any other markings, blemishes or blotches can also be added using dry brush work to complete a realistic effect.

THE DRY BRUSH TECHNIQUE

Unlike the wet-into-wet technique, dry brush painting involves using very minimal quantities of water with the pigments. It is a technique often used towards the end of the painting process to add details to illustrations over base washes, however some artists prefer to use the technique much earlier on in painting to describe details and 3D first. They may then follow this towards the end of painting with 'glazes' of dilute colour to tint highlights, and water glazes to help blend the brush strokes and colours together. Using your paintbrush rather like a pencil to 'draw' detail is the best way to describe this technique.

Dry brush painting requires much control to handle the brush well (a size 0 or 1 with a good point is ideal), to apply the paint carefully. It is necessary that your brush is not completely dry – as you may expect, given the name of the technique – but is instead just slightly damp. Using tube paints can be significantly easier to produce a good result since they already contain gum Arabic binder, but it will still be necessary to combine the paint with a little water.

Conventionally, dry brush technique involves applying the paint using tiny brush strokes, which should follow the natural direction of the contours of the specimen. At the end of painting, it is then usually necessary to add a glaze over the brush strokes so that they blend together evenly.

As with the wet-into-wet technique, it is well worth practising beforehand on a few scraps of hot-pressed paper. Try drawing some small 3D shapes to paint first, and then follow the method for painting a small sphere. Use a size 0 or 1 pointed brush.

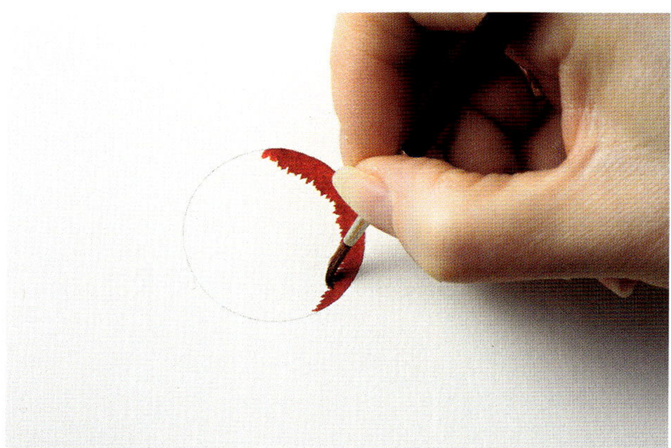

Step 1. Draw yourself a small sphere. Mix up some paint to a reasonably thick consistency, so that you can track the path of the brush through it (tube paints will give a better result for this). Dip your brush into the paint so that it is reasonably loaded and start by painting a small linear block of colour on the shadow side of the sphere. Carefully begin to pull and push the paint towards the position of a highlight area. Work with small movements, trying not to pull or push the paint too much.

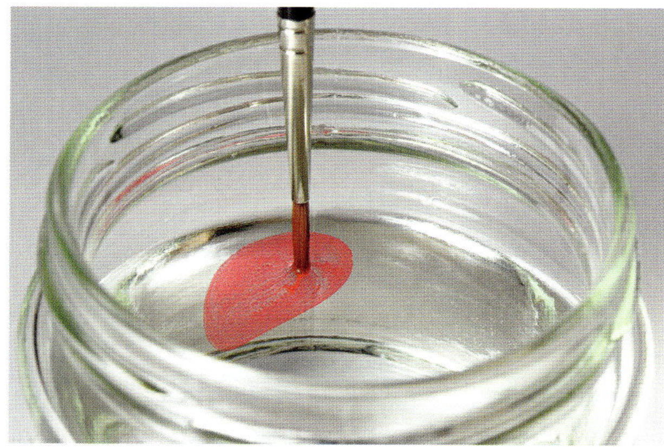

Step 2. Dip the brush partially in the water to take out some of the paint, and then dab excess water from the point of your brush onto your rag.

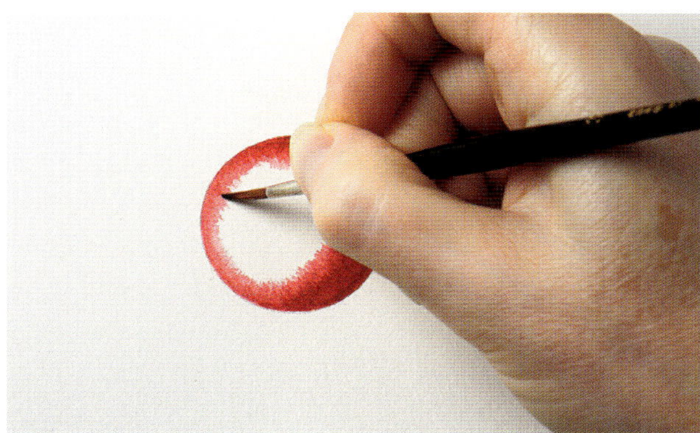

Step 3. Pick up the leading edge of the paint already applied and continue pulling and pushing the paint towards the highlight area of the sphere. You will notice how the strokes you are now applying are tonally lighter. Repeat the process from Step 2, working your way around the whole sphere, gradually painting lighter and lighter strokes towards the highlight area. As the paint dries, you will probably notice tiny brush marks appearing – don't worry about these for now.

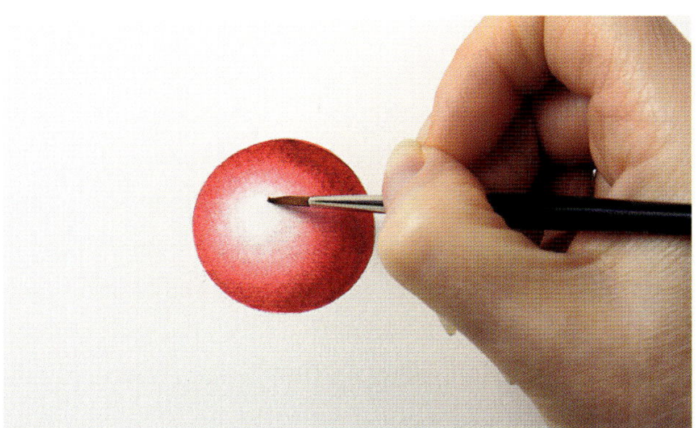

Step 4. Rinse your brush completely and blot off excess water on your rag. Gently feather the edges of the paint into the whiteness of the paper at the highlight area.

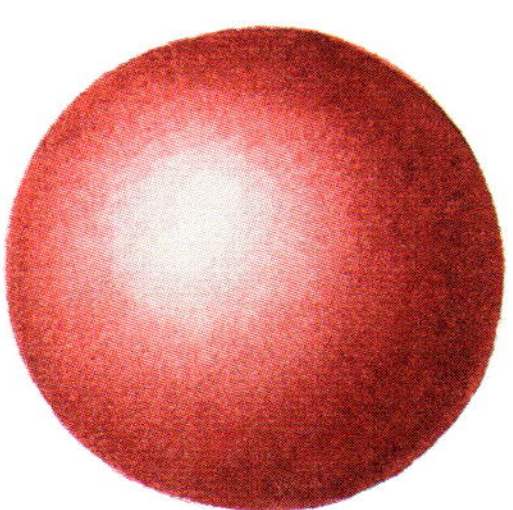

Step 5. Finally, to complete the sphere, gently smooth out any brushstrokes by blending them together with a clean, damp brush. Apply a very dilute wash of colour over the highlight area (never leave a highlight pure white).

OTHER PAINTING TECHNIQUES

Other techniques to consider using are flat washes and layers of wash. These are popular amongst botanical painters as they are generally considered the most effective way of modelling the painting, and bringing about a 3D quality to the work. They are also controllable, as they can be applied in different consistencies.

PRELIMINARY FLAT WASH

A flat wash is generally quite easy to apply and often used by artists as the first stage of the painting process. The wash is achieved by diluting the hue of each colour being used, and carefully painting the relevant areas. When dry, the diluted wash should be very subtle (it is often referred to as a tea wash), which allows the artist to see the distribution of colours over the entire painting, and to gain an overall 'feel' for how the painting will look once finished.

When the flat washes are dry, it is then possible to build layers of richer, more intense washes over the top, in addition to using dry brush work to depict details at the end and to complete the painting.

A preliminary flat wash is sometimes referred to as a 'tea wash'.

Building up layers of wash will intensify your colour.

BUILDING LAYERS OF WASH

For many artists, a technique between the two methods of wet-into-wet and dry brush is favourable. Laying down a series of washes allows you to still have the flexibility of using some water but still maintain control over how and where the paint is applied and worked. The layers of wash can be applied more intensely each time to build up the modelling of a 3D shape. If you use this technique always remember to allow the previous wash to fully dry each time, otherwise you may experience paint lifting as you apply a new wash over the top.

Finally, dry brush work can be added to increase depth of shadows and add details.

MODELLING

Modelling is the stage of your painting when you will need to convey a sense of three-dimensional structure in your work. In addition, creating contrast between highlighted and shadowed areas, achieving a subtle sense of depth of field, and adding details such as veins in petals and hairs on stems also help to establish reality into your illustration, and contribute to the modelling process.

When you are beginning to think about modelling, it is sensible to have some strategy in place before you begin painting, so consider deciding beforehand the techniques you could use. For example, a large expanse of variegation in a leaf is probably best achieved by first using the wet-into-wet technique, and the finer, threadlike structures of filaments on a stamen are probably best created using the dry brush technique.

Whichever methods and techniques you choose, practise them beforehand so that you have confidence to work with them on your actual illustration.

ACHIEVING A SENSE OF 3D

Creating a 3D effect in your work is by far the most important and challenging aspect of the painting process. Achieving a believable and naturalistic result requires forethought and vision, as well as skill in using relevant techniques. It will take time to become proficient, so allow yourself plenty of practice time and don't be afraid of making mistakes.

Artists normally create form and structure in their work by using a combination of layers of wash and the dry brush technique. By carefully studying how the light falls on your subject matter, you can begin to replicate the same in your illustration using the techniques in a controlled manner. Before you progress however, you should always double-check that you have set the lighting up correctly for your specimen, and that if you are using artificial light, you are using a daylight simulation bulb to achieve accurate colour matching. If you have already made a tonal pencil drawing of your subject, then you will have already done much of the work in studying how the light forms highlights and shadows. This will help you with your painting, as essentially your task is to convert the grey tones of your pencil work into colour. A tonal pencil drawing is also extremely helpful if you are painting your subject out of season, when it may be unlikely that you will have the specimen in front of you, and you are relying on your botanical sketchbook to help you complete your illustration.

As you study the highlights and shadows on your subject, decide which are the very lightest and which are the very darkest areas, and, if it helps, demarcate them in light pencil on your drawing. For example, indicate the highlights on a leaf or berry, and the shadow area at the point where two leaves or two berries overlap.

It is largely up to you how you progress your painting. Some artists like to concentrate on small, individual areas and bring each to a nearly finished state, for example laying a wash, modelling, and adding details. Others however will prefer to work systematically around the painting and paint each part to the same level of finish before continuing, for example laying all of the initial washes before modelling. Each artist is unique; there is no right or wrong way to go about what you do, so try experimenting to see what works best for you.

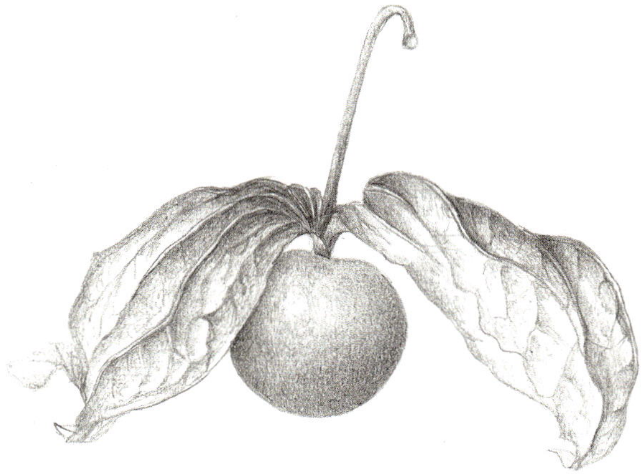

A tonal drawing is useful to refer to when painting.

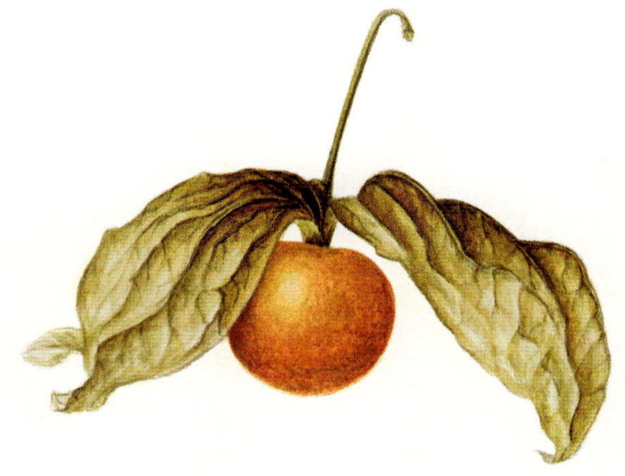

Refer to the tonal drawing you made to help you add shadows and highlights in the correct places.

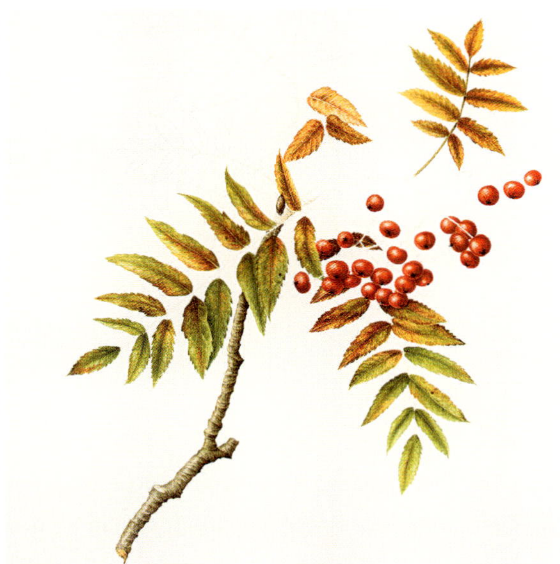

An example of a painting in progress where small sections are worked on to an almost finished state before moving on.

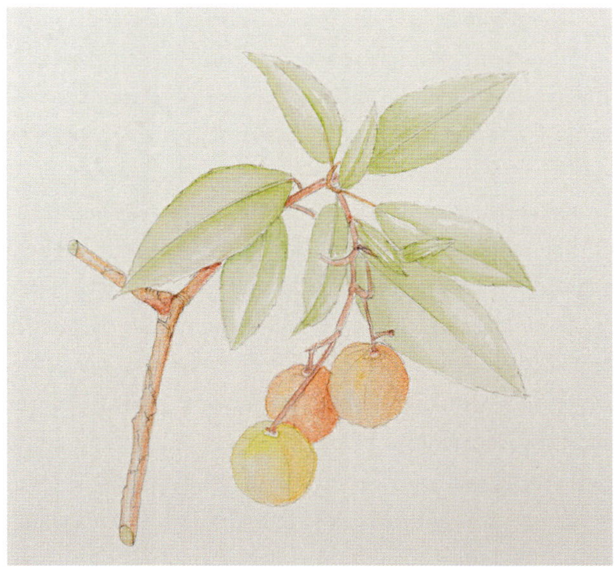

Progressing a painting equally, here, laying initial washes altogether before adding modelling and details.

COLOUR MATCHING

During the painting process, you should be conscious of the colours in your specimen and how you will go about matching them accurately. Refer to Chapter 5 to learn about colour theory if this helps. It is very important that you develop a good eye for colour matching – which can only be achieved with practice – as this shows that you have observed well and understand how the colours work in your subject. Above all, in combination with your accurate drawing it demonstrates that you are illustrating the species you have set out to illustrate. It is quite possible that a subtle difference in colour matching could suggest a similar species is illustrated, so accuracy is key.

Use your colour theory knowledge to help you with matching colours to your specimen. Identifying whether the colours you are trying to match are either cool or warm is usually your first challenge, and once you have

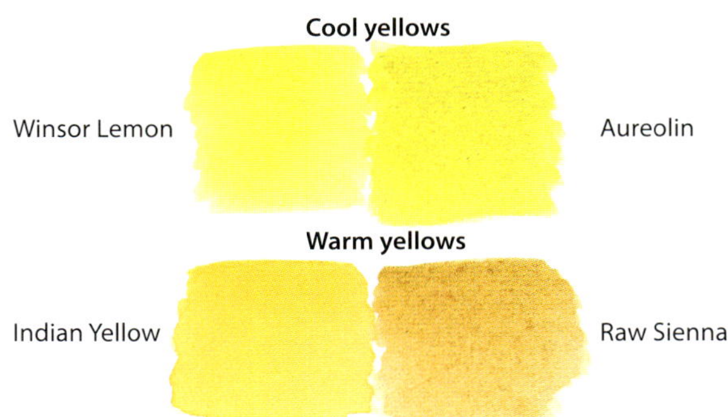

Learn your colour theory; be able to identify cool and warm groups of colours in your palette.

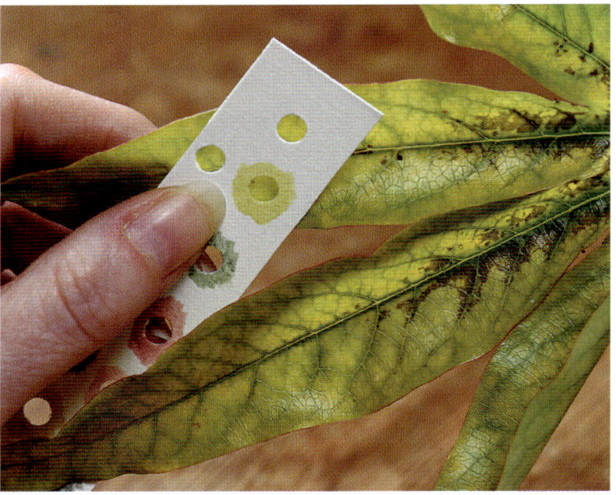

Paint around punched holes in watercolour to help with colour matching. Hold the painted area against the specimen.

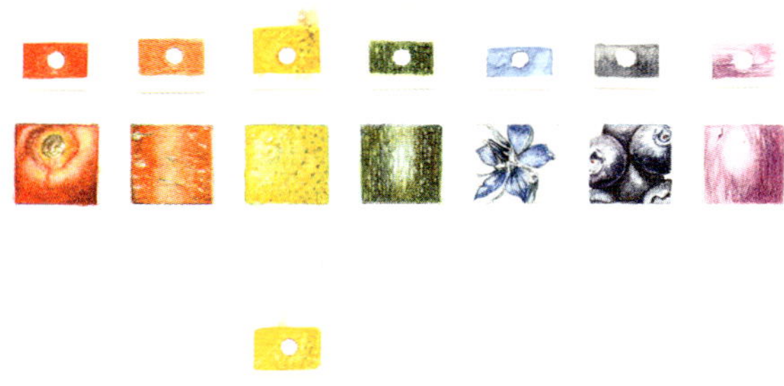

An exercise in colour matching using the punched hole method. Botanical rainbow of vegetables, fruit and flowers. VICKY SHARMAN

decided this, ensure you choose relevant cool or warm colours from your palette. For example, if the yellow you can see is cool, then choose perhaps Winsor Lemon or Aureolin rather than Indian Yellow or Raw Sienna. Sometimes, it can be hard to decide if the colour is cool or warm, so you may have to experiment with your mixes, especially if colour matching is relatively new to you. If you have made some colour charts – especially for greens – then use them against the specimen, and this will help you decide between cool and warm. With practice, you will soon develop an eye for colour and be able to identify the colours you need to use. When colour matching, remember you need to match the hue (colour), rather than the intensity (richness) of the colour. You can dilute and strengthen the colour later if you need to.

If you are unused to colour matching, and not using colour charts, you may find it helpful to write down combinations of colours as you try different mixes. This will help you learn the names of your paints and what happens when you mix them together.

Whenever you are colour matching, you should always test your mix first on scraps of paper before committing yourself to your painting. You can do this by painting swatches on the very edge of a piece of paper, but an increasingly popular method is to paint around holes that have been punched out with a hole punch. By painting around a hole and holding it directly against the specimen you will see if the colours blend. You will get an even better idea of the match if you squint; if you can see differences whilst squinting then the colour needs adjusting, but if not, then your mix is accurate. Remember also that watercolours dry slightly lighter than when wet, so wait a minute or so before assessing the likeness.

ADDING AERIAL PERSPECTIVE

A common misconception exists that aerial perspective is somehow to do with looking down at the subject from a height. In fact, it is the atmosphere that is referred to, so a more accurate label would be atmospheric perspective, which is sometimes how it is known.

As an object recedes into the distance it appears to get smaller. This is known as perspective (*see* Chapter 3), but the object also changes in colour and intensity of detail due to particles such as water vapour and dust in the atmosphere. These particles cause the object to appear

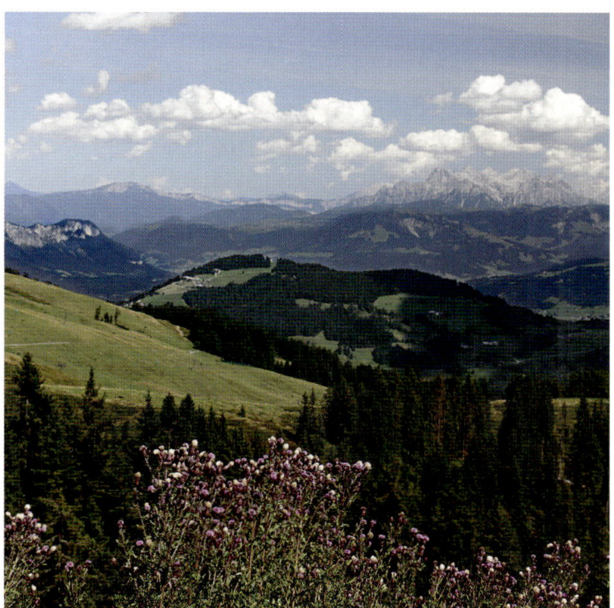

The receding mountains take on a smaller, hazy appearance, compared with the brighter, more detailed flowers in the foreground.

duller and less contrasting because they bend the light in different directions. Objects appear 'hazy' or blurred as a result. A typical example is a landscape scene with mountains in the distance. The mountains appear hazy, or sometimes blue, whilst details in the foreground remain bright, crisp, and clear.

In botanical illustration, it is seldom that the depth of field is that great, and is only fractional compared with the mountain landscape example above. However, it is worth employing a little aerial perspective into your painting to help define the foreground and background. For example, by painting leaves which recede into the background from a stem slightly duller with less detail clearly gives the illusion of depth, which will in turn help to establish an overall 3D effect.

BUILDING IN THE DETAILS

Adding details to your work will most likely be done once you have completed the modelling in your painting. The finer details, such as veins in a petal, hairs on a leaf or stem or the delicate bloom on a bunch of grapes, should all be dealt with once you are happy that you no longer need to build up the three-dimensionality of your work. Details

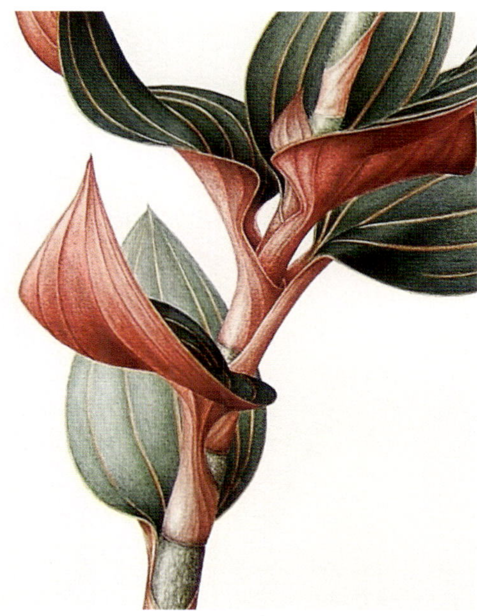

Aerial perspective on leaves. *Ludisia discolor* 'Red Velvet'. LEIGH ANN GALE

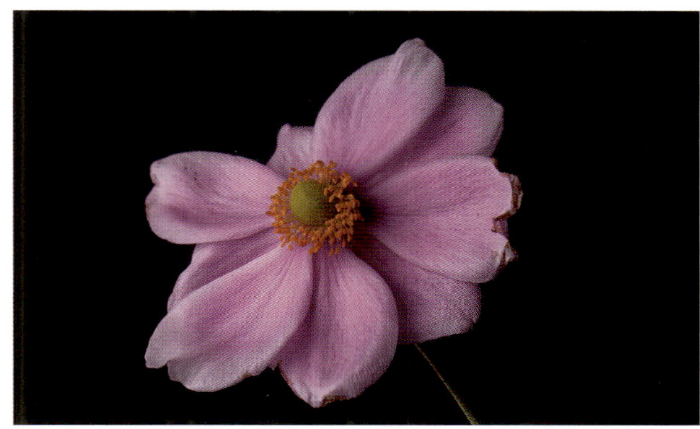

The majority of detail (such as veins in petals) are seen in the midtones.

will also include any areas where it may be necessary to emphasize shadows, or perhaps lift a little paint in a highlight to brighten it, for example.

You should be careful not to 'overdo' the details you add. They should be sufficient that your viewer will be able to identify them without them being the dominant feature. Striking a happy balance will come with practice but be mindful that most of the details you add should occur in the foreground, and in the mid-tones of your painting. Details will be less prevalent in areas of strong highlight and shadow. This is because these areas are either flooded with lots of light or are not receiving enough light for the details to be clear.

SOME USEFUL BRUSH TECHNIQUES FOR ADDING DETAILS

It is worth building a repertoire of different brush techniques to use for creating different effects in botanical illustration. These could include painting fine lines to replicate the hairs of the pappus on a dandelion 'parachute'; using small flecks of paint to capture the furry texture of *Stachys byzantina* (lamb's ear); or suggesting the central section of disc florets of an Asteraceae (daisy) flower by the careful use of stippling. (*See* Chapter 9 for some ideas.)

ADAPTING YOUR TECHNIQUES

As you progress from painting to painting you will probably find that you will develop your own routine to follow. This will involve not only your ideas at the drawing and composition stages, but also the strategies you put in place during the painting process. It will become clear to you which painting techniques you favour most and those that you don't, but sometimes you may take on a subject that is very different or new to you. When this happens, it is worth addressing whether your tried and tested methods are suitable or relevant for the job in hand. You may need to adapt or alter your techniques, or use some that you wouldn't normally use. For example, each time you paint, you may always begin with a flat wash to lay down the foundations of blocks of colour, but in the case of painting a colourful autumn leaf that consists of subtle merges of varying colours, this may not be entirely appropriate as a starting point. Instead, using a wet-into-wet technique may be a more suitable way of achieving the subtle transitions and blends of colour in the leaf.

You should always use techniques for painting your subject matter that are relevant, as this will help to ensure you create an illustration which harnesses the true character and detail of the species.

CARING FOR YOUR WORK DURING THE PAINTING PROCESS

Whilst you are painting, you should make every effort to ensure your work is kept as clean as possible. Try to avoid splashing paint, dropping your brush or accidentally smudging wet paint with your hand, as this will cause your work to look untidy and unprofessional. Obviously, accidents do happen from time to time and can usually be rectified, but it is best to try and avoid them happening in the first place. It is wise to mask your painting as you work on it. This can simply be done by partially covering your work with a piece of paper or tracing paper, or better still, by cutting a square hole roughly 4in × 4in in a large piece of clear acetate that you can then work through. The advantage of using acetate is that you can still see the rest of your painting whilst working on a small area.

You will also need to consider how you will protect your work between painting sessions. Your painting may take you many hours to complete, so leaving it out during times when you are not painting can make it prone to attracting dust, pet hair or worse still, vulnerable to spillages, items being dropped on it or simply being knocked off the work surface and so on. After every painting session, always put your work away, either in a plan chest or portfolio to protect it.

USING PREPARATIONS AS AIDS

From time to time, it is possible that the use of preparations such as ox gall liquid, gum Arabic or masking fluid might be useful. Such preparations have been used for many years by watercolour artists; they are designed to make working with this medium easier, and to assist with achieving the effects you want. The following is a guide to some of the preparations available.

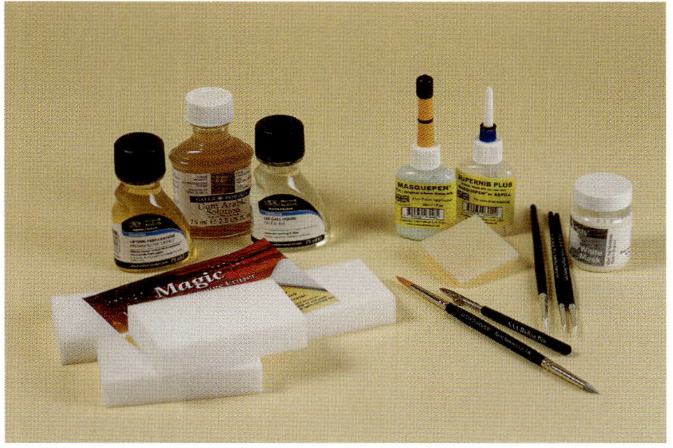

Ox gall liquid, gum Arabic, lifting preparation and masking fluid are all useful preparations in botanical illustration; use a magic erasing sponge with care to eradicate unwanted smudges and paint splashes.

OX GALL LIQUID

An additive used by watercolourists to aid and improve the wetting and flow of paint, ox gall liquid is obtained from cattle. It works by reducing the surface tension of the water. A few drops to your water before mixing paint will allow your watercolour to move more freely on the paper when applied as a wash. It is ideal for using on hot-pressed paper, which can be prone to repelling liquid if it is heavily sized (as in the case of watercolour blocks).

GUM ARABIC

If you are using tubes of watercolour paint then gum Arabic is already present in the composition as a binder, but it can be bought separately and added to your mixing water. It is ideal for making watercolours rich and glossy, and intensifying the consistency and transparency. It is particularly helpful if you are creating gloss, perhaps on a leaf or berry, but should be used sparingly. It is best not to over use gum Arabic as it can be susceptible to cracking or reflecting light when dry.

MASKING FLUID

Masking fluid is used by many artists as a means of preserving areas of paper that need to remain white during the painting process. It is a liquid suspension formed of thin latex solution, which is applied with a special masque pen or silicone brush. It is advisable not to use a sable brush as the latex is difficult to remove from the bristles and may leave it permanently damaged. Masking fluid is applied to the surface of the paper and allowed to dry, before painting takes place. Once painting is completed, the areas of masking fluid are simply erased using an eraser.

For botanical painters, masking fluid is usually used to mask off areas where fine details are to be depicted, or where light-coloured attributes butt up to dark-coloured backgrounds, such as light-coloured stamens against dark-coloured tepals of a hellebore or clematis.

Some botanical painters find that masking fluid can be too messy to work with, usually because of the fine, small areas that need to be masked. Diluting the masking fluid with a little water first will help to improve its flow.

To use masking fluid, follow this method:

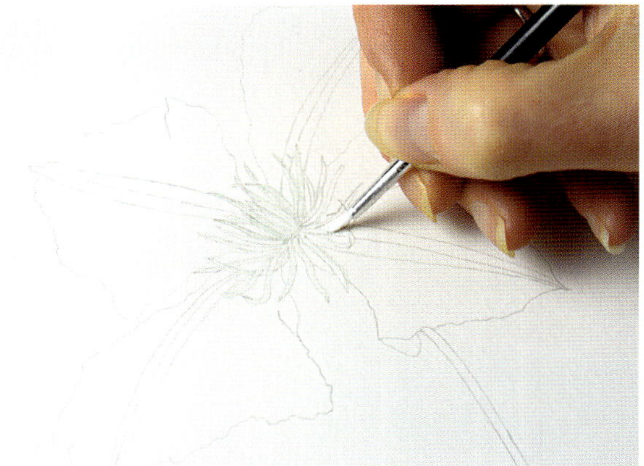

Step 1. Carefully paint the areas to be masked.

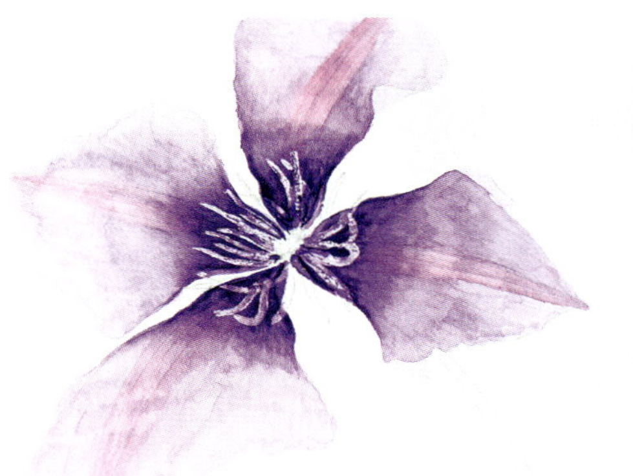

Step 2. Progress your painting as you would normally, painting over the masked areas.

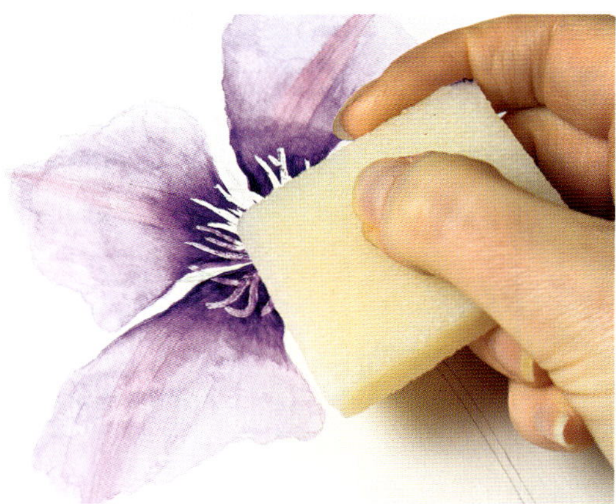

Step 3. Once you have completed your painting and it is dry, carefully remove the masking fluid by lifting with an adhesive pick-up eraser.

LIFTING PREPARATION

Lifting preparation allows you to easily lift paint from your painting and can be used as an alternative to masking fluid. The liquid is painted onto the surface before painting takes place, and allowed to dry. Once painting has been completed, the areas to be lifted can be gently raised by using a clean, damp brush. It is a useful preparation for preventing colours such as reds and maroons from staining the surface of the paper when lifted.

LIFTING SPONGE

Although not a preparation, a lifting sponge (sometimes called a magic eraser) is ideal for removing areas of paint or small smudges from around your painting. It works in a similar way to a ceramic wall tile stain-removing sponge, and is a relatively new product to enter the art world. A handy item, the lifting sponge is lightweight and can be cut down in size as required. It is simply used, just dipped lightly into clean water and the excess squeezed out, before using on your painting.

COMMON PROBLEMS

Even the most accomplished artists will from time to time experience problems during their painting. It is seldom that a piece of work will run totally smoothly without a hiccup along the way, so you should not become disheartened should you encounter a problem, it is quite normal.

Occasionally, problems arise when a new product is being used for the first time. For example, a new brand of watercolours, when the artist may not be familiar with the staining and granulating properties of some of the colours, or perhaps a new brand of watercolour paper whereby the paint lifts more readily than a previous paper which was more absorbent. It is understood that problems such as these can be minimized if the artist invests time to practise with the new materials before starting a painting, to avoid being 'caught out' during the painting process.

Some common problems occur which are technique-based. It is wise to suggest that an artist should employ techniques that he/she has tried and tested, and which demonstrate appropriateness to the subject being painted, but problems do arise from time to time. When they do, they should always be dealt with in a calm and confident manner, as overreacting and trying to deal with the problem immediately or without thinking can cause it to become worse.

If you are new to botanical painting – or using watercolours for the first time – it is often the most immediate and natural response to panic when something doesn't go well. However, watercolour is a versatile medium; a resolution to a problem can usually be sought, so with a little knowledge of how you might overcome a problem, there is usually no call for immediate concern.

DEALING WITH COMMON PROBLEMS DURING PAINTING

As you paint, try to do so in a relaxed and confident manner, as very often problems occur when the artist feels nervous or worried about the finished outcome of their work. This will come with practice, like many things; as you encounter problems and deal with them logically and successfully, they will begin to minimize over time. Here are a few common problems and how to deal with them.

HARD WATER LINES IN WASHES

Hard water lines occur at the edges of a wash if too much water has been used to apply the paint. Often, they are not visible until the paint has dried so you may not notice them at first. You can solve the problem by taking a clean, damp, pointed brush to gently re-wet the paint line, and move or 'feather' it to create a softer edge. The brush must not be too wet, so ensure you remove the excess moisture by dabbing it on your rag. The paint should merge sufficiently with the background, and the hard, visible line will be eradicated. If necessary, once the area is dry again, apply an additional wash over the top to blend even more.

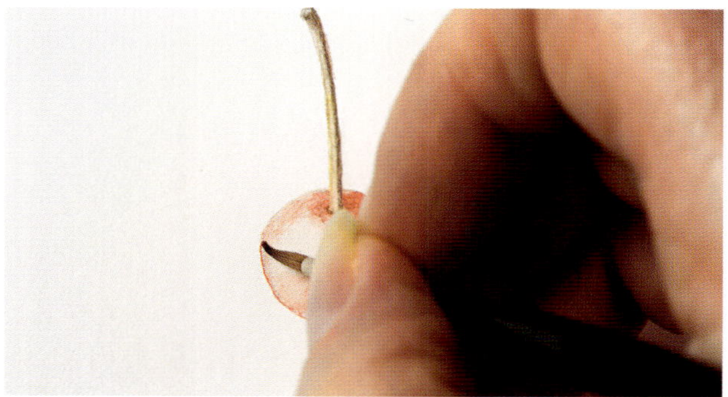

Eliminate the hard line at the edge of a wash by gently dampening it with a pointed brush, and feathering it into the surrounding paint.

'CAULIFLOWER' EFFECT IN WET-INTO-WET TECHNIQUE

This usually unwanted effect is the result of wetter paint being added to the dampened surface too soon. It is known as the 'cauliflower' effect because usually the pattern left behind resembles that of a cauliflower head. Timing is key during the wet-into-wet technique to achieve the correct effect; the damp surface must not be too wet (glossy) before adding the paint, so through practice, this problem can be avoided. However, if you do encounter a 'cauliflower', the easiest solution is to wait until it is fully dry before doing anything. Do not be tempted to fiddle with it, as this will usually make the problem worse. Once the area is dry, the method used for eradicating hard water lines can be applied to soften the edges.

PAINT LIFTING OFF DURING WASHES

Discovering that underlying paint suddenly lifts off as you apply multiple layers can be quite disheartening. This will happen if you have not left initial washes to dry properly before adding more, or there are so many layers that the paint simply will not adhere to the paper surface any more. The simple solution here is to ensure you allow sufficient time for initial washes to dry in between applications, or make your initial washes stronger and more intensely coloured, which will alleviate the need for multiple washes. If this doesn't solve the problem, simply allow any damp paint to thoroughly dry before

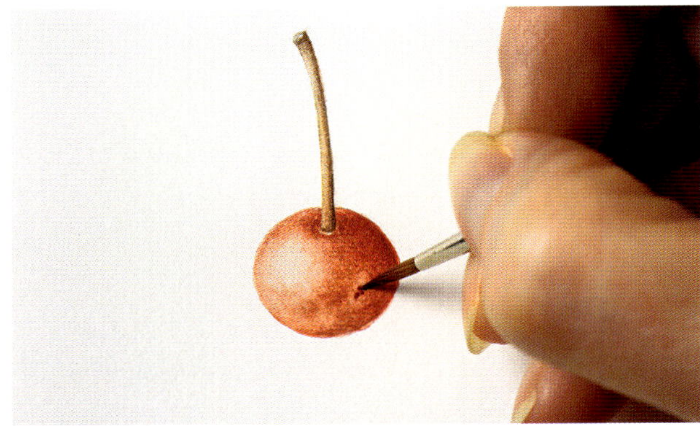

Carefully stipple colour into a 'hole' in the paint, before gently smoothing it into the surrounding area with a damp brush.

carefully stippling paint into any holes that have occurred, and then feathering gently with a slightly damp brush, to blend with the surrounding paint.

VISIBLE BRUSH STROKES IN PAINT WORK

Ugly brush strokes in the paint, usually caused by mixing a thin consistency, can be unsightly and often rebuked. However, this is quite a common problem for inexperienced artists who are still learning about watercolours and colour mixing. Learning through practice is the only way to deal with this problem; adjusting the ratios of paint and water will help, and will yield differing results. You may find you encounter this problem more if you are using student colours, or if you are using pans instead of tubes. If you are using pans, which are dry, it will take longer to achieve a thicker consistency of paint compared with tubes, which are already malleable.

All watercolours are unique in their composition, which you will discover as you use them more and more. You may find in some tube paints that a separation has occurred between the pigment and the gum Arabic binder, so that when you first squeeze the tube only a clear oily substance comes out. This happens if the tube is new, or it has been stored for a long time since it was manufactured. Do not be tempted to mix the binder into your palette, as this will cause oily brush strokes to appear in your work. Instead, discard the binder, replace the cap on the tube and knead it a little so that the binder becomes mixed properly with the pigment.

Some watercolour pans, despite generally taking longer to 'work' than tubes, may appear excessively difficult to use and you constantly end up with brush strokes in your work. Occasionally, the only answer is to discard them and replace with new ones, or invest in a different brand such as Rembrandt, which offer pans containing some gum Arabic.

Checklist for Developing a Painting

- Start in the right frame of mind; be positive.
- Consider the techniques you might use for painting, in advance of starting.
- Practise new painting techniques such as wet-into-wet on scraps of paper first.
- Use your brush like a pencil for drawing when adding details using the dry brush technique.
- Show good contrast between highlights and shadows when modelling and developing 3D.
- Take care to colour match accurately to your specimen.
- Add some aerial perspective to differentiate between foreground and background.
- Use relevant techniques to help convey texture.
- Try using some preparations to help with your painting.
- Deal with common problems without panicking, and don't be afraid to make mistakes.

Case Study

As the shapes of the berries of *Fuchsia magellanica* were relatively simplistic, these were painted first. The tonal studies were referred to in the sketchbook, to ensure the nuances of detail were captured in the vertical ridges evident in each berry. A dry brush technique was used to work from dark to light across each berry, and to create the 3D structure of the internal locules; each ridge was emphasized slightly using darker paint.

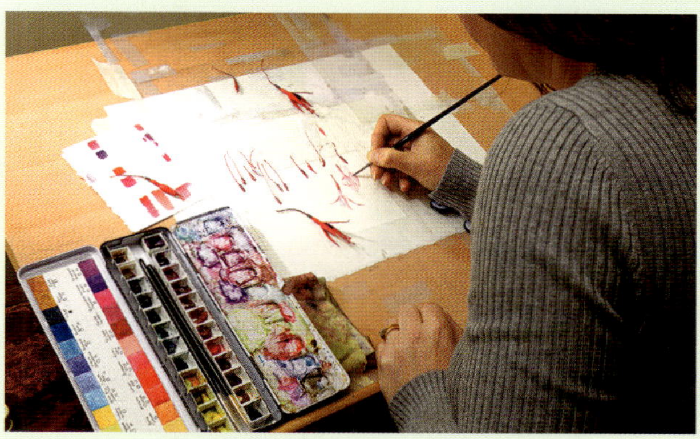

Painting in progress of *Fuchsia magellanica*.

Once the berries were completed, enough mix of Quinacridone Magenta and Winsor Red was made to begin painting the sepals of the flowers. Individual flowers were collected and brought to the studio for reference, and to clarify the colour choices already decided for the mix, and were used in conjunction with the sketchbook drawings and notes to create realistic shapes. The Anglepoise lamp was used to help determine where the highlights and shadows should fall on each sepal, and a dry brush technique was used to emphasize modelling and add detail after a preliminary flat was applied. The petals were also worked on at this stage using the same technique. Once all the sepals and petals of each open flower had been painted, the stamens, stigmas and styles were added in, followed by the flower buds. A suggestion of aerial perspective was indicated at this stage, but would need to be emphasized further, once more of the painting was complete.

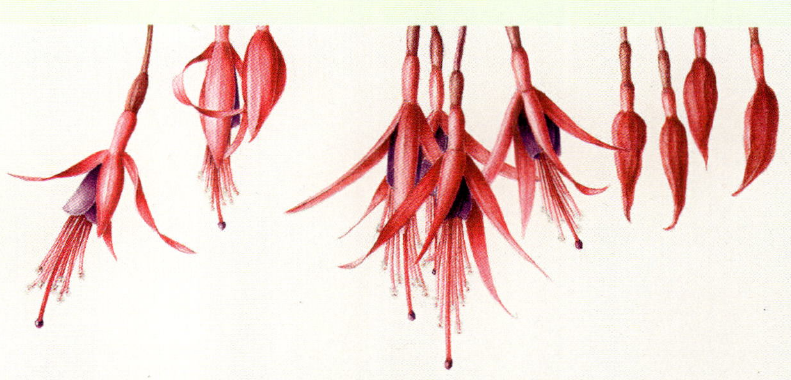

Details of the painted flowers of *Fuchsia magellanica*.

To put the flowers and berries into context within the composition, the next area to be worked on was the flowering and supporting stems. Each group of flowers and berries evolves from nodes along the stems, so it was important to anchor these to the stems before painting the leaves.

There is a distinct difference in the colouration of different parts of the stems, with the growing tip of the main stem and side stem being predominantly pink. The gradual transition of this colour to the browner, thicker part of the main stem was achieved using a blend of the correct colours in a preliminary flat wash, before being intensified with a dry brush technique over the top. An indication of the darker shadow areas on the undersides of the stems was also suggested, but would be worked on further once the leaves have been painted fully.

Finally, at this stage, a preliminary flat wash of green was used on each leaf (ensuring more Transparent Yellow was added to the mix for the younger leaves), and the petioles and midrib of the pink colour were also suggested, before further work to include details such as venation on the leaves would be applied later on.

At the end of this middle stage of the painting process, each part of the composition had been worked on, and an idea of how the final painting would look began to evolve.

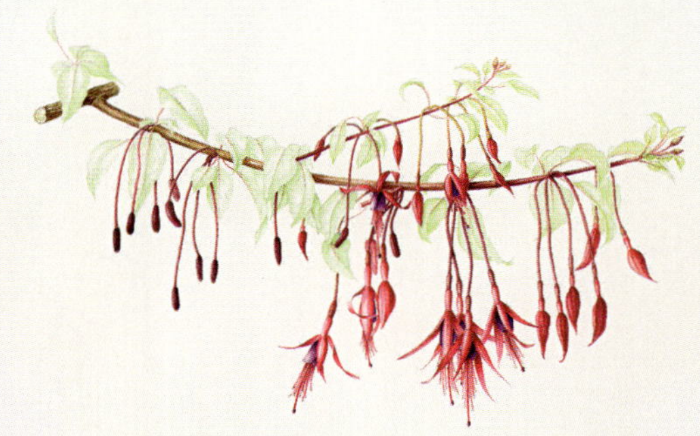

Painting of *Fuchsia magellanica* ready to be completed.

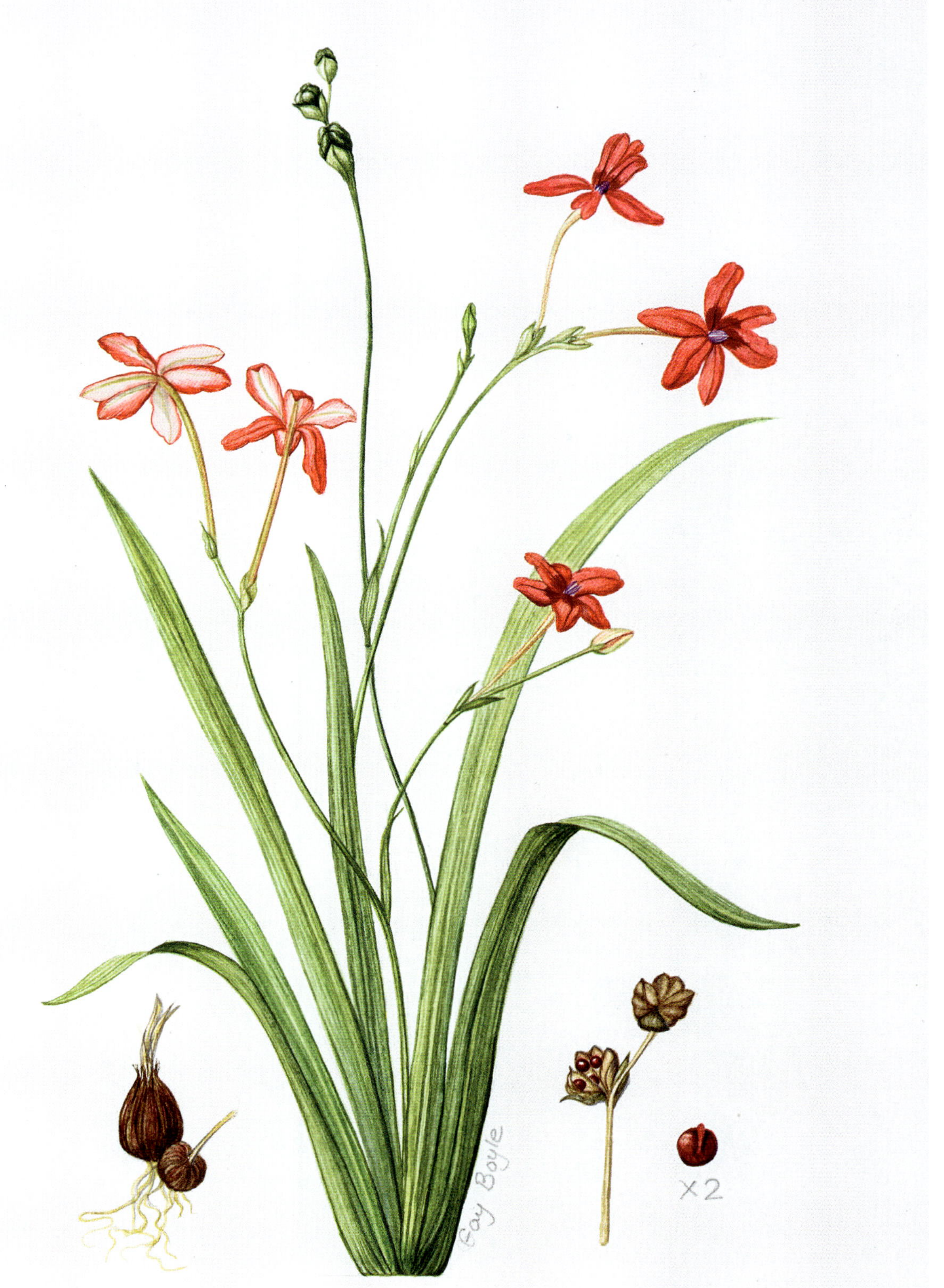
Gay Boyle
×2

CHAPTER 8

Completing a Painting

When you start a painting, it is somewhat outside you. At the conclusion, you seem to move inside the painting.

– Fernando Botero (Colombian figurative artist)

Without doubt, seeing a painting through to completion is one of the most satisfying aspects of botanical illustration. It is the point at which you will see the fruits of your labour harnessed together into a single image for the first time, and which you have come to know and feel extremely familiar with. The painting may have taken you many hours, days, weeks or even months to finalize, but hopefully you will have achieved your aim. Whether the painting is purely for yourself, a friend, or relative – or maybe even for an exhibition – the sense of achievement and satisfaction can be very rewarding. For professional artists, completing an illustration may simply be just one more to add to an already full portfolio, but for the amateur, completing a first project can be a truly momentous occasion.

A dilemma for some artists, and quite understandably, is knowing when a painting is considered finished. How do you actually know when a painting is finished? What are the deciding factors? It is common for these questions to be raised each time a painting nears completion, but with experience and practice, the answers will emerge and become clear.

Working through the stages of developing your painting towards completion usually indicates that you have worked carefully and consistently through the process. When you consider your painting to be virtually finished, then it will be time to check that you have everything accurate and correct, that there are no errors or other ambiguities, and to apply some finishing touches.

Anomatheca. GAY BOYLE

At this stage, you should check that all your edges are neat, clean, and crisp and any rogue paint splatters or other paint or graphite marks are cleared. If you are including magnifications and dissections, then you should also ensure you have indicated them or included scale bars where necessary. These final few tweaks to your illustration count for a lot, and can clearly make the difference between a good and a very good piece of work.

The final stage of the painting process is described in this chapter. Work through each process to ensure that you achieve a completed illustration that will be ready to mount and frame.

HOW DO I KNOW WHEN MY PAINTING IS FINISHED?

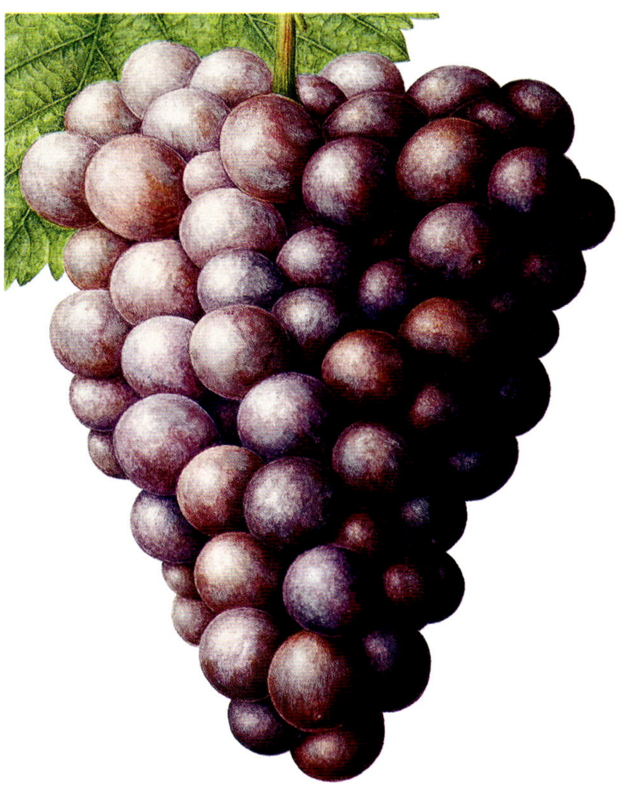

Check that your painting is complete. For example, on a bunch of grapes, that the shadows are strong enough when the grapes overlap each other, and reflected light has been added. The Great Vine at Hampton Court Palace. LEIGH ANN GALE

If you have painted your illustration using a series of washes and dry brush detail, then you will have a virtually completed piece of work in front of you. Although fundamentally your illustration is finished, it can often be difficult to judge whether your painting might benefit from adding a few extra washes (known as glazes at this stage of painting), or a little more detail in one or two places. However, it is all too easy to overwork the painting, so knowing when to stop is key. It may be helpful – if time allows – to put your work away or out of sight for a few days, because up until this point you will most likely have spent so many hours working on your painting that it has in a way become too familiar to you, and you may not be able to make an informed assessment of it to know whether it needs more work or not. Once you see your painting again after a period of time, it will be fresh to your eye, and it may now be clear that you could easily add more to it. For example, it may be obvious that you could fill an awkward gap of negative space you hadn't noticed before with an extra bud or leaf, to enhance the composition. However, care should be taken when making such decisions, and they should only be made if it is conceivable that an extra bud or leaf could actually exist in the space on the specimen. You should never add extra details if they wouldn't naturally exist in the space you want to add them to. Conversely, you should not deliberately look for gaps, holes, or other open spaces either, just for the sake of wanting to add extra information, as this could also be inaccurate or make your work look too contrived.

Whilst you are assessing your work, look to see if all the botanical structures you have painted appear finished. For example, with a group of fruits or berries, that they are all of an equally finished state (allowing for some aerial perspective if applicable), that any overlapping berries have cast shadows onto underlying ones, and you have included any areas of reflected light if they are shiny berries. Now is the time to also darken any pockets of shadow which may be a little too light, or to enhance the 3D form of a bud or a stamen for example.

You should pay attention to how well you have matched the colours to your specimen, that you have studied them in natural light (or daylight simulation), and that they are completely accurate. If they need adjusting, then it is possible to do this by adding glazes to alter the hues.

Only when you are completely satisfied that you have checked all your painting for information, accuracy, and consistency of finish, will you know whether it is finished or not. Remember your overall aim is to accurately illustrate a species, so your painting must represent and describe that species fully.

Sometimes an artist may seek guidance from a fellow artist whose opinion they trust. An additional pair of eyes to scan over your work can be very helpful, particularly if you regularly struggle to evaluate whether your painting is finished or not, which can be the case if you work alone, or without the regular support of other artists around you. Someone else's opinion can help to highlight areas that may need attention, which you may not have otherwise spotted for yourself, or the other person may offer a suggestion for an addition to your illustration. Trusted opinions are invaluable, so it is advisable to make asking for them a regular exercise when you near completion of a painting.

The following are some suggestions to consider when completing your painting, and which, once addressed, will help you determine when your painting is finished.

CHECKING FOR ERRORS AND AMBIGUITY

As you near completion of your illustration you should allow time to check that you have painted everything in accordance with your specimen and your original drawings. This is a fundamental requirement, in that it should be clear that you haven't introduced any errors (such as unintentionally painting in negative space areas), and there is no ambiguity such as misleading or confusing information being shown. Occasionally, as you look carefully at your work, you may come across parts where you ask yourself, 'what is happening here?' If you find yourself doing this, then it is highly likely that your viewer will also have difficulty in understanding your painting, in which case you need to address the problem and correct it. Ideally, you should not come across such errors, but from time to time they can creep in without you realizing, or they may only become obvious after you have finished painting.

Double-check your painting against your original drawing, as most introduced errors at the painting stage occur because of poor transferral of the image to final painting paper. If you can see where you have gone wrong, then set about correcting the error or ambiguity before doing anything else. Common ambiguities often include the edges of two leaves touching side by side awkwardly; the misalignment of a stem as it travels behind a leaf or flower and then does not realign at the correct place, and the juxtaposition of two structures where it is not clear which one is in front and which one is behind.

Check that your colour matching is accurate; add glazes if necessary to alter a hue (*see* 'Adding glazes' in this chapter).

It is usually possible with careful attention to alter or amend errors at the painting stage. If you are unsure about if or how you could make an amendment, practise first on a spare piece of paper.

CHECKING LINES ARE PARALLEL OR STRAIGHT

Another common error in an illustration is the case of parallel lines. Although many stems and veins tend to taper towards their extremities, not all do so. Parallel lines often occur in botanical structures such as the filaments of a stamen and the square-sided stem of a pansy flower. You must ensure that you have observed them accurately and that you draw and paint them as parallel lines.

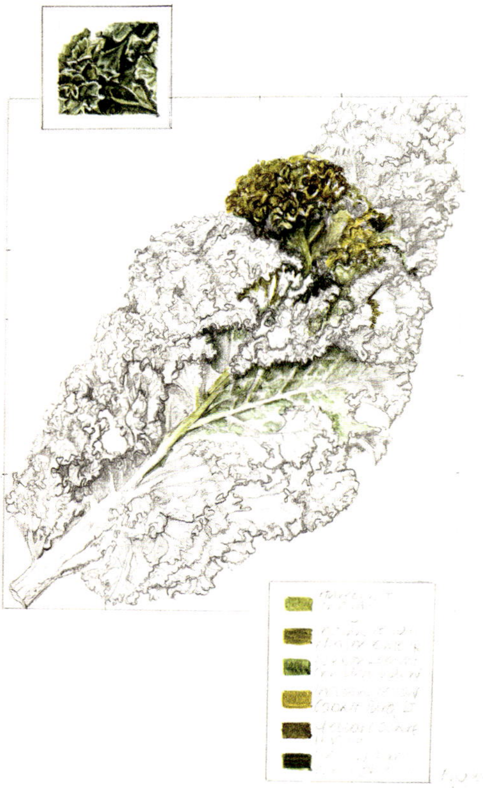

Correct any errors such as incorrect colour matches. Here, the artist corrected the kale leaf colour before finalizing her painting. Kale Leaf sketch. VICKY SHARMAN

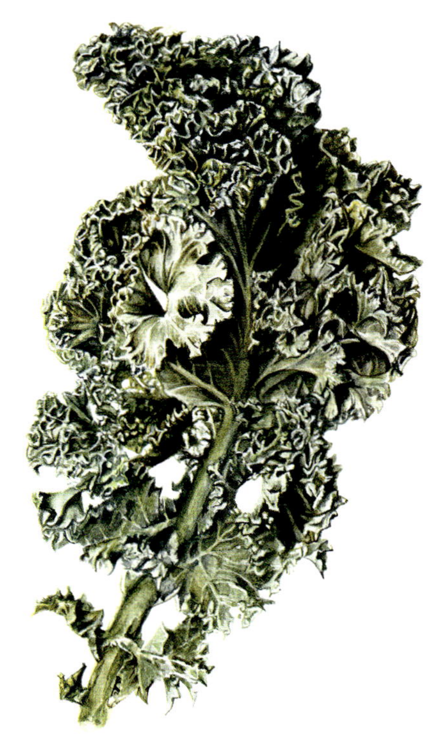

Kale Leaf. VICKY SHARMAN

You should also check whatever lines you are painting for bulges and kinks, and minimize any that you can see by carefully applying or lifting paint. A good test for checking that you have all your lines straight is to view them as foreshortened lines. You can do this by picking up your painting, bringing it up to eye level, then tilt it away from you. Rotate the painting so that you appear to be looking down the line you have painted, so that you see a foreshortened view. You will soon spot any anomalies in the straightness of your painted lines. Adjust them by carefully adding or lifting paint, then re-check what you have done.

CHECKING SYMMETRY

You should always check carefully that you have indicated the symmetry of flowers and leaves correctly. Refer to Chapter 3 for descriptions of the different types of symmetry.

THE FINISHING TOUCHES

Putting the last-minute finishing touches to a painting can be a very satisfying job. Just a few minutes spent at this stage can dramatically change how your illustration looks. The few little tweaks you make now should be the absolute final amendments or adjustments you make, so try not to be tempted to 'fiddle' any further with your work once you have made them. This can be quite a difficult discipline, but can make the difference between a beautifully finished painting and a spoilt or overworked one.

ADDING GLAZES

Adding a glaze, which is another term for a wash added at the end of painting, can be successfully carried out to slightly alter the hue in parts of your painting. It is quick to do, but skill is needed so as not to disturb the underlying painted area.

The process of applying a glaze is rapid; ensure your painting is totally dry before attempting to add a glaze. Load your brush with a dilute mix of pigment and water, and paint over the area briskly, taking care not to settle the brush over one particular area for too long. You will notice how the glaze sits on top of the paint rather than soaking in to the paper, and the hue of the painted area will change.

A water glaze can also be added, if you do not wish to actually change the colour of your painting. This is a useful glaze, as it will enable you to smooth out any areas of underlying paint and eradicate brush strokes for example. Apply a water glaze in the same way as a normal glaze, ensuring that your painting is completely dry before you begin.

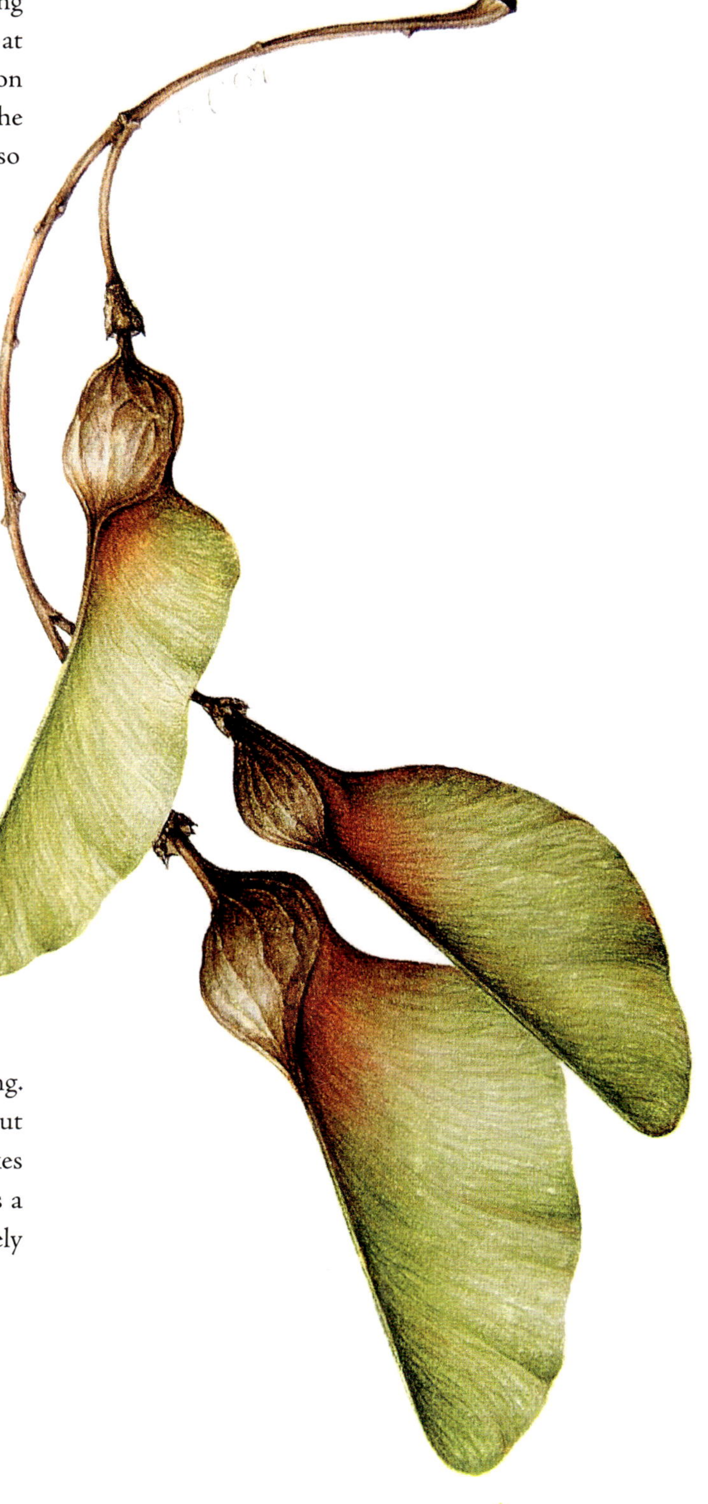

Tipuana Tree Samaras. LEIGH ANN GALE

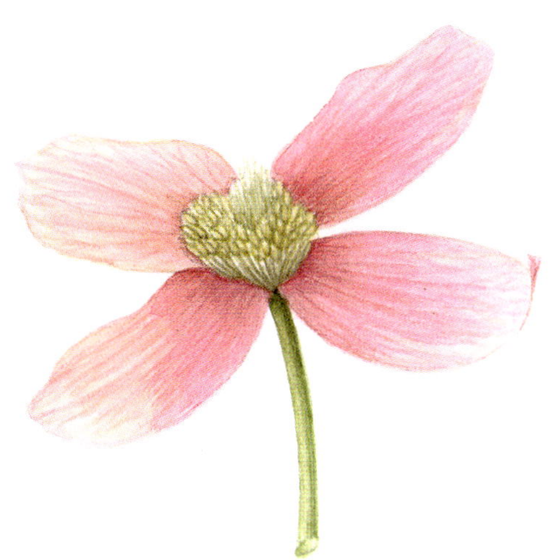

Add a glaze over parts of your painting to alter the colour.

CHECKING EDGES

Crisp and tidy edges should be one of your priorities when applying the finishing touches to your painting. Sadly, many a painting is let down because the artist has failed to address any 'fuzzy' painted edges, which greatly detracts from the overall quality of the work. This usually happens because the brush has not been formed to a good point before painting, or it has not been held upright enough to ensure only the point of the brush has been used.

The edges of your painting should clearly replicate what you can see on your specimen. For example, if the margin of a leaf is entirely smooth, so should your painted leaf margin be entirely smooth. If it appears fuzzy, you could unintentionally be describing a slightly hairy leaf margin for example, which wouldn't be correct for the species you are painting.

As you complete your painting, cast your eye over the edges you have painted. If you spot any fuzzy edges, now is the time to smooth them out with a well-pointed, slightly damp brush, or add a little more paint, or gently feather the existing paint into a finer line.

CHECKING YOU HAVE ADDED MAGNIFICATIONS OR SCALE BARS

If you have been painting an illustration that includes extra scientific drawings to better describe more complex structures of your specimen, then you will no doubt have included some magnifications and possibly dissections. To enable your viewer to have a clearer understanding of what you are trying to portray, it is vital that your drawings are not only drawn accurately, but there is also some indication of their size as well. You will do this by adding a magnification or a scale bar. (*See* Chapter 3 for more information about magnifications and scale bars.) Generally, unless your work is being reproduced in print, a magnification such as ×2 or ×5 is usually sufficient.

If you have included magnifications and dissections, then check that you have included an indication of their size with a written magnification or scale bar alongside each image.

CLEANING UP

A task often overlooked is cleaning up around your finished painting. You should take the opportunity to remove any excess graphite, small paint splatters or other marks that have appeared during the painting process. Unsightly marks detract from your illustration, and once noticed are very hard to ignore.

Ideally, you will have kept any potential for splashes and marks appearing to a minimum, however it is not uncommon for the odd accident to happen, so do your best to eradicate them.

If you notice any marks, clean them up carefully. A nylon brush can be used for marks in awkward, small places, as the bristles are slightly abrasive and should easily lift the mark. However, you should not overwork the area; only use single directional strokes. Do not be tempted to brush backwards and forwards as this will only aggravate the paper fibres and cause them to potentially lift. If you notice this happening, then allow the area to completely dry before burnishing the paper fibres back down through a piece of tracing paper using a metal burnishing spoon or equivalent.

For larger mistakes, such as paint smudges and splashes, use a piece of damp lifting sponge to eradicate the mark. Again, use single directional strokes to avoid damaging the paper fibres.

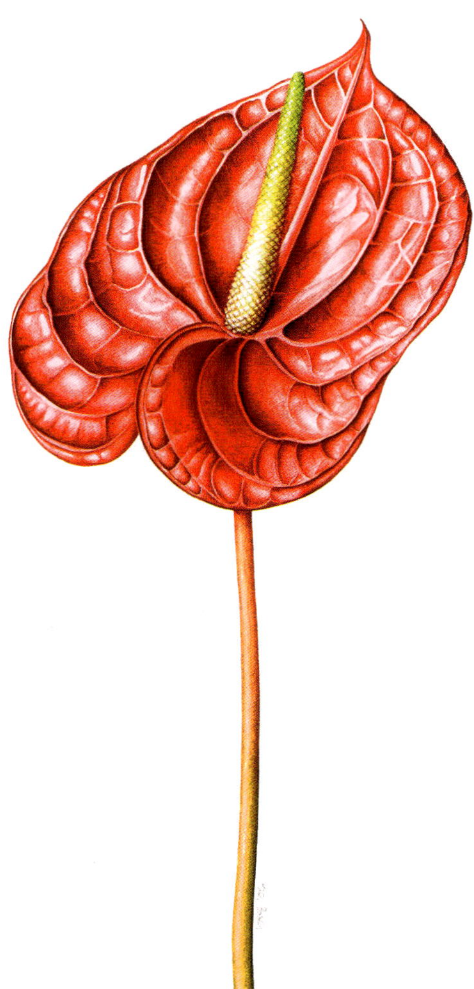

Check that edges are clean and crisp on your painting. *Anthurium andreanum*. LEIGH ANN GALE

Checklist for Completing a Painting

- Put your work away when it is virtually finished, before considering whether to add or adjust anything.
- When assessing your work, check that you have painted all the botanical structures well, and the colours are a true likeness to the specimen.
- Check for errors or ambiguity and make amendments.
- Ensure parallel lines are parallel and straight lines are straight. Correct any bulges and kinks.
- Check the symmetry of flowers and leaves; adjust any that are incorrect.
- Add glazes to alter the hue of parts of your painting if necessary.
- Tidy up any fuzzy edges.
- Ensure you have indicated magnifications or added scale bars to magnifications and dissections.
- Clean up splashes and marks around your painting.
- Ask a trusted fellow artist for their opinion of your painting; add any conceivable suggestions if they enhance the composition.
- When you have finished your painting leave it alone. Don't be tempted to fiddle with it and potentially overwork it.

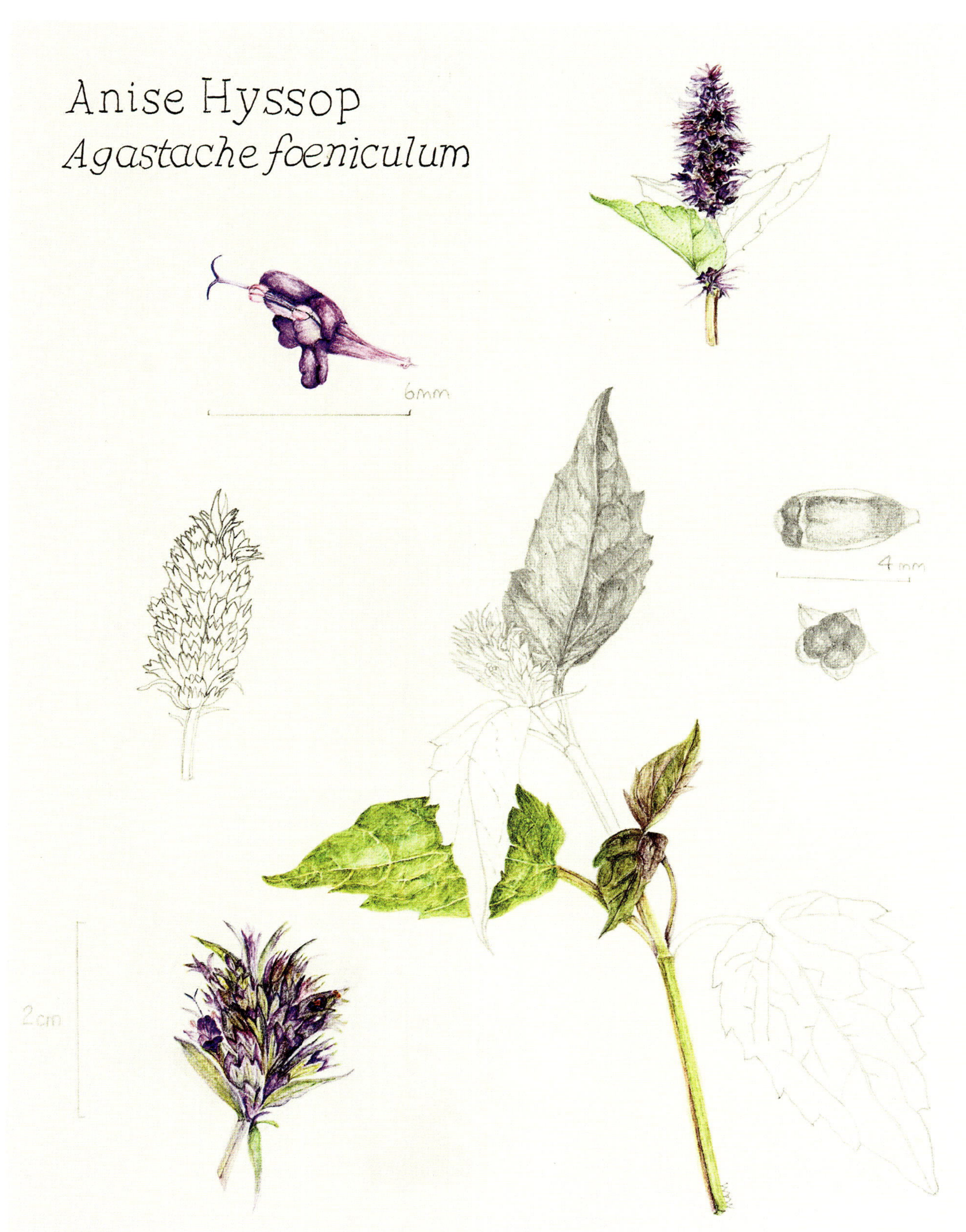

If you have added magnifications and scale bars to your work, check that they are accurate. *Agastache foeniculum*, Anise Hyssop. MURIEL MCINTOSH

Case Study

Progressing the painting of the leaves of *Fuchsia magellanica* was the next task towards completing the painting. By working progressively from left to right, painting the more mature leaves first, it was possible to ensure the very subtle transition between the darker, bluer green, to the slightly more yellow green of the younger leaves growing at the tips of the flowering stems. This was done by gradually adding more Transparent Yellow to the mix.

A small amount of aerial perspective was applied to some of the leaves falling away into the distance, and emphasis was given to the venation on the backs of any leaves that were visible. Care was taken to model the leaves according to where the highlights and shadows fell, and blend the paint between light and dark tones in such a way that would emulate the texture of the reasonably smooth, soft surfaces of the leaves.

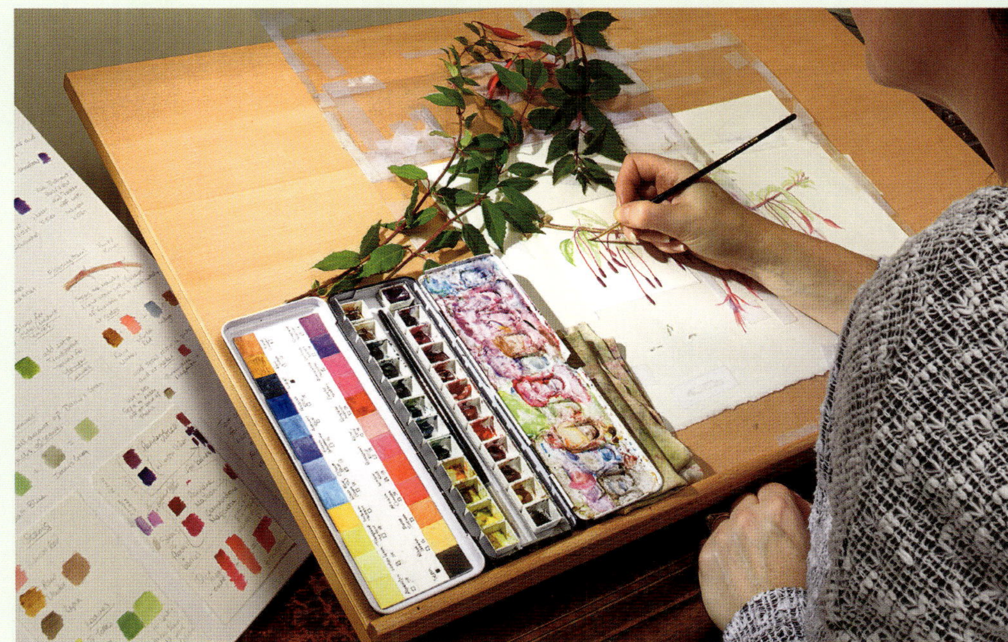

The leaves of *Fuchsia magellanica* being painted.

Once the leaves were completed, more definition was given to the stems to make them appear more three-dimensional. This was done by darkening up the areas of shadow where leaves, flowers or stems overlapped the wood, using Sepia in the darkest shadows. The subtle markings on the wood were also enhanced, as was the colouration of the stems from the cool brown of the mature wood on the left, to the warmer pink wood of the tender flowering tips.

Attention was then given to the flowers and buds, defining areas of shadow where overlaps occurred, and subtly enhancing the saturation of colour in the flowers and buds that appear in the foreground of the composition. A light pink/red glaze was also applied to the Fuchsia berries, to slightly intensify their warmth.

As the painting reached completion, checks were made around the edges of all leaves, stems, flowers and berries, to ensure the painted edges were neat and tidy. A water glaze was added to several leaves to further soften some of the colour blends, and the whole painting was checked for any signs of ambiguity in any of the botanical structures. Finally, a putty rubber was used to erase any tiny areas of graphite left over from the transferral process at the composition stage, and to lift any particles of dust that had fallen on the painting during the painting process.

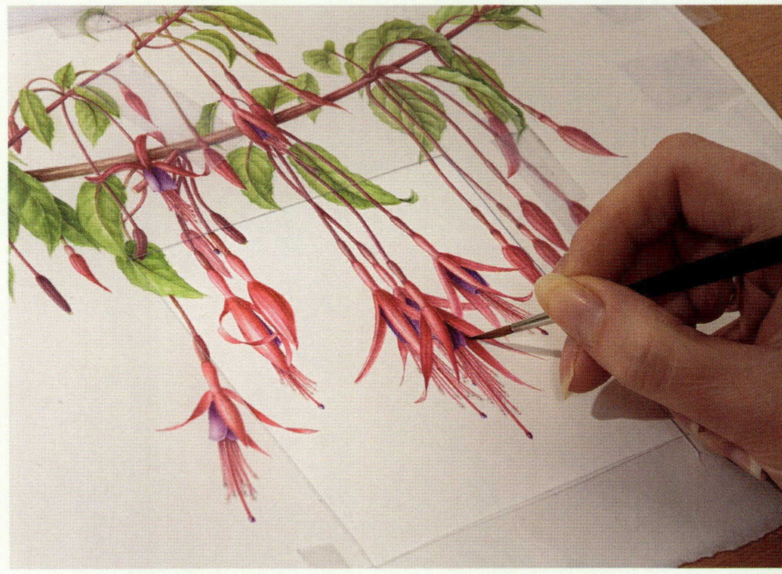

Adding the finishing touches to the flowers of *Fuchsia magellanica*.

The painting was now complete, and ready to be covered and protected before being mounted (*see* Chapter 11).

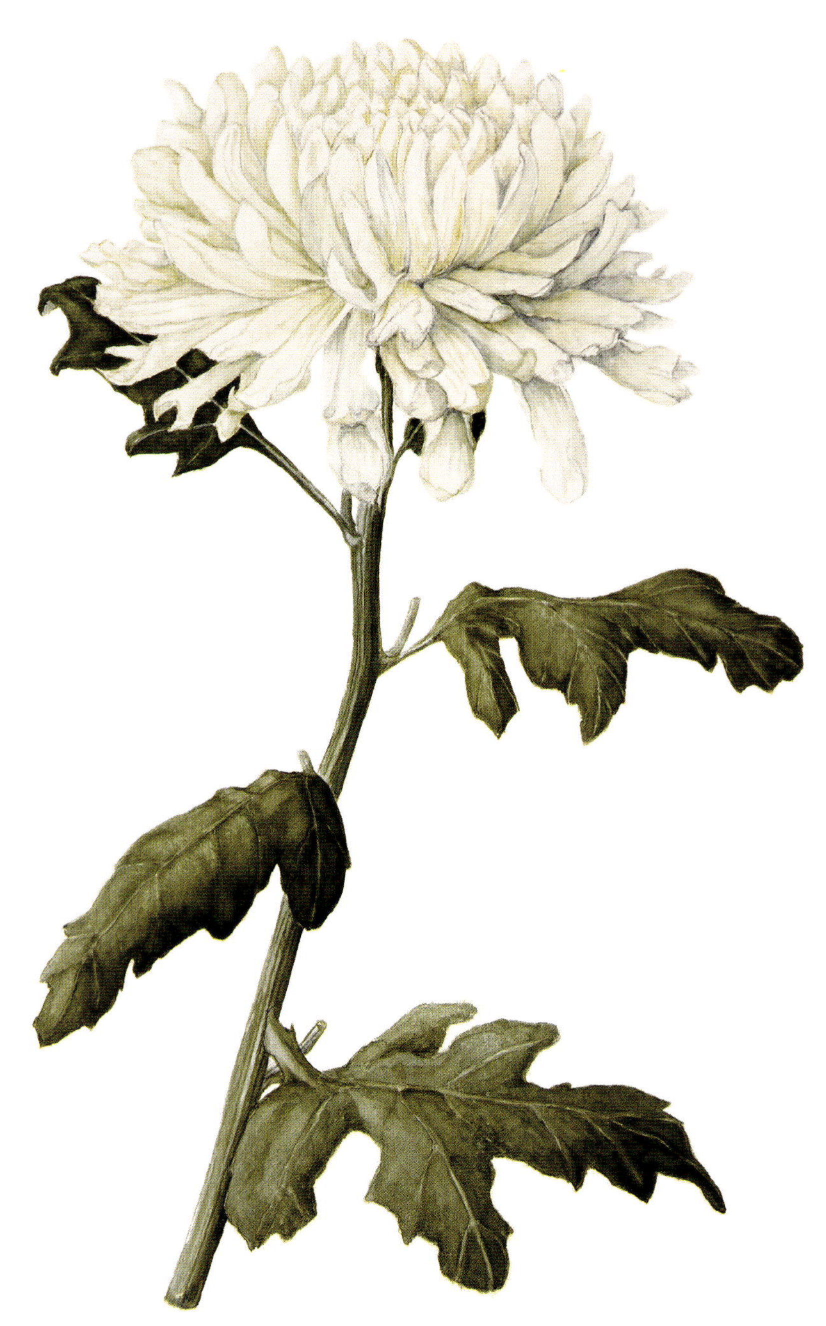

CHAPTER 9

Specific Painting Techniques

When your technique and your ideas support each other and the image becomes the vehicle of that expression, then you will have found your voice or niche.

– Henry Bateman (British cartoonist, 1887–1970)

Throughout the painting process you will from time to time need to use specific painting techniques to accurately describe the details of your subject matter. For example, the shiny or textured surfaces of leaves, or the bloom on plums and grapes. Techniques such as creating hairs on stems, building up the rich velvety texture of pansies, or forming the finest point of a thorn, are as much about the practical skills involved as the vision of how these effects should appear in your final painting. You will need to closely observe the thickness, length, and direction of the lay of hairs for example, or the mix of colours needed to subtly depict 'grey' shadows on a white flower, so that the effects look as real and naturalistic as possible.

Some of the most common specific painting techniques in botanical illustration are described in this chapter, using a step-by-step format. Before committing yourself to trying any of the techniques on your painting, make sure you observe your subject matter very closely (maybe with a magnifying glass in some cases), and then practise the techniques first on scraps of paper. You may find that you need to adapt some of the methods to suit you personally, and this is fine to do, as long as you work carefully and accurately to obtain the correct effects.

As you progress with more and more painting, you may also discover entirely new methods for achieving results, as and when you come across new features and characteristics of your subject matter.

White Chrysanthemum. SUE HANNELL

TECHNIQUES FOR PAINTING BOTANICAL FORMS, TEXTURES AND SPECIAL EFFECTS

The structures of flowers, fruits and berries are generally regarded as being more three-dimensional than leaves, which in the main, we tend to perceive as appearing much flatter. Although all botanical structures are three-dimensional, it is easier to separate the specific painting techniques for painting leaves into a separate section for the purposes of this book.

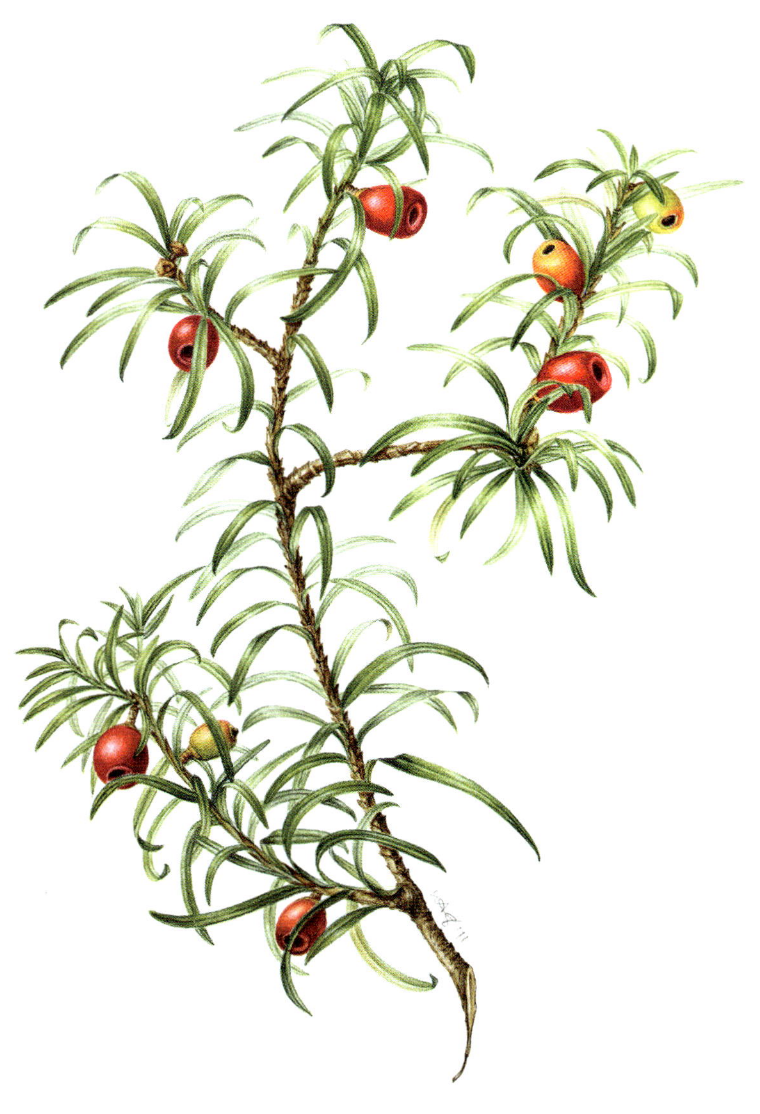

Taxus baccata 'Fastigiata'. LEIGH ANN GALE

CREATING HIGHLIGHTS ON SHINY BERRIES

To make a berry look shiny you will need to show the highlights very distinctly. It will be necessary to show a hard edge around the highlight on the smoothest reflective surface, such as a rowan or holly berry.

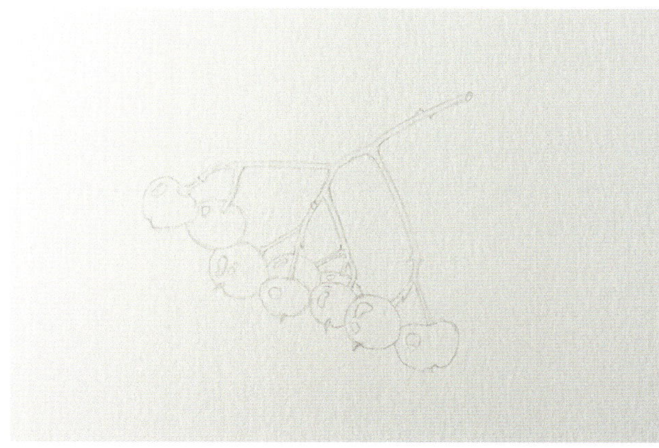

Step 1. To paint a small group of rowan berries. Firstly, note where the highlight(s) appear and draw them in lightly with a pencil.

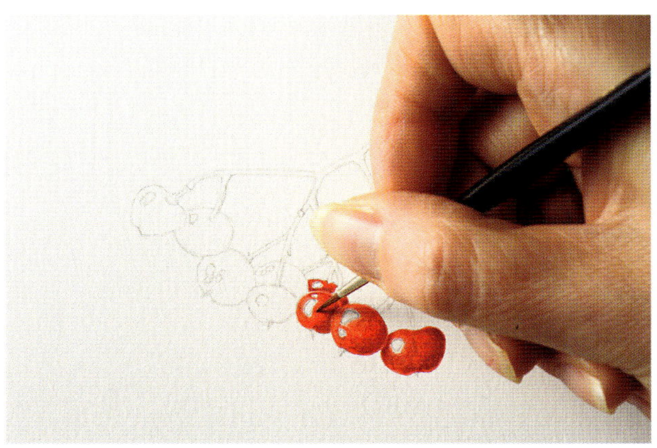

Step 2. Paint the berries using your preferred painting method, paying attention not to paint over the edge of the highlight.

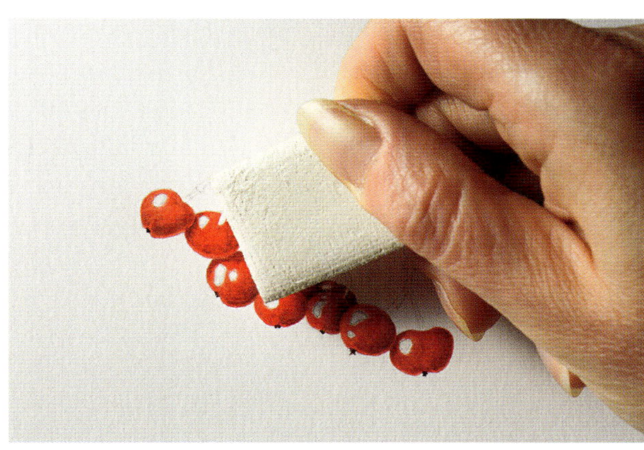

Step 3. Once the paint is dry, carefully rub out the pencil lines of the highlight.

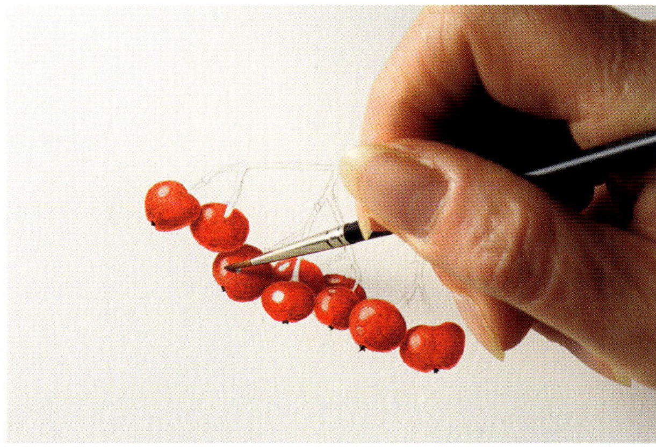

Step 4. Briskly apply a very pale, dilute wash over the highlight. Never leave a 'white' highlight as pure paper white.

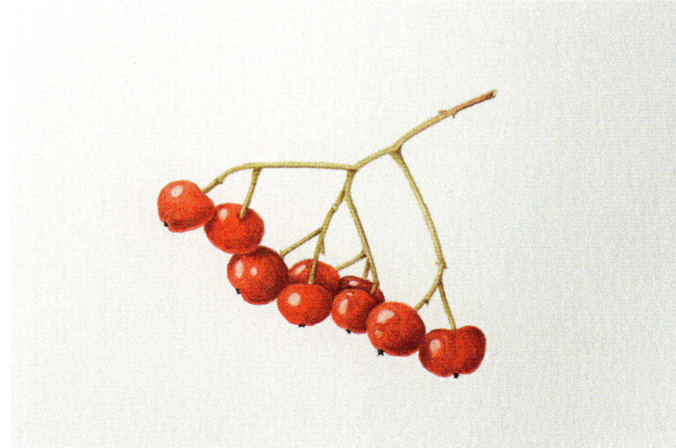

Step 5. Complete the painting by adding in the stalks for each berry.

CREATING SOFT HIGHLIGHTS ON FRUIT

For softer highlights on fruits, such as those on a peach, you will need to create a soft edge around the highlights because the surface of the peach is less reflective.

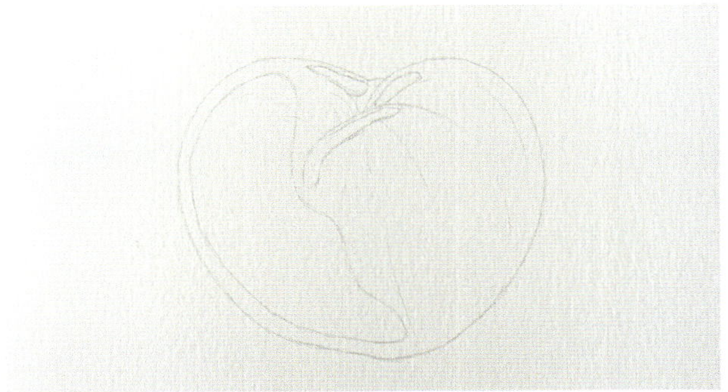

Step 1. Begin by drawing the outline of the peach and noting where the highlight(s) appear. Draw them in lightly with a pencil.

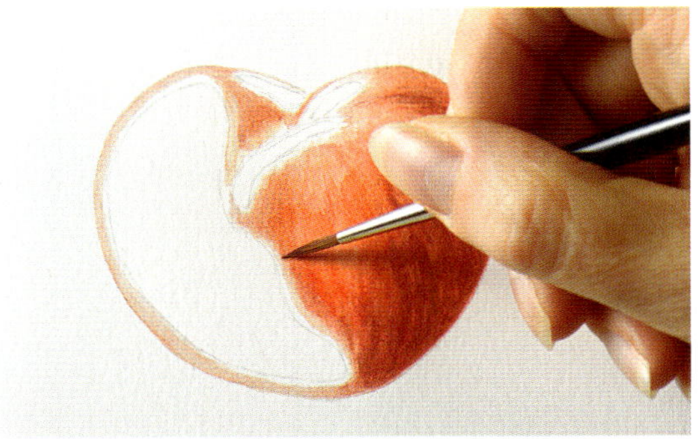

Step 2. Paint the peach using your preferred painting method, taking care not to paint over the lines for the highlights.

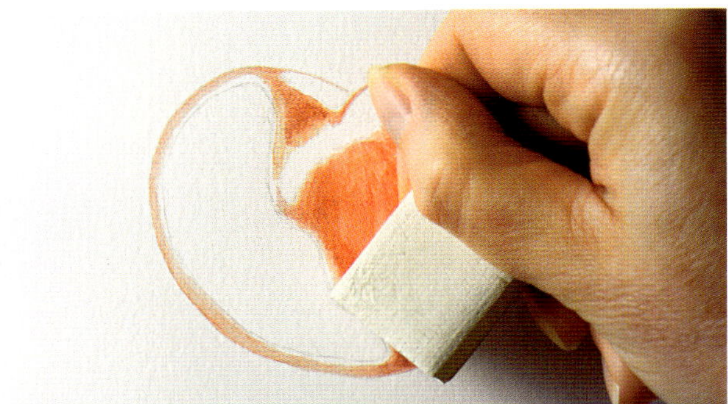

Step 3. Carefully rub out the pencil lines of the highlight when the paint is almost dry.

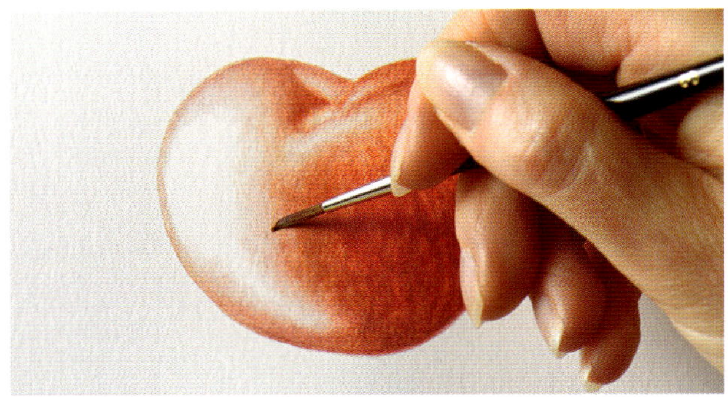

Step 4. Feather the edges of the paint into the highlight areas with a slightly damp brush, making a gradual transition.

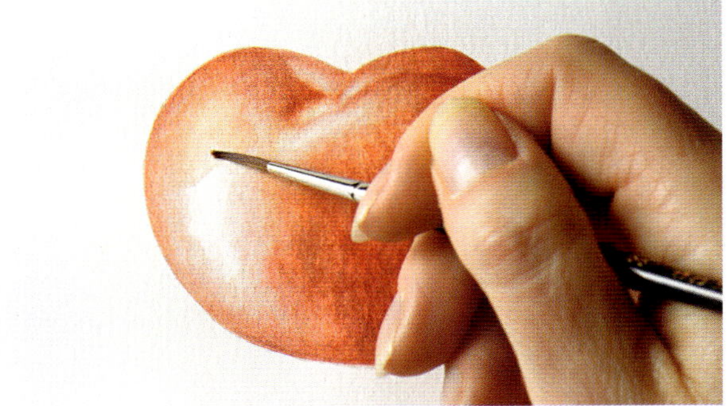

Step 5. Once the paint is dry, briskly apply a pale, dilute wash over the highlight and blend with the surrounding paint. Never leave a 'white' highlight as pure paper white.

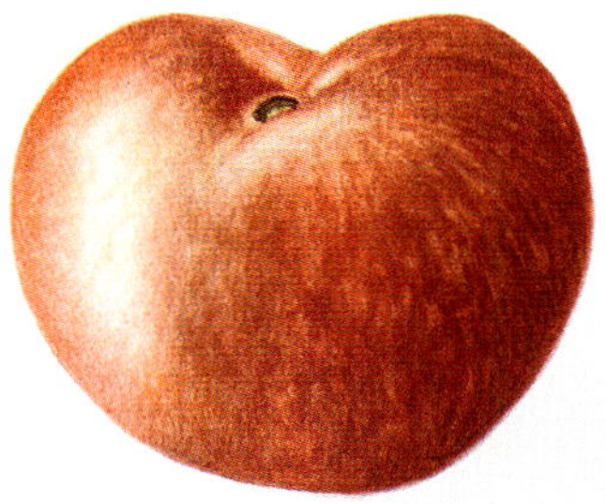

Step 6. Complete the painting by touching up any areas of paint that need further blending or extra shadows, and add detail to indicate the position of the stalk.

PAINTING THORNS

Painting a convincingly sharp-looking thorn can appear challenging, but is actually quite a straightforward process. Looking carefully at the shape of a thorn and its attachment to the stem is key, and is the first step in painting a believable sharp thorn.

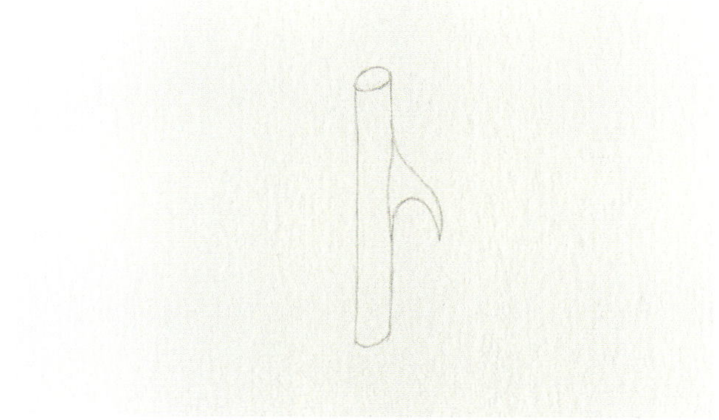

Step 1. Make an accurate drawing of your thorn, which should look like a protrusion from the stem, rather than looking as though it is 'stuck on'. To draw a convincing shape, begin and finish drawing on the stem line. This will help you make a convincing curved line between the stem and the thorn.

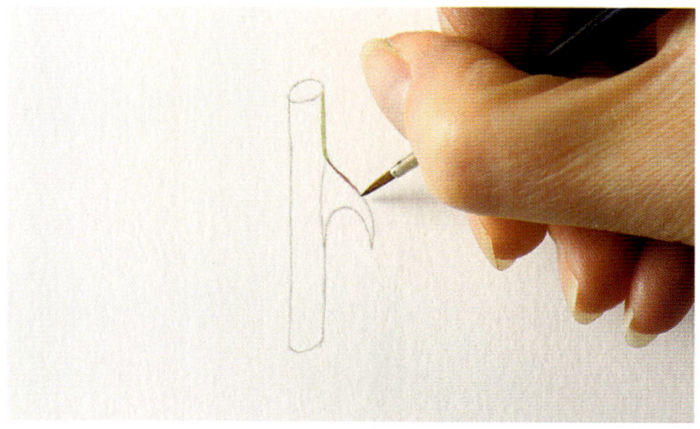

Step 2. Paint the outline of the thorn using dry brush technique, starting at the point on the stem where the thorn evolves. Holding the brush in an almost upright position, paint towards the tip of the thorn, to achieve a good, sharp point. If necessary, rotate the paper when painting what would be the upward stroke from the bottom.

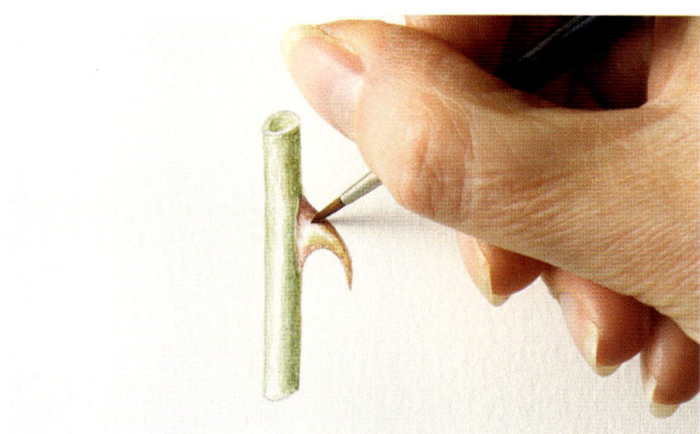

Step 3. Once the outline is painted, continue painting the thorn with your chosen technique, taking care not to paint over the outline. Take note of any colour differences between the stem and the thorn, and remember that the thorn is a 3D shape, so allow for highlights and shadows.

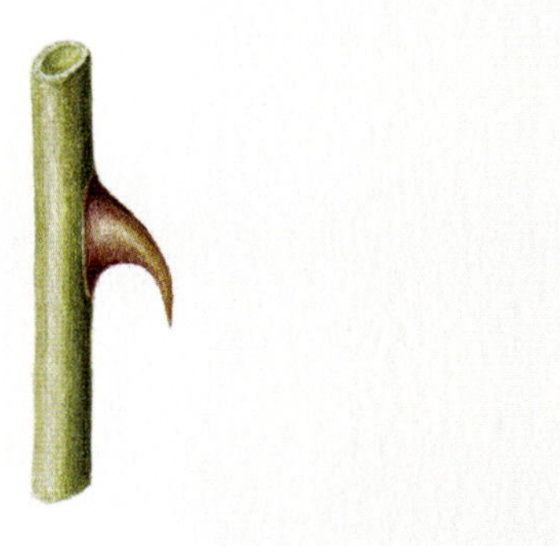

Step 4. Complete the painting by intensifying the shadows and highlights to make the thorn look three-dimensional.

PAINTING PRICKLES

Prickles on a stem may be very thin and abundant so the challenge lies in positioning the prickles around the stem convincingly, to include foreshortened and real-length views, or any other pattern of protrusion that you can identify.

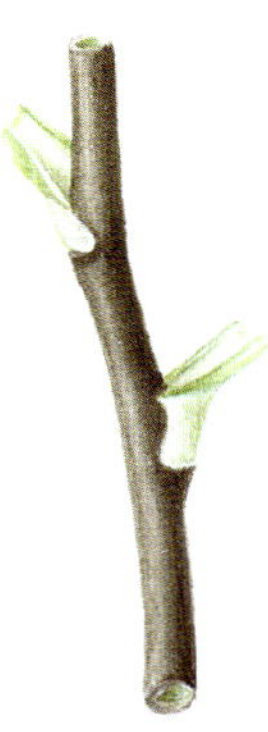

Step 1. Start by painting the stem completely, imagining that the prickles are not present. It is seldom that you will use white paint for botanical illustration but in this instance, it is possible to do so. Mix up some white watercolour, or you could use gouache. Add a little of the stem colour to the mix to give a realistic colour. You will not want them to look unnaturally pure white.

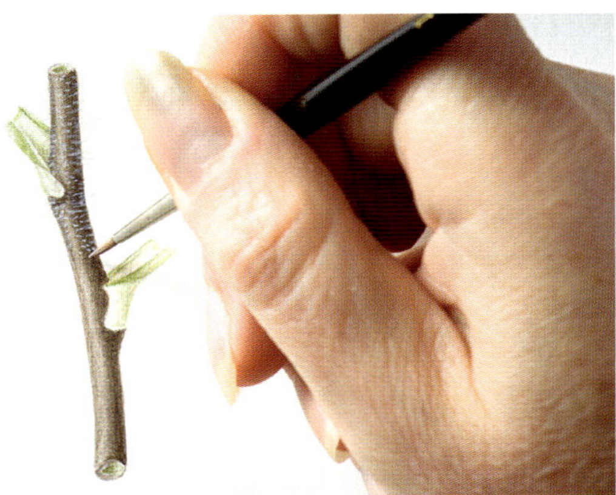

Step 2. Using the dry brush technique, carefully paint the prickles onto the stem, observing the specimen as you go, and paying attention to the length of the prickles especially as foreshortened ones come into view. Hold the brush almost upright to obtain clean, crisp lines.

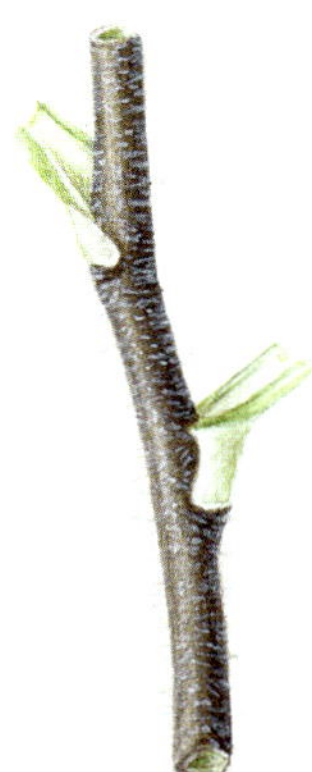

Step 3. Once you have painted the prickles, complete the painting by adding small shadow lines in a slightly darker colour underneath a few of the prickles.

PAINTING YELLOW SUBJECTS

It is extremely easy to create a 'muddy' effect when painting yellow subjects, and this is often because the choice of shadow colours used is inaccurate. To avoid the muddy effect, it is helpful to understand which colour to select for your shadow colour. You will need to primarily choose the complementary colour (opposite colour) on the colour wheel, which for yellow is violet, plus tones either side, depending on the temperature (coolness or warmth) of your yellow subject.

It is very easy to 'overdo' the shadows, causing your painting to very quickly look too dark or overworked, so an air of caution should be exercised when adding them.

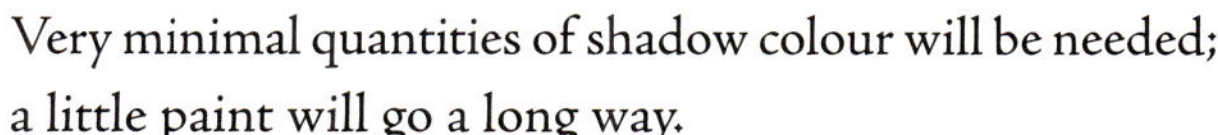

Very minimal quantities of shadow colour will be needed; a little paint will go a long way.

Some artists like to use underpainting as the technique to add shadows (a method of laying down the shadows before adding colour), which works well for painting darker subjects which are red, green, or blue for example. This is because there is more scope to subtly blend the shadows within the overriding colours, which are naturally darker tones. When painting a pale colour however, unless the artist is very skilled, there is often a tendency to use underpainting too heavily, which can prove irreversible after the subject has been fully painted. In this example, shadow colours will be added after painting a yellow coreopsis flower.

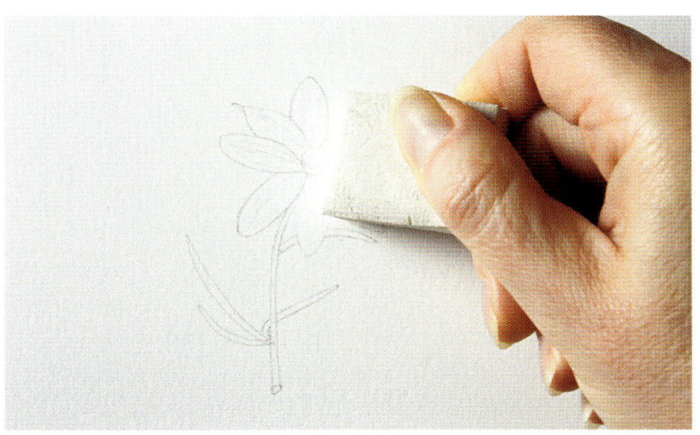

Step 1. Firstly, ensure your pencil drawing is very light; you do not want any graphite to show after you have finished painting. If necessary, dab off any excess graphite with a putty rubber before starting to paint.

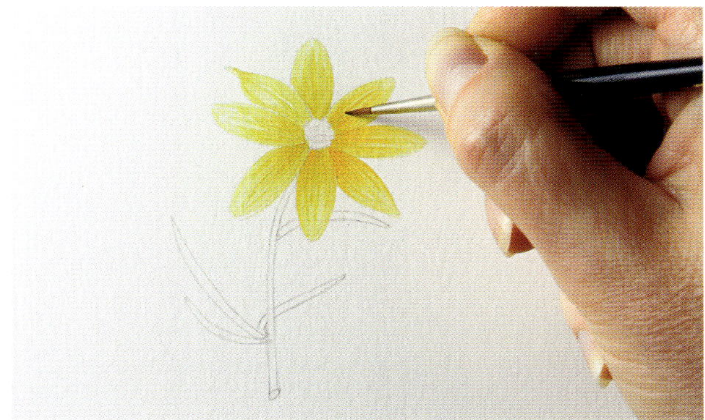

Step 2. Paint your yellow subject by building up layers of wash and depict any finer details such as veining in petals using the dry brush technique.

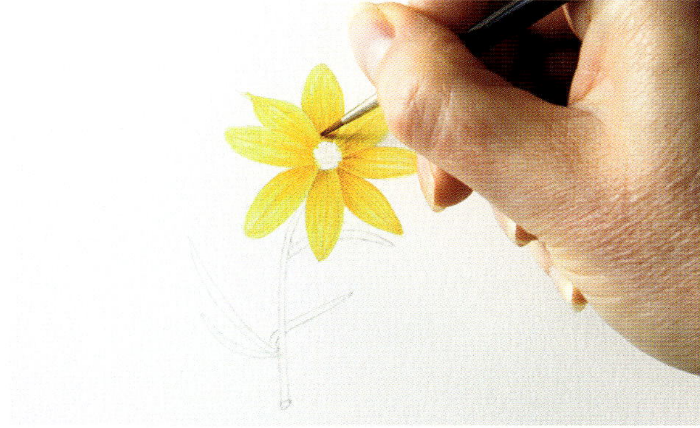

Step 3. Apply shadows. To begin with, mix very small amounts of cool violet shadow colour to some of your yellow mix in your palette. The ratio will be approximately 10% violet, 90% yellow.

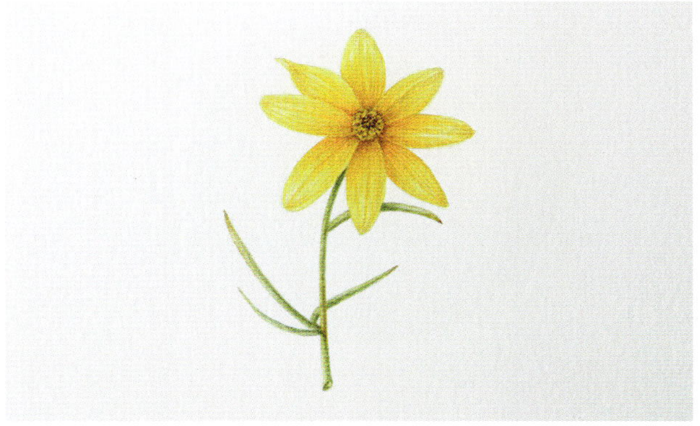

Step 4. Finally, if necessary, carefully add stronger shadows by intensifying the mix in your palette, and add stalks, leaves and so on to complete the painting.

BLOOM ON FRUIT

The naturally occurring 'bloom' found on fruits such as plums, grapes and blueberries is a thin, waxy substance believed to help decrease moisture loss and protect the skin surface from the effects of the environment, such as ultraviolet light. Bloom is also found on some leaves, typically those of the monocotyledons, such as daffodils, tulips, and irises.

To create bloom, you will need to apply an opaque layer of primarily white paint, once painting of the fruit or leaf has taken place. White paint by itself will appear too harsh and unnatural looking, so the addition of a small amount of Cobalt Turquoise Light (by Winsor & Newton) is recommended.

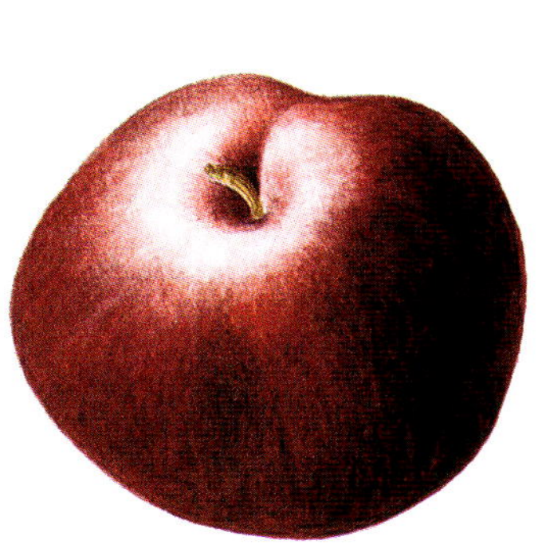

Step 1. To begin, paint the fruit completely, using your preferred technique, and ignoring the bloom. Allow to dry.

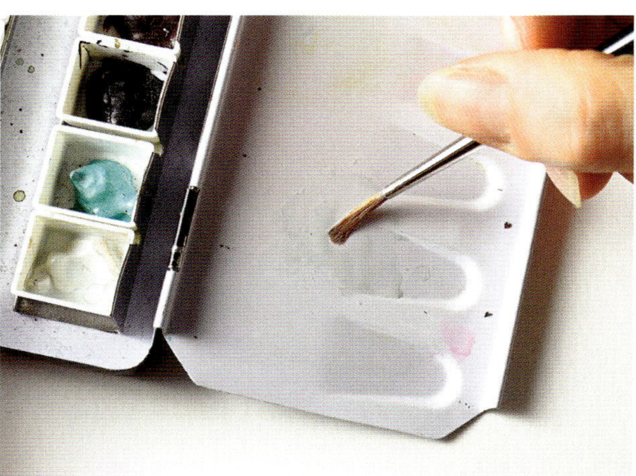

Step 2. Make a solution of white paint and add a small quantity of Windsor & Newton Cobalt Turquoise Light (ratio approximately 90% white, 10% Cobalt Turquoise Light). Aim for a consistency of paint similar to that of semi-skimmed milk. (If the dilution is too weak it will not show on the painted surface; too thick, and it will show too much.)

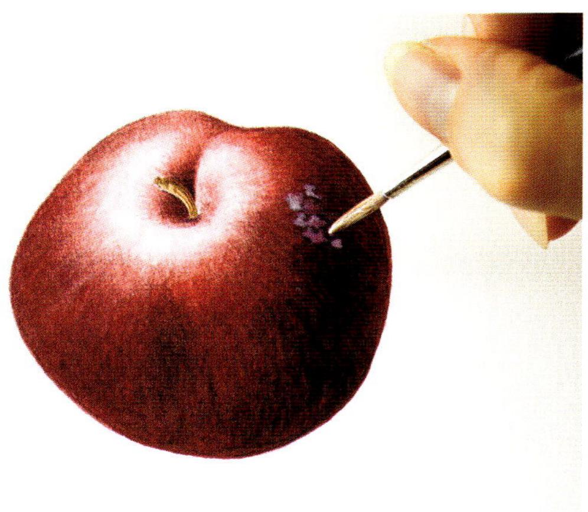

Step 3. Apply the mix of bloom colour directly onto the painted surface in the areas where you can see it. Do not brush the mix on; instead, gently stipple using the brush rather like a pipette.

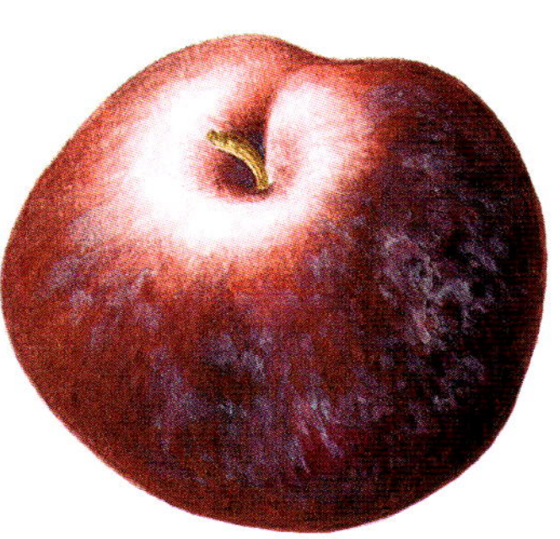

Step 4. Finally, gently spread the paint by nudging the drops together. The mix should be lightly visible on the painted fruit once dry. Apply a little more where it is thicker in some areas.

THE VELVET TEXTURE

The soft texture of velvet is commonly found on flowers such as pansies, petunias and cockscomb, as well as on some leaves. The velvety effect is the result of numerous tiny papillae (tiny outgrowths on the petal surface), which are invisible to the naked eye. As the papillae stand upright, they form a thick bed of soft tissue on the petal surface, and are absorbent of light rays. In dark, violet, or maroon-coloured pansies for example, this can be clearly seen when compared to the reverse of the petals, which do not contain papillae.

To create the velvet effect of a purple-coloured pansy, you will first need to study the different colours within the flower itself, which are seen on the reverse of the petals. There is usually a myriad of colours: yellow, cyan, magenta and so on, and it is these colours which you will lay down one by one to build the intense, rich, velvety texture. It is worth noting down the colours you can see and checking that you have them in your palette before you begin painting.

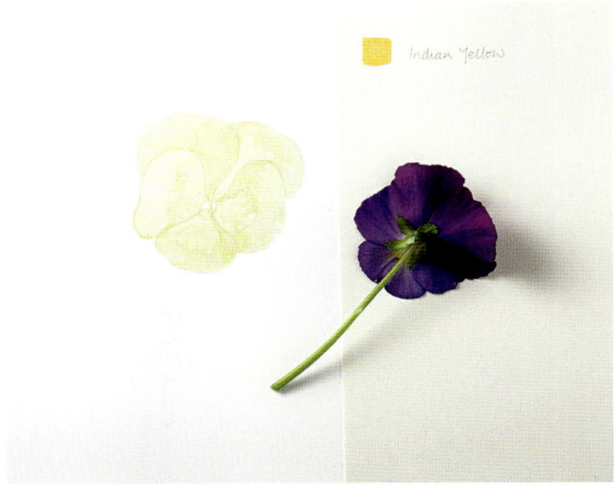

Step 1. Once you have drawn the pansy, you will need to build up layers of single colours, the first being a fairly wet solution and the latter ones becoming drier as you progress. Leaving aside any whitish areas around the middle of the pansy face, apply the lightest colour you can see as a wash, over the entire flower (often yellow found around the base of the bottom petal), and allow to dry.

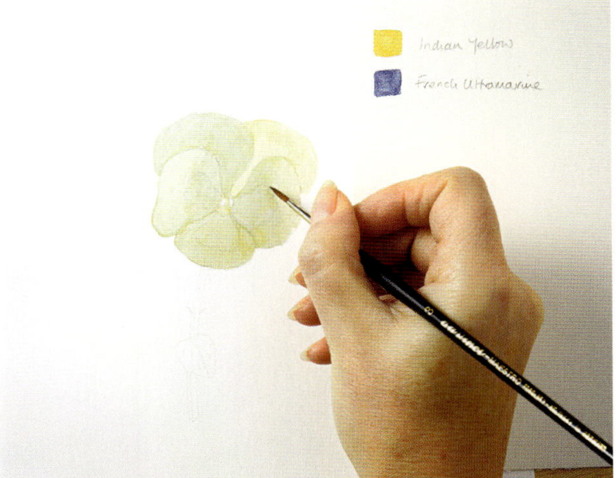

Step 2. Choose the next lightest colour and repeat the process, avoiding any areas of the 'face' that should remain yellow. It is wise to keep a list of each colour that you apply by painting a small swatch on a separate piece of paper, as you will most likely need to repeat layers of some of the colours as you go.

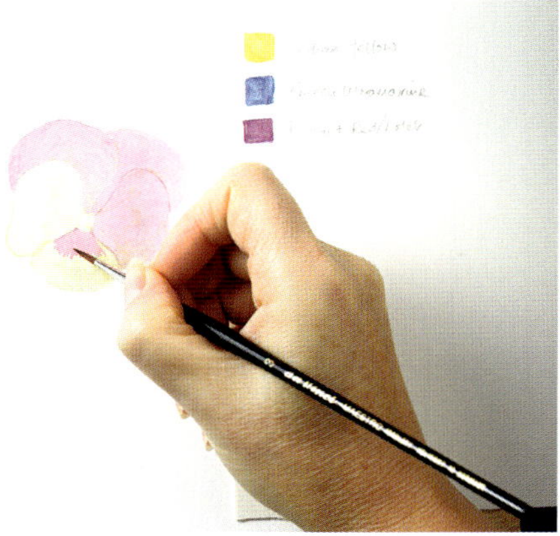

Step 3. Repeat the layering process, slowly building up all the colours as single layers, and thickening each to a drier consistency as you go. Allow each application to dry before applying the next, and pay attention to the pattern of the face if there is one, avoiding painting colours where they do not appear.

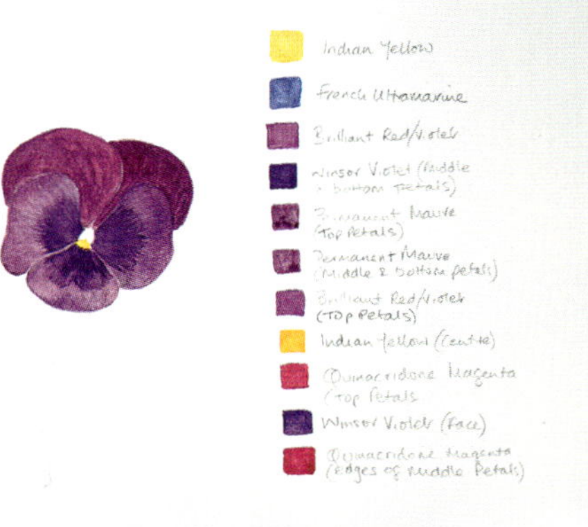

Step 4. Build up the layers further still; for extremely dark-coloured pansies, or those with intricate faces or patterns, it is not uncommon to apply upwards of twenty layers.

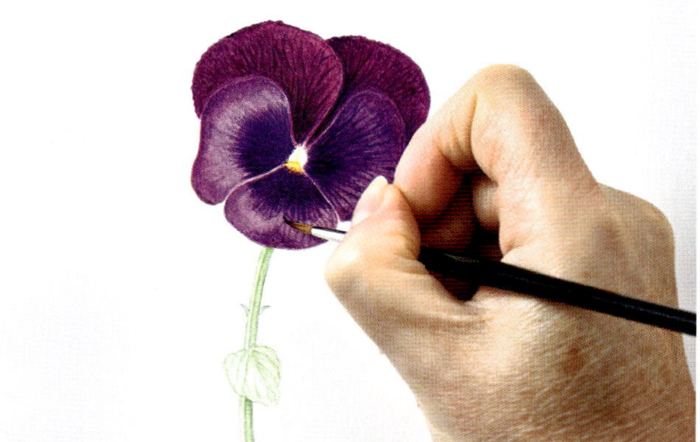

Step 5. Once your layers are rich and intense, add any finer details such as veins over the top using the dry brush technique. You could also paint in the stem of the pansy, to put the flower into context.

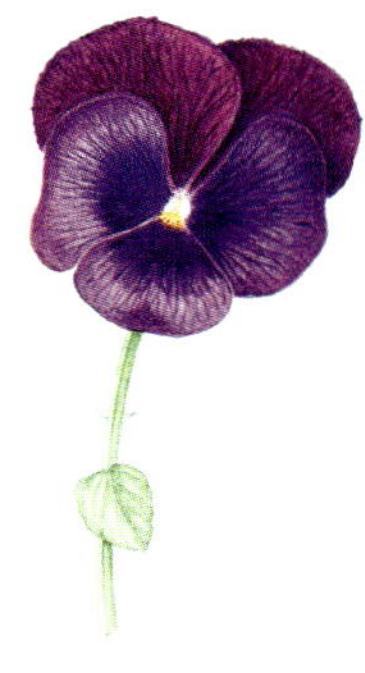

Step 6. To complete the painting, intensify any shadows where petals overlap and add details to the central area of the face of the pansy.

MULTIPLE PETAL FLOWERS

The prospect of painting a flower consisting of multiple petals, such as a camellia or peony (or multiple flowers in the case of the Asteraceae family, such as chrysanthemums, dahlias, and sunflowers), can appear quite overwhelming. However, the technique can be simplified by breaking the process down into manageable tasks, and working through them systematically. The most important considerations are the structure of the flower and its growth pattern. The petals of many flowers are formed in whorls and if you can identify these at the drawing stage, your painting task will be much easier. It is also worth noting that some growth patterns of flowers (as with many other botanical structures) are formed in a spiral formation, most commonly the Fibonacci sequence. You should check you have identified such features and have included them in your drawing. You will also need to look carefully to see how the light falls on multiple-petal flowers. For example, (for a right-handed artist) if the flower is virtually spherical there will be more shadows on the right-hand side towards the bottom of the flower head, and highlights will appear in the upper left-hand quadrant. On flatter, more open cup-like structures, the highlights will appear on the inside of the flower to the right-hand side, with the shadows on the left. There is little point painting your flower if you paint all the shadows and highlights with equal tonality, as this will create a very flat-looking image.

Considering your approach to painting multiple-petal flowers will help you plan your painting. It is worth thinking about the numerous petals as not petals at all, but instead as a series of shapes that happen to fit together, rather like a jigsaw puzzle. Largely, this type of psychological disassociation may help you to see the flower in a more abstract way, which can make it easier for you to construct your painting.

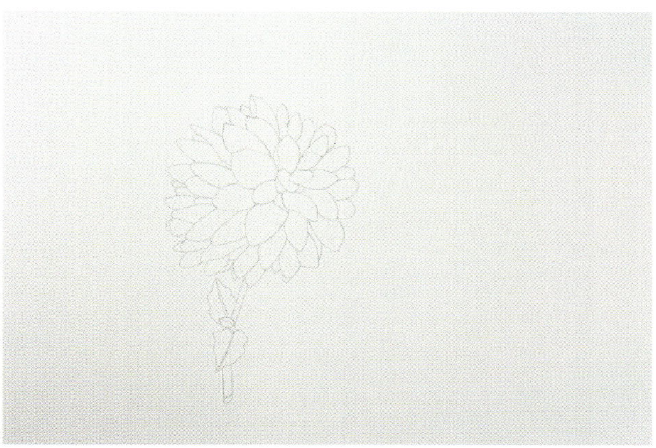

Step 1. To paint a red dahlia, you will first need to make an accurate drawing, by carefully identifying the whorls of petals and the flower head structure. If there are many, many petals, it is not necessary to draw every single one, but you should still convey their abundancy and growth habit convincingly in your drawing.

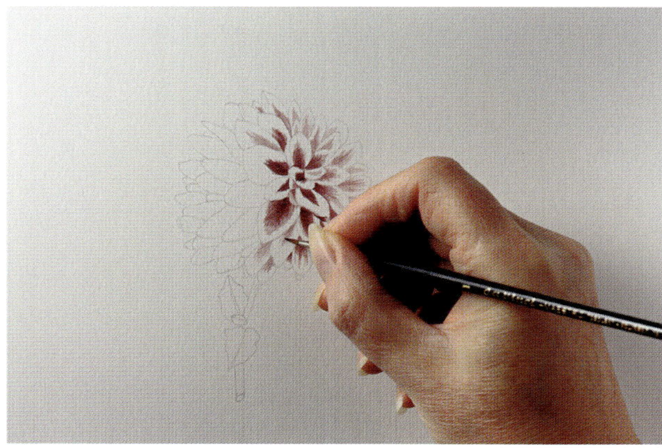

Step 2. If you are painting a dark-coloured multiple-petal flower, it is worth considering using an underpainting technique to add the shadows first (a method of laying down the shadow colours before adding colour). Use your colour theory knowledge (*see* Chapter 5) to select the right colours for making shadows.

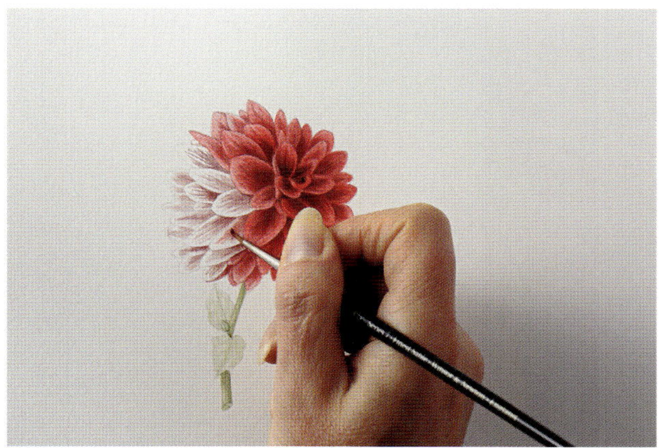

Step 3. Once you have painted in the shadows, begin building up the colour of the flower by using layers of wash, and use dry brush technique for adding details. Work systematically from petal to petal. Always keep in mind where the highlights and shadows are on the overall flower.

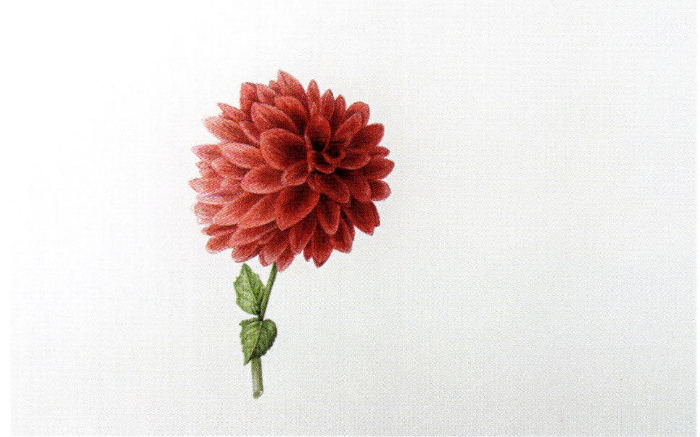

Step 4. To complete your painting, increase tonal contrast between highlights and shadows if necessary, and tidy up the edges of the petals so they are neat and crisp.

The Fibonacci Sequence

The medieval Italian mathematician Leonardo Pisano Fibonacci devised this unique numbering sequence, whereby each number starting at 0 is the sum of the previous two numbers, so 0, 1, 1, 2, 3, 5, 8, 13, 21 and so on. When applied diagrammatically as a series of abutting squares, a spiral can be seen if arcs are then drawn between the diagonally opposite corners of each square, to form the continuous line of a spiral. It is these spirals which are commonly visible in the growth patterns of many species such as sunflowers, daisies, and chrysanthemums of the Asteraceae family, and other plants and fruits such as some succulents, fern croziers, pineapples, and cones. They are recognizable in both clockwise and counter-clockwise directions.

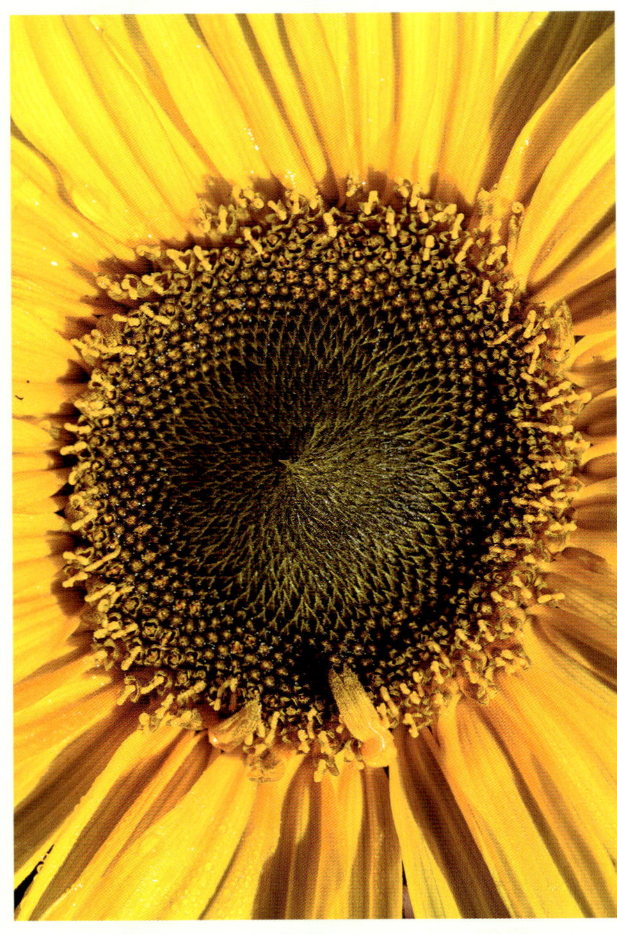

The spiralling Fibonacci sequence is clearly visible in the disc florets of a sunflower.

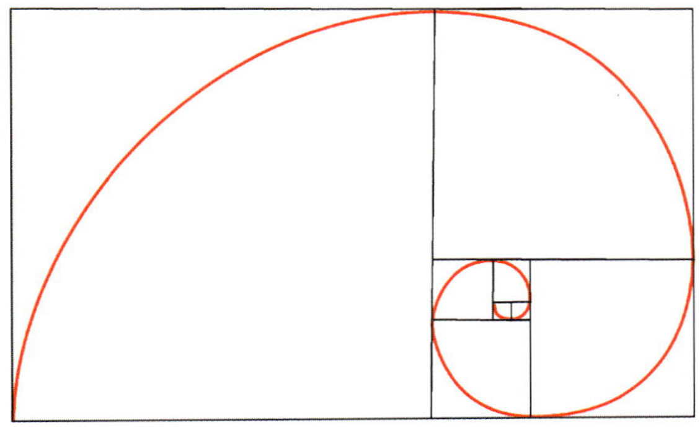

The recognizable spiral of the Fibonacci sequence.

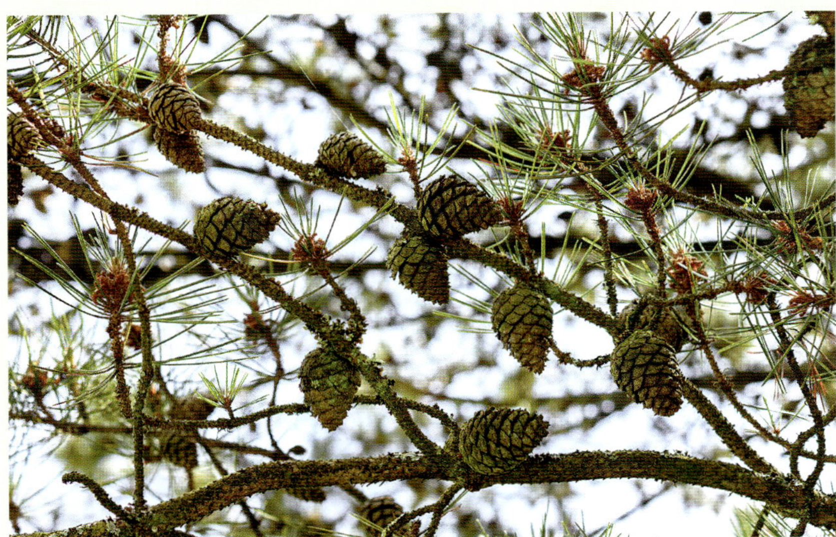

The Fibonacci sequence is identifiable in pine cones.

REFLECTED LIGHT

Reflected light is the small amount of light (often crescent-shaped on a spherical form) that bounces from one reflective surface into another. For example, it is typically noticeable on bunches of grapes hanging on a vine, or a cluster of apples on a tree, when the fruits naturally overlap each other. It does not however appear on a single grape at the edge of the bunch, or a single apple growing on the tree, if there is no other reflective surface in close enough proximity to reflect light back. Therefore, in studio conditions, if you are painting a single fruit with a reflective surface situated on a light-coloured tabletop or white sheet of paper, do not make the common mistake of adding reflected light, as this is not a naturally occurring phenomenon. Instead, to minimize the effect of reflective light in this situation, it is a good idea to place a sheet of mid-grey or mid-blue paper underneath your subject.

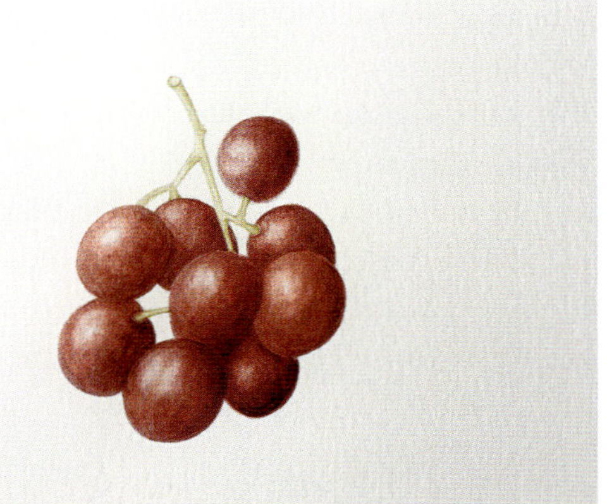

Step 1. To add reflected light to a small bunch of red or black grapes, you will first need to paint each grape as if there is no reflected light visible. Include shadows and highlights to emphasize the overlapping nature of the fruit. Also, lightly paint in the stalks of the grapes to put them into context with each other.

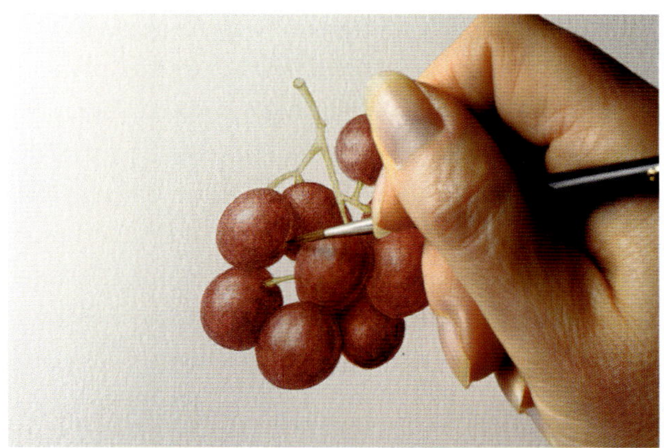

Step 2. Once the grapes are painted, lift out some of the paint where the reflected light occurs, using a clean, dampened brush. Lift the paint only in a situation where the grapes overlap each other, leaving any fruits that do not overlap anything without reflected light.

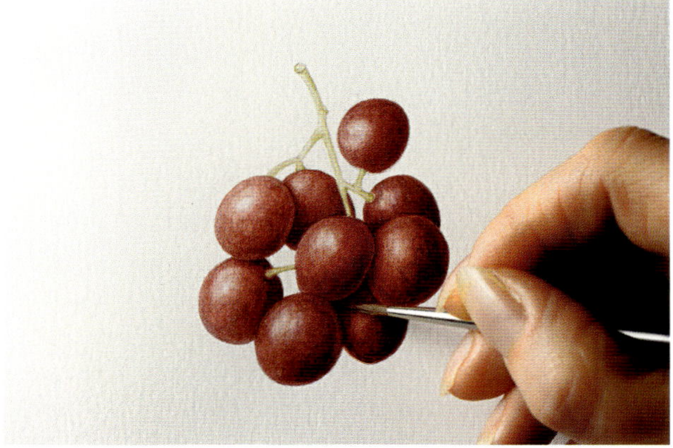

Step 3. Strengthen the pockets of cast shadow of the overlapping grapes in the background, which will help to create contrast and a strong outlined edge to the grapes in front. Ensure that you consider and vary the tonality of the highlights and shadows over the entire bunch of grapes, as well as each grape individually.

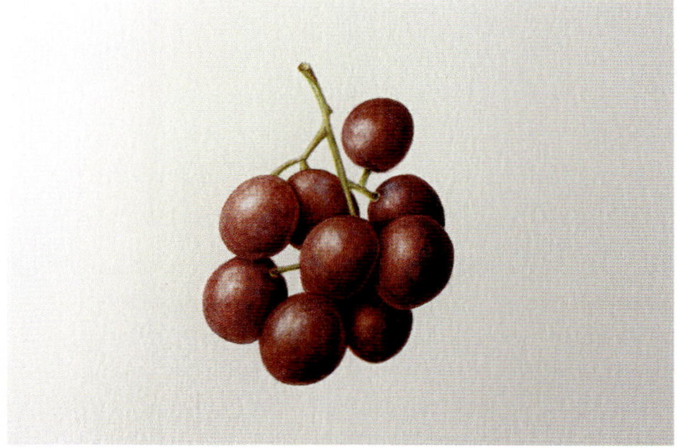

Step 4. Finally, add bloom to some of the fruits (described earlier in this chapter in the 'Bloom on Fruit' section) and finalize painting the stalks to each grape.

WHITE FLOWERS

It is very easy to feel daunted by the prospect of painting white flowers, although you should not feel overwhelmed. You will learn here how such a minimal quantity of paint goes a very long way, as you will need to apply paint very delicately to create realistic effects.

One of the biggest challenges of course is how to depict a white flower against a white background. The traditional method is quite simply to colour the background behind the flower, which quite visibly depicts the white flower. This is an easy way to create outlines to the flowers. Botanical artists and illustrators over the years have used this technique, which is common in floras and other published reference books. However, a portrait of a white flower painted botanically for display arguably does not warrant the same treatment, and so other techniques need to be considered to show the white flower painted on white paper. One method of doing this is to compose a good majority of the white flowers positioned against their foliage. This works well in the case of white lilies or white camellias for example, which may naturally have leaves growing near flowers, but in the case of white flowers sitting at the top of long stems with foliage much lower down, such as a white *Phalaenopsis* orchid, this technique cannot be used. There becomes no choice but to paint white flowers against white paper.

The key to successful white flower painting is using minimal quantities of paint, and being able to carefully depict details such as veins, and shadows falling onto the petal surfaces to help describe form. Shadows are cast according to the curvature and natural undulations of the 3D structure, and are typically noticeable in flowers such as chrysanthemums but are less obvious in petals, which are smoother or flatter.

The technique described here addresses the problem of painting the lone, white, smooth-textured flowers of a *Phalaenopsis* orchid against white paper, when it is not possible to consider positioning them against foliage.

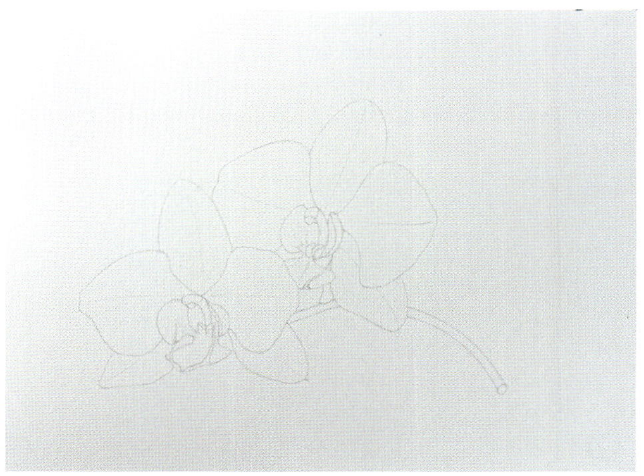

Step 1. As you will be painting a flower that is extremely pale, firstly make sure your outline drawing is as light as possible. You will not want any graphite to show, so minimizing this to begin with is beneficial. You may find it easier to draw a slightly darker outline, then gently rub out as much graphite as possible as you paint.

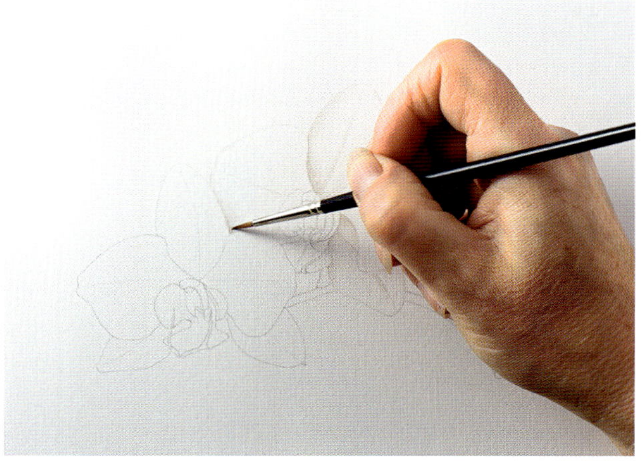

Step 2. Identify the colours you can see in the shadows of the petals, which will appear as cool (blue) or warm (red) grey tones. Bear in mind that these may vary if nearby buds or stems are reflecting colours into the whiteness of the petals. Mix up your shadow colour and paint outlines and cast shadows onto background petals using small amounts of paint. Slowly build up washes, and allow paint to dry between applications.

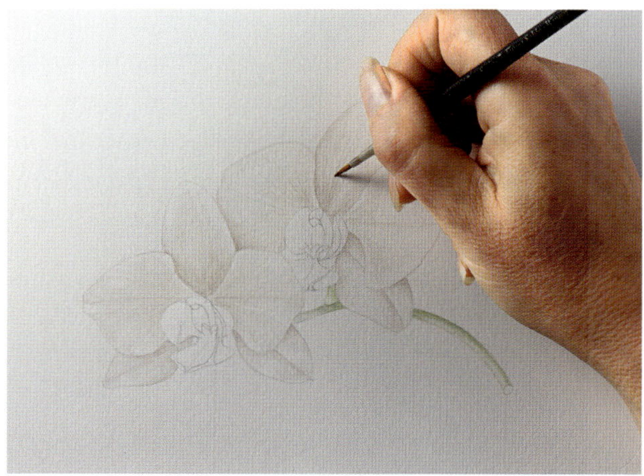

Step 3. Gently paint the edges of foreground petals and add light shadows, being careful to allow for any highlights you can see near the edges. Paint details such as subtle veins by pulling lines towards the edges of the petals. Vary the length and thickness of the veins to give a naturalistic effect.

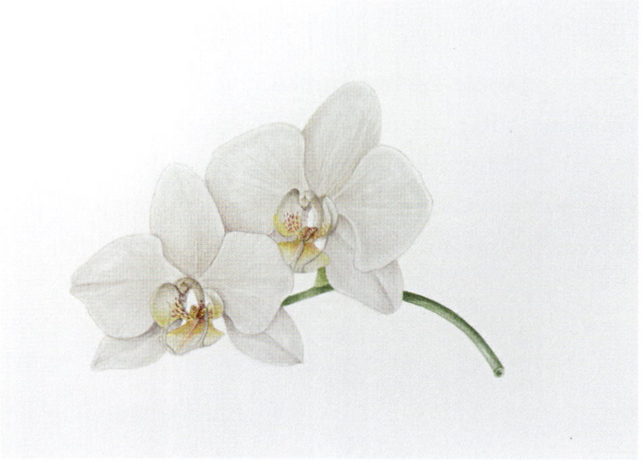

Step 4. Finally, paint in other coloured details, such as stems, buds, markings, stamens and so on to complete your painting.

SPECIFIC TECHNIQUES FOR PAINTING LEAVES

Textures such as sheen on thick, leathery leaves, hairy leaves such as those of *Stachys byzantine* (lamb's ears), or the cushioned surface texture of primula leaves, all present a challenge to botanical painters. Other issues such as variegation, pale veined leaves, and leaves with finely toothed margins also need to be considered carefully and the most appropriate techniques used to create realistic effects.

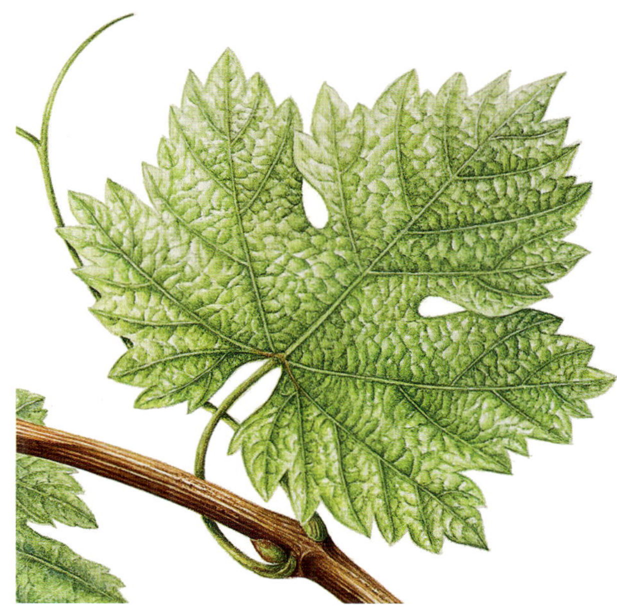

The Great Vine at Hampton Court Palace (leaf detail).
LEIGH ANN GALE

SHINE AND SHEEN

Shine and sheen are very similar, and distinguishing one from the other when studying the light fall on leaves can be difficult. Shine is the term generally used when light is reflected from a leaf, so usually the leaf surface is extremely smooth, such as holly leaves or very new, very young leaves. Sheen on the other hand describes more of a lustre coming from the leaf surface, such as on an ageing leaf, or one that may be slightly less smooth in texture.

To paint a very shiny leaf, the method described for creating highlights on berries can be used. To paint sheeny leaves, such as camellia leaves, use the following method.

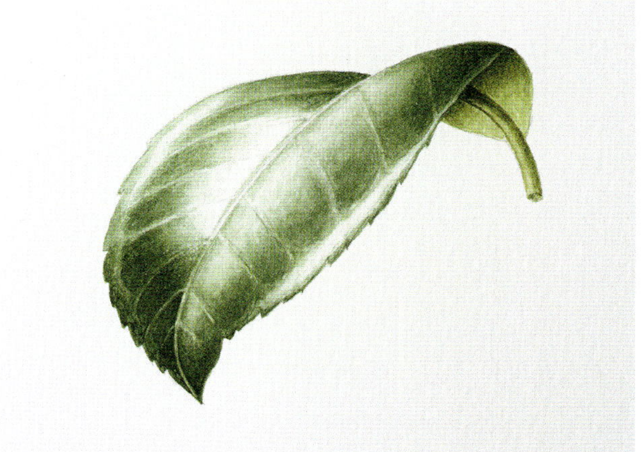

Step 1. Begin by painting the leaf, building up layers of wash, leaving the very lightest highlights paper white. Do not create hard edges where the highlights are; remember you are creating a sheen rather than a shine.

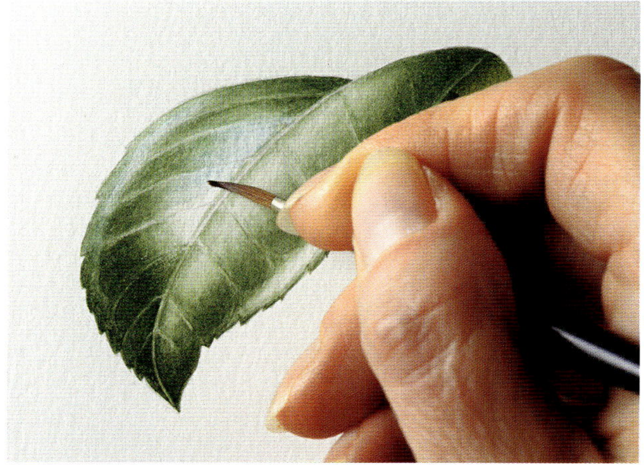

Step 2. Very dark green leaves often take on a bluish hue in the highlights. This can be easily achieved by applying a dilute wash of Cobalt or Cerulean Blue to the highlighted areas after painting the leaf.

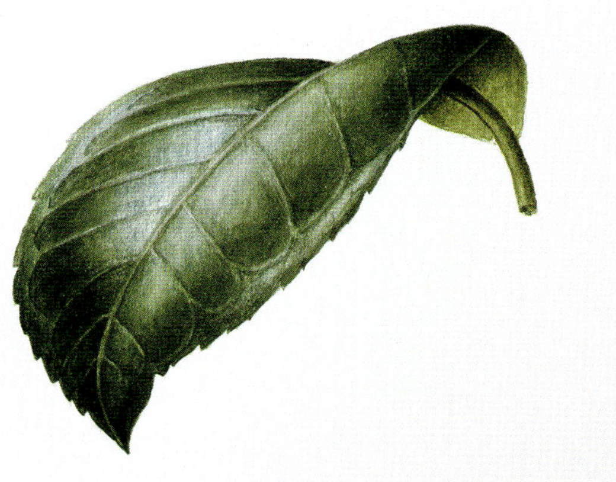

Step 3. Once the wash is dry, complete the painting by carefully suggesting the veins with added shadows along the bottom edge of each one.

DEPICTING FINE, LIGHT-COLOURED VEINS ON A DARK LEAF

The technique of lifting out paint to depict fine, light-coloured veins on dark leaves such as ivy can be very effective.

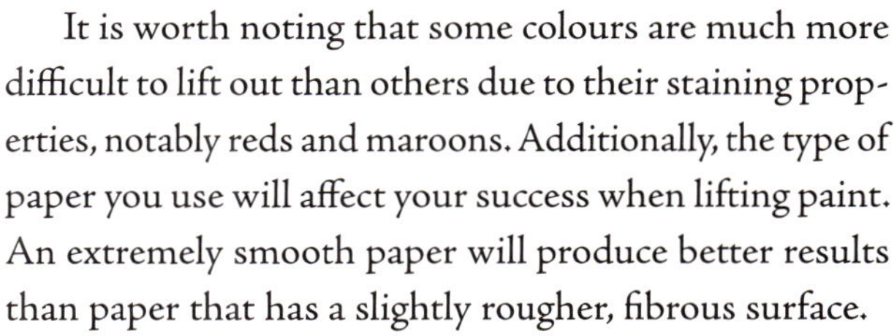

It is worth noting that some colours are much more difficult to lift out than others due to their staining properties, notably reds and maroons. Additionally, the type of paper you use will affect your success when lifting paint. An extremely smooth paper will produce better results than paper that has a slightly rougher, fibrous surface.

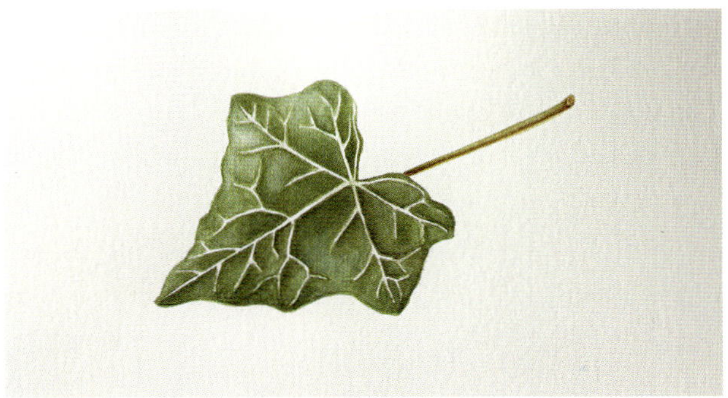

Step 1. Paint the leaf using your preferred technique, including up to the edges of the midrib and the thickest lateral veins. Also paint the petiole (the leaf stem) gently indicating the highlights and shadows.

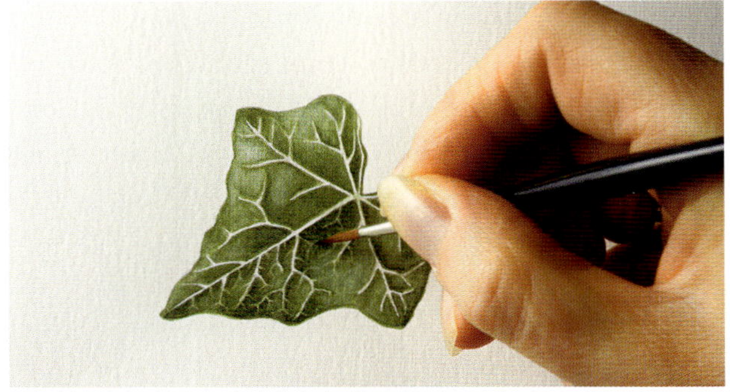

Step 2. Gently apply a pointed, damp brush to lift out paint for the fine veins. Use single directional strokes along the line of each vein. Do not try to lift paint using backwards and forwards brush strokes, as this could damage the paper surface fibres. It may take several strokes to penetrate the paint.

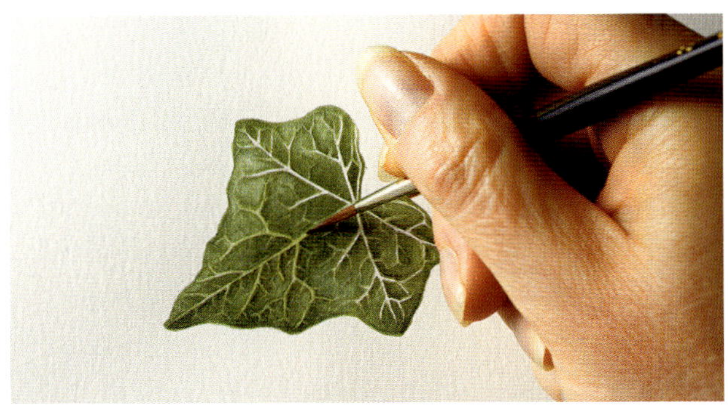

Step 3. As you continue lifting out veins, pay attention to whether they taper to a point. Once all the veins have been revealed, allow to dry and apply a wash of the vein colour over the veins to make them pale green.

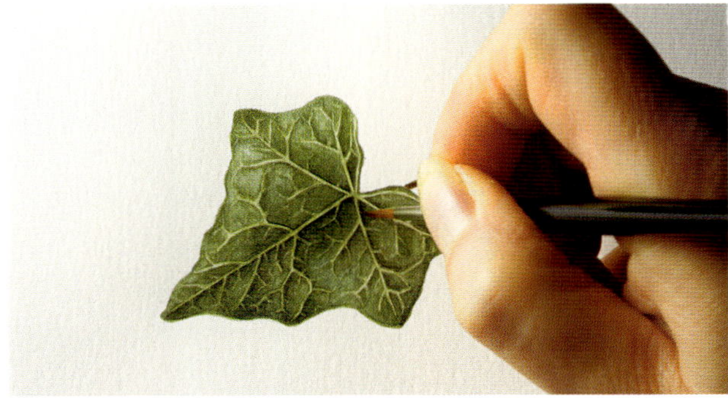

Step 4. Using dry brush technique, start to add shadows to one side of each vein to create a realistic 3D effect.

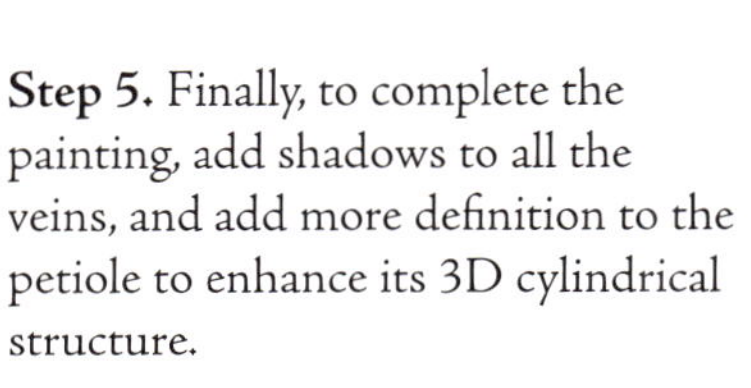

Step 5. Finally, to complete the painting, add shadows to all the veins, and add more definition to the petiole to enhance its 3D cylindrical structure.

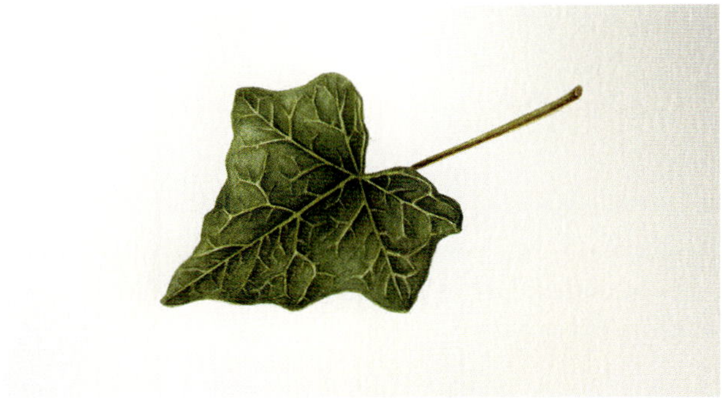

FURRY AND HAIRY LEAVES

The degree to which a leaf is 'furry' or 'hairy' varies enormously, depending on the reason for the 'furriness' or 'hairiness'. Many species that grow at high altitudes for example often have furry or hairy leaves either to conserve warmth or to protect the underlying leaf surface from intense ultraviolet light rays. Some leaves of climbing plants may display hairs of a much coarser, hook-like nature, which aids climbing and grasping of the support, and some very young hairy leaves often secrete unpleasant-tasting chemical substances as well, to ward off predators.

Painting the fur or hairs on leaves will involve your close observation of the hair structures, so it is worthwhile spending some time assessing what type of hair you can see with a magnifying glass, hand lens, or possibly a microscope. Some hairs will be large and coarse enough for you to paint individually, such as those on an oriental poppy leaf, in which case you can use the technique for painting prickles. Other leaves of a finer, denser, 'furry' nature will require you to paint using the following method.

Step 1. Begin by painting the lightest hair colour as a wash. You may need to use a little white paint in your mix depending on the opacity of the furry texture.

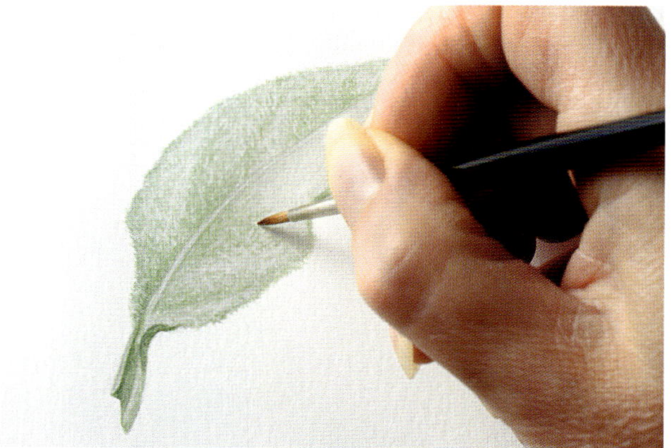

Step 2. Add darker colour using a thicker mix of paint, allowing areas of the lightest wash already applied to show through. Use small, dashed strokes to start creating a 'furry' texture.

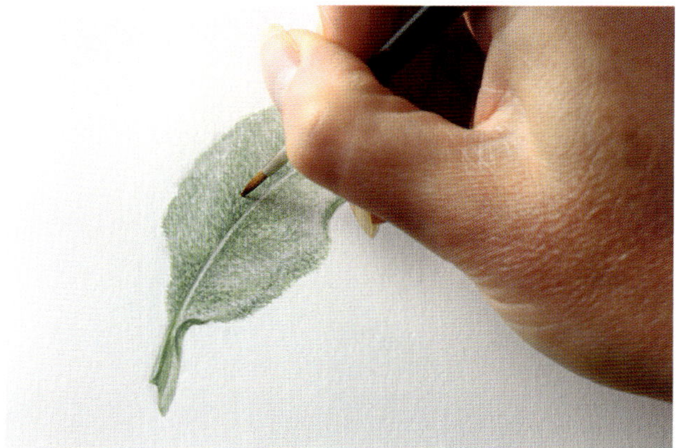

Step 3. Repeat the process, paying attention to the lie of the hairs on the leaf surface, and allowing for both thinner and thicker patches of 'fur'.

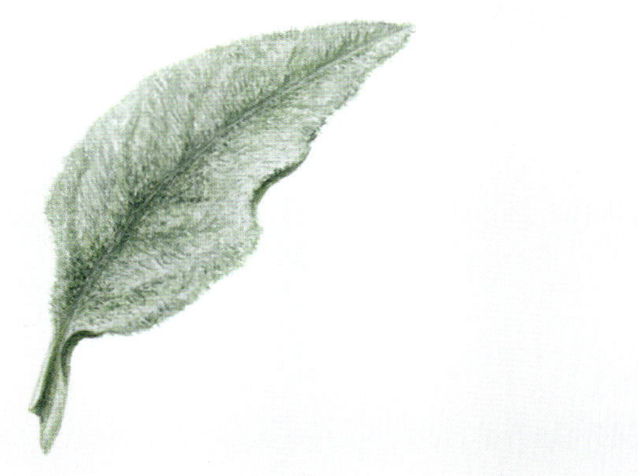

Step 4. Finally, in a few areas, add very dark tones to give the illusion of depth in the 'fur' and to depict the veins if they are visible.

CUSHIONED LEAVES

Of all the 'cushioned' effect leaf textures, those of the primula are commonly known. However, other species including viburnum, hydrangea and salvia also present with a cushioned effect on their leaves.

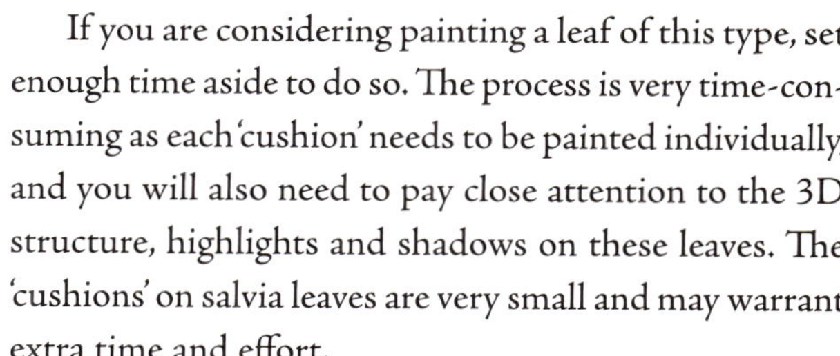

If you are considering painting a leaf of this type, set enough time aside to do so. The process is very time-consuming as each 'cushion' needs to be painted individually, and you will also need to pay close attention to the 3D structure, highlights and shadows on these leaves. The 'cushions' on salvia leaves are very small and may warrant extra time and effort.

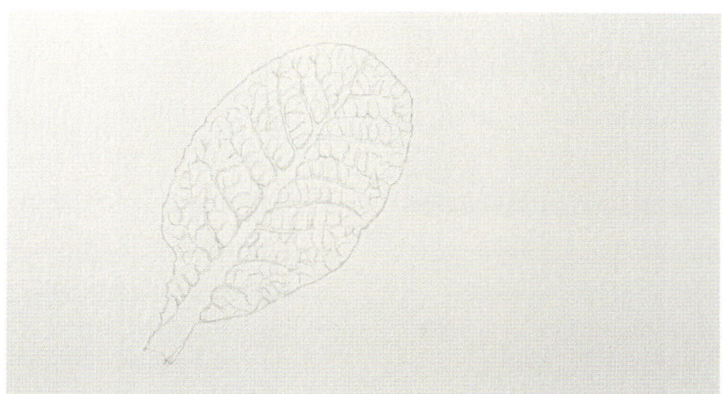

Step 1. To paint a primula leaf, start by drawing the leaf, ensuring that it contains sufficient accurate information to enable you to paint the leaf without becoming confused or lost during the process. Most importantly, identify and draw in the tapering lateral veins and the midrib.

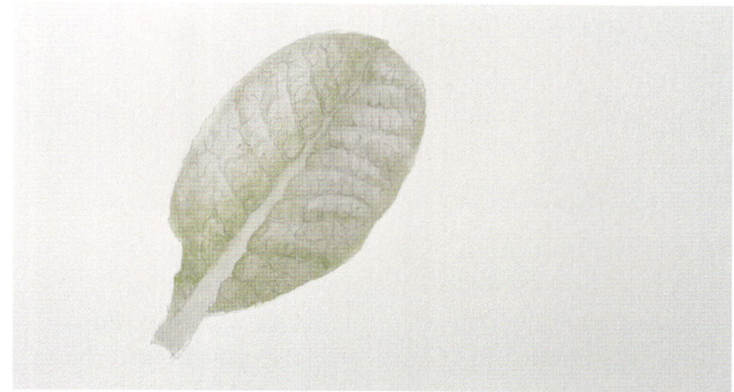

Step 2. Using the wet-into-wet technique, drop in the mid-green tone of the overall leaf colour, taking care to leave the lightest highlight areas untouched. Allow the paint to dry.

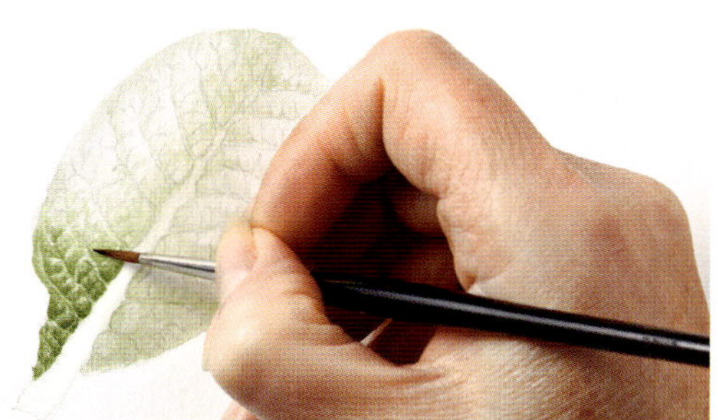

Step 3. It is best to tackle painting the leaf by splitting it into smaller areas, typically each section between two lateral veins works well. Using the dry brush technique, begin painting the 'cushions' in one section before progressing to the next.

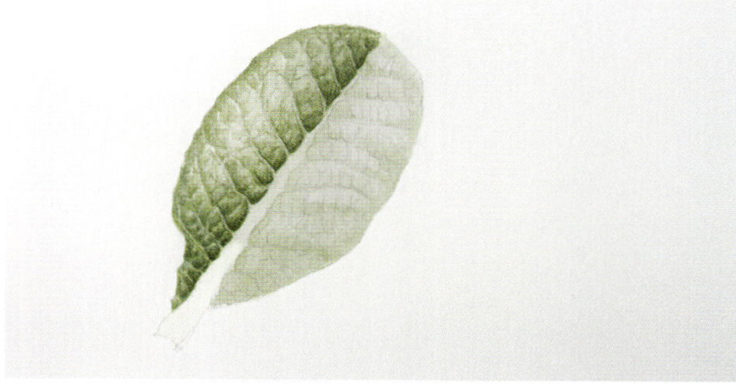

Step 4. Keep painting the sections, building up the 3D effect by using darker paint in the shadow areas and keeping lighter areas paler. As you shape each 'cushion', note how the light falls on it. Paint up to the edges of the thicker, lateral veins.

Step 5. Complete the leaf by painting in the rest of the sections, emphasizing shadows and highlights where necessary, and depicting the concave nature of the midrib.

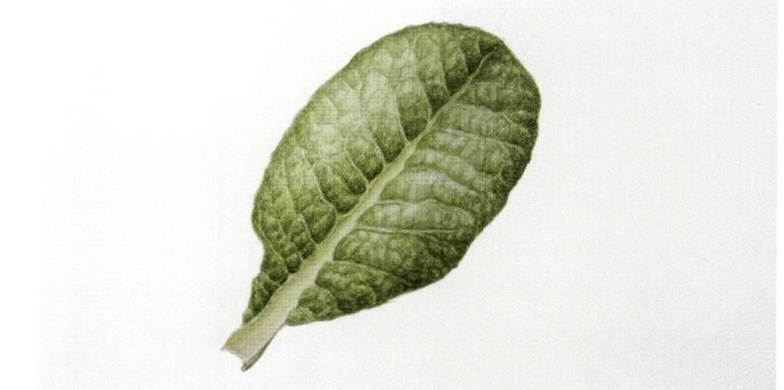

Step 1. To paint a long, smooth (entire) leaf with long veins, typically that of a monocotyledon such as an ornamental grass, begin by making an accurate drawing showing the veins.

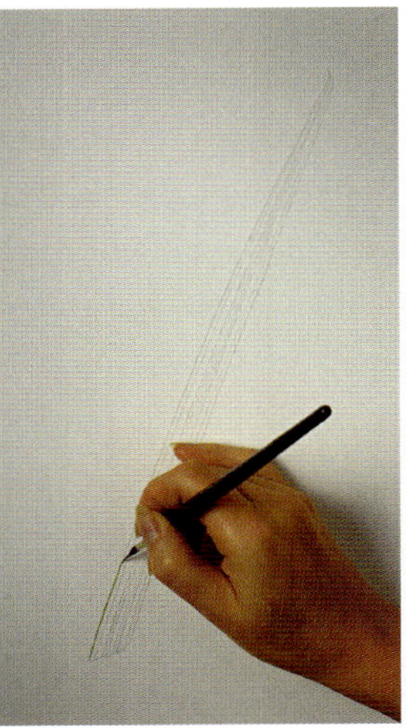

Step 2. Position your paper so that it is moveable, as you will no doubt want to turn the paper as you paint. Keep your hand in a comfortable position to apply paint. Hold the brush in a virtually upright position, and begin painting the leaf margin either from the top or the bottom (whichever feels most natural). You may find it helpful to use your little finger to support the rest of your hand as you travel along the length of the line.

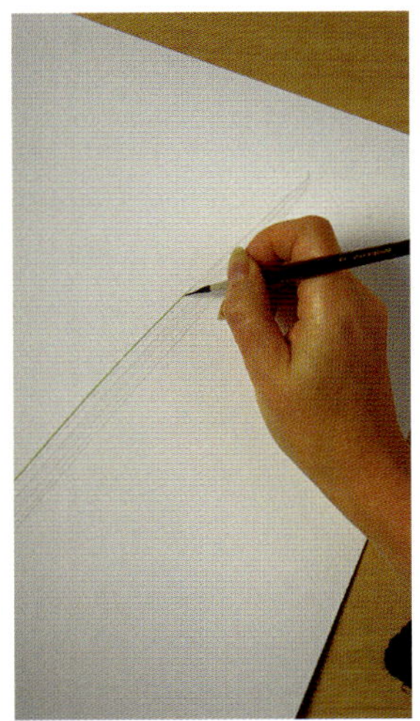

Step 3. You will obviously need to stop and start painting, so when starting a new section, carefully return your hand and paintbrush to the previous stopping point on the paper to continue. Rotate the paper as you go if it helps.

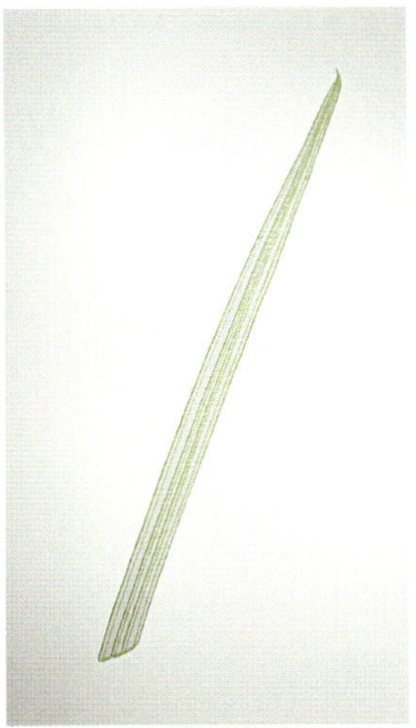

Step 4. Continue painting all the way around the margin, and then add the internal veins in a similar manner. Always ensure your hand is in a comfortable position.

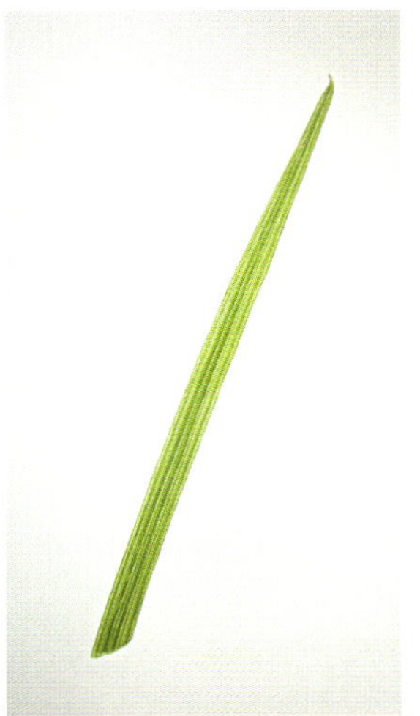

Step 5. Once you have finished painting the whole leaf margin and veins, check them carefully and smooth out any bumps and joins using a damp, clean brush to blend the paint into the surrounding area. Finally, to complete the painting, add shadows and highlights where they appear against the veins to create a 3D effect.

LONG LEAVES

Painting long leaves with smooth-edged margins and long veins is amongst the most difficult of techniques in botanical illustration. Such leaves are typical of the monocotyledons, for example iris, narcissi and grasses. Being able to keep a steady hand to paint continuous crisp, neat lines is most challenging, and it may take several attempts to perfect the technique to achieve consistency in painting them.

When painting long veins, it is necessary to create convincing, unbroken lines, which often may taper towards a point at the apex of a leaf. The veins may be close together or further apart, or be a combination of both, and may cause the leaf to undulate to reveal a corrugated effect. To make long leaves look three-dimensional you will therefore need to pay attention to the highlights and shadows either side of the veins.

The key to painting the lines of long leaves requires constancy of application. It can be beneficial to use an extra long needle point brush for this work.

VARIEGATED LEAVES

Variegated leaves are usually an attractive feature of a plant. Indeed, some plants are grown specifically for their leaf variegation, to add interest to a garden border or as a feature indoor plant. Variegation occurs for several different reasons. Most commonly in cultivation, it is the result of a lack of the green pigment chlorophyll in some of the plant cells, which is sometimes replaced by pinks and reds. Mineral deficiencies or viral infections can also cause leaf variegation. In natural habitats, variegation occurs predominantly in plants of tropical forests, and some species such as bromeliads will produce variegation in their leaves to attract pollinators such as hummingbirds just before flowering. Other species may produce variegated leaves to ward off predators.

The often precise, neat distribution of colour and pattern in variegated leaves such as those of begonia can be a joy to paint. Whichever species with variegated leaves you choose, you will need to closely study the colours and match them carefully with the paints in your palette. Planning to paint your variegated leaf too will involve some logical thinking and planning, as well as time and patience to complete the task.

Extremely colourful variegated leaves with crisp edges between the patches of colour benefit from being painted by using layers of wash and a dry brush technique; however some variegated leaves, such as those appearing in autumn, can be treated differently. Autumn leaves often display large patches of merging colours as the chlorophyll gradually breaks down in the leaf. These leaves can be painted effectively starting with a quicker, wet-into-wet technique, and completed with dry brush detail over the top.

Follow the step-by-step methods for the wet-into-wet and dry brush techniques described in Chapter 7 to paint variegated and autumn leaves.

CREATING SOME OF YOUR OWN TECHNIQUES

The more varied your choice of subjects to paint, the greater your repertoire of techniques will become. You may find that you can use some of the techniques described in this chapter to paint alternative subjects, or you could combine techniques to achieve effective results.

Creating your own techniques too will involve a good deal of experimentation, or even evolve as the result of the occasional 'happy accident'. Whenever using any specific painting techniques, it is crucial to remember that they should be relevant, that they describe exactly the effect you are trying to achieve, and that they are used accurately.

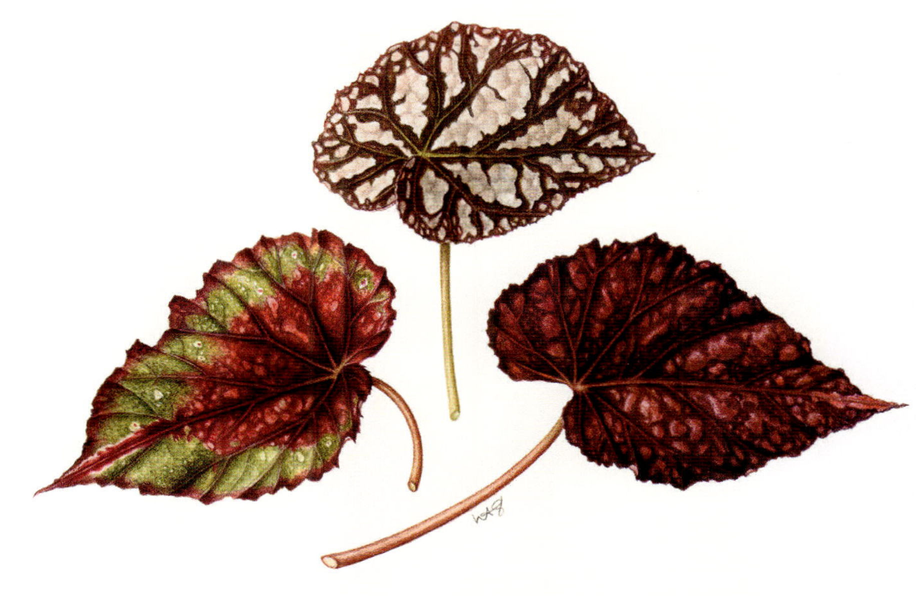

Begonia Leaves. LEIGH ANN GALE

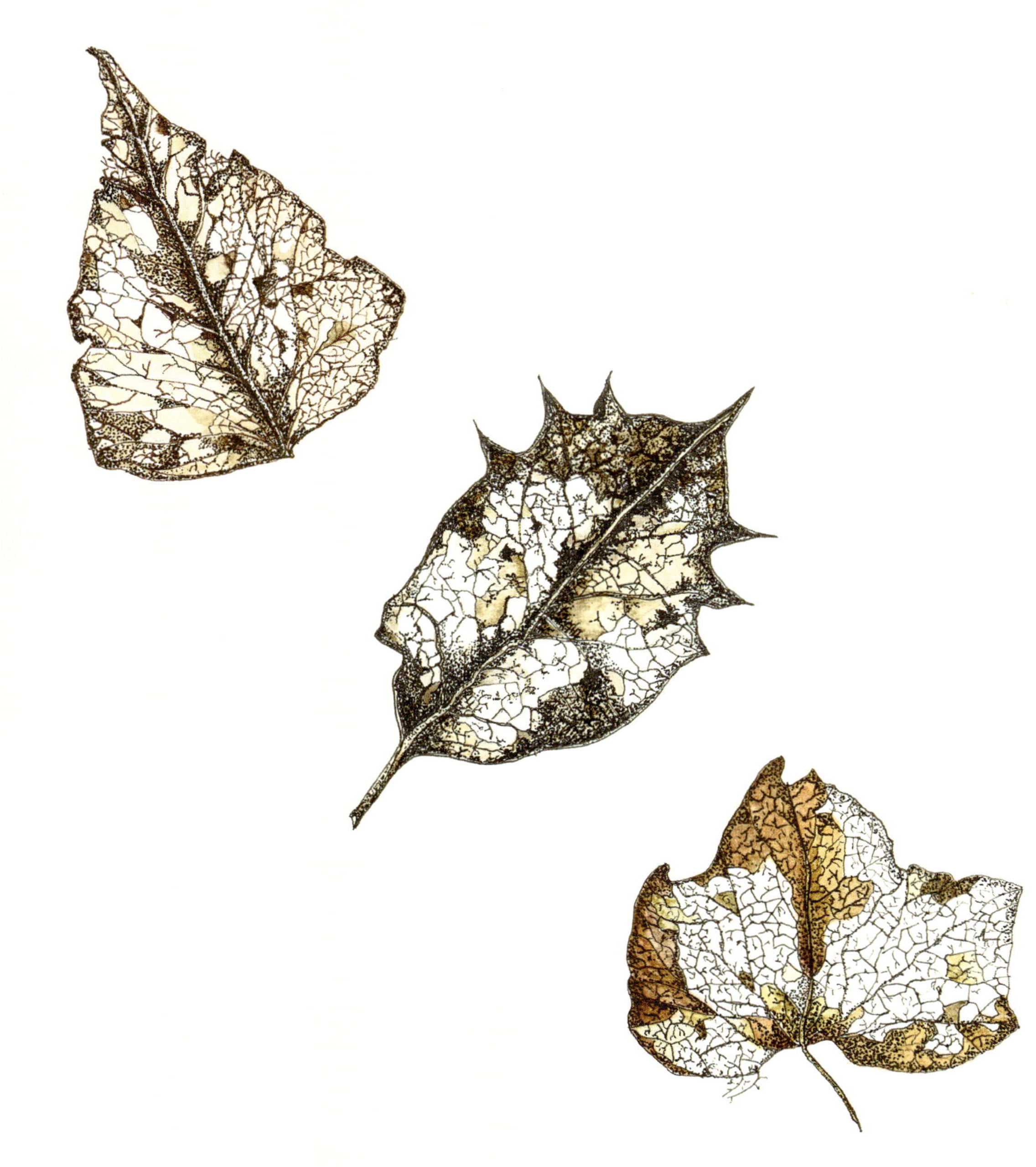

CHAPTER 10

Alternative Media

I work in whatever medium likes me at the moment.

– Marc Chagall (French artist)

Besides watercolour, it is quite possible to create botanical illustrations using other media. Some professional botanical artists and illustrators use alternatives, most notably coloured pencil, and pen and ink. As in watercolour, both media require the finite skills of the artist to render the nuances and details of the subject matter in a scientific way, yet the final appearance of the work created will look and feel quite different.

Most like watercolour, the medium of coloured pencil requires the artist to have a very good understanding of colour theory and an aptitude for layering and blending single colours on the paper, in place of colour mixing in a palette. For pen and ink illustration, the skill of rendering light and shade is highly important to convey three-dimensional form effectively, and the choice of ink mark used needs to demonstrate varying textures in different specimens.

Here, we will consider alternative brands and ranges of coloured pencils and ink pens and think about some of the basic techniques you will need to use for each, to get you started. We will also think about combining media to create different effects, such as using graphite pencil with coloured pencil, and pen and ink with watercolour wash.

If you have been using watercolours up until now – or have been struggling with them – it may be worth considering an alternative medium to see how you get on or adapt. You may simply like the idea of a change from the norm or alternatively want to set yourself a new challenge!

Three Diagonal Leaves: Pen and ink with watercolour wash. VICTORIA WILKINSON

COLOURED PENCIL

The medium of coloured pencil has rapidly grown in popularity over the last twenty years or so, and there are now several botanical artists who specialize in using them. The UK Coloured Pencil Society, which was founded in 2001, has helped promote awareness and use of coloured pencil as an accepted medium, whilst other countries such as Canada, the USA and Australia have also formed their own societies over recent years, giving rise to the popularization of this versatile medium on a global basis.

Traditionally, coloured pencils were usually very hard, being clay-based in composition, and often associated with the pencils or 'crayons' familiar in childhood. Nowadays however, softer pencils that are wax- or oil-based are most often used, allowing for intense coverage of paper and vibrancy of colour. With much more choice available, ranges of coloured pencils also include water-soluble varieties, and harder, thinner leads which allow for finer details to be added to an illustration.

If you are unfamiliar with coloured pencils, it is worth experimenting with a few varieties in the first instance to see which suit you best.

POPULAR COLOURED PENCIL BRANDS

The availability of wax-based and oil-based coloured pencils has contributed significantly to the quality of pencils used today. They are much softer to apply on the paper and have good lightfastness, meaning that they will not fade.

A coloured pencil consists of a 'core', which combines both pigment and binder. The binder is either oil- or wax-based and may or may not be water-soluble. For botanical illustration work, it is wise to invest in good quality brands that offer an extensive colour range and are rich in pigment. It is also advisable to buy individual pencils to build a collection, rather than full sets or tins. This is because some of the colours included in standard sets are too vivid to use, such as some greens and some blues.

The following is a list of popular, recommended brands to try:

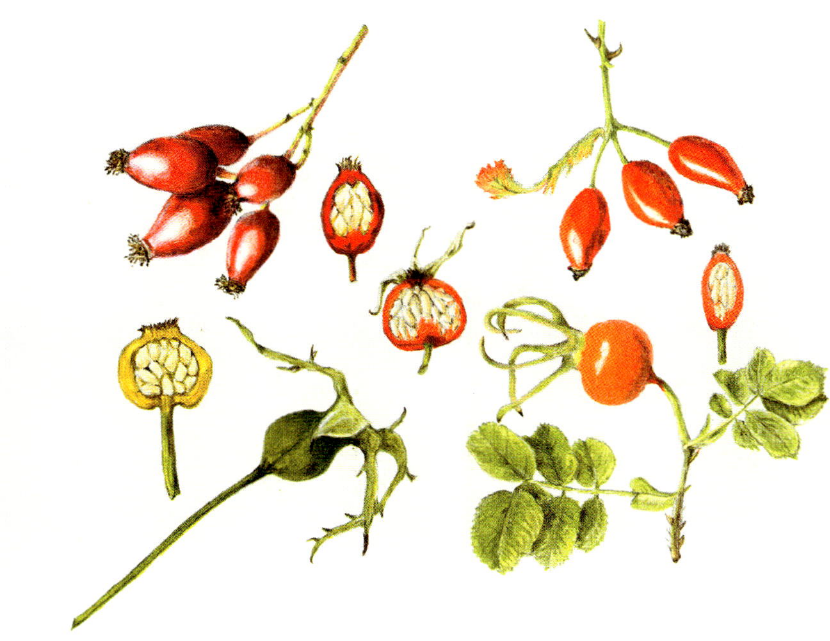

Rosehips: Coloured pencil. VAL FORSTER

Polychromos by Faber-Castell

Polychromos are amongst the finest quality coloured pencils available and are particularly favoured by some botanical artists for their renowned smoothness, superior pigments and blending qualities. These oil-based pencils are available in over a hundred colours, so selecting pencils for a botanical palette is highly achievable. This range is also recommended because they are smudge-proof and water-resistant.

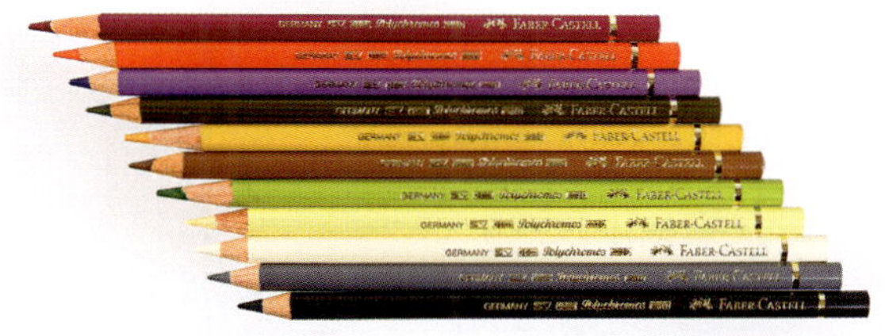

Polychromos are amongst the finest quality coloured pencils available.

Prismacolor Premier by Sanford

These quality wax-based pencils can be successfully used in conjunction with Polychromos and with an excellent colour range and good bendability, make an excellent choice for artists. However, due to being wax-based, standard Prismacolor pencils are a little less sturdy and have a tendency to snap at the point, which is not ideal for fine detail work. To overcome this issue, Prismacolor have introduced a limited colour range of finer, harder pencils known as Prismacolor Verithins, which are narrower and perfect for creating detail and producing crisp line work.

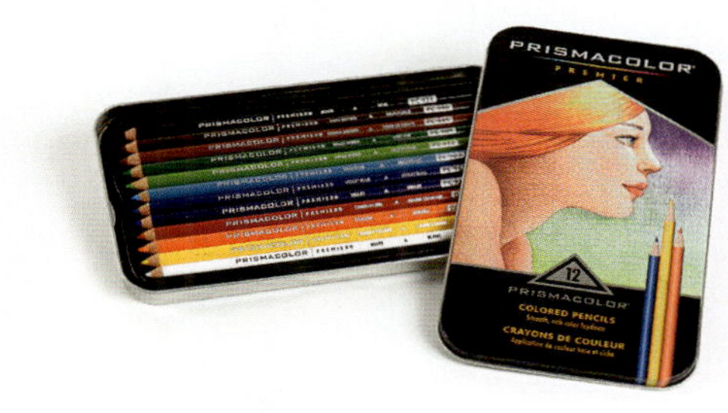

Prismacolor Premier by Sanford is a good quality, wax-based brand.

Derwent Studio and Derwent Artists ranges

Derwent is synonymous with the manufacture of pencils and stationery in the UK, having produced quality products since 1832.

Derwent Studio coloured pencils are of fine quality and a perfect choice for detailed work due to the slightly harder core. With a maximum range of seventy-two colours, they offer a good selection to produce vibrant illustrations, and they hold a point well.

Derwent Artists coloured pencils complement the Studio range very well, due to their slightly waxier texture, which allows for layering and blending with relative ease.

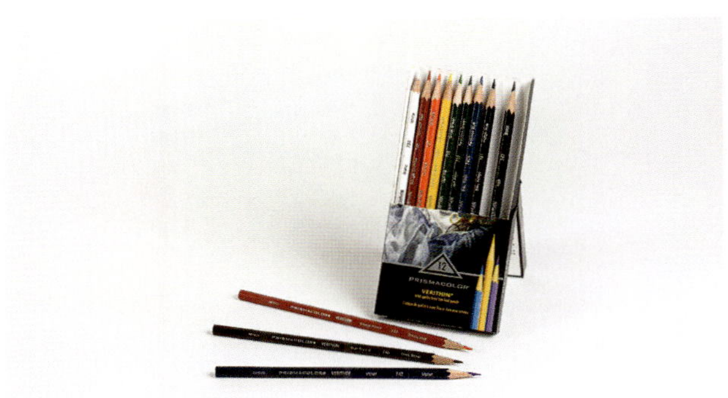

Use Prismacolor Verithins to achieve details and crisp lines in your work.

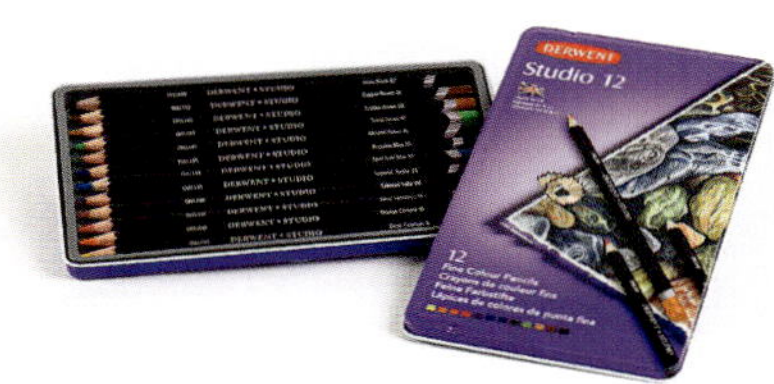

A harder colour core in the Derwent Studio range makes them a good choice for creating fine, detailed work.

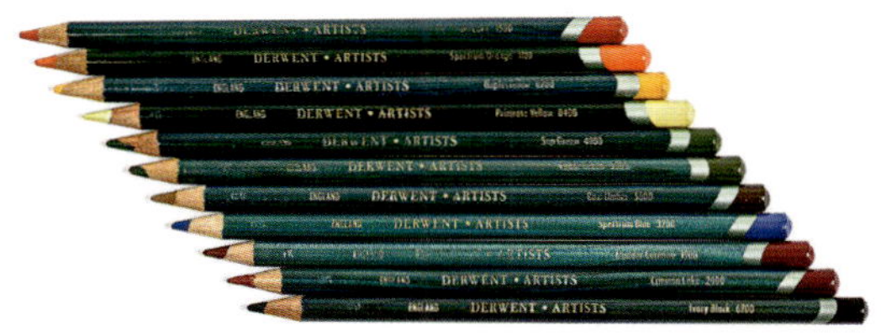

Derwent Artist coloured pencils with their waxier texture complement the Derwent Studio range.

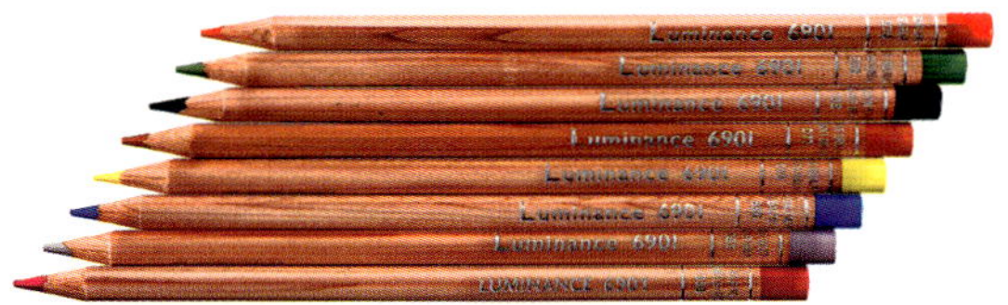

Luminance by Caran D'ache are renowned for their strong, vibrant, and durable colours.

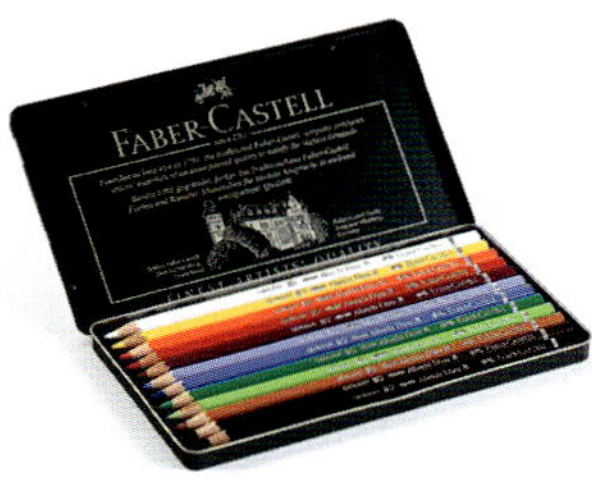

Albrecht Durer watercolour pencils maintain strong colour vibrancy and break-resistant leads.

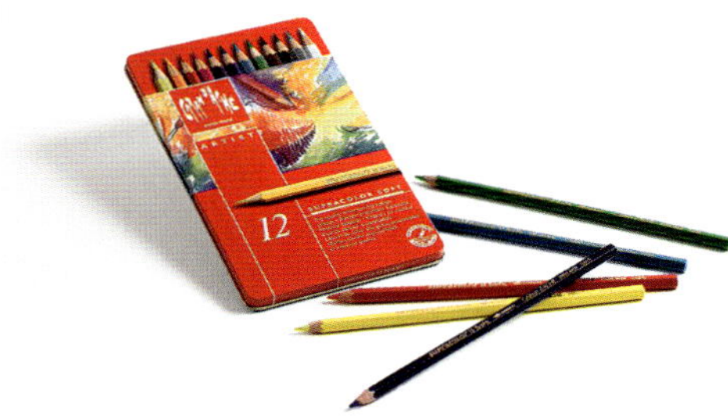

Supracolor water-soluble pencils offer excellent blending capabilities.

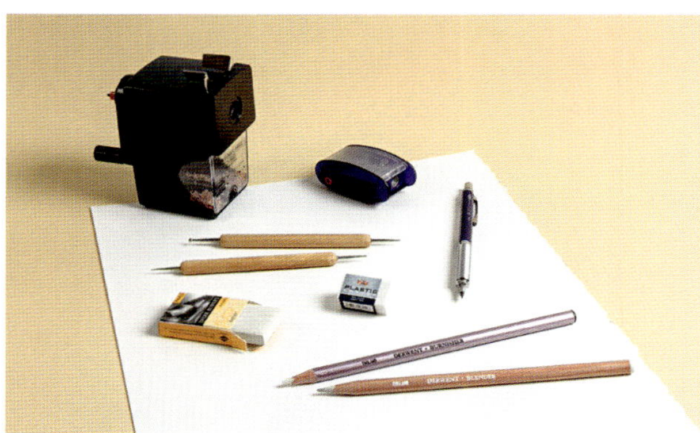

Equipment for coloured pencil illustration: hot-pressed watercolour paper, standard or mechanical pencil sharpener, graphite pencil, eraser, blender, burnisher and embossing tool.

Luminance 6901 by Caran D'ache

This range of soft, vibrant colours produced by Swiss company Caran D'ache are suitable for creating strong, vibrant illustrations. Caran D'ache offers a lightfastness guarantee on most of the colour range, meaning that these pencils can be used with confidence in the knowledge that the colours will remain true for many years to come.

WATER-SOLUBLE OPTIONS

The versatility of coloured pencils is such that it allows for the use of water to be added to some ranges. Water-soluble pencils can also be used dry, enabling a combination of techniques to be used without having to swap pencils. To create washes with water-solubles, the colour is first laid down and then water is applied with a paintbrush.

Albrecht Durer Watercolour pencils by Faber Castell

The Albrecht Durer watercolour range is an established range of water-soluble coloured pencils, and consists of 127 different colours, which are soft to apply and maintain a strong colour vibrancy. They are made with strong, thick, break-resistant leads, which blend well when wet. However, it is worth noting that the colours become permanent once dry, so re-wetting and blending is not possible.

Supracolor by Caran D'ache

This range offers slightly fewer colours than the Albrecht Durer option, but are nevertheless a popular choice. The application of Supracolor is soft, and blending is good. The range is also fully water-soluble meaning that they can be used in a similar way to watercolour regarding mixing and blending.

EQUIPMENT NEEDED FOR COLOURED PENCIL ILLUSTRATION

Besides a range of coloured pencils there are a few other items of equipment necessary to complete coloured pencil illustrations. You will most likely have some equipment already which is similar to that required for graphite drawing.

Colour charts

As with watercolour illustration it is wise to create a chart of the colours in your collection. You can do this however you wish, but it is sensible to make a chart using the hot-pressed paper you will use for your illustrations. Use your colour chart to then match hues to your subject matter.

Paper

Primarily, you will need some paper. The best option is to use hot-pressed (HP) paper such as Arches or Fabriano, which are both quality papers with smooth textures. This will ensure that as you layer your colours up, no texture will appear (*see* Chapter 1 for more information about paper).

It is quite possible to use the reverse side of hot-pressed paper, which may sometimes be marginally smoother than the front surface. This varies between manufacturers, so it is best to choose whichever side feels smoothest to you before you begin.

Pencil sharpener

This is an essential piece of equipment for the coloured pencil artist. Several types are available, however a standard hand-held wedge shape sharpener is not advised, since the blades become blunt quite quickly. Excellent results can be achieved using a rotary pencil sharpener especially or you could also try an electric or battery-operated variety, which also give good results.

Graphite pencil

Before you begin to use your coloured pencils, you will first need to lightly sketch out your drawing with an H or 2H pencil. You can use the same process as for watercolour illustration, by transferring your drawing using either a lightbox or tracing paper onto your hot-pressed paper.

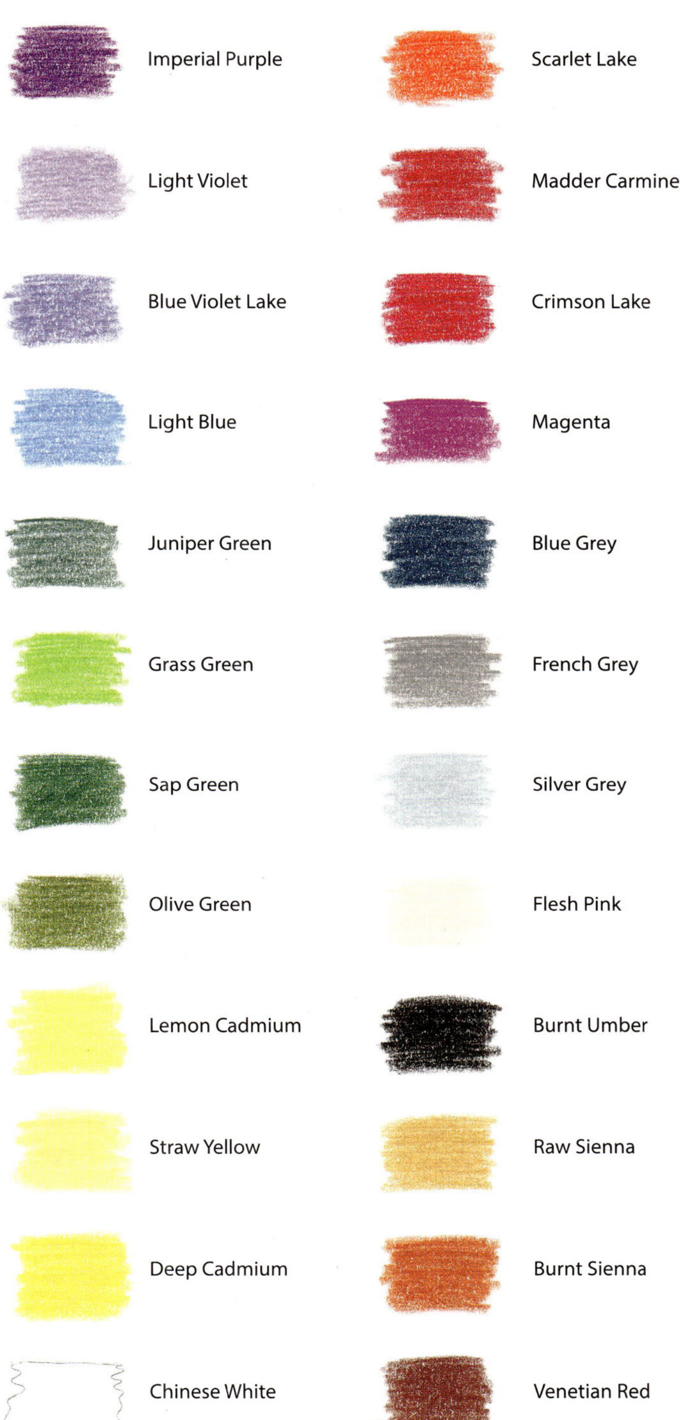

Make a colour chart of all your coloured pencils.

Eraser

If you happen to make a mistake whilst drawing your subject, it is best to use a soft, kneadable eraser such as a putty rubber, or a clean plastic eraser (*see* Chapter 1). Both types of eraser should not damage the fibres of your paper if used correctly.

It is also possible to erase areas of coloured pencil. Refer to the section 'Coloured Pencil Techniques' later in this chapter on how to do this.

Blender

A colourless blender is a useful tool to intensify layers of colour. Blending is achieved when the particles of colour are pushed together and into the grain of the paper, which in turn effectively mixes them together to create a very smooth, painterly effect.

Burnisher

Using a burnisher over layers of coloured pencil creates shine on your subject. The burnisher pencil will polish the surface of the coloured pencil but will not alter the colour. As an alternative, you could use the lightest colour in your mix to achieve a similar effect.

Blender and burnisher pencils can be purchased together in a pack from Derwent. Caran D'ache and Sanford also manufacture their own brands of colourless blending pencils.

Embossing tool

From time to time you may have use for an embossing tool, which can be used to create fine details such as hairs on stems or veins on leaves, for example.

An embossing tool is a stainless-steel stylus with a blunt head. Various thicknesses are available, and some are provided with easy-grip handles. For details such as hairs, you would need to use a fine-sized embossing tool.

BASIC COLOURED PENCIL TECHNIQUES

The overall biggest challenge is to layer the colours on top of each other to acquire both adequate saturation of colour and precise colour matching, in addition to creating the illusion of 3D. This process is the equivalent of mixing watercolours in a palette and then applying washes and shadow colours when painting. With coloured pencil work, the paper becomes the mixing palette and as the individual translucent colours are overlaid on one another, they begin to mix and blend together.

Layering

There are no fixed rules about how to lay down the colours in your illustration. Some artists will choose to lay down the lightest colours first, such as yellow, and then build the layers on top. However, a common method of working is to lay the shadow colours before applying the main subject colours. To do this, the same theoretical process of using the opposite (complementary) colours on the colour wheel to create shadow colours still apply (*see* Chapter 5). To layer coloured pencils, use the following method:

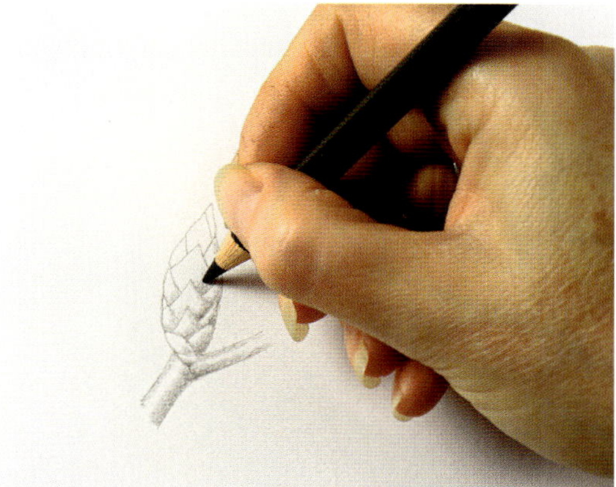

Step 1. Draw an outline of your subject first. Begin by laying down shadow colours in the darkest areas.

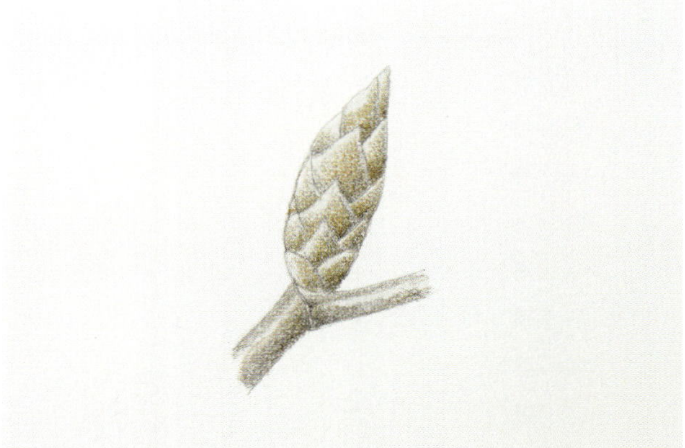

Step 2. The main subject colours can then be applied over the top of the shadows, lightly at first.

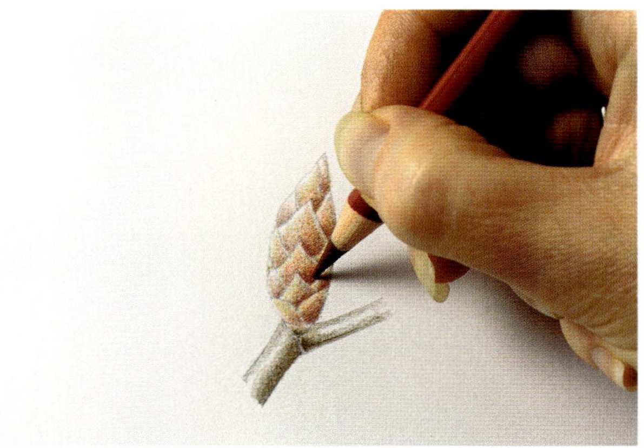

Step 3. Use tones either side of the main colours to help build the colour intensity, model your subject and create a 3D effect.

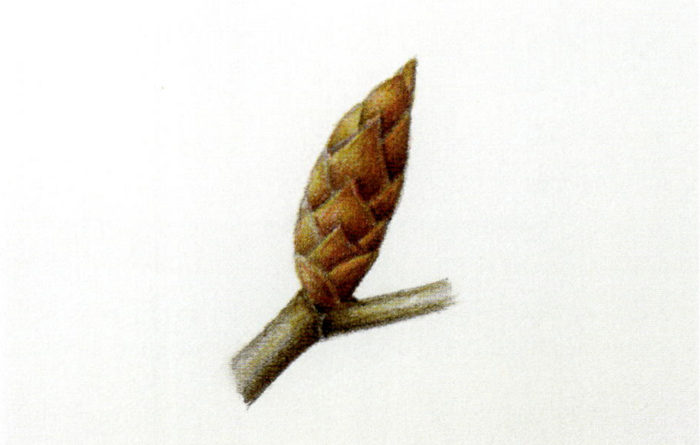

Step 4. Ensure you add any details and enough shadows if parts of the subject overlap. If you have highlights to include, they can remain paper white until near the end of the colouring process, and then be lightly coloured with a faint 'wash' of colour.

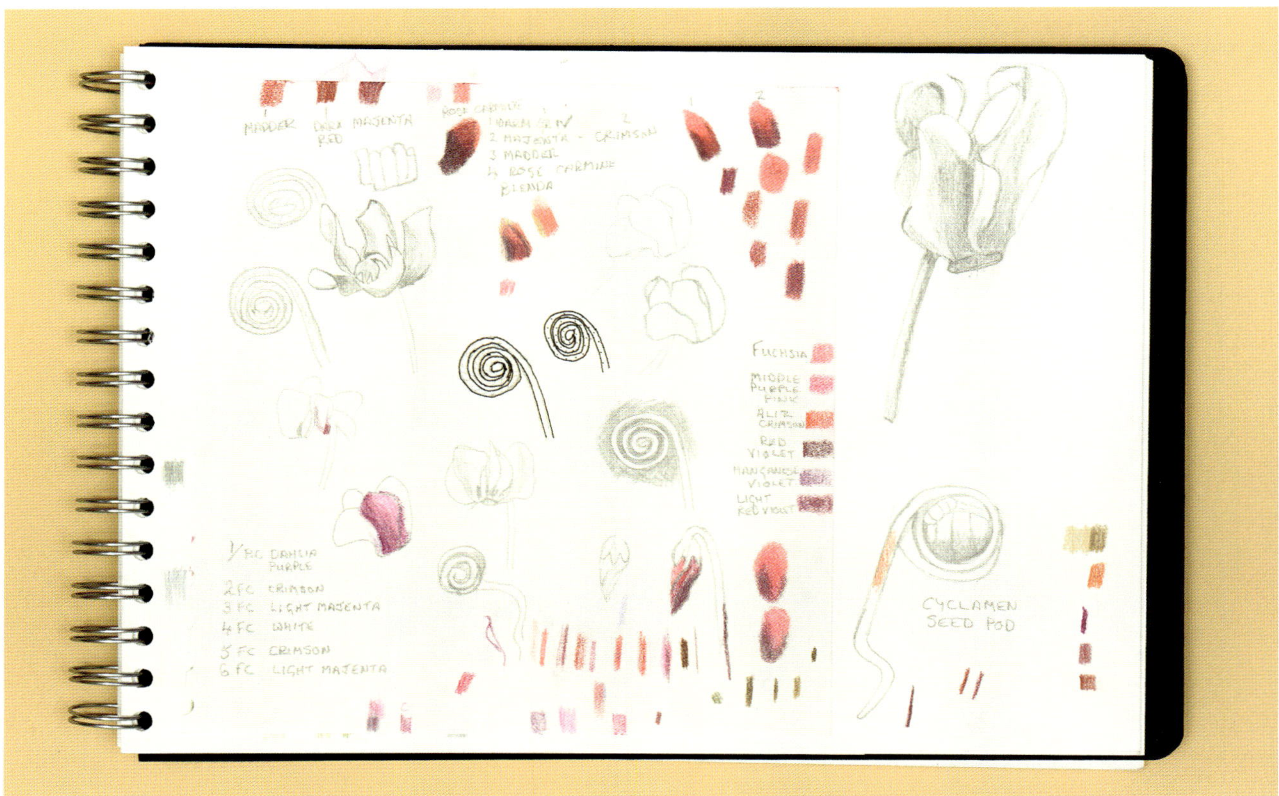

Laying the same colours down in different orders will give different results. Cyclamen: sketchbook work in coloured pencil. VAL FORSTER

Colour matching

Unless you are extremely fortunate, the chances of a coloured pencil completely matching your subject is minimal, in which case you will need to use two or more colours together to make the correct colour. The process of colour matching may take some time, so making several swatches of test colour on a spare piece of paper beforehand is advisable. Once you have made a match, it is then essential to remember the sequence of layering. You will discover that a different colour is made if you do not use the same sequence for subsequent applications, so make a note before you begin – especially if you need to use several colours.

Application

Rather like graphite tonal shading, using small elliptical movements to cover an area is the best method of achieving a smooth continuous tone. Check that your pencils are ready and sharpened before you begin, and remember to alter the pressure of your hand as you shade; more pressure for darker areas and less for lighter areas. Use a colourless blender pencil as you layer the colours together. Adding finer details and neatening and crisping up any edges can be done towards the end of the process with very sharp pencils.

Burnishing

Only when you have applied all your colour completely should you burnish your work. Burnishing will help to improve the lustre and brightness of your coloured pencil work, and can help to blend the colours still further. You will need to use a reasonable amount of pressure to do so, as this will ensure the wax or oil in the coloured pencil is polished and a shine is achieved. Once you have burnished your work, it will be very hard to apply further coloured pencil over the top, so ensure that you have completely finished before you start the burnishing process.

Once you have burnished your work, it is wise to 'fix' the coloured pencil in place using fixative, which will help to avoid smudging once your work is complete.

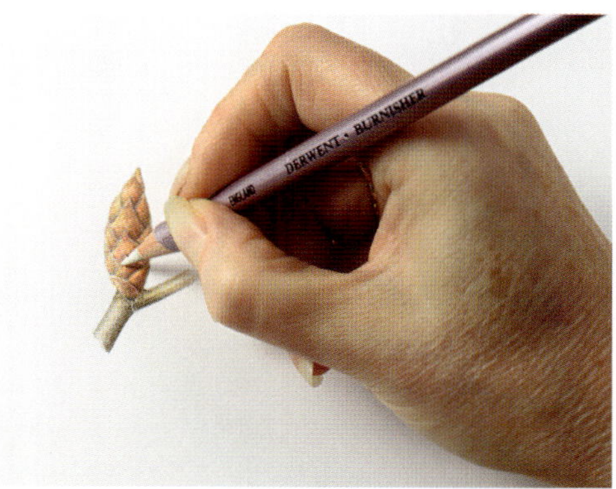

Use a burnishing pencil to brighten and blend the colours together.

Lifting off

Undoubtedly, from time to time you may need to lift some colour from your work, either because you have smudged some colour accidentally or you have made some other error, but you could also lift colour off to reveal highlights that appear on your subject.

There are several ways to remove unwanted colour, such as using a putty rubber kneaded into a fine point or chisel shape to lightly remove small areas or lines of colour, or areas of smudged colour around the edges. For major areas of colour removal, a battery-operated eraser will effectively lift coloured pencil. However, it is advisable to practise this technique on a spare piece of paper first so that you do not overwork the area and make a hole in the paper.

Sticky-back plastic or low-adhesive clear tape can be used to lift colour to reveal highlights. Use the following method:

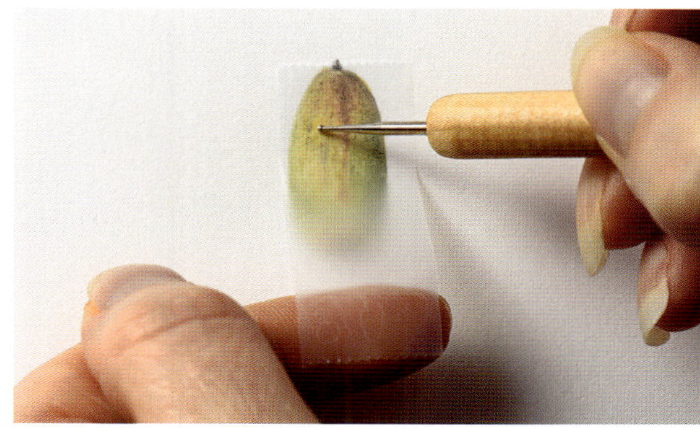

Step 1. First, lay the sticky-back plastic or low-adhesive clear tape over the area of coloured pencil to be lifted. Gently press down onto the plastic or tape with a pointed pencil or use an embossing tool lightly and 'draw' over the area to be lifted.

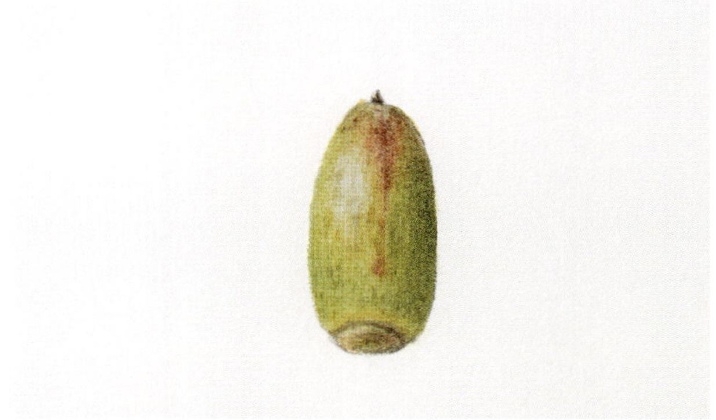

Step 2. Lift the tape carefully to reveal your highlight and tidy up any hard edges left behind. Blot off any excess coloured pencil particles with a putty rubber.

Using an embossing tool

Sometimes it may be necessary to use special techniques to show fine details in your specimen. Many subjects have fine structures and features such as the intricate venation on some leaves or the fine hairs on stems. A relatively quick and straightforward method of acquiring these effects is to use a fine point embossing tool.

For creating light-coloured veins on a dark leaf, use the same method of indenting after an initial light vein colour has been laid. Veins on leaves are seldom white, so you should ensure you have colour matched the vein accurately prior to indenting with an embossing tool.

Use the following method to indicate pale-coloured hairs on stems:

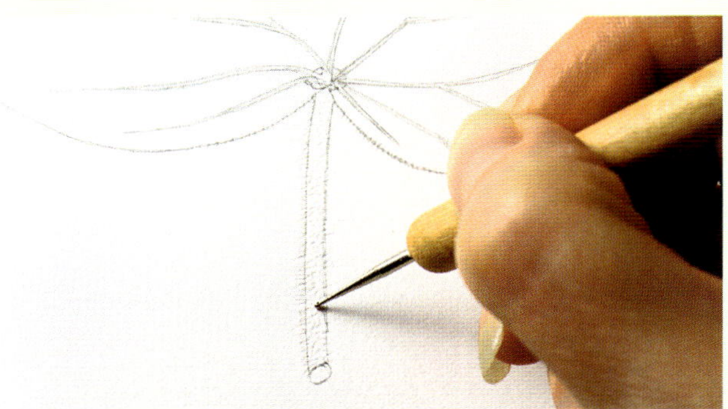

Step 1. Make small indentations with the embossing tool where the hairs appear on the stem. (Remember to draw them foreshortened when they are visible directly in front of you and lengthen them as they move out to the sides.)

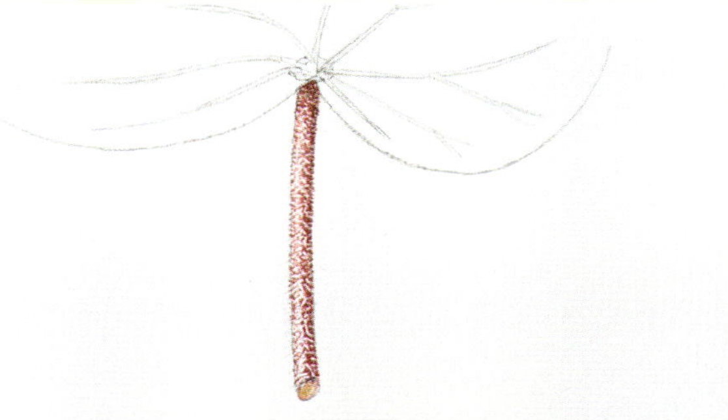

Step 2. Layer up the colours of the stem over the indentations you have made.

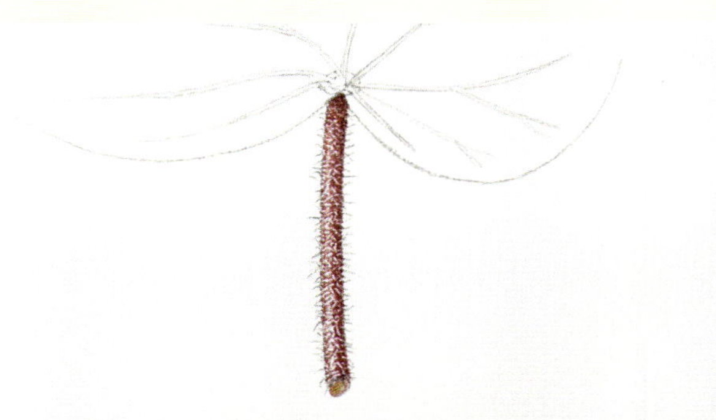

Step 3. Carefully define the hairs projecting at the sides by adding a delicate underline to each hair in a shadow colour. You may find it helpful to use a magnifying glass whilst doing this, so that you can see each indented hair clearly.

PEN AND INK

With the advent of the printing process in the fifteenth century, taxonomists began to use ink to produce precise, meticulous scientific studies of botanical specimens. This became the conventional method of describing plants and their complexities, and illustrations often included magnified and dissection drawings. As printing processes developed, botanical ink drawings were used to produce floras around the world.

The term 'pen and ink' implies the traditional technique of dipping a nib attached to a suitable holder into ink, and applying it to the paper. Nowadays, with the introduction of disposable fibre-tip pens, dipping is no longer a necessity, although we do still tend to refer to the process as 'pen and ink' illustration. It is most common practice to use black ink for illustrations, but options such as sepia, and 'graphite' (which mimics graphite pencil) can be used as alternatives.

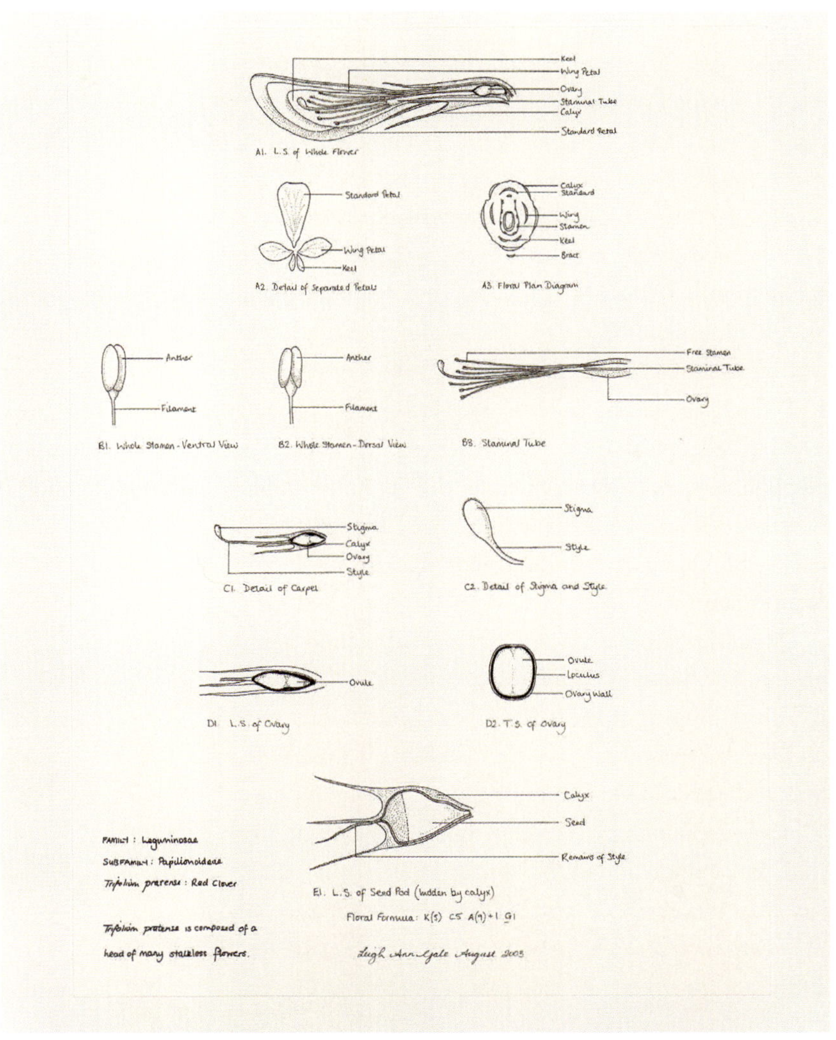

Floral structure of *Trifolium pratense*, Red Clover. LEIGH ANN GALE

As with coloured pencils, pen and ink is increasing in popularity. Several professional botanical illustrators specialize in this medium and some have been awarded medals for their work. The Margaret Flockton annual international award for scientific botanical illustration attracts submissions from artists around the world, and has helped promote the use of pen and ink as a pure and scientific method of illustrating botanical species.

TYPES OF PEN

Many artists enjoy the convenience of disposable fibre-tip pens; however, some still prefer to work with traditional dipping pens. Technical drawing pens are also popular,

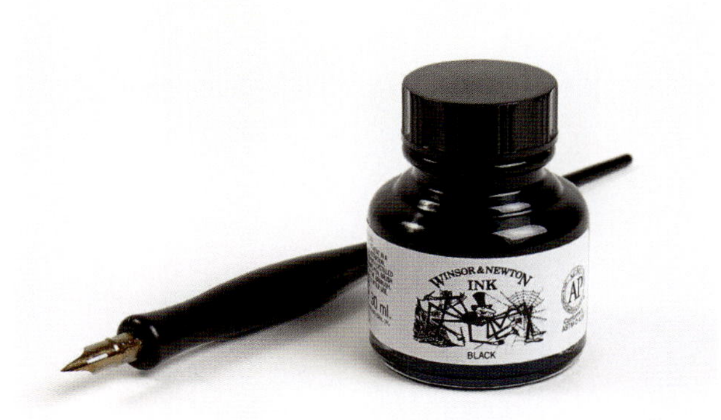

Traditional dipping pen and ink.

especially if the artist has used them professionally in other types of work, such as graphic design or architecture drawing.

It is a matter of personal preference as to which type of pen to use, so it is worth exploring some options before deciding which you prefer for your own work.

Fibre-tip disposable pens

Without doubt the most convenient types of pen to use for ink drawing are the fibre-tip varieties. There are many brands that are long lasting and available in several thicknesses. It is always best to choose brands from quality manufacturers rather than cheaper alternatives. PITT artist's pens by Faber Castell are excellent quality. The ink is 'archival' India ink, which is both waterproof and lightfast, making these pens a perfect choice for both professional and amateur artists. They are available in packs of four, which include varying thicknesses, ranging from 0.1mm to 1.5mm.

Staedtler Fineliner pens offer a similar good quality option, and are also available in a pack of four assorted nib sizes ranging from 0.1mm to 0.7mm. They boast up to eighteen hours of continuous cap-off time, which makes them suitable for continued periods of long use.

Coloured inks can make a refreshing change from traditional black, and could be used especially if the subject warrants it. For example, sepia for wood and bark illustrations. Derwent have produced a range of sepia and graphite effect coloured ink pens in their Graphik Line Maker brand. Both colours are available in sets of three pens from 0.1mm to 0.5mm nib widths.

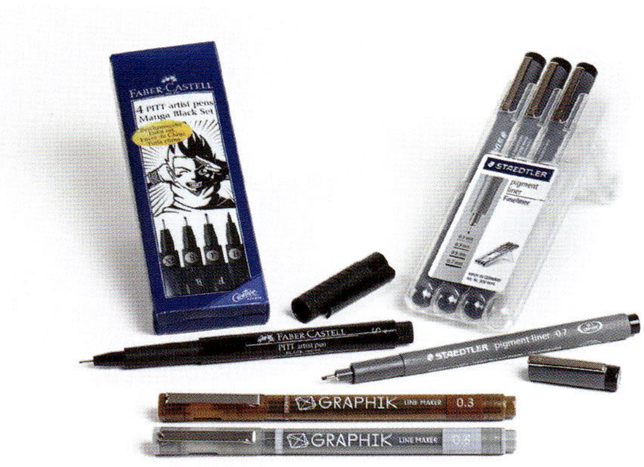

Fibre-tip disposable pens are convenient to use.

Technical drawing pens

Technical drawing pens, once the mainstream tool for ink drawing amongst graphic designers, draughtsmen, architects and so on, are still used today. Professional botanical illustrators like them for their sturdiness and extensive nib thickness options.

Rotring, a popular brand, produce both Rapidograph (ink via capillary cartridge) and Isograph (ink via refillable reservoir) technical pens, both available in a range of thirteen line widths from 0.1mm. The quality of the Rotring brand is insurmountable; these pens have hard-wearing chrome plated tips and opaque, lightfast ink which is waterproof and fast drying. Available individually or in sets, they are ideal for fine and very detailed drawings.

Staedtler also produce fine quality technical pens such as their Marsmatic range, which can be purchased individually or in sets, and are available in a range of line widths.

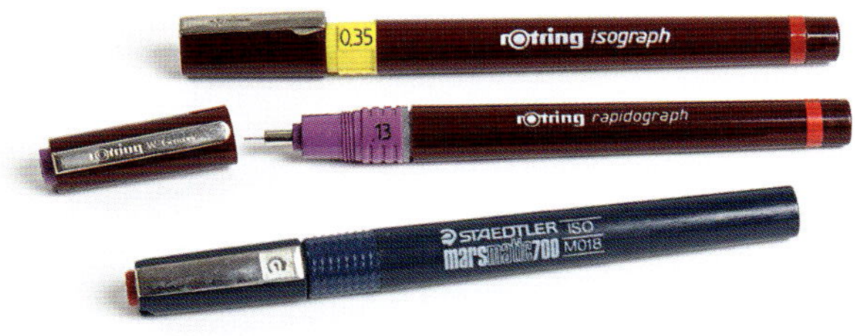

Technical drawing pens are sturdy and available in a multitude of nib thicknesses.

ADDITIONAL EQUIPMENT NEEDED FOR PEN AND INK DRAWING

Other than your chosen style of ink pen, you will also need smooth paper or smooth board, a pencil eraser, and an ink eraser to produce your illustration. You should work over a faint drawn outline of your composition and then gently erase pencil lines once you have finished and the ink is completely dry.

Paper and board

Ink pens work best when applied to good quality rag-based hot-pressed paper or Bristol Board. If you choose

Useful additional equipment for pen and ink illustration: hot-pressed watercolour paper, Bristol Board, eraser, and ink eraser.

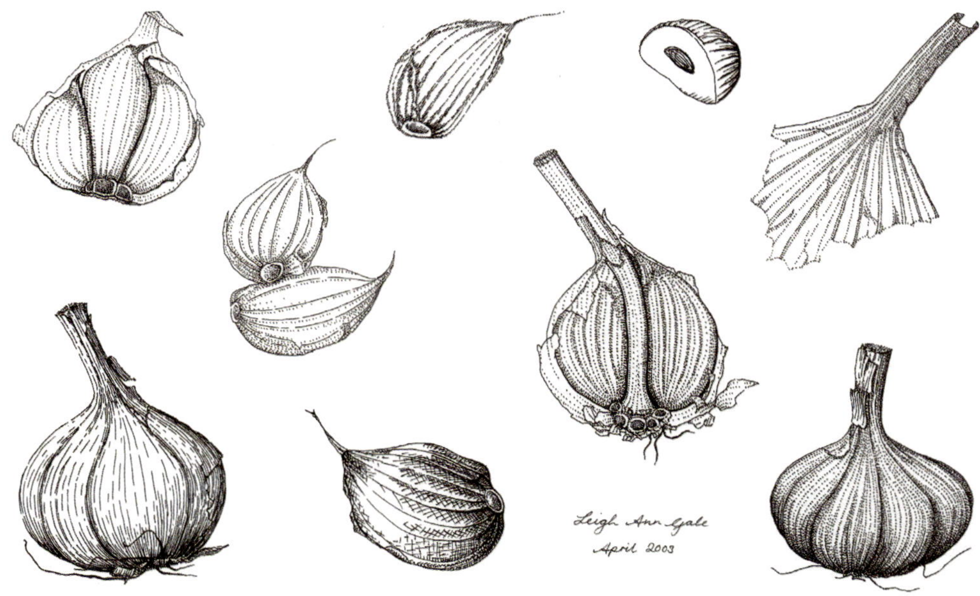

Garlic studies in pen and ink. LEIGH ANN GALE

paper, you will notice that the pen will just very slightly 'drag' over the surface, especially when using a very fine width nib. If you intend to make extremely fine detailed studies, then it would be wise to use Bristol Board instead, which provides an even smoother surface to work on.

Erasers

To remove pencil lines from Bristol Board, use a clean plastic eraser to avoid leaving any residue or smears, which a gum-based eraser may otherwise leave behind. For erasing pencil lines from paper, either use the plastic eraser or a kneadable putty rubber.

If you need to erase ink, then a more abrasive eraser can be used, such as the type used in traditional typewriting. These erasers are usually coloured pink or blue, and are often combined in a block with a standard graphite eraser.

BASIC PEN AND INK TECHNIQUES

When drawing in ink, you will need to be mindful that the marks you make should help to define the three dimensions of your subject, as well as any textures and patterns. Unlike pencil shading or watercolour painting, you will make solid marks every time, there is no grey or opposite hue available to create tonal variations. Tones must be made using a choice of mark such as stipple, line, or cross-hatch, and placed in close proximation to make dark tones or spread further apart to make lighter tones.

The choice of ink mark you make is important and you should consider them carefully, so that they are relevant to indicate the textures and patterns of your specimen as well as indicating tone. For example, a smooth-surfaced cylindrical stem could be indicated with stipple, a woody textured stem could be indicated with small broken and unbroken lines, and the pattern of a snake's head fritillary could be indicated by using an arrangement of chequered blocks of solid black and white.

More often than not, a combination of different marks is used together in one drawing, and a solid outline used to depict the edge of a drawing is common practice.

Stipple

The technique of using dots is known as 'stippling' and is an excellent way to show effective modelling of a subject. By varying the quantity of dots laid down, subtle tonal

Vary the quantity of dots laid down to indicate darker and lighter tones.

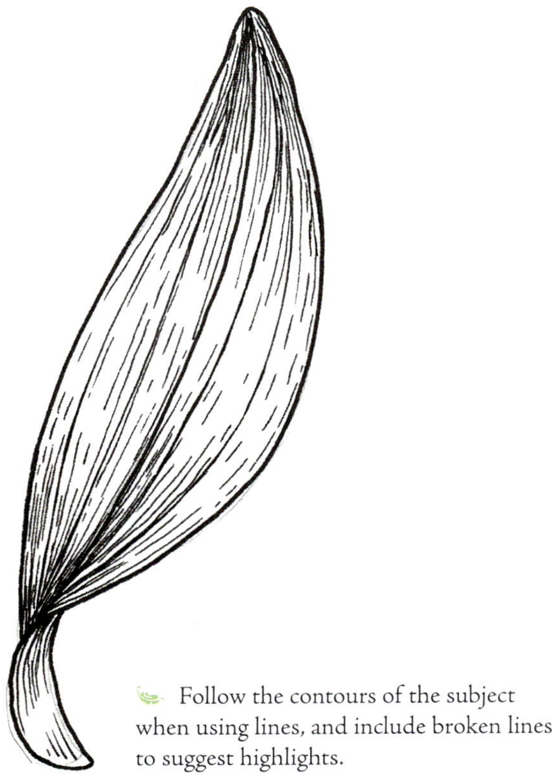

Follow the contours of the subject when using lines, and include broken lines to suggest highlights.

differences can be achieved to show lighter and darker tones. The technique is especially useful when finer, intricate details need to be shown on magnifications and dissections.

Lines

Solid line is generally used to show the outline of a drawing and the main structures of a specimen. However, care should be taken not to make solid lines too thick as this will give a heavy, clumsy feel to your work.

Lines can also be used to show linear venation on leaves, such as those of iris, bluebell, and orchid. Drawing lines on long leaves requires good concentration, to ensure that the lines are drawn over the whole leaf and follow the leaf contours. If you need to stop and reposition your hand whilst doing this, carefully join the ends of the lines together. To indicate highlights, use broken lines in a few places.

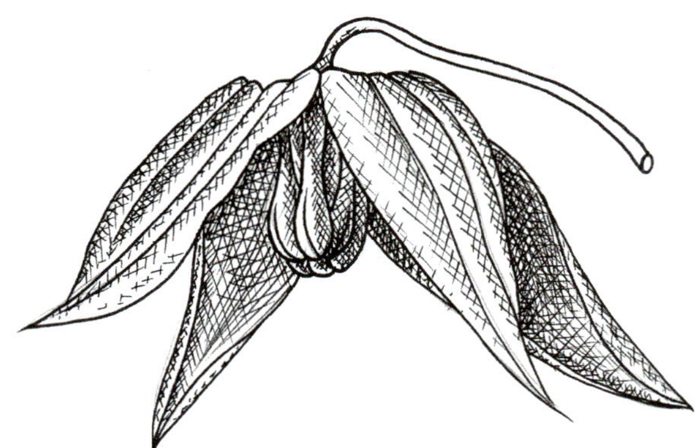

Diagonal hatching with added vertical and horizontal lines increase the illusion of dark shadows.

Hatching

Hatching is used as another method of indicating tones, particularly if an area is dark, and can be achieved by using lines in a criss-cross fashion. Adding further lines over the top in a vertical and horizontal direction will further intensify any very dark shadow areas.

Combining techniques

Most botanical ink drawing will be achieved by using a combination of fine ink marks, most commonly stipple and line. This combination works well, as light and shade, form, texture, and pattern can all be shown satisfactorily whilst still maintaining essential scientific accuracy and detail. However, combinations of line weights or line, stipple and block work can also be effective.

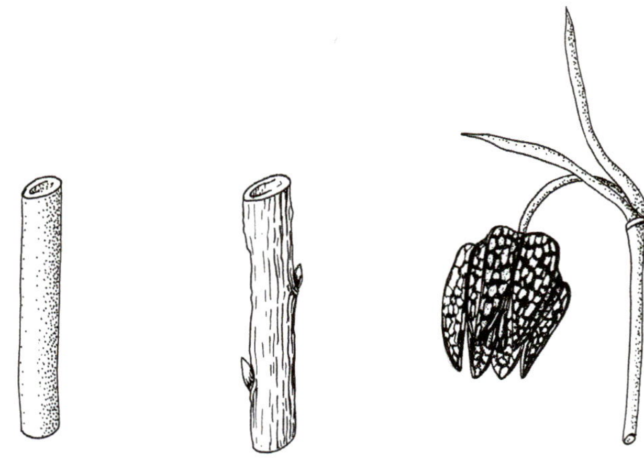

Light, shade, form and texture can be shown by combining techniques.

COMBINING MEDIA

The idea of combining media is common among artists but is less practised by botanical artists and illustrators. However, that is not to say you should avoid it altogether, so long as the aim of producing your illustration is comparable with that of using a single medium – that it is scientifically accurate – then a combination of media can be a fresh and contemporary approach.

You may like to experiment and try out various combinations for yourself on your own projects. Even with the limited choices discussed in this chapter plus graphite and watercolour, the results might surprise you! Here are a few ideas to get you started.

GRAPHITE AND COLOURED PENCIL

Graphite pencil can enhance a coloured pencil illustration quite significantly, especially as it can be used to enhance the 3D shape of your subject. Graphite pencil is first used to apply the darkest tones and shadows, before coloured pencil glazes are overlaid. The result gives excellent tonal contrast between highlights and shadows, and is quite quickly achieved. Note: to avoid smudging or 'muddying' the coloured pencil glazes, you should first 'fix' the graphite. Use a workable fixative such as Krylon Workable Fixatif or Winsor & Newton Artist's Workable Fixative and allow to dry before applying coloured pencils.

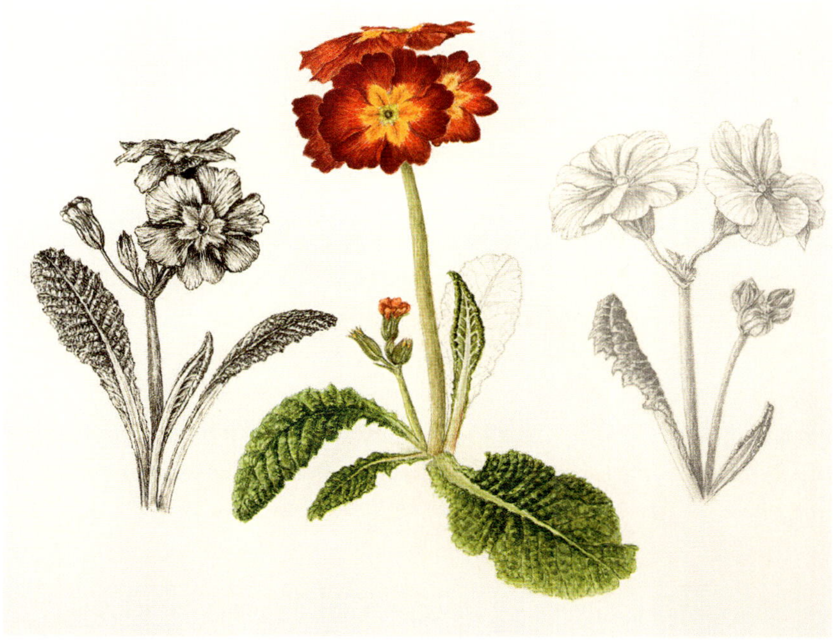

Primulas – mixed media. COLLEEN BALLONE

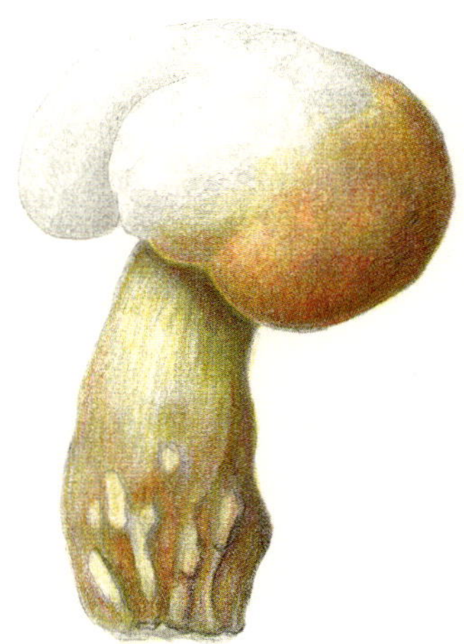

Apply graphite to indicate shadows and 3D before adding coloured pencil work over the top.

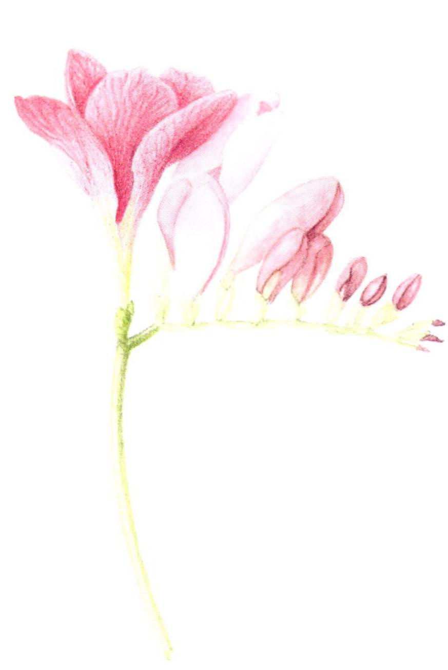

Lay watercolour washes before applying details in coloured pencil over the top.

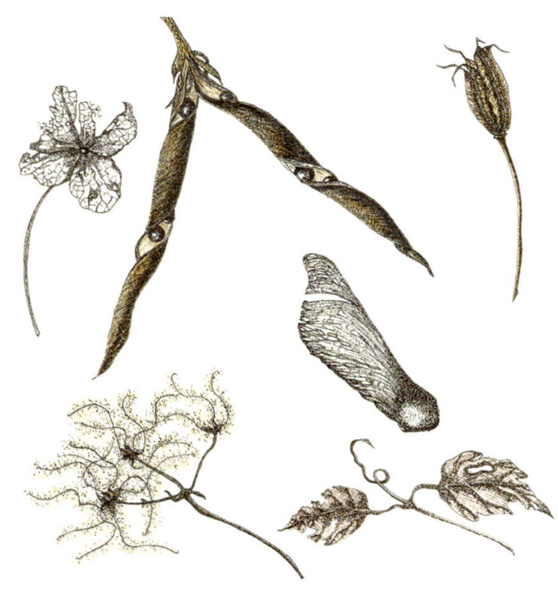

Seed heads: Pen and ink with watercolour wash. VICTORIA WILKINSON

WATERCOLOUR AND COLOURED PENCIL

In this combination, watercolour is usually laid down in washes before coloured pencil detail is applied over the top. You could use water-soluble pencils instead if you wish. It can be relatively fast to work with this combination, as larger areas can be covered initially with the watercolour washes. Allow each wash to dry before applying the next, and reserve the fine detailed work for the coloured pencils. Make sure your coloured pencils are sharp.

INK AND WATERCOLOUR

Watercolour applied over a pen and ink drawing can look especially effective and is quick to achieve. It is fine to use either pale washes to lightly tint your drawing, or stronger washes can be used to give greater saturation, giving the illusion of more form and structure to your work.

For this combination, you will need to ensure that the ink you use is permanent, otherwise mixing will occur when watercolour is applied.

GRAPHITE AND WATERCOLOUR

Similar in application to graphite and coloured pencil, but remember to fix the graphite with workable fixative before applying watercolour washes.

Some artists use this combination in a different way; part of the illustration remains purely in graphite whilst other areas are coloured. This can look very effective, especially if you need to emphasize specific parts of your illustration, in which case the areas to be depicted can be reserved for the watercolour application. Alternatively, graphite in this combination could emphasize aerial perspective (*see* Chapter 7), with it being used to depict background details.

If additional details such as enlargements, dissections and scaled habit drawings are needed, it is quite acceptable to add them using graphite to complement the main watercolour illustration.

Checklist for Alternative Media: Coloured Pencil

- Try out and experiment with different brands of coloured pencil before starting an illustration.
- Use the smoothest side of hot-pressed paper to work on.
- Prepare in advance. Make a colour chart of all your coloured pencils on hot-pressed paper and use it for colour matching.
- Consider laying down shadow colours first, before applying the main subject colours.
- Colour match carefully. Make test swatches before you begin, and remember the application sequence when layering two or more colours.
- Keep coloured pencils sharp at all times by using a rotary, electric or battery-operated pencil sharpener.
- Blend colours together with a blending tool as you work, and only use a burnisher once you have finished.

Checklist for Alternative Media: Pen and Ink

- Before starting an illustration, experiment with different types of pen such as fibre tip and technical drawing pens to see which you prefer using.
- Consider using Bristol Board for very fine, scientific illustrations rather than hot-pressed paper.
- Use appropriate ink marks to define areas of tone, texture, and pattern.
- Outline your drawing and its main structures using a continuous solid black line.
- Use a slightly abrasive ink eraser to erase ink.

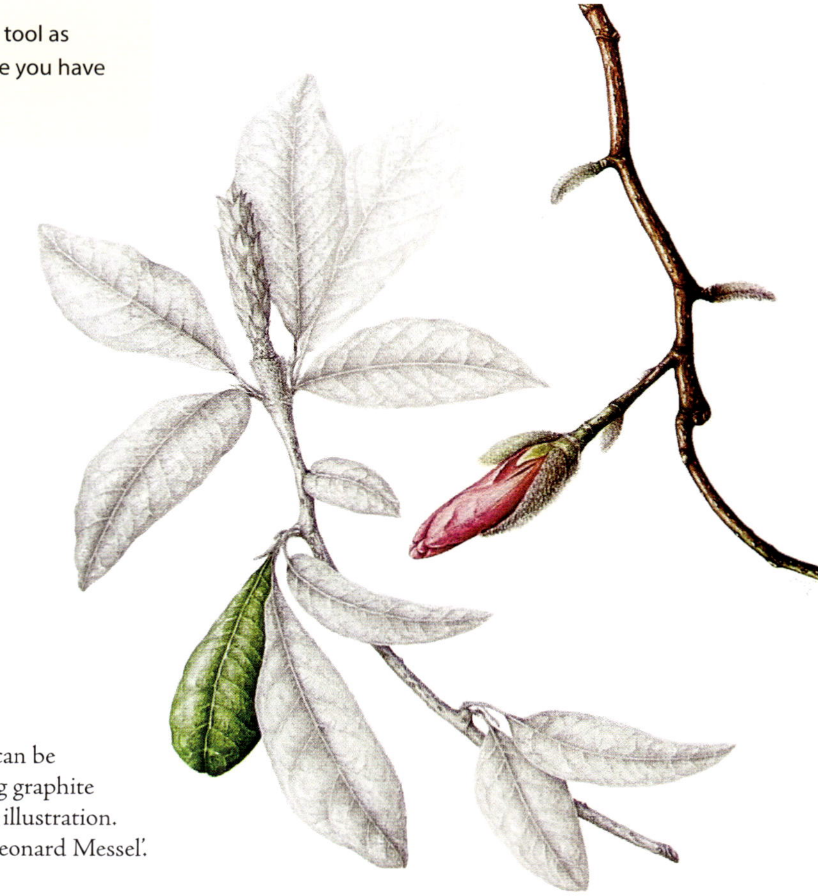

Dramatic effects can be achieved by combining graphite and watercolour in an illustration. *Magnolia x loebneri* 'Leonard Messel'. LEIGH ANN GALE

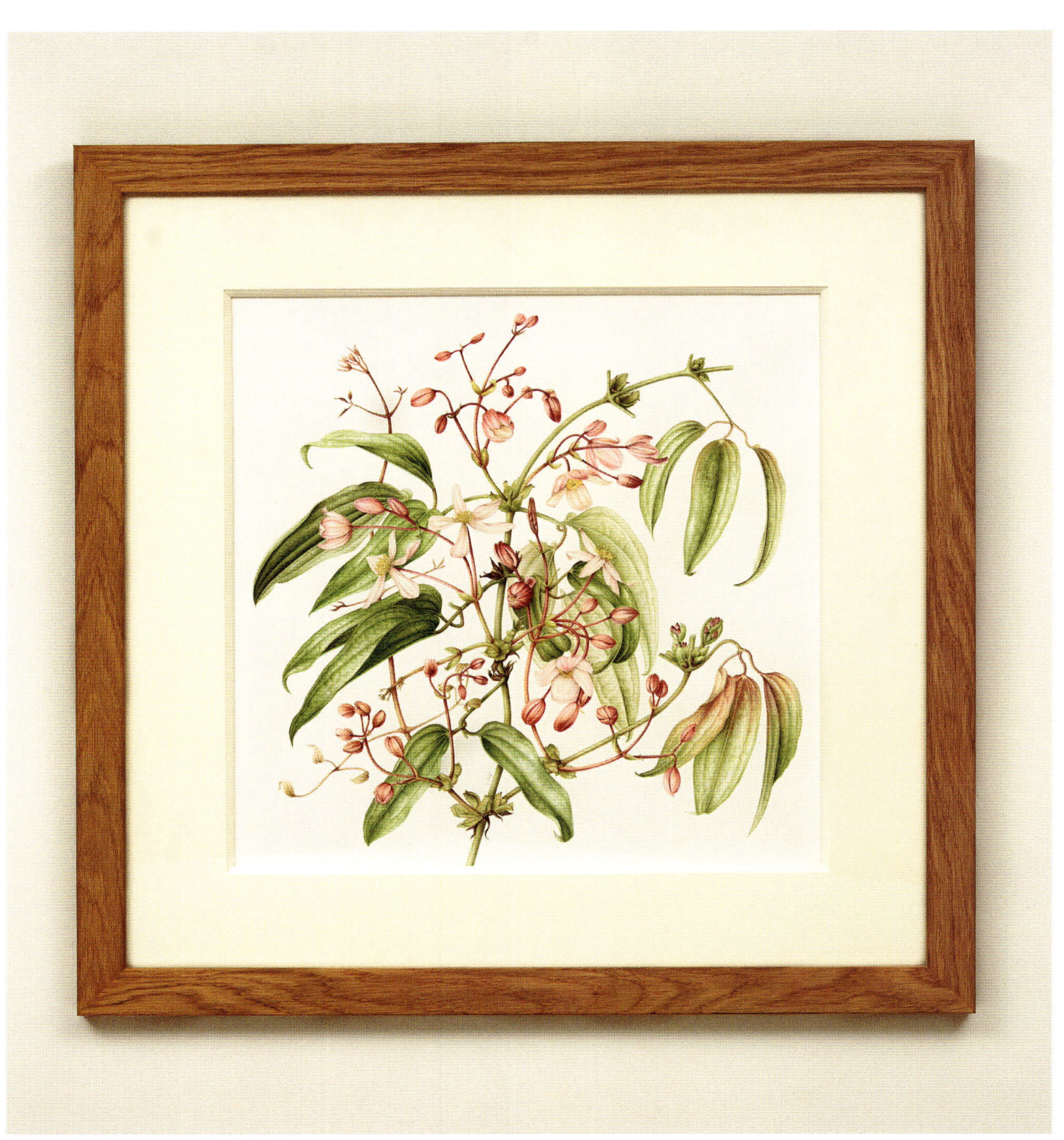

CHAPTER 11

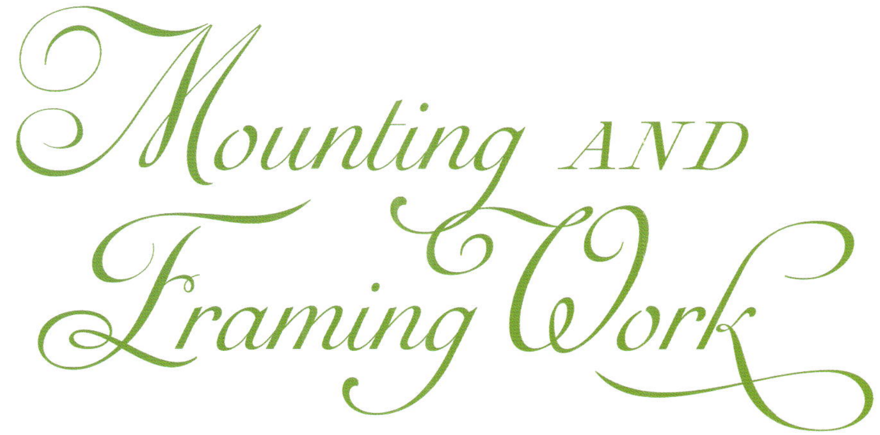

Mounting and Framing Work

Art consists of limitation. The most beautiful part of every picture is the frame.

– Gilbert K. Chesterton (English writer, journalist and art critic)

Simplicity and timelessness are key for mounting and framing botanical illustrations. Whether your intention is to exhibit, fulfil a commission, or simply to hang on a wall in your own home, making good, well-informed choices about the mounting and framing process is a major consideration. You will have spent many hours of hard work up to this point; it would be imprudent to consider the style of mount and frame without a thoughtful approach.

The mount and frame you choose for your illustration will become part of the overall finished artwork. It is the point at which the work 'comes to life' and is finally completed.

Learning to make well-informed decisions about styles and colours of mounts and choosing compatible frames will all be part of the final process of completing your artwork. In this chapter, we will consider these decisions, explore the options of choice and learn about the mounting and framing of artworks.

Clematis armandii 'Apple Blossom'. LEIGH ANN GALE

MOUNTS

It is without doubt that a botanical illustration will look better if it is mounted, and arguably even more so if it is subsequently framed. Simply placing a mount around your artwork immediately gives a sense of near completeness, the painting process is finally over, and it is now time to put your work on show.

The primary function of a mount is to create a gap between the artwork and the glass so that they do not touch one another over time when the painting is framed. However, besides this important role the appearance and style of the mount you choose is equally significant, and needs to be considered carefully.

Most often simplicity will work best. For example, there are many textured boards available, but a smooth texture will always be more sympathetic for mounting botanical illustrations. The focus should be the painting itself; choosing a distracting textured mount board will only detract, causing an effect of competitiveness with the painting.

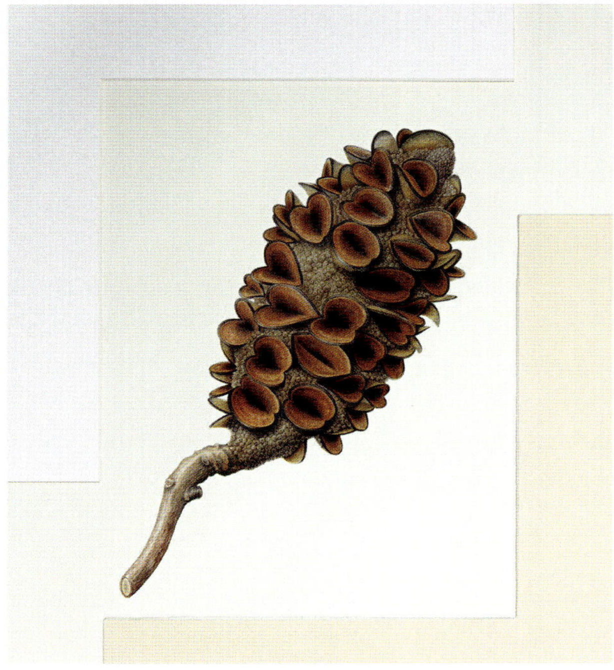

Choose an off-white mount for botanical illustrations. Ensure you choose a mount to harmonize with the tones of your painting. In this example, the warmer tone (bottom) is more appropriate than the cooler option (top).

CHOOSING A COLOUR AND STYLE

The first part of the mounting process will be to choose a colour. In botanical illustration, it is important that the mount does not become the focus, or detract from the work itself. It needs to act as a 'support'; a way of presenting the work. The general convention is to use an off-white colour but there are many variations on this, for example ivory, pale cream, vanilla. Each tends to take

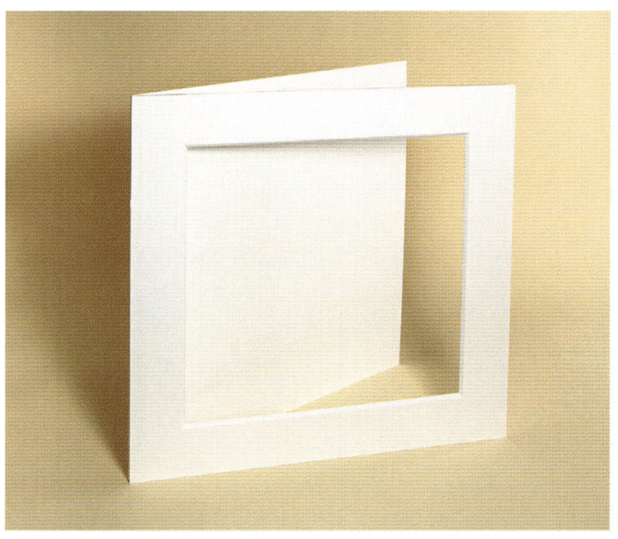

A book mount is ideal for mounting botanical paintings, allowing you to hinge your work to the backing board using archival tape.

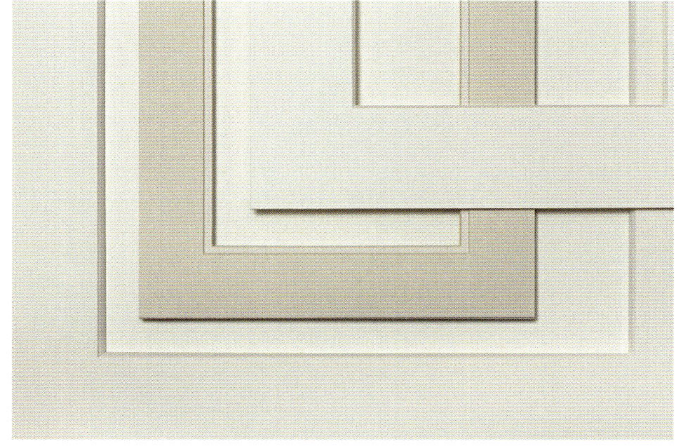

Examples of single, double, and thicker, foamcore mounts.

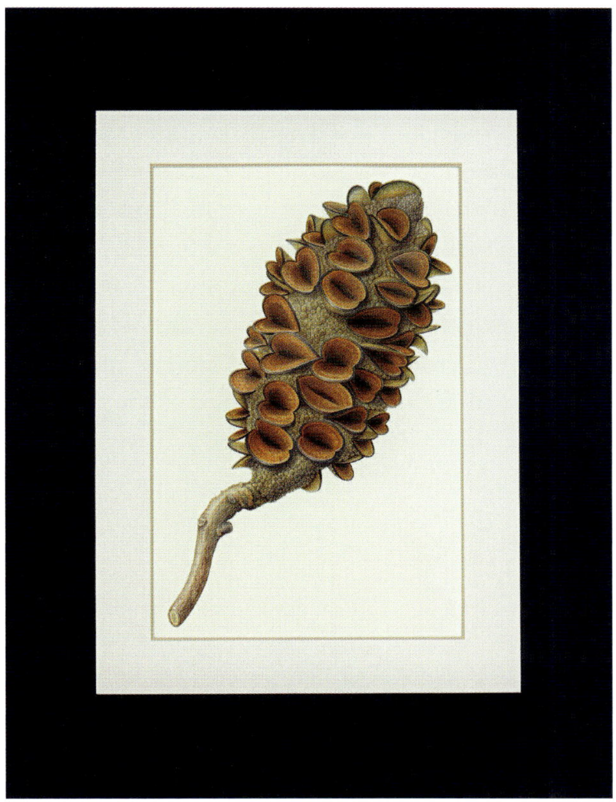

The narrow border mount looks unbalanced around the painting.

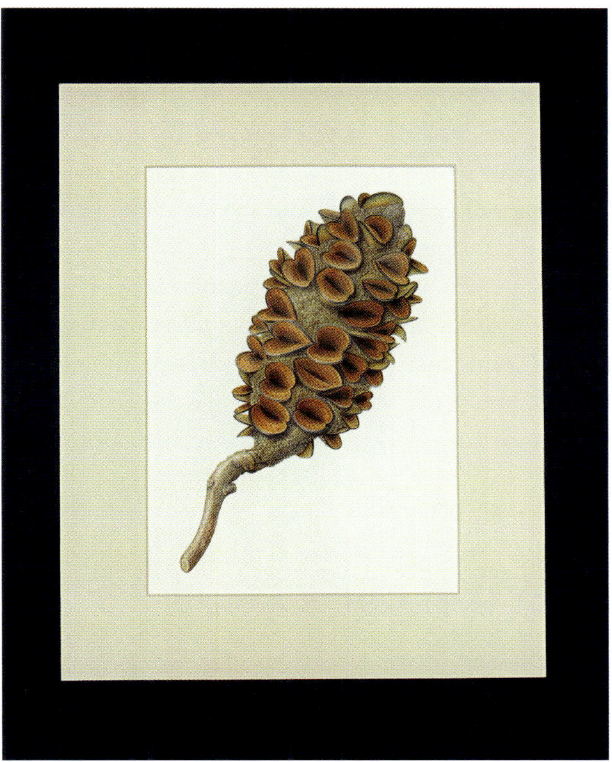

Use a wider border width mount to balance the effect.

on either a cool or warm tone. Studying the colours in your painting will help you decide whether you need a warm or cool tone. For example, if your painting depicts warm tones of red berries, it would be wise to choose an off-white colour with a warm tone. Conversely, if your painting depicts foliage of a deep blue/green with pale, perhaps lemon-coloured flowers, a mount suggesting a cool tone would be the best option.

As well as the colour of the mount, you will also have to select a style. Are you going to opt for a single or double mount, or possibly a thicker mount made of foam core? A good, reputable picture framer (even if you don't intend to frame your artwork) should be able to advise you and offer suggestions, or you may have very clear ideas of your own.

Your mount should be constructed of acid-free board, which is necessary to minimize the process of deterioration which acidity promotes. It should be borne in mind that your painting is likely to remain mounted (and possibly framed) for many years to come, so preserving it in the best possible condition is in your own interest to avoid degeneration over time.

The way in which your mount is made is equally important. It should consist of a front board with a mitred, bevelled aperture cut into it, plus a backing board upon which the artwork will be attached. The construction of the mount can be such that it is rather like an opened book, hinged along the left edge. The hinging mechanism should be made of archival quality tape, which is available either gummed or sticky on one side. If the gummed variety is used, then it will need to be dampened with water to make it sticky and adhere to the boards.

CHOOSING A MOUNT SIZE

Once you have decided on the colour and style of your mount, the next decision to make is the size. There are no set rules about this, other than what looks visually appealing and well balanced with the painting. It will be easy to ascertain that if a mount consisting of very narrow-width borders placed on a large painting for example, will look very unbalanced as the mount border widths will look too thin. However, by increasing the border widths of the mount, the visual ratio of mount to painting will be corrected, and the mount and artwork will harmonize much more.

Often, it is a good idea to ensure that the bottom border width is slightly greater than the remaining three sides. It could be as little as an increase of just 5mm, but this is enough to create an optical illusion that all four borders are of equal width. Without this increase, the bottom border can appear visually narrower, causing an effect of the painting sitting too low in the mount.

If you have chosen to use a double mount, you will need to consider how much overlap to allow for the two boards at the aperture. Again, there are no rules about this, but the effect should be one of balance and proportion. Usually, an overlap of about 5mm works well. The thickness of the two boards you use is up to you. Sometimes, a thicker board sits nicely against a thinner board on top, creating an impact of contrast and a sense of depth within the painting.

Affixing a painting to a picture mount

- Place your painting on the backing board and position it until you are happy that it looks visually balanced when the aperture is laid on top.
- Mark in pencil with a small dot where the four corners of the paper appear against the backing board of the mount.
- Take away your painting. Cut two lengths of acid-free archival tape approximately 2in long.
- Attach each piece of tape to the reverse of the illustration, along the top edge, approximately 2in in from the left hand side and the right hand side. Attach the tape so that only 1in is fixed to the reverse and the other inch stands above the height of the paper.
- Reposition your illustration onto the backing board of the mount, using the pencilled marks to help you find the exact positions.
- Cut two more lengths of archival tape, approximately 3in long.
- Affix a piece of tape across the front of each of the first tapes. Press the tape down firmly against the backing board.
- Repeat the process for the second piece of tape.
- The painting is now attached to the backing board. Replace the aperture over the top.

In the case of very large paintings, you may need to affix three primary pieces of tape to support the extra weight of the paper.

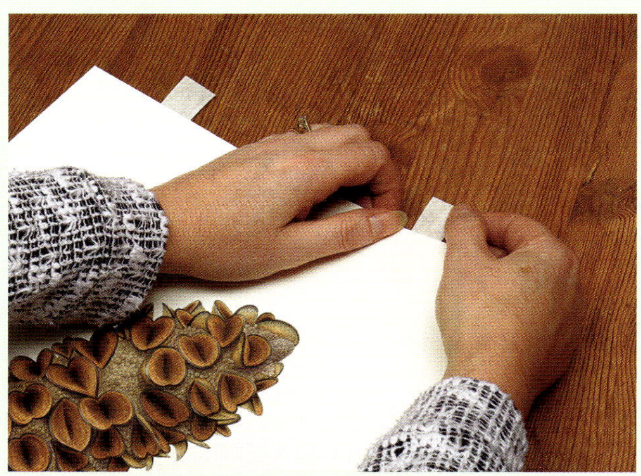

Attaching first tapes.

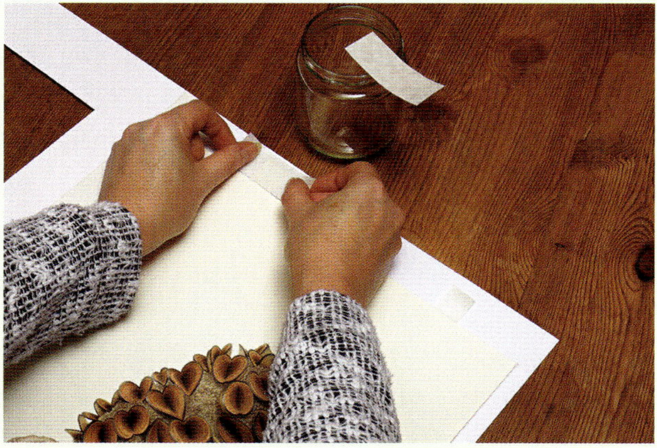

Attaching second tapes.

PRE-CUT MOUNTS

There is a wide selection of pre-cut, mass-produced mounts available commercially. They are readily available online, in art shops and other outlets selling picture and photograph frames. The problem with using these mounts is one of compromise. Very often the sizes and range of colour is quite limited, meaning that you may end up using a mount which doesn't quite fit comfortably, or the colour is not quite the right tone to blend suitably with your painting. It is much better to work with a picture framer, who can make a bespoke mount for you that will be exactly the right proportion, style, and colour to suit your painting.

FRAMES

To finish your painting, you may decide to have it framed or frame it yourself. This will quite possibly be the case if you intend exhibiting your work, or you are creating a painting to hang in your own home. If you are working to commission, it is possible that your client will want to choose a frame for themselves once they receive the painting, especially if they have a specific location in mind to hang the work. If not, you could offer to have it framed for them instead, considering any guidance for the style and finish of frame they may give you. In this instance, working with a reputable picture framer will help you realize a suitable choice for both the mount and frame together.

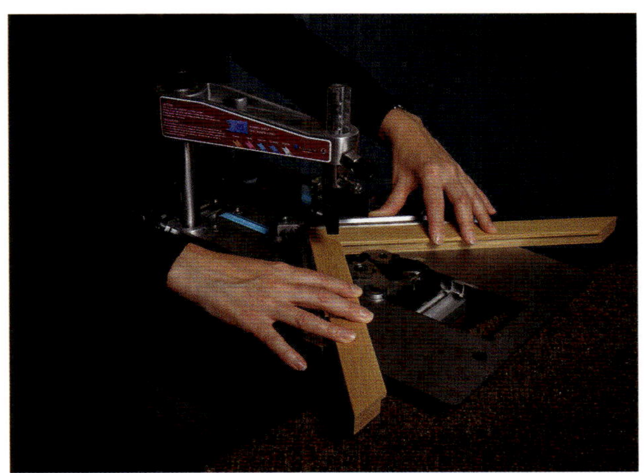

A professional picture framer will make a bespoke frame to your exact requirements.

USING A PROFESSIONAL PICTURE FRAMER

A reputable, professional picture framer is very often the first choice for an artist who would like to – or has been requested to – frame a piece of work. Leaving the job to a professional, knowing that your work will be cared for and framed to a high standard, can clearly give you peace of mind. Obviously, it will be up to you to instruct your picture framer regarding your choice of frame, mount, and glazing, but you should also seek their advice and recommendations. They are experienced professionals, used to framing many styles of art, and will be able to give clear judgements about aesthetics that you may not have considered yourself.

CHOOSING A SUITABLE PROFILE

Rather like mounting a painting, framing your work is about aesthetics. The frame will also become part of the overall picture, so that everything will become one entity. Sometimes there is a tendency to be rather lavish or extreme in the choice of frame – which may be suitable for some genres of art – but in botanical illustration it is the content of the painting that should be the most dominant feature. The choice of profile needs to blend and harmonize with the painting. Very often a choice of natural material, such as wood, is suitable for most botanical paintings. For example, a painting of oak leaves, twigs and acorns would sit comfortably in a natural wood frame, quite possibly made of oak.

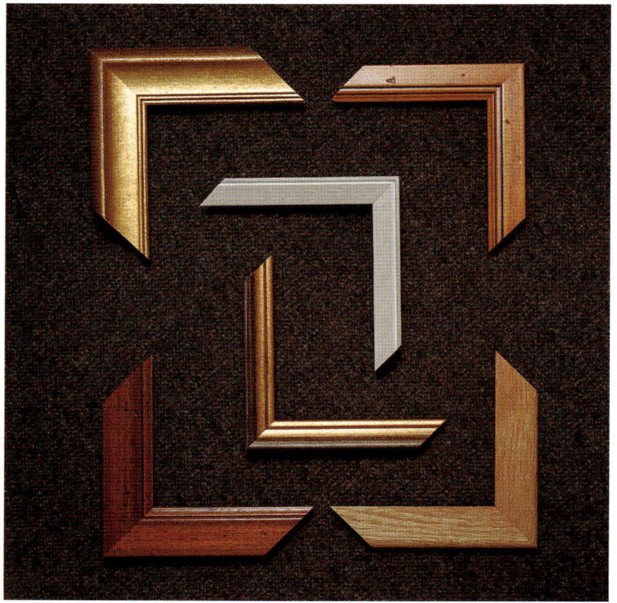

Making the right choice of profile for your painting is important.

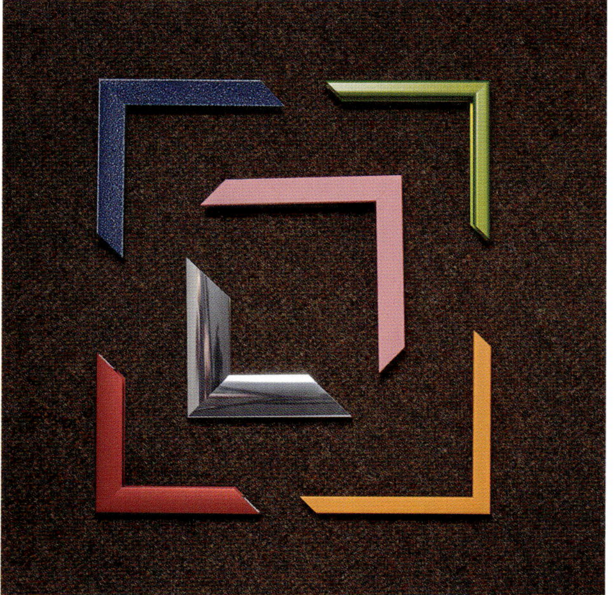

Avoid harsh, bright colours that detract from the painting.

Keeping the choice of profile relevant and unobtrusive, yet tasteful, is a wise move. Complex, intricate styles or bright colours may be attractive, perhaps too attractive, but tend to detract from the painting itself.

FASHIONS

From time to time, fashions in picture framing, as with anything else, occur. For example, purposely 'antiqued' wooden frames, where a vintage, older style or weathered look is deliberately added; metal or gilt frames, or embellished and highly decorated profiles have all enjoyed being the height of fashion in recent times.

Whether there is a trend for certain styles at the time, and whether you choose to opt for any of them is ultimately your own choice. However, you should always remind yourself of the main purpose of your work; that being the scientific study and replication of the species you have studied, which should be presented in an aesthetically appealing way and be the dominant part of your painting.

GLAZING

As part of the framing process you will need to decide on the type of glazing to use with your frame and mount. Your decision should be driven by thinking about where your painting may be displayed. We tend to naturally assume that 'glazing' involves the use of glass but you may opt to settle for a quality acrylic (Plexiglas) covering instead, especially if you wish to hang your painting at home.

If you have decided that traditional glazing is your preferred option, then it is useful to know a little about the different types of glass available. Standard, regular glass is quite acceptable and the cheapest option, but it is quite possible that you may want to choose a low reflective surface so that you can see your painting much better. Etched low reflective and coated low reflective glass are used to greatly reduce reflection and glare, but are more costly.

If you are likely to be hanging your painting in an exhibition, then the criteria for glazing may have already been set in advance. If this is the case, it is important that you follow any guidelines carefully if mounting and framing your work becomes your responsibility. It may however fall to the organizers of the exhibition to decide on mounting, glazing and framing, in which case such decisions will be made on your behalf.

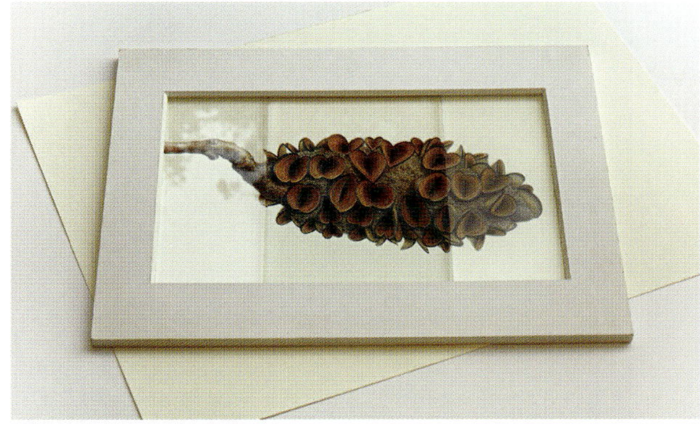

Examples of glazing choices for your painting: regular, etched low reflective, and coated low reflective.

MOUNTING AND FRAMING A PICTURE YOURSELF

It can be more cost effective to consider mounting and framing work yourself, especially if you are likely to want to frame several paintings. You will need to make an initial investment in the correct equipment, but once purchased, you will be able to use it repeatedly.

To make your own mounts, you will need a mount board cutter consisting of two cutters; one straight, and one bevelled. (You can purchase mount cutting kits that contain all the correct equipment.) You will use the straight cutter to cut the mount board down to the size you want, and the bevelled one to cut the aperture in the centre. The bevel is cut to an angle of 45 degrees and there should be no over cuts at the corners, which can look unsightly and unprofessional.

To make your own picture frames, a picture framing kit will supply you with everything you need, often including hardware such as picture hooks, screws, and D-rings. Ensure you read any instructions or guidelines from a kit carefully before you begin.

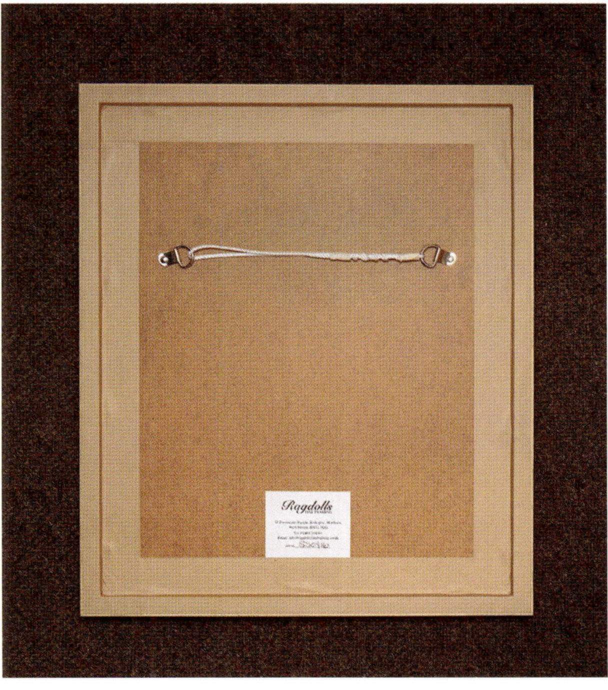

A professionally framed picture will be completed to the highest standard, and will be ready to hang on a wall.

HANGING A PAINTING

If you have used a professional picture framer to frame a painting for you, then it will be ready to hang after you have collected it.

If, however, you have framed your painting yourself, you will need to consider some means of attaching some cord or wire to the reverse of the frame and backing board.

Picture wire and cord is readily available from commercial suppliers, along with suitable fixings. Both wire and cord do the job equally well, but it is worth understanding a little about them to help you decide which to use.

Picture cord

Picture cord made of strong nylon is probably the most common material used for hanging pictures and it is used commonly amongst commercial picture framers. It is important that the weight of the framed picture (inclusive of the glazing) is considered beforehand, and that the correct strength of cord is then chosen for the job. Once attached, picture cord can be neatly tied in a knot and is strong enough to support the weight of the framed painting on the wall without fraying or splitting.

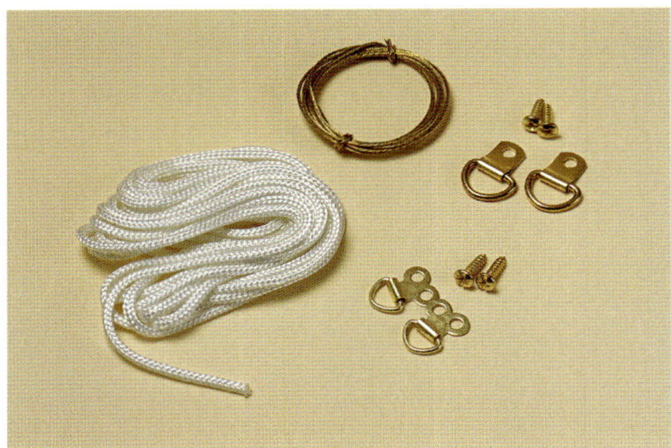

Use picture cord or wire, D-rings and screws to prepare a home-framed painting for hanging.

Picture wire

Before the advent of picture cord, wire was commonly used for hanging pictures. Picture wire is constructed of a stainless-steel core, with strands of brass braided around it. As with cord different strengths are available, depending on the weight of the picture to be hung.

D-rings

You will need to affix your picture cord or wire to fixings against the picture frame. Known as 'D-rings', these fixings are available in varying sizes according to the weight of the picture and the width of the frame profile you are using. As with picture wire, they are made from a base metal and then brass or nickel-plated. It is important that you select the correct size of D-ring fixing and check that the screws supplied are short enough to embed only within the frame without protruding through to the front.

For aesthetic purposes, it is recommended that a match in metal finish of both D-rings and screws is obtained.

Checklist for Mounting and Framing Work

- Choose a smooth-textured, off-white mount, which reflects the warm or cool tones of your painting.
- Check that the mount size and aperture are proportional to the painting.
- If you mount a painting yourself, ensure you use an acid-free archival-quality mount board and tape.
- Select a frame that complements the painting but does not overpower it.
- Trust the judgment of a reputable, professional picture framer; they will be best placed to advise you and make recommendations about mounts and frames.
- Ensure the type of glazing you choose is appropriate for your painting depending on the location in which it will hang.
- If you choose to mount and frame your work yourself, ensure you use the correct equipment, including D-rings and picture cord, or wire.

BOTANICAL ILLUSTRATIONS AS 'WORKS OF ART'

What do we consider to be 'a work of art'? Why would a botanical illustration be considered a work of art? The answers to these questions are not easy because aesthetics in the context of 'art' are purely subjective. What appeals to one person may equally be to the distaste of another. However, in the context of botanical illustration, the criteria by which the illustration is created helps us to determine whether it could be considered 'a work of art'.

The function of a botanical illustration as we now know is to inform and educate the viewer. The information conveyed needs to explain the species scientifically: its growth habit, structure, appearance, colour, diagnostic features and so on. It can be argued that it is these scientific accuracies combined with their artistic presentation through the skilfulness and precision of the artist that makes a work completely unique and 'a work of art'.

Case study

The painting process of *Fuchsia magellanica* was finished and the painting ready to be mounted for submission to the Nymans Florilegium.

Adding a signature or initials

Most botanical artists and illustrators like to add their signature or initials to their work so that they can be identified as the creators of individual paintings. Adding your signature or initials however should be secondary to the painting itself and should not dominate the work in any way. Your signature or initials should be applied in a suitably discreet place, such as a natural 'gap' in your painting or along a stem or the edge of a leaf for example. You can find the best position for your signature or initials by writing them first on a small piece of tracing paper. It is then possible to move the tracing paper into different positions until you find the best location.

Mounting the painting

To complete the overall painting of *Fuchsia magellanica,* an acid-free, off-white, double aperture book mount was applied. It was important to ensure that the mount was made to the correct size visually, whereby a visual equilibrium could be achieved between the painting and the mount. Therefore, in this respect, the mount should not look too small or too large, so that neither the painting nor the mount dominated the overall visual effect. In addition, the left, right and top sides of the mount were all cut to the same depth, whilst the bottom side was made 5mm deeper. This creates an optical illusion to the viewer, whereby this very small increase actually makes the mount look of equal depth on all four sides. Without it, the bottom side would look visually narrower. The internal aperture size was also a critical consideration. Enough visual marginal space was necessary between the 'edges' of the painting and the aperture window, so that the painting neither touched the aperture window, nor looked lost in the centre.

With the mount cut to the correct size, the painting was then positioned accurately and secured in place using acid-free strips of tape, following the method described in this chapter.

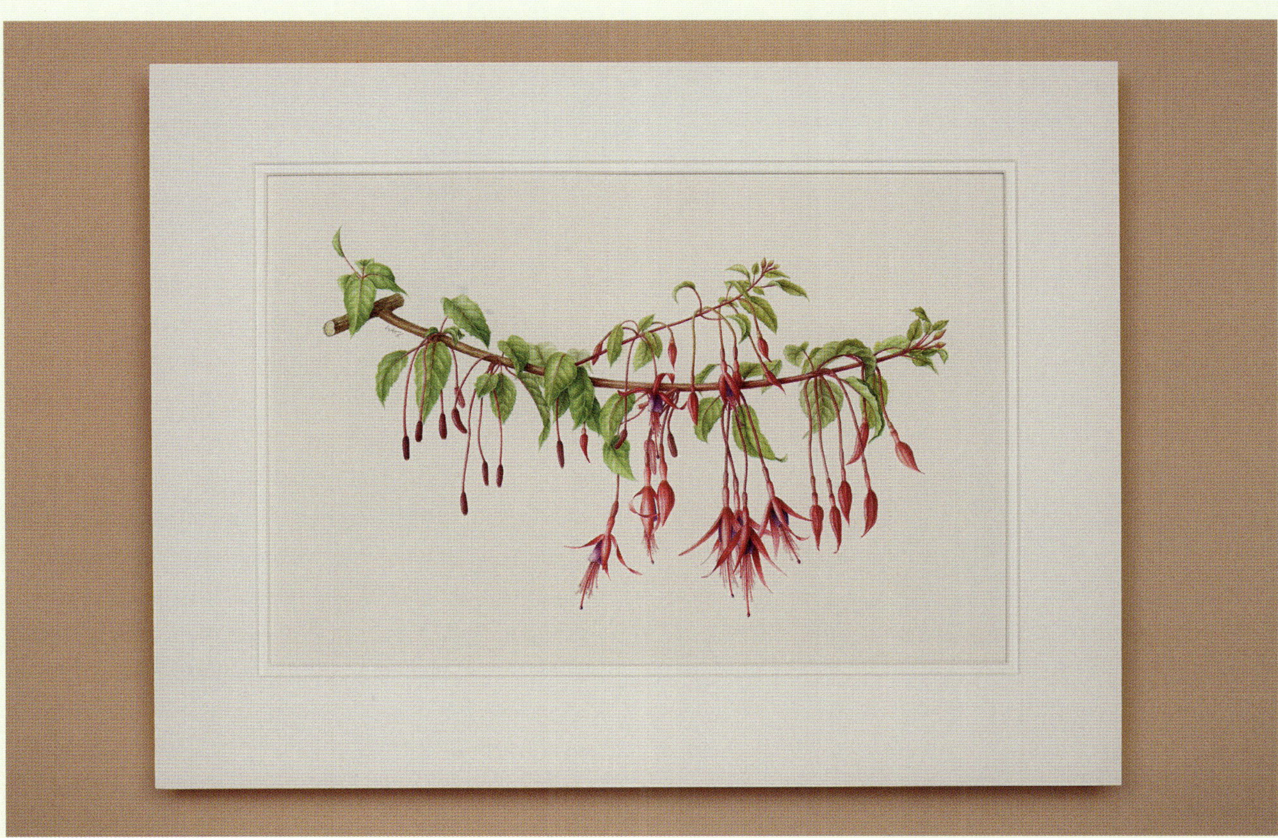

Mounted painting of *Fuchsia magellanica.*

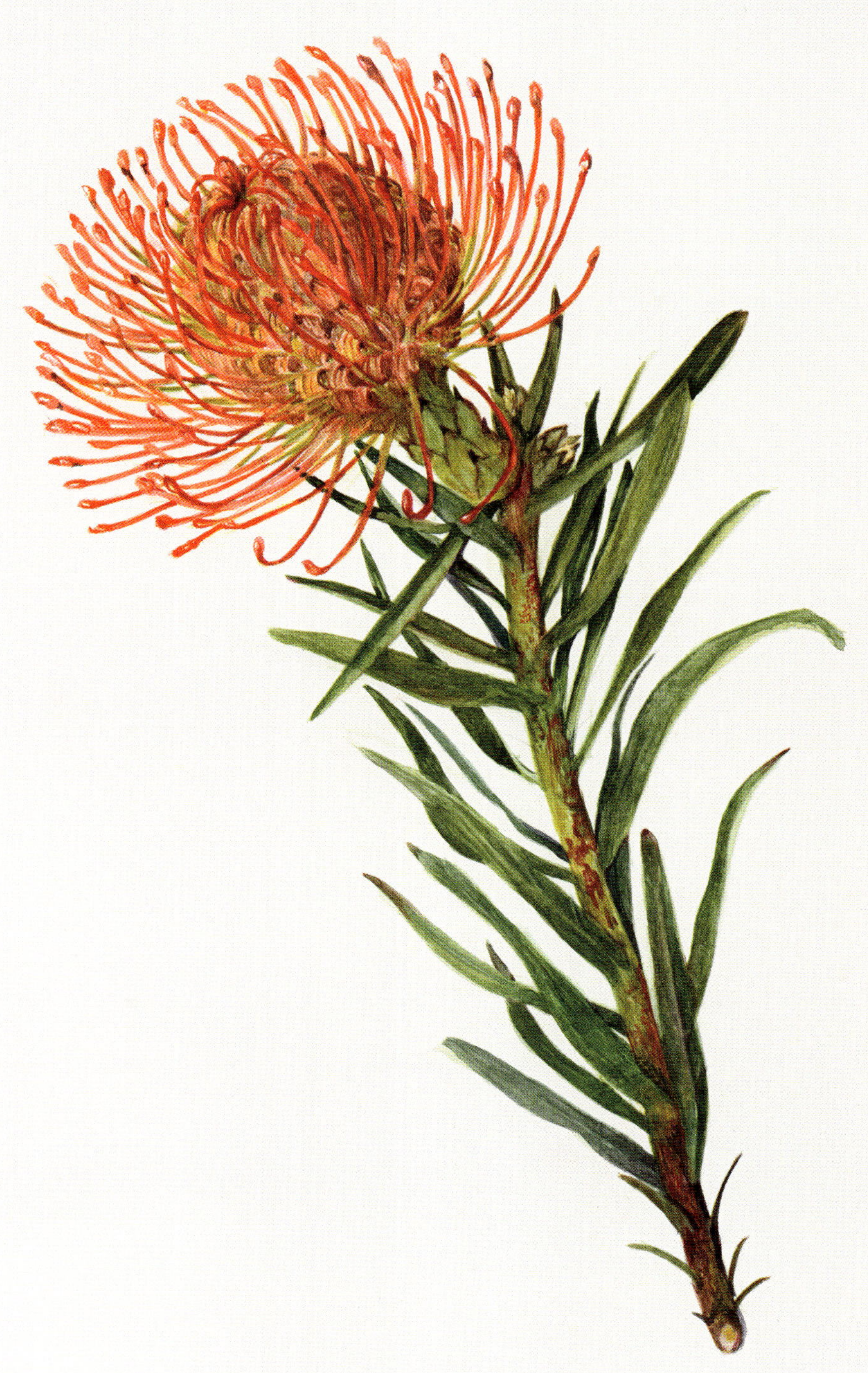

CHAPTER 12

Further Learning, Continued Practice and Individual Style

I'm still learning.

– Michelangelo, aged eighty-seven

In order that you progress in botanical illustration to achieve a high degree of skill, it is advisable to seek out opportunities to learn more and continue to practise as much as you can. The processes of botanical illustration are such that each demands a considerable investment of time, effort, and practice – just like any other practical skill such as driving a car – and it is only through doing so that you will achieve your aim.

There are several ways to attain proficiency in this art and most will involve some form of alliance with other people.

Learning from, and alongside others is the most common method of progressing. These are effective ways to help you develop a discipline for regular practice, learn and share new skills and techniques, evaluate your work, and receive feedback and constructive criticism from professional teaching artists. You could also consider visiting exhibitions to observe the work of accomplished botanical artists and illustrators, join groups or societies, or learn from subject-specific publications and online tutorials.

Over time you will notice the uniqueness of your own work when comparing it with others. No two artists will ever be identical in the way they draw or paint – even if they receive the same instruction and subject matter – so recognizing that you do have your own individual style can be fascinating and quite revealing about your nature and personality. It is also the one thing that you have which will distinguish you from any other artist.

In this chapter we will explore in more detail the opportunities for further learning and continued practice, and learn about the characteristics of your work that will identify you and your individual style.

Leucospermum cordifolia, Protea. KATE TILBURY

LEARNING FROM OTHERS

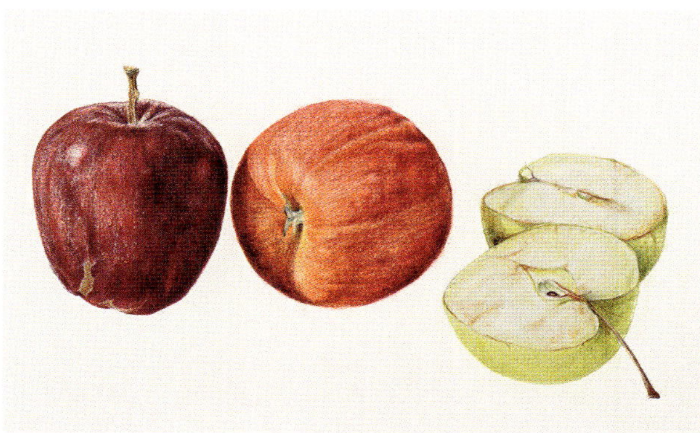

Three Apples: Coloured pencil. LOREN DIXON

One of the most effective ways of learning is to acquire new knowledge or modify existing knowledge of a subject. As botanical illustration is a skill-based subject, this process takes time, but can be achieved in several ways, most notably by learning from others.

ATTENDING COURSES AND WORKSHOPS

Prior to the 1980s, relatively few specialized botanical illustration courses existed. This was mainly due to progressive printing processes and the growth of photographic plates being preferred in printed materials over and above illustration. However, in recent years, due in part to an increased interest in the changing natural world, the realization and urgency to scientifically record diminishing species, and the commercial popularity of the art form as 'wall art', botanical art and illustration are now enjoying a lively renaissance. This has highlighted the need for specific botanical painting courses as a means of combined study of art and science, rather than the individual routes of botany and fine art, enabling the next generations of botanical artists and illustrators to emerge.

Courses

Formal qualifications including diplomas and certificates taught by prominent teaching artists and botanists are now offered by institutions such as The Chelsea School of Botanical Art and the Society of Botanical Artists (SBA). Diploma and certificate courses are generally lengthy and will require a considerable investment of time, effort, and practice to achieve the necessary high standards of skill and expertise, but they will provide you with a recognized, solid foundation on which to build your reputation as a botanical artist of excellent pedigree.

Shorter, less formal courses, including residential courses, are also popular with students and usually require less financial investment. Whilst the majority do not offer a formal qualification upon completion, they are still taught by leading, reputable teaching artists, and cover all the fundamental skills and techniques necessary for proficient botanical illustration. These courses too are generally more accessible, being taught in more regional centres and locales.

Workshops

Botanical illustration workshops offer the student a focus of study, for a short, intense period of time, most likely with an emphasis on a single topic or theme. Workshops by nature are much shorter in length than courses and can be beneficial to first-time students. They can act as a 'taster' in botanical illustration, which gives the student the opportunity to try out the suitability of the subject before making a serious commitment onto a longer formal or informal course.

LEARNING ALONGSIDE FRIENDS

For some, learning in a very relaxed and informal setting can be a good idea. Meeting up and sharing knowledge perhaps on an ad hoc basis with a few friends or sharing hints, tips and ideas gleaned from online tutorials and instructional books can all help instil confidence amongst students. However, this method of learning can have its drawbacks. The combination of differing information relating to approaches, methods and techniques can cause confusion and become misleading.

It is best to obtain an equilibrium of informal group gatherings and participation in professionally led courses and workshops, to ensure fundamental skills are correctly identified and acquired.

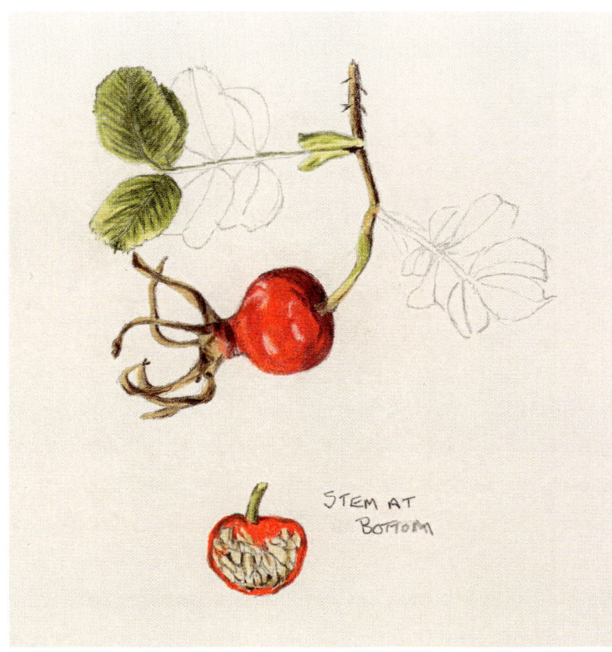

Rosehip rugosa: Sketchbook work in coloured pencil. VAL FORSTER

ONE-TO-ONE LEARNING

Tailor made, one-to-one tuition is a suitable option if you feel hesitant about learning within a group setting or lack confidence in your ability. Building a good rapport with a professional tutor can increase your level of confidence, provide instruction and constructive feedback in specific areas of the discipline, and allow you to work at your own pace, often with assigned personal goals for you to reach along the way.

After several one-to-one sessions, you may feel this is the best way for you to continue your learning, or you may feel ready to integrate with other students by attending courses and workshops. Alternatively, of course, you may opt for a combination of both methods of learning.

PRINTED REFERENCE MATERIAL

There is something quite endearing about being able to pull a book down from a bookshelf, refer to the contents or index, and immediately access the information you are seeking, or simply flick through the pages at your leisure. Nowadays, with many instructional, historical, and scientific books available, accessing all kinds of information about botanical illustration can be a very easy process.

Many instructional books have been published by professional artists which detail their own unique approaches, skills, and techniques, whilst leading authorities on the subject seek to educate us about botanical illustration in an historical context. There are also several leading publications focussing on botany, which is a clear necessity for all budding botanical artists and illustrators.

Much can be learned from simply studying the vast array of information available in published books and such material is often identified in reading lists to support learning on formal botanical illustration courses.

DIGITAL REFERENCE MATERIAL

As the interest in botanical illustration grows, more and more digitally published instructional material is becoming available at an increasing rate. Being able to access such material can be quick and easy, introducing another form of learning from others.

ONLINE TUTORIALS AND COURSES

With the advent of the digital age it is now possible to learn many skills and techniques from online tutorials. This is a convenient, flexible, and cost-effective method of immediately accessing tuition whenever you wish; all you need is a computer with an internet connection. There are many online tutorials published by professional botanical artists and illustrators, and some are also incorporated into online courses.

An online course is a form of distance learning that includes tuition (online tutorials) and feedback from a tutor(s). Like a conventional course, exercises, projects, or assignments are set throughout the duration, although some online courses do allow flexibility for students to work at their own pace and complete courses in their own time.

VISITING EXHIBITIONS

Exhibitions of botanical art and illustration are fast becoming popular features on the botanical art calendar. Some exhibitions, notably the London shows of

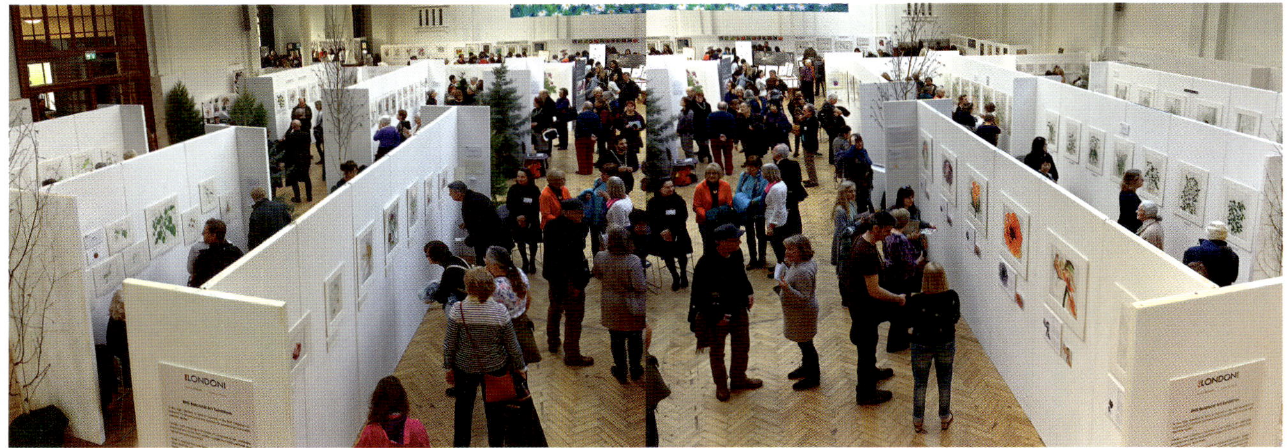

Attending exhibitions to view work closely will help you observe, learn, and understand techniques and processes.

the RHS and Society of Botanical Artists (SBA) in the UK, are now well-established annual events which thousands of people attend each year. It is very often at these exhibitions that the artists themselves are present, enabling current and prospective students to meet, greet and discuss their work with them. This can be a most useful and valuable learning experience when artists are usually very generous with their time and happy to discuss their skills, methods, and techniques with you.

Being able to witness at close range the hand of a skilled botanical painter is clearly one of the most beneficial ways to learn. Studying 'real' paintings rather than printed or digital ones reveals application techniques, colour mixes, as well as the fine nuances of observed detail, all carefully rendered. Observing paintings close up really helps you to understand all the processes involved in the art of botanical illustration.

CONTINUED PRACTICE

If you have completed a course in botanical illustration – especially an intensive programme – it is vital that you continue to practise to sustain and implement your newly acquired skills. Sometimes it is very easy to complete a course, afford yourself a rest, and then promise yourself that you will be disciplined enough to continue, but for some this can sometimes be very difficult if there are other distractions to divert your attention. The best way to continue is to consider joining a botanical painting group, a society, or consider marketing or exhibiting your work or even perhaps becoming an artist tutor. You will discover that having an end goal in mind will keep you sufficiently motivated to inspire your continued practice.

JOINING GROUPS AND SOCIETIES

Painting alongside others – and networking with other artists – is an avenue worth considering if you are serious about becoming a proficient artist and building a good reputation for yourself. Nowadays, with the resurgence of interest in botanical art and illustration, painting groups and botanical art societies are flourishing globally. Many societies offer membership based on the successful submission of your work to a required standard. Some also offer associate membership, allowing you to partake in meetings and so on but not necessarily to paint. The latter option may be desirable if you are just starting out and still receiving tuition in the art.

With the renewed awareness of the importance of botanical illustration being the preferred method of recording plants, florilegium societies are also becoming popular. With many skilled and esteemed artists taking up membership, joining these groups to record significant and often endangered plant collections is taking on a serious role in the natural world. The standard of work required to become a member of a florilegium needs to be consistently high, so that an accurate archive of plant paintings can be established. Membership of florilegia is usually offered upon recommendation, submission and acceptance of several examples of an artist's work, but is a goal that can be achieved through the successful completion of highly regarded courses and continued practice thereafter.

An illustration prepared for The Florilegium Society at the Royal Botanic Gardens, Sydney. *Rhododendron oldhamii*. LEIGH ANN GALE

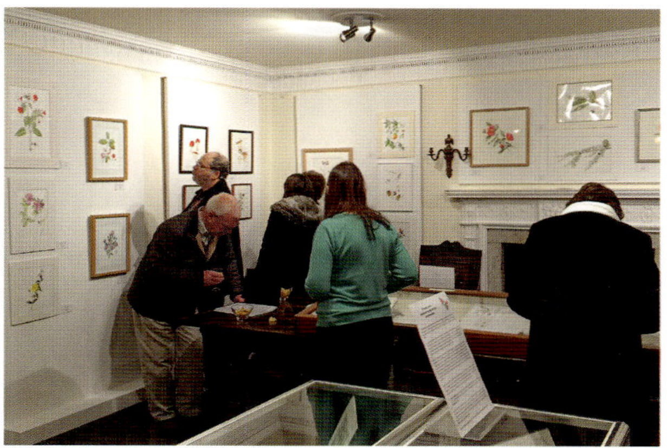

Exhibiting your paintings helps develop your confidence in sharing your work with others. Here, an exhibition of student work on display at Horsham Museum and Art Gallery, West Sussex.

EXHIBITING YOUR WORK

Once you feel confident and reach a good standard you might want to think about exhibiting some of your work. You may have joined a local group or society which holds exhibitions of its members' work from time to time; this can be a good way to become familiar with how exhibitions are organized and run, and how well your work is received by the public and your fellow exhibitors. Exhibitions are an excellent way to promote yourself and your work. You could even consider handing out business cards to visitors, so they remember you and can contact you in the future.

COMMISSIONS

As you continue to practise your art there could be the possibility that you may be asked, or you might like to consider, taking commissions. To start, this may seem a rather daunting prospect, but working for friends and family initially will help you grow in confidence and get you used to the idea of creating work to commission. You may in time consider taking on more commissions from other sources; you could even begin to tender for work if you seek out companies or individuals looking to commission botanical artists and illustrators for specific projects.

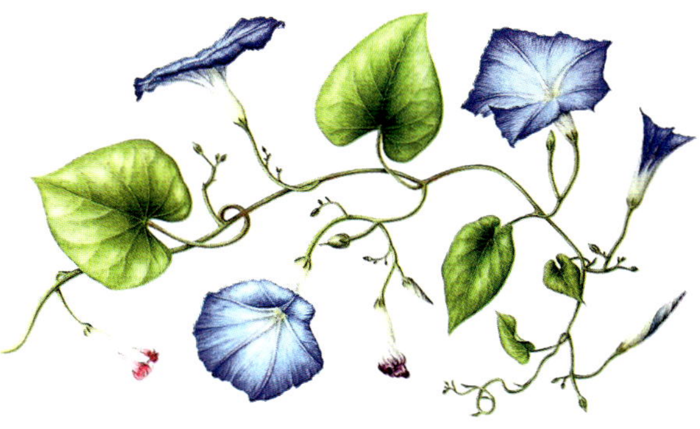

Morning Glory. LEIGH ANN GALE

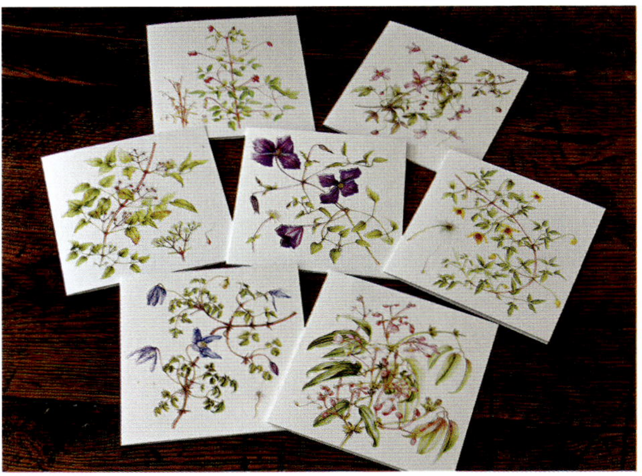

Reproducing and selling your work as greeting cards is an easy form of self-promotion.

Commissions are a good way to develop yourself, have the advantage of earnings potential, and could help to establish you in a larger competitive market.

MARKETING AND SELLING YOUR WORK COMMERCIALLY

If you are interested in selling your work on a commercial basis, then planning is key. With the digital age now fully upon us, marketing your work can be a straightforward process but one that will still require some research beforehand to ascertain which markets will be right for you. You could market your work by yourself, perhaps by hosting your own website or webpage, or find a gallery willing to represent you to sell your work on your behalf. You could even consider taking a stall at an art fair if that is more appropriate. It is always a good idea to consider in advance who your potential clients are going to be and where they will look to buy their art. For example, if you are hoping to sell original paintings to a botanical art collector, it is unlikely they will attend your local art fair to do so. Instead, you would need to approach a prestigious gallery renowned for selling original botanical illustrations.

You will need to make good preparations to market and sell your work, such as having at the very least a supply of business cards so that you can distribute them to any potential customers you meet. Writing an artist's statement about you and your work for your website or webpage will help people engage with you, and understand what it is that drives your passion for botanical illustration, or talking to visitors at exhibitions to discuss your style and technique are all good ways to promote yourself.

You may consider that selling reproductions of your work, such as greeting cards or prints, is the best way forward for you, and there are several ways of doing this successfully. It is worth approaching greeting card agencies to see if they would be interested in publishing your illustrations; printing sufficient cards yourself and marketing them to high street and online shops, and garden centres; or targeting organizations associated with gardens and buildings of interest.

Becoming successful at marketing and selling your work commercially takes time. If you are looking for career opportunities, allow yourself plenty of time and room for your business to grow and develop.

BECOMING AN ARTIST TUTOR

For practising botanical artists and illustrators, becoming an artist tutor can be one of the most satisfying and rewarding experiences. With the increased interest in botanical art and illustration, many people are keen to try their hand, and there is no better way to learn than from an experienced and respected professional. More and more artists are becoming artist tutors, sharing their knowledge and passion with a new generation of students. Passing on years of honed skills and techniques and keeping this traditional genre of art alive becomes part of their ongoing quest and ultimate legacy.

To become a tutor there are several routes you could take. In the public sector, there is often demand for professional artist tutors at educational institutions, and whilst you may be suitably qualified in your subject field, it may be necessary to undertake a professional qualification for this type of teaching. This will equip you with Qualified Teacher Learning and Skills (QTLS) status, a designation given to tutors specifically in the Further Education and Post-Compulsory Education and Training sectors. Colleges and universities usually offer post-graduate teacher training courses.

Alternatively, you could opt to teach privately, by running your own courses and workshops. You could also offer classes in botanical illustration at your own home studio or at privately hired venues, or museums, heritage conservation centres, and charities with alliances to gardening, art, floristry and so on.

As an artist tutor, you will gain immense satisfaction in seeing your students grow and develop by honing the skills and techniques that you have taught them. Following their progression can be very motivational, and knowing that you have contributed to their achievements and made a difference in their lives is very gratifying. Teaching is also an excellent stimulus to keep up your own continued practice, thereby developing your own skills whilst handing them on to your students at the same time.

INDIVIDUAL STYLE

Sometimes people refer to an artist's 'style', but exactly what are they talking about?

If you have been working hard and regularly at botanical illustration, you will have probably noticed your own individual style developing. This may not be entirely apparent to you immediately, and is quite possibly something that you are not even conscious of. However, the more work you produce, the greater your own unique style will evolve.

Very often art tutors will say that once they have been teaching their students for a period of time, and have got to know them well as individuals, they will be able to identify each student's style of work simply by recognizing the characteristics or strategies each of them uses. It is well known that students who are set the same project brief will produce their own unique piece of art, but all will be recognizable and will answer the brief. No two students' work will ever be identical. It is a similar scenario if several musicians were to play the same piece of music individually; each version will be recognizable but slightly different depending on the interpretation of the musician.

Individual style in the context of botanical illustration is exactly what makes us all entirely unique, but what, if anything, influences our style and how does it develop?

STYLE INFLUENCES

There could be many factors that influence your style of botanical illustration. Perhaps you are particularly fond of how the great nineteenth-century master Pierre-Joseph Redouté, known for his exquisite illustrations of roses and lilies, composed and painted his subjects. Or maybe you have developed an interest in painting specific groups of subjects such as palms, ferns, or fungi for example, because you relish in depicting the nuances of the fronds, sporangia or gills. There may be certain characteristics of some plants, fruits or vegetables you find particularly appealing, or it could simply be because you enjoy using a medium other than watercolour, such as coloured pencils or ink.

You may discover that you can recognize your style being influenced by your own personality. If, for example, you are a talkative and sociable person you might discover

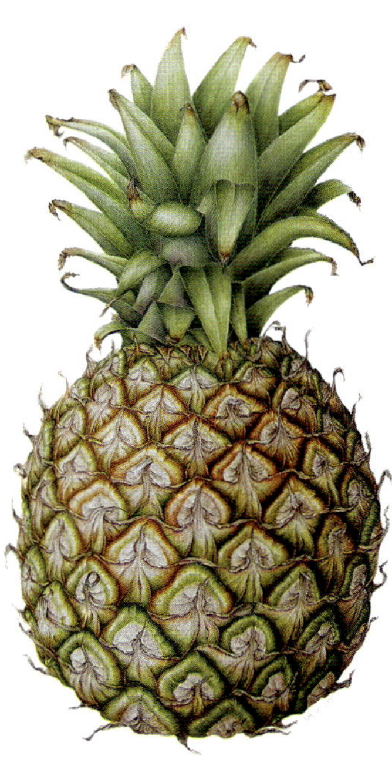

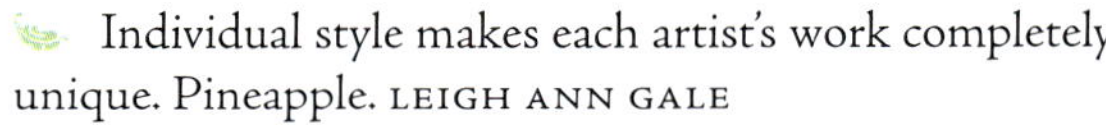

Individual style makes each artist's work completely unique. Pineapple. LEIGH ANN GALE

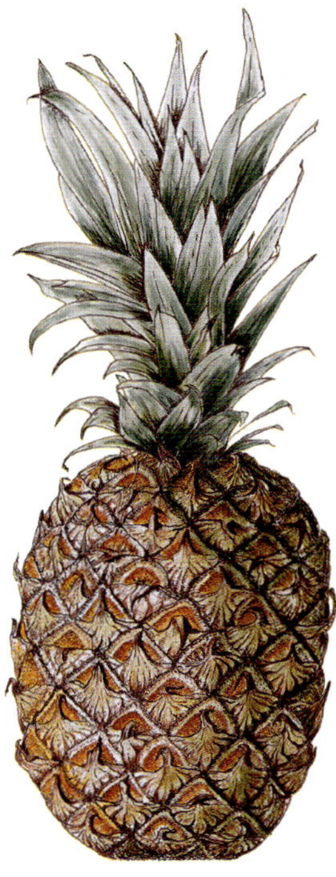

Here, the artist has chosen to use her preferred style of pen and ink with wash. Pineapple: mixed media. CATRIONA ARNOLD

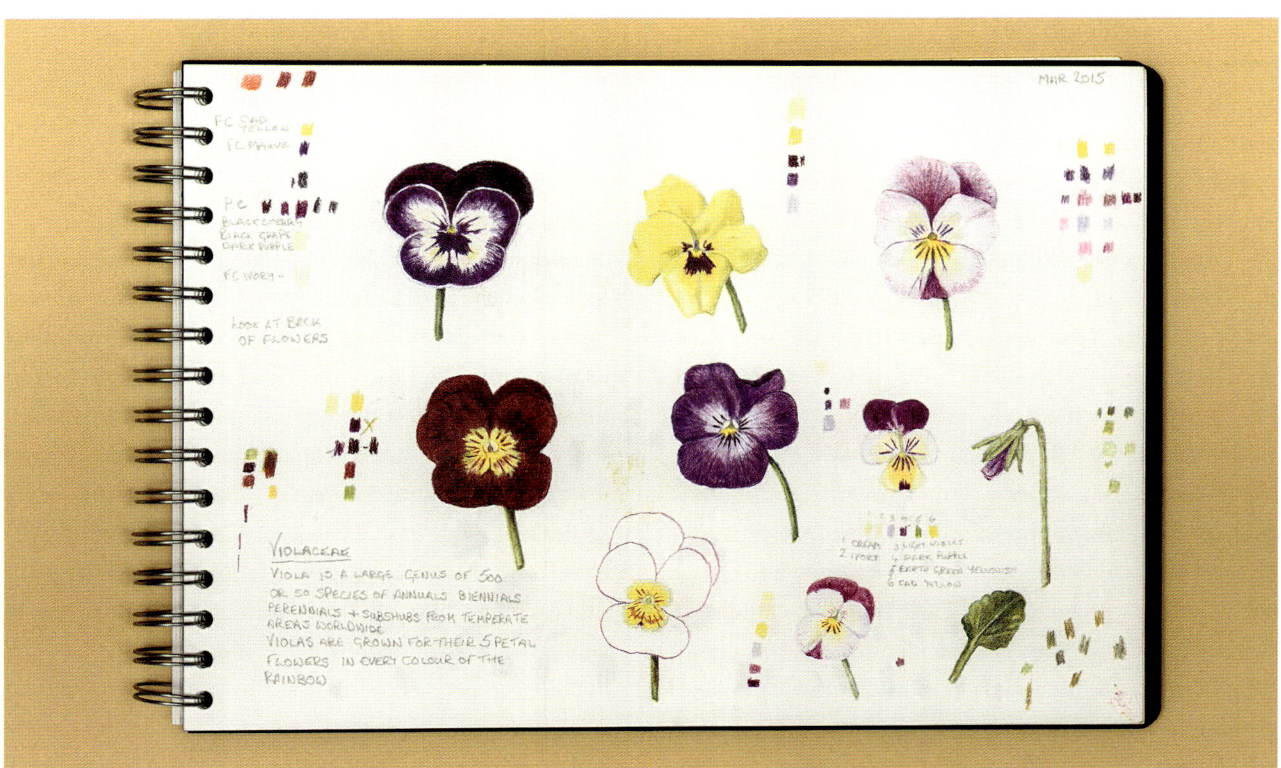

Pansies: sketchbook work in coloured pencil. VAL FORSTER

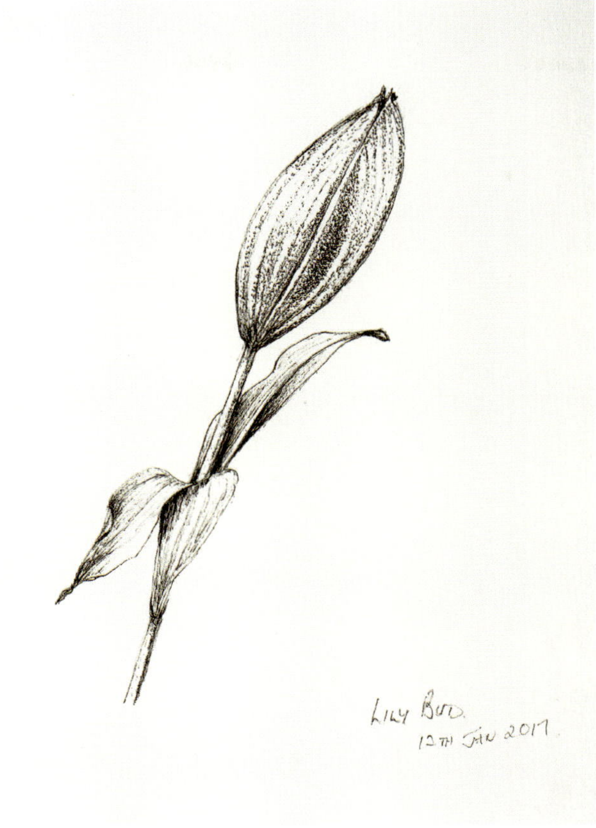

Lily Bud: Pen and ink. CATRIONA ARNOLD

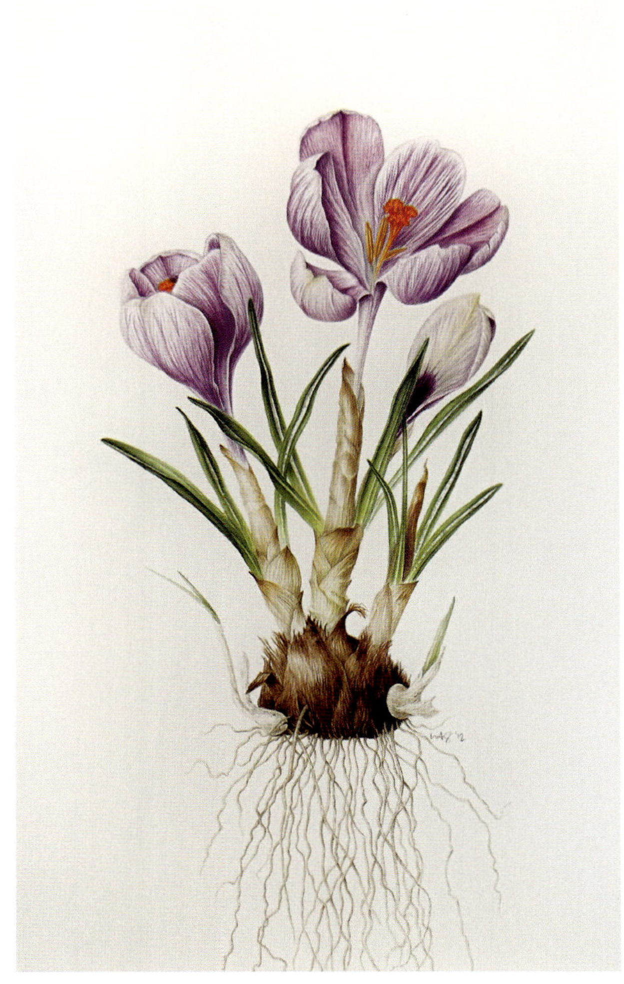

Crocus 'Pickwick'. LEIGH ANN GALE

you enjoy painting large subjects in lively compositions or that you use a slightly looser approach to your work. Conversely, a naturally quiet and reserved person may prefer to paint the finer details of a complex thistle flower or the numerous tiny thorns of a *Rosa rugosa* stem.

DEVELOPING YOUR OWN STYLE

Developing your own style will largely depend on how much work you produce and the speed at which you produce it. If you are prolific and spend most of your time drawing and painting, then the process will be much quicker than if you can only draw and paint for short periods of time. It could take just a few months or several years for your style to fully emerge and as mentioned previously, may be something that you are not entirely conscious of as it happens.

Your own individual style is clearly what distinguishes you from another artist. It is usually defined by the specific characteristics that feature routinely in your work; the way in which you handle your preferred medium, and the strategies and techniques you use to produce your paintings. It is a constant process and one that in time will naturally evolve, making you and your work unique.

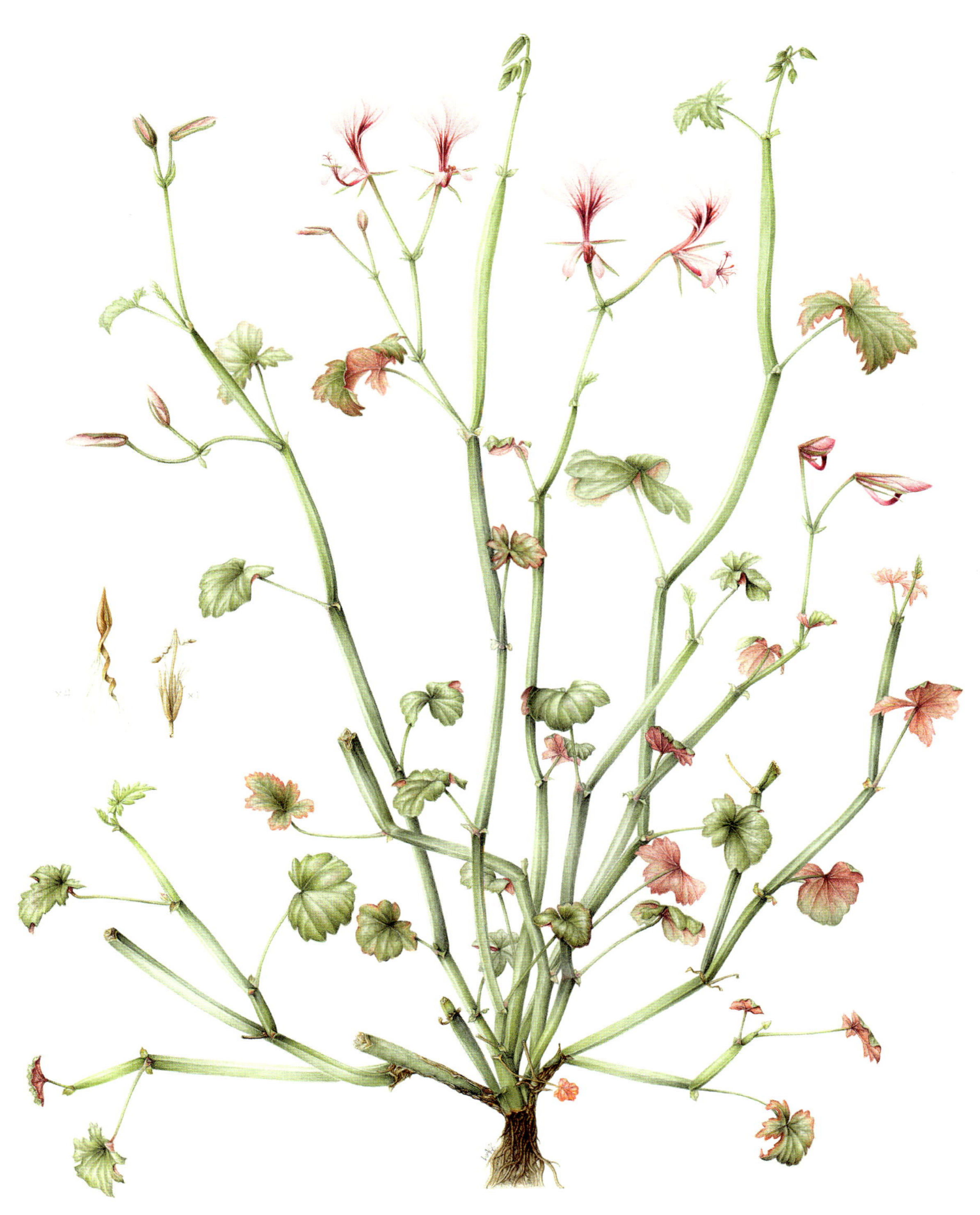

An Introduction to Botanical Terms

Your botanical knowledge does not need to be exhaustive, however it is beneficial to familiarize yourself with some of the most common characteristics and features of flowers, fruits, leaves and seeds as early as possible. By making frequent drawings of botanical specimens you will quickly begin to identify common structures, and using a glossary of botanical terms will help you describe them. Below is a simple glossary of some of the most useful vocabulary you will need, ideal as a first glossary for beginners and a useful reference to those already with some mastery of botanical illustration.

Pelargonium tetragonum. LEIGH ANN GALE

Achene A small, dry, indehiscent fruit formed from one carpel, typically in the genus *Ranunculus* and *Rosa*.

Actinomorphic symmetry (otherwise known as radial symmetry) When a flower can be cut in half in any direction and both halves are identical.

Aggregate fruit The fruit formed from several carpels joining together in a single flower, for example a blackberry.

Androecium A collective term for the male stamens of a flower.

Anthecology The study of pollination including the relationship between flowers and their pollinators.

Asymmetrical When no symmetry exists at all.

Basifixed The attachment of an anther at the base of the filament.

Calyx A collective term for the outer whorl of free or united sepals on the outside of a flower.

Carpel One of the female reproductive structures of a flower consisting of ovary, style, and stigma.

Class A principal taxonomic rank positioned between division and order.

Corolla A collective term for the inner whorl of petals in a flower.

Cotyledon A seed leaf.

Dehiscent To open spontaneously at maturity, for example a pea pod.

Dicotyledon An embryonic flowering plant having evolved from two cotyledons (seed leaves). The leaves are typically stalked and consist of branching veins.

Dioecious Separate male and female flowers borne on separate male and female plants.

Disc-floret One of a number of small tubular structured flowers at the centre of a flowerhead, typically of the Asteraceae family.

Division A taxonomic rank positioned between kingdom and class.

Embryo A young and developing plant growing from the seed.

Endocarp The layer surrounding the seed of a fruit, which is often woody and inedible.

Epicarp The outermost layer (skin) of a fruit.

Family A principal taxonomic rank positioned between order and genus.

Filament The supportive stalk-like structure of an anther.

Fruit The seed-bearing structure of a flowering plant.

Funicle The stalk attachment of a seed to its placenta.

Genus A principal taxonomic rank positioned between family and species.

Gynoecium A collective term for the female reproductive organs comprising a single or several free or fused carpels.

Hermaphrodite A flower that consists of both male and female reproductive organs.

Hilum The scar or mark left behind on a seed, where it was once attached to the funicle.

Indehiscent A fruit such as a seed pod which does not split open at maturity.

Inflorescence The arrangement of a group or cluster of flowers on a stem.

Infructescence A cluster of fruits having evolved from an inflorescence.

Internode The intervals along a stem between nodes.

Keel (petal) The lower almost united two petals in flowers of the subfamily Papilionoideae in the Fabaceae family, for example sweet pea.

Kingdom The principal taxonomic rank.

Lamina (blade) The thin, flat surface material of a leaf.

Lateral veins The major side veins protruding from the midrib of a leaf.

Legume A pod containing seeds attached to one edge of the two split valves as in the Fabaceae family, for example broad bean.

Locule One compartment of an ovary or anther.

LS Longitudinal section.

Margin (leaf) The outermost edge of a leaf, which may be entire, toothed, lobed or indented.

Mesocarp The central fleshy layer of a fruit.

Midrib vein The central vein of a leaf.

Monocotyledon An embryonic flowering plant having evolved from one cotyledon (seed leaf). The leaves are typically stalkless and consist of parallel veins.

Monoecious Plants bearing both separate male and female flowers.

Node The point on a stem at which one or more leaves are borne.

Nutlet A small nut-like fruit.

Order A principal taxonomic rank positioned between class and family.

Ovary The lower section of a carpel, which contains the ovules.

Ovule A botanical structure that develops into a seed after fertilization.

Papillae A small, nipple-like projection.

Pappus A modified calyx consisting of hairs or scales typically of the Asteraceae family, for example dandelion.

Pedicel The name given to the stem of a single flower.

Perianth A collective term for the non-reproductive parts of a flower, consisting of the calyx and corolla.

Petal A non-reproductive (usually coloured) part of a flower.

Petiole The stalk of a leaf.

Photosynthesis The process of green plants using sunlight to convert carbon dioxide into oxygen. Photosynthesis also produces glucose to feed the plant.

Pin-eyed Typically in primroses, where the style is long and the stamens fall below the stigma.

Placenta The surface of the ovary to which the ovules are attached.

Pollen Fine grains containing the male reproductive cells, situated on the anther.

Pollination The transferral process of pollen onto the stigma.

Ray-floret One of a number of petal-like structured flowers surrounding the centre of a flowerhead, typically of the Asteraceae family.

Receptacle The expanded top of a flower stem at which point the flower parts are attached.

Secondary veins The numerous veins on a leaf, which are usually smaller and narrower.

Seed The fertilized ovule of a plant containing the embryo.

Sepal A protective segment of the usually green calyx surrounding the flower. Sepals may be free or united (gamosepalous).

Serrate Having a sharp saw-like appearance (leaf margin).

Serrulate Minutely serrated (leaf margin).

Simple (fruit) An individual fruit formed from a single flower.

Species The lowest principal taxonomic rank; a group of closely related plants having similar characteristics.

Sporangia Typically in ferns, a vessel in which spores are formed.

Stamen The collective name for the male reproductive structure consisting of a filament and anther.

Standard (petal) The larger upper petal in flowers of the subfamily Papilionoideae in the Fabaceae family, for example sweet pea.

Stigma The receptive female reproductive organ located on the style of a flower.

Style The supportive structure connecting the carpel to the stigma.

Tegmen The inner protective coating of a seed.

Tepal An outer part of the perianth that resembles both a petal and sepal but cannot be clearly defined as either.

Testa The hard outer covering of a seed.

Thrum-eyed Typically in primroses, where the style is short, and the stamens are above the stigma.

TS Transverse section.

Venation The arrangement of veins on a leaf.

Whorl The circular arrangement of at least three organs around an axis, such as sepals and petals.

Wing (petal) One of two lateral petals in flowers of the subfamily Papilionoideae in the Fabaceae family, for example sweet pea.

Zygomorphic symmetry (otherwise known as bilateral symmetry) When a flower can only be cut in half lengthways for both halves to be identical.

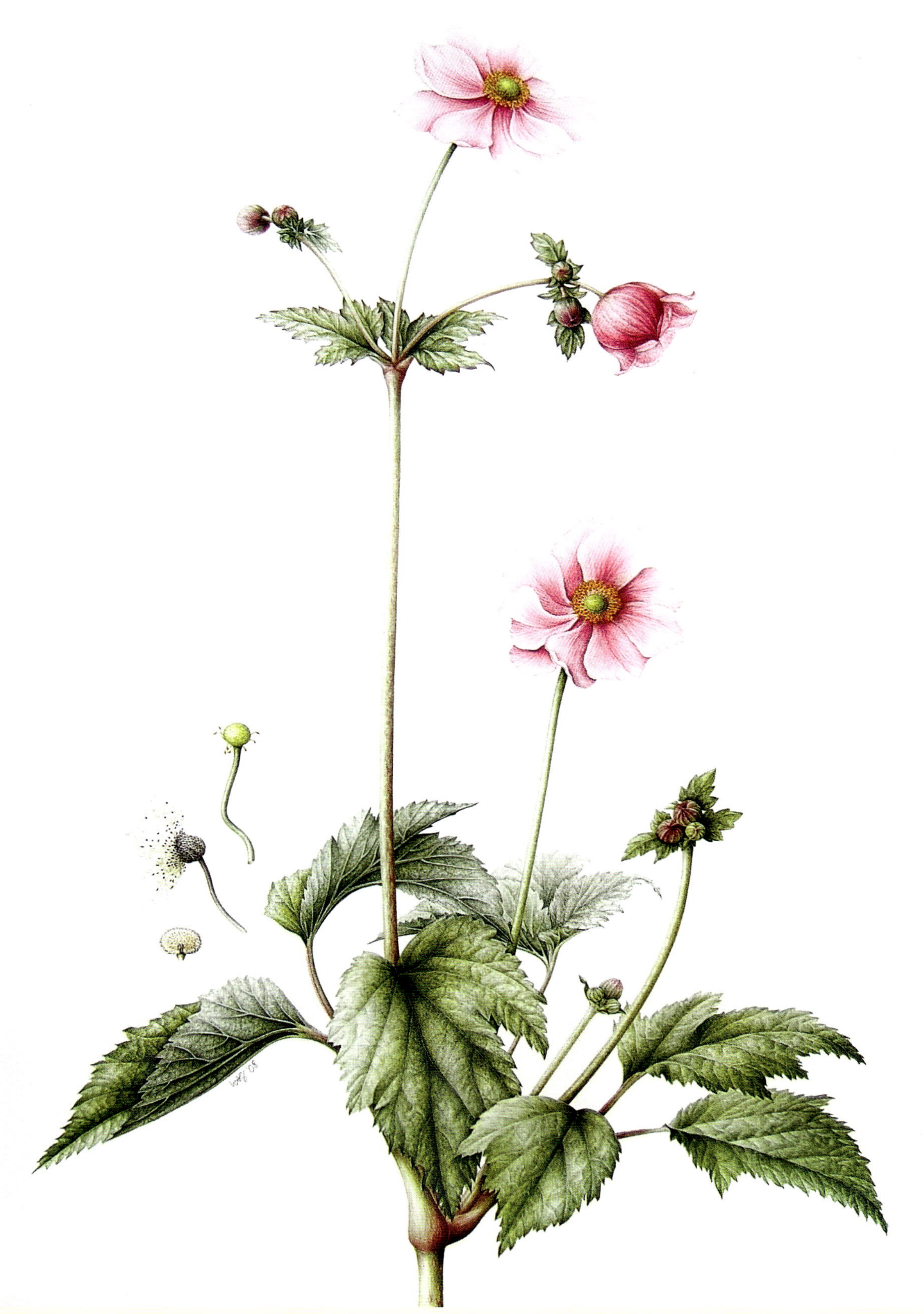

List of Contributors

As this book is geared primarily to students of botanical illustration, a number of artworks by the author's students have been included, not only to help illustrate the pages but to demonstrate what can be achieved through an enthusiasm and determination to succeed, and continued further learning to achieve a competent standard.

The students listed below all attend the author's regular classes in botanical illustration, many for several years. Additionally, some have also completed certificated courses such as the Society of Botanical Artists Distance Learning Diploma course and the Certificate in Botanical Illustration run by the Royal Botanic Garden Edinburgh. Others have also gained membership to The Hampton Court Palace Florilegium Society through the author's recommendation. Such achievements are indicated as (SBA Diploma), (RBGE Certificate) or (HCPFS) after their names.

Anemone hupehensis. LEIGH ANN GALE

Catriona Arnold: Lily bud: pen and ink; Pineapple: mixed media.

Colleen Ballone: Primulas – mixed media.

Gay Boyle (HCPFS): *Koelreuteria paniculata*; *Anomatheca*; *Nicandra physalodes*; *Nicandra physalodes* sketches.

Loren Dixon (SBA DIPLOMA): Three Apples: coloured pencil.

Val Forster: Rosehips: coloured pencil; Cyclamen: sketchbook work in coloured pencil; Pansies: sketchbook work in coloured pencil; *Rosehip rugosa*: sketchbook work in coloured pencil.

Sue Hannell: White Chrysanthemum.

Muriel McIntosh (RBGE CERTIFICATE): *Agastache foeniculum*, Anise Hyssop.

Linda Pitkin (HCPFS): Rose Hips, *Rosa* sp.; Ornamental Gourds, *Cucurbita pepo*; Red Chicory, *Cichorium intybus* 'Rossa di Treviso'; Orchid × *Oncidopsis* 'Nelly Isler' (flower enlarged).

Vicky Sharman: Pear 'Invincible'; Strawberry study; *Rosa rugosa*, sketchbook study; Botanical rainbow of vegetables, fruit and flowers; Kale Leaf; Kale Leaf sketch.

Kate Tilbury (SBA DIPLOMA): Sketchbook work: *Leucospermum cordifolia*, Protea; *Leucospermum cordifolia*, Protea; Wild Flowers in my Garden: *Mysotis sylvatica* – Forget Me Not, *Pentaglossis sempervivens* – Alkanet, *Geranium phaeum*, *Hyacinthoides non-scripta* – Bluebell; Tulip 'Rococo'; *Cleome spinosa*, American Spider Flower.

Elanor Wexler: Seeds composition; Autumn Leaves.

Victoria Wilkinson (SBA DIPLOMA), (HCPFS): Three Diagonal Leaves: pen and ink with watercolour wash; Seed Heads: pen and ink with watercolour wash.

Photographer who has supplied photograph for inclusion: Malcolm Elliott: *Carpobrotus edulis*, Hottentot Fig.

Acknowledgements

I am deeply indebted to my husband Rupert who, besides giving me much support and encouragement to write this book, kindly and very ably took on the role of photographer along with his assistant Waspie. Without Rupert's help, this book wouldn't have been possible; I am extremely grateful for his care and attention to detail in taking what seemed to be a never-ending list of photographs. We got there eventually. My grateful thanks also to my family and friends for their continual encouragement, regular progress checks, and for so patiently waiting for me to 'finish the book'. I would like to thank all my students, past and present, for showing their interest and enthusiasm, and my sincere thanks go to those students who have generously allowed me to use their artworks – with my gentle persuasion in some cases – to illustrate parts of this book. Their names and artworks are included in the List of Contributors. I also thank my great friend Malcolm Elliott for the use of his photograph of 'that pink flower', otherwise known as *Carpobrotus edulis*, Hottentot Fig, in Chapter 5. I would like to express my gratitude to the National Trust for allowing me to feature Nymans Gardens in Sussex in this book, and to the gardeners at Nymans for letting me take cuttings of *Fuchsia magellanica* for the case study. The painting, now complete, will be my next contribution to the Nymans Florilegium. My thanks also to Winsor & Newton for permission to reproduce their opacity system diagram in Chapter 5. I especially thank my good friend Liz Leech for her practical advice and tips, and for so kindly stepping in for me at the beginning of my adventure to take on the role of Chairman of the Hampton Court Palace Florilegium Society, allowing me sufficient time to write this book before I take office. My grateful thanks go to Sandra Stevens at Ragdolls Fine Framing in Horsham, Sussex, for generously giving her time, and allowing us to take over her shop to photograph equipment, mounts, and frames. Finally, I must thank my adorable cats Florence and Harry; to Florence for her tremendous and timely 'helping' skills of sleeping on my notebook, iPad and keyboard, and to Harry for his unconditional affection and cuddles during the slightly more stressful times.

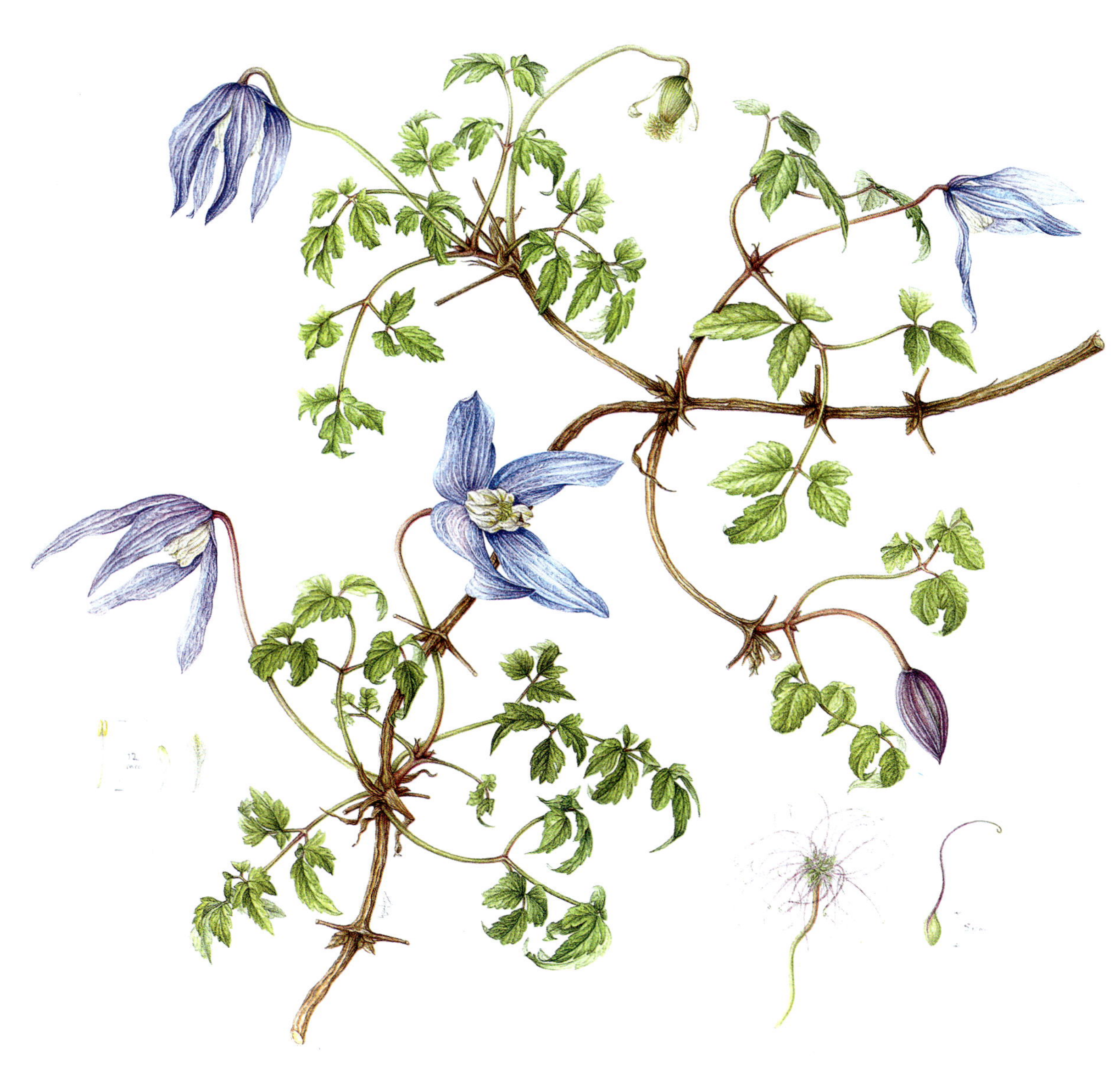

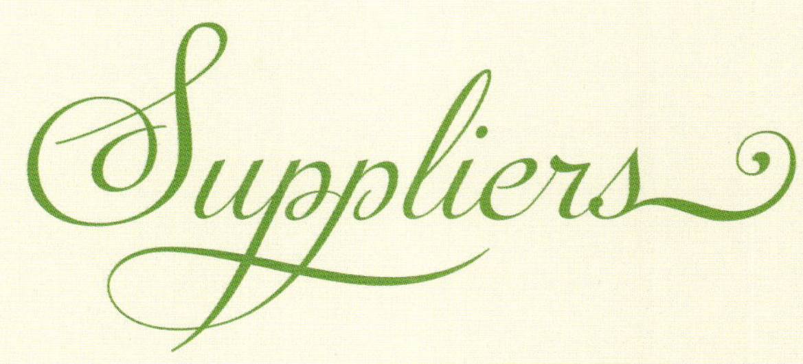

ART SUPPLIERS

Green & Stone of Chelsea
259 King's Road
London, SW3 5EL
+44 (0) 20 7352 0837
Email: sales@greenandstone.com
Website: www.greenandstone.com

Jackson's Art Supplies
1 Farleigh Place
London, N16 7SX
+44 (0) 20 7254 0077
Email: customerservices@jacksonsart.co.uk
Website: www.jacksonart.com

Ken Bromley Art Supplies
Unit 13, Lodge Bank Estate
Crown Lane
Horwich
Bolton, BL6 5HY
+44 (0) 1024 690114
Email: sales@artsupplies.co.uk
Website: www.artsupplies.co.uk

L. Cornelissen
105 Great Russell Street
London, WC1B 3LA
+44 (0) 20 7636 1045
Email: info@cornelissen.com
Website: www.cornelissen.com

Lawrence Art Supplies
208, Portland Road
Hove, BN3 5QT
+44 (0) 1273 260260
Email: artbox@lawrence.co.uk
Website: www.lawrence.co.uk

SAA
PO Box 50,
Newark, NG23 5GY
0800 980 1123
Email: info@saa.co.uk
Website: www.saa.co.uk

PICTURE FRAMING SUPPLIERS

Ragdolls Fine Framing
33 Freshwater Parade
Bishopric
Horsham, RH12 1QD
+44 (0) 1403 218091
Email: info@ragdollsfineframing.co.uk
Website: www.ragdollsfineframing.co.uk

Clematis alpina 'Frances Rivis'. Leigh Ann Gale

Index